# RESPONSIBILITIES

TER
JER

## Compensation and Benefits

| | |
|---|---|
| Ensure the compliance of compensation and benefits with applicable federal, state, and local laws. | 6 |
| Analyze, develop, implement, and maintain compensation policies and pay structure consistent with the organization's strategic objectives (includes broad definitions and designs). | 6 |
| Analyze and evaluate pay rates based on internal worth and external market conditions (includes wage and salary surveys). | 6 |
| Develop/select and implement a payroll system. | 6 |
| Administer payroll functions. | 6 |
| Evaluate compensation policies to ensure that they are positioning the organization internally and externally according to the organization's strategic objectives (refers to 'tweaking,' 'refinement,' or 'alterations;' turnover issues related to compensation also belong under this responsibility). | 6 |
| Conduct a benefit plan needs assessment and determine/select the plans to be offered, considering the organization's strategic objectives. | 6 |
| Implement and administer benefit plans. | 6 |
| Evaluate benefits program to ensure that it is positioning the organization internally and externally according to the organization's strategic objectives. | 6 |
| Analyze, select, implement, maintain, and administer executive compensation, stock purchase, stock options, and incentive, and bonus programs (includes profit sharing). | 6 |
| Analyze, develop, select, maintain, and implement expatriate and foreign national compensation and benefit programs. | 6 |
| Communicate the compensation and benefits plan and policies to the workforce. | 6 |

## Employee and Labor Relations

| | |
|---|---|
| Ensure compliance with all applicable federal, state, and local laws and regulations. | 7 |
| Develop and implement employee relations programs that will create a positive organizational culture. | 7 |
| Promote, monitor, and measure the effectiveness of employee relations activities. | 7 |
| Assist in establishing work rules and monitor their application and enforcement to ensure fairness and consistency (for union and non-union environments). | 7 |
| Communicate and ensure understanding by employees of laws, regulations, and organizational policies. | 7 |
| Resolve employee complaints filed with federal, state, and local agencies involving employment practices (formal, legal complaints). | 7 |
| Develop grievance and disciplinary policies and procedures to ensure fairness and consistency. | 7 |
| Implement and monitor grievance and disciplinary policies and procedures to ensure fairness and consistency (includes investigation). | 7 |
| Respond to union organizing activity. | 7 |
| Participate in collective bargaining activities, including contract negotiation and administration. | 7 |

## Occupational Health, Safety, and Security

| | |
|---|---|
| Ensure compliance with all applicable federal, state, and local workplace health and safety laws and regulations. | 8 |
| Determine safety programs needed for the organization. | 8 |
| Develop and/or select injury/occupational illness prevention programs. | 8 |

SYBEX

| RESPONSIBILITIES | CHAPTER NUMBER |
|---|---|
| **Workforce Planning and Employment** *(continued)* | |
| Implement selection procedures, including interviewing, testing, and reference and background checking. | 4 |
| Develop and/or extend employment offers. | 4 |
| Perform or administer post-offer employment activities (for example, employment agreements, completion of I-9 verification form, relocation agreements, and medical exams). | 4 |
| Facilitate and/or administer the process by which non-US citizens can legally work in the United States. | 4 |
| Design, facilitate, and/or conduct the orientation process, including review of performance standards for new hires and transfers. | 4 |
| Evaluate selection and employment processes for effectiveness and implement changes if indicated (for example, employee retention). | 4 |
| Develop a succession planning process. | 4 |
| Develop and implement the organizational exit process, including unemployment insurance claim responses (includes severance, turnover and outplacement). | 4 |
| Develop, implement, manage, and evaluate affirmative action program(s), as may be required. | 4 |
| **Human Resources Development** | |
| Conduct needs analyses to identify and establish priorities regarding human resources development activities. | 5 |
| Develop training programs. | 5 |
| Implement training programs. | 5 |
| Evaluate training programs. | 5 |
| Develop programs to assess employees' potential for growth and development in the organization. | 5 |
| Implement programs to assess employees' potential for growth and development in the organization. | 5 |
| Evaluate programs to assess employees' potential for growth and development in the organization. | 5 |
| Develop change management programs and activities. | 5 |
| Implement change management programs and activities. | 5 |
| Evaluate change management programs and activities. | 5 |
| Develop performance management programs and procedures. | 5 |
| Implement performance management programs and procedures. | 5 |
| Evaluate performance management programs and procedures. | 5 |
| Develop programs to meet the unique needs of particular employees (for example, work-family programs, diversity programs, outplacement programs, repatriation programs, and fast-track programs). | 5 |
| Implement programs to meet the unique needs of particular employees (for example, work-family programs, diversity programs, outplacement programs, repatriation programs, and fast-track programs). | 5 |
| Evaluate programs to meet the unique needs of particular employees (for example, work-family programs, diversity programs, outplacement programs, repatriation programs, and fast-track programs). | 5 |

Exam specifications and content are subject to change at any time without prior notice and at the Society for Human Resource Management's Human Resource Certification Institute's sole discretion. Please visit HRCI's website (www.hrci.org) for the most current information on their exam content.

| RESPONSIBILITIES | CHAPTER NUMBER |
|---|:---:|
| **Occupational Health, Safety, and Security _(continued)_** | |
| Implement injury/occupational illness prevention programs. | 8 |
| Develop and/or select safety training and incentive programs. | 8 |
| Implement safety training and incentive programs. | 8 |
| Evaluate the effectiveness of safety prevention, training, and incentive programs. | 8 |
| Implement workplace injury/occupational illness procedures (for example, worker's compensation, OSHA). | 8 |
| Determine health and wellness programs needed for the organization. | 8 |
| Develop/select, implement, and evaluate (or make available) health and wellness programs. | 8 |
| Develop/select, implement, and evaluate security plans to protect the company from liability. | 8 |
| Develop/select, implement, and evaluate security plans to protect employees (for example, injuries resulting from workplace violence). | 8 |
| Develop/select, implement, and evaluate incident and emergency response plans (for example, natural disasters, workplace safety threats, evacuation). | 8 |
| **Core Knowledge Required by HR Professionals** | |
| Needs assessment and analysis | 2 |
| Third-party contract management, including development of requests for proposals (RFPs) | 2 |
| Communication strategies | 2 |
| Documentation strategies | 2 |
| Adult learning processes | 2 |
| Motivation concepts and applications | 2 |
| Training methods | 2 |
| Leadership concepts and applications | 2 |
| Project management concepts and applications | 2 |
| Diversity concepts and applications | 2 |
| Human relations concepts and applications (for example, interpersonal and organizational behavior) | 2 |
| HR ethics and professionals standards | 2 |
| Technology and human resource information systems (HRIS) to support HR activities | 2 |
| Qualitative and quantitative methods and tools for analysis, interpretation, and decision-making purposes | 2 |
| Change management | 2 |
| Liability and risk management | 2 |
| Job analysis and job description methods | 2 |
| Employee records management (for example, retention, disposal) | 2 |
| The interrelationships among HR activities and programs across functional areas | 2 |

Exam specifications and content are subject to change at any time without prior notice and at the Society for Human Resource Management's Human Resource Certification Institute's sole discretion. Please visit HRCI's website (www.hrci.org) for the most current information on their exam content.

# PHR/SPHR: Professional in Human Resources Certification® Study Guide

## HRCI Test Specifications

| RESPONSIBILITIES | CHAPTER NUMBER |
|---|---|
| **Strategic Management** | |
| Interpret information related to the organization's operations from internal sources, including financial/accounting, marketing, operations, information technology, and individual employees, in order to participate in strategic planning and policy making. | 3 |
| Interpret information related to the general business environment, industry practices and developments, and technological developments from external sources (for example, publications, government documents, media, and trade organizations), in order to participate in strategic planning and policy making. | 3 |
| Participate as a partner in the organization's strategic planning process. | 3 |
| Establish strategic relationships with individuals in the organization, to influence organizational decision-making. | 3 |
| Establish strategic relationships/alliances with key individuals in the community and in professional capacities to assist in meeting the organization's strategic needs. | 3 |
| Evaluate HR's contribution to organizational effectiveness, including assessment, design, implementation, and evaluation of activities with respect to strategic and organizational measurements in HR objectives. | 3 |
| Provide direction and guidance during changes in organizational processes, operations, planning, intervention, leadership training and culture that balances the expectations and needs of the organization, its employees, and other stakeholders (including customers). | 3 |
| Develop and shape organizational policy related to the organization's management of its human resources. | 3 |
| Cultivate leadership and ethical values in self and others through modeling and teaching. | 3 |
| Provide information for the organizational budgeting process, including budget development and review. | 3 |
| Monitor legislative environment for proposed changes in law and take appropriate action to support, modify, or stop the proposed action (for example, write to a member of Congress, provide expert testimony at a public hearing, lobby legislators). | 3 |
| **Workforce Planning and Employment** | |
| Identify staffing requirements to meet the goals and objectives of the organization. | 4 |
| Conduct job analyses to write job descriptions and develop job competencies. | 4 |
| Identify and document the essential job functions for positions. | 4 |
| Establish hiring criteria based on the competencies needed. | 4 |
| Assess internal workforce, labor market, and recruitment agencies to determine the availability of qualified applicants. | 4 |
| Identify internal and external recruitment methods and implement them within the context of the organization's goals and objectives. | 4 |
| Develop strategies to market the organization to potential applicants. | 4 |
| Establish selection procedures, including interviewing, testing, and reference and background checking. | 4 |

SYBEX

# PHR/SPHR:
## Professional in Human Resources Certification
### Study Guide

# PHR/SPHR:
## Professional in Human
## Resources Certification®
### Study Guide

Anne M. Bogardus, SPHR

San Francisco • London

SYBEX

Associate Publisher: Neil Edde
Acquisitions Editor: Elizabeth Hurley Peterson
Developmental Editor: Heather O'Connor
Production Editor: Leslie E.H. Light
Technical Editor: Cynthia Erickson
Copyeditor: Sally Engelfried
Compositor: Interactive Composition Corporation
Graphic Illustrator: Interactive Composition Corporation
CD Coordinator: Dan Mummert
CD Technician: Kevin Ly
Proofreaders: Nancy Riddiough and Laurie O'Connell
Indexer: Lynnzee Elze
Book Designer: Bill Gibson and Judy Fung
Cover Designer: Richard Miller, Calyx Design
Cover Photographer: Getty Images

Library of Congress Card Number: 2003106717

ISBN: 0-7821-4252-4

SYBEX

To Our Valued Readers:

Sybex® is excited to be publishing the *PHR/SPHR: Professional in Human Resources Certification Study Guide*, the first of its kind for the increasingly critical business area of Human Resources. The skills and concepts covered here are certainly different from the technical topics one usually finds in Sybex Study Guides, but the relevance and importance to businesses of all kinds will be immediately evident to all who peruse this invaluable book.

Just as the Human Resource Certification Institute is committed to establishing measurable standards for certifying human resource professionals, Sybex is committed to providing those professionals with the skills and knowledge needed to meet those standards. The author and editors have worked hard to ensure that this study guide is comprehensive, in-depth, and pedagogically sound. We're confident that this books will meet and exceed the demanding standards of the certification marketplace and help you, the PHR or SPHR exam candidate, succeed in your endeavors.

Good luck in pursuit of your PHR and SPHR certifications!

Neil Edde
Associate Publisher
Sybex, Inc.

*For Kit, who taught me to love reading; Bob, the best manager of people I've ever known; and to both of them for their unwavering support and love.*
*—With love and gratitude*

# Acknowledgments

Having dreamed of writing a book for a very long time, I was thrilled when this opportunity was presented to me. The team at Sybex provided the encouragement, cheerleading, and whip-cracking that got me through the process. Thanks to Elizabeth Peterson for putting the deal together, to Heather O'Connor for helping to shape the book, and to Leslie Light for making sure that the final product was the best it could be. Thanks also to Sally Englefried whose attention to detail was immensely helpful and to Rozi Harris and the group at Interactive Composition Corporation who made the pages of this book so accessible. I'm grateful for the level of professionalism and expertise that each of them brought to the project.

I am most grateful to the book's technical editor, Cynthia Erickson, SPHR, whose feedback helped me to express my thoughts more clearly and who knew exactly what to ask to help me clarify some of the information. Aside from that, your support and encouragement were always there when I needed them. You are awesome! Thanks also to Hal Anjo, SPHR, who wrote fabulous questions and provided feedback that made the book better. Carolyn Way, PHR, was a great help on the compensation section—thanks for your hard work on it!

Thanks to the students in my certification classes, especially those who put me on the spot by asking questions that I didn't know the answers to—I learned so much from all of you! Special thanks to Gayle Holmlund, SPHR, for her encouragement and support.

Thanks also to Bob and Rita for their support and to Linda, Gene, and Alison for understanding. To my clients, from whom I learn more every day, thank you; Chad, thanks for waiting patiently for *just one more week* while I finished this book. And thanks to Bill—he knows why. Finally, thanks to my friends for their understanding and patience while I finished this project—all of you are the best!

# Contents at a Glance

# Contents

# Introduction

Congratulations on taking the first step toward achieving your Professional in Human Resources (PHR) or Senior Professional in Human Resources (SPHR) certification! The process you are embarking upon is rewarding and challenging and, as more than 59,000 of your fellow human resource colleagues have already discovered, it's an excellent opportunity to explore areas of human resource management with which you may not work every day. In the next few pages, you will find some general information about human resource certification, some suggestions for using this book, information about what to expect in the following chapters, and a discussion of the organizations involved in certification.

Before we begin, a word about what you should already know. This study guide was designed to serve as a refresher for experienced professionals who have practiced HR for a minimum of two years. I assume that those who are pursuing certification have the basic HR knowledge that comes not only from education in human resources but also, more importantly, from exempt-level experience. If your daily work is truly generalist in nature, you likely have touched upon many of the topics I cover, but you may not have in-depth knowledge in all of them. Conversely, if you specialize in one or two areas of HR, you probably have extensive experience in those areas, but may need to refresh your knowledge in other areas.

The goal of this study guide is to provide enough information about each of the functional areas of human resource management to enable candidates in either situation to find what they need to prepare themselves for successfully completing the exam. There are more than 22,000 books related to human resources listed on Amazon.com alone, and there is obviously no way that I can cover all the aspects of HR in a single book. So I've organized the information around the test specifications (test specs) established by the Human Resource Certification Institute (HRCI), the certifying body for our profession. I'll talk more about the test specs in Chapter 1, but for now, suffice it to say that the key to success on the exam is a thorough understanding of and ability to apply the test specs in answering questions on the exams.

# About Human Resource Certification

What exactly *is* human resource certification? Briefly, let's just say that certification is a way of acknowledging individuals who have met the standard of competency established by HR practitioners as that which is necessary to be considered a fully competent HR professional. To understand if this book is for you, you'll want to know why you should become certified and how.

## Who Certifies HR Professionals?

There are three organizations involved in the certification of human resource professionals: the Human Resource Certification Institute (HRCI), the Society for Human Resource Management (SHRM), and the Professional Examination Service (PES).

## The Human Resource Certification Institute

HRCI is the certifying body for the human resource profession. It was formed by the American Society of Personnel Administrators (ASPA) in 1972 when it was known as the ASPA Accreditation Institute (AAI). In its early stages, HRCI was financially dependent upon SHRM, but it is now financially independent. Both HRCI and SHRM have individual boards of directors that govern their operations. While HRCI and SHRM have a long history of affiliation and mutual support, the certification process is a separate and distinct function of HRCI, and SHRM has no more control over or access to the certification process than does anyone else in the profession.

 You can find HRCI's organizational mission statement at www.hrci.org/about/2002stateinstituterpt.html.

## The Society for Human Resource Management

SHRM is the largest organization of human resource professionals in the world, representing more than 170,000 members worldwide in 2002. From its beginning in 1948 as the American Society for Personnel Administrators (ASPA), SHRM has been a leader in the endeavor to gain recognition for the human resource profession. Today's certification program is a direct result of efforts by the first volunteer members of SHRM who recognized the need for a defined body of knowledge and set about to develop it along with a certification process that evaluates the abilities of practitioners in the field.

## Professional Examination Service

PES is a nonprofit organization that conducts license and credential examinations for a wide variety of professions, including psychology, pharmacy, real estate appraisal, and security management, among many others. PES maintains the database of test items developed by HRCI and is responsible for ensuring that applicants for the PHR and SPHR exams meet the eligibility requirements, administering and scoring the tests, and notifying candidates of the results. In 2000, PES conducted the most recent review of the body of knowledge, called a practice analysis study, to ensure the continued relevance of the credentialing process to current business practices.

I will refer to these organizations frequently in Chapter 1 as I discuss the body of knowledge and the certification process.

# Why Become Certified?

Over time, the certification offered by HRCI has become the industry standard for determining competence in the field of human resources. There are many reasons that individuals may decide to seek professional certification. Let's talk about just a few of them.

First, certification is an acknowledgement that you have met the standards of excellence determined by other HR professionals to be those which are necessary to be fully competent in the field. Because the standards are developed by working professionals, not just by those who teach and consult in the field, this credential demonstrates that you are a fully competent HR practitioner based on a standard set by your peers.

Second, certification is a way to increase your marketability. In difficult economic times, when there is tough competition for jobs, certification provides an edge that can be advantageous in your job search. With an abundance of job seekers for a limited number of jobs, whatever you can do to set yourself apart from the crowd can give you the edge when potential employers are making the final hiring decision.

Third, those who spend the time to advance their own knowledge and achieve certification have demonstrated their ability to continue learning and growing as times and business needs change. A person who is willing and able to set a significant goal and do what is necessary to achieve it demonstrates characteristics that are in great demand in business today: results orientation, technical competence, commitment, and excellence.

Finally, certification enhances your credibility with coworkers and customers. It demonstrates to those with whom you come in contact during your work day that you have met the standard that has been determined by others within the field to be that which is required to demonstrate competence.

Whether your reason for seeking certification falls into one of these categories, or you are motivated to do so for some other reason, it can be a great opportunity to validate how much you already know about the practice of human resources as a profession.

## How to Become Certified

To become a certified HR professional, you must pass either the PHR or SPHR exam, both of which have been developed by HRCI in a comprehensive process described in Chapter 1.

Beginning with the May 2004 exam, HRCI will utilize a computer-based testing (CBT) process during two time periods each year: between the beginning of May and the end of June and from mid-November through mid-January. One advantage of the CBT process is that exam candidates will know before they leave the testing center whether or not they are certified.

Each exam, PHR and SPHR, consists of 225 questions. Of these questions, 200 are scored to determine whether or not you pass the exam. The additional 25 questions are being "pretested" in order to determine their reliability and validity for inclusion in future test cycles. A detailed discussion of how the questions are developed and scored can be found in the HRCI *PHR & SPHR Certification Handbook*, which can be viewed and/or downloaded at the HRCI website (`www.hrci.org`), or you can request a hard copy from HRCI by calling (866) 898-4724. The handbook is an essential guide to all aspects of the exams and includes test dates, application deadlines, fee information, and answers to frequently asked questions about the certification process, as well as the full list of test specifications.

Chapter 1 explains in greater detail how much and what kinds of experience are required for each exam level and how the questions differ on each level.

# How This Book Is Organized

I've talked a little bit about Chapter 1, which provides information about requirements for certification and the testing process. Chapter 1 also provides some suggestions on the best ways to study for the exam.

Chapter 2, "Core Knowledge Requirements for HR Professionals," provides a brief discussion of knowledge with implications in multiple functional areas. Reading this chapter first gives exam candidates a base for understanding topics covered in subsequent chapters.

Chapters 3–8 are where we get down to business and discuss the test specifications in detail. Each of these chapters consists of a list of objectives, an overview of the functional area, the federal employment laws applicable to that area, and a discussion of the test specs, including appropriate court cases.

I have also provided three appendices to facilitate your study. Appendix A, "Federal Employment Legislation and Case Law," is a chronological listing of the federal legislation appearing throughout the book, as well as significant court decisions with implications for human resources. In this appendix, I've also included additional court decisions that were not discussed in the chapters but have significance for HR practice and with which you should be familiar, so be sure to review these. They are included in a separate section of the appendix.

Appendix B, "Resources," is just that: a list of additional sources of information about each of the functional areas of human resources.

Appendix C, "Employment Documents and Retention," compiles the various requirements of federal laws and regulations pertaining to documents that must be collected and archived.

Finally, I have included a Glossary, an alphabetical listing of all of the key terms throughout the book with their corresponding definitions.

## The Elements of a Study Guide

You'll see many recurring elements as you read through the study guide. Here's a description of some of those elements.

**Summary**   The summary is a brief review of the chapter to sum up what was covered.

**Exam Essentials**   The Exam Essentials highlight topics that could appear on one or both of the exams in some form. While I obviously do not know exactly what will be included in a particular exam, this section reinforces significant concepts that are key to understanding the functional area and the test specs HRCI has developed.

**Key Terms**   Throughout each chapter, I've identified and defined key terms that exam candidates will need to understand.

**Chapter Review Questions**   Each chapter includes ten practice questions that have been designed to measure your knowledge of key ideas that were discussed in the chapter. After you finish each chapter, answer the questions; if some of your answers are incorrect, it's an indication that you need to spend some more time studying that topic. The answers to the practice questions can be found after the last question in each chapter. The chapter review questions are designed to help you measure how much information you retained from your reading and are different from the kinds of questions you will see on the exam.

## What's on the CD?

I worked really hard to provide some essential tools to help you with your certification process. All of the following gear should be loaded on your computer when studying for the test.

## The Sybex Test Preparation Software

The test preparation software, made by experts at Sybex, prepares you to pass the PHR/SPHR exams. In this test engine you will find all the review and assessment questions from the book, plus four additional bonus exams that appear exclusively on the CD. You can take the assessment test, test yourself by chapter, take the practice exams, or take a randomly generated exam comprising all the questions. Finally, you can be graded by topic area, so you can assess the areas where you need further review.

 Just as on the certification exams, the bonus exam questions on our CD will contain questions that draw upon your experience as an HR professional. Be on the lookout for questions based upon your everyday activities in HR and not just on the material in the PHR/SPHR study guide.

## Electronic Flashcards for PC and Palm Devices

Sybex's electronic flashcards include 150 PHR and 150 SPHR questions designed to challenge you further for the PHR and SPHR exams. Between the review questions, practice exams, and flashcards, you'll have a wide variety of materials to help you prepare!

### *PHR/SPHR Study Guide* in PDF

Sybex offers the *PHR/SPHR: Professional in Human Resources Certification Study Guide* in PDF format on the CD so you can read the book on your PC or laptop if you travel and don't want to carry a book, or if you just like to read from the computer screen. Acrobat Reader 5 is also included on the CD.

# How to Use This Book and CD

This book has a number of features designed to guide your study efforts for either the PHR or the SPHR certification exam. All of these features are designed to assist you in doing the most important thing you can do to pass the exam: understanding and applying the test specs in answering questions. This book helps you do that by listing the current test specs at the beginning of each chapter and by ensuring that each of them is fully discussed within the chapter. The practice questions at the end of each chapter and the practice exams on the CD are designed to assist you in testing your retention of the material you've read to make you aware of areas in which you should spend additional study time. I've provided web links and other resources to assist you in mastering areas where you may require additional study materials. Here are some suggestions for using this book and CD:

1.  Take the assessment test before you start reading the material. These questions are designed to measure your knowledge and will look different than the questions you will see on the exam. They are designed to give you an idea of the areas in which you need to spend additional study time, as well as those areas in which you may just need a brief refresher.

2. Review the test specs at the beginning of each chapter before you start reading. Make sure you read the associated knowledge requirements in HRCI's *PHR and SPHR Certification Handbook* as these may help you in your study process. After you've read the chapter, review them again to make sure you understand and are able to apply them.

3. Answer the review questions after you've read each chapter; if you missed any of them, go back over the chapter and review the topic, or utilize one of the additional resources if you need more information.

4. Make sure you understand the laws that apply to each functional area, what they cover, and to which companies or government agencies they apply.

5. Download the flashcards to your handheld device and review them when you have a few minutes during the day.

6. Take every opportunity to test yourself. In addition to the assessment test and review questions, there are bonus exams on the CD. Take these exams without referring to the chapters and see how well you've done—go back and review any topics you've missed until you fully understand and can apply the concepts.

Finally, find a study partner if possible. Studying for, and taking, the exam with someone else will make the process more enjoyable, and you'll have someone to help you understand topics that are difficult for you. You'll also be able to reinforce your own knowledge by helping your study partner in areas where they are weak.

# Assessment Test

1. An employee has come forward with an allegation of quid pro quo harassment by her supervisor. As the HR manager, you are responsible for investigating the charges. The supervisor in question is someone with whom you have become quite friendly. In this case, the best person to conduct the investigation is

    **A.** You.

    **B.** The corporate attorney.

    **C.** The direct manager of the accused supervisor.

    **D.** A third party investigator.

2. The motivation theory that suggests people are motivated by the reward they will receive when they succeed and that they weigh the value of the expected reward against the effort required to achieve it is known as:

    **A.** Vroom's Expectancy Theory

    **B.** Adams' Equity Theory

    **C.** McClelland's Acquired Needs Theory

    **D.** McGregor's Theory X and Theory Y

3. Which of the following is an example of a passive training method?

    **A.** Vestibule training

    **B.** Demonstration

    **C.** Distance learning

    **D.** Self-study

4. One purpose of a diversity initiative is to:

    **A.** Increase workplace creativity

    **B.** Increase the effectiveness of the workforce

    **C.** Increase the organization's ability to attract customers

    **D.** All of the above

5. The concept that recognized businesses as social organizations as well as economic systems and recognized that productivity was related to employee job satisfaction is known as:

    **A.** Human resource management

    **B.** Strategic management

    **C.** Human relations

    **D.** Human resource development

6. Before selecting an HRIS system, which of the following questions should be answered?

   **A.** What information will be converted to the HRIS?

   **B.** Who will have access to the information stored in the HRIS?

   **C.** How will the HRIS be accessed?

   **D.** All of the above.

7. The correlation coefficient is a statistical measurement that is useful for:

   **A.** Determining whether or not one variable affects another

   **B.** Compensating for data that may be out of date

   **C.** Determining which variables are outside acceptable ranges

   **D.** Describing standards of quality

8. The process of identifying risks and taking steps to minimize them is referred to as:

   **A.** Liability management

   **B.** Risk management

   **C.** Qualitative analysis

   **D.** Risk assessment

9. Examples of workplace ethics issues include:

   **A.** Workplace privacy

   **B.** Conflicts of interest

   **C.** Whistle-blowing

   **D.** All of the above

10. Which of the following points is important to effective lobbying, that is, attempting to influence or persuade an elected official to pass, defeat, or modify a piece of legislation?

    **A.** Learn how the legislative and political process works.

    **B.** Begin by using persuasion to convince the elected official to accept your position.

    **C.** Make big financial contributions.

    **D.** Let the elected official choose a solution rather than present a proposal solution.

11. An HR audit is designed to help management

    **A.** Improve employee morale.

    **B.** Analyze HR policies, programs, and procedures against applicable legal requirements.

    **C.** Improve HR effectiveness.

    **D.** All of the above.

**12.** Which of the following is a productivity type of statistical HR measurement?

  **A.** Turnover and retention

  **B.** Cost per hire

  **C.** Revenue per employee

  **D.** Job satisfaction

**13.** A statement of cash flows is a financial report that tells you:

  **A.** The financial condition of the business at a specific point in time

  **B.** Where the money used to operate the business came from

  **C.** The financial results of operations over a period of time

  **D.** How much money is owed to the company by its customers

**14.** Which of the following activities is *not* a responsibility of the operations function of a business?

  **A.** Designing the product

  **B.** Scheduling production runs to coincide with customer demand

  **C.** Ensuring that products or services meet quality standards

  **D.** Determining what new products will be produced

**15.** A PEST analysis is used during the strategic planning process. PEST is an acronym for:

  **A.** Political, environmental, strengths, threats

  **B.** Political, economic, specific, timely

  **C.** Political, economic, social, technology

  **D.** Product, environment, social, technology

**16.** Which of the following is a characteristic of the Delphi technique?

  **A.** It is a quantitative tool used to build consensus.

  **B.** It is a structured meeting format.

  **C.** The participants never meet.

  **D.** It requires a facilitator to guide the process.

**17.** Which of the following alternative staffing methods would be *most* appropriate for a company with ongoing yet sporadic needs for a specific job to be done?

  **A.** Intern program

  **B.** On-call worker

  **C.** Seasonal worker

  **D.** Temp worker

**18.** A standard employment practice that seems to be fair yet results in discrimination against a protected class is a description of:

 **A.** Disparate treatment

 **B.** Disparate impact

 **C.** Adverse impact

 **D.** Unfair treatment

**19.** Measuring staffing needs against sales volume could be done most effectively by using which of the following techniques?

 **A.** A multiple linear regression

 **B.** A ratio

 **C.** A simulation model

 **D.** A simple linear regression

**20.** When an interviewer is aware that a candidate scored particularly high on an assessment test, this bias is known as the:

 **A.** Halo effect

 **B.** Knowledge-of-predictor effect

 **C.** Cultural noise effect

 **D.** Stereotyping effect

**21.** According to the WARN Act, an employer with 200 employees is required to provide 60 days' notice of a mass layoff when:

 **A.** The employer is seeking additional funding and will lay off 70 employees if the funding falls through.

 **B.** A major client unexpectedly selects a new vendor for the company's products and the company lays off 75 employees.

 **C.** The employer lays off 5 employees a week for 3 months.

 **D.** A flood requires that one of the plants be shut down for repairs and 55 employee are laid off.

**22.** The Vietnam Era Veterans Readjustment Assistance Act (VEVRA) requires that

 **A.** All contractors list all job openings with state employment agencies.

 **B.** All employers list all job openings with state employment agencies.

 **C.** State employment agencies give preference to Vietnam veterans for senior-level management position referrals.

 **D.** State employment agencies give preference to Vietnam veterans for positions lasting 3 days or longer.

**23.** A high involvement organization is an example of what type of OD intervention?

   **A.** human process

   **C.** techno-structural

   **B.** human resource management

   **D.** strategic

**24.** The _____ seating arrangement is best for case discussions where everyone can observe each other and a trainer.

   **A.** theater style

   **B.** U-shaped style

   **C.** classroom style

   **D.** banquet style

**25.** According to the Copyright Act of 1976, which of the following is most likely to be considered a fair use of copyrighted material?

   **A.** Distributing 30 copies of a chapter in a book to a study group

   **B.** Copying a book for 10 staff members of a non-profit organization

   **C.** Distributing 30 copies of a paragraph in a book to a study group

   **D.** None of the above

**26.** A process for reducing the impact of bias during performance reviews by using multiple raters is known as:

   **A.** Inter-rater reliability

   **B.** An MBO review

   **C.** A rating scale

   **D.** Paired comparison

**27.** To increase the chances for successful repatriation of employees, the process should include:

   **A.** Development of a qualified pool of candidates for global assignments

   **B.** A formal repatriation program that includes career counseling

   **C.** Setting expectations for repatriation before employees begin global assignments

   **D.** All of the above

**28.** Total quality management focuses all employees on producing products that meet customer needs. This is done by:

   **A.** Eliminating processes that waste time and materials

   **B.** Developing a high level of expertise in all employees

   **C.** Sharing information with all levels in the organization

   **D.** Balancing the needs of all stakeholders in the organization

**29.** Which of the following is an example of a strategic OD intervention?

    **A.** Leadership development

    **B.** Total quality management

    **C.** A learning organization

    **D.** Teambuilding activities

**30.** The most effective method of performance evaluation is

    **A.** A field review process

    **B.** A continuous feedback process

    **C.** A forced ranking process

    **D.** A behaviorally anchored rating scale process

**31.** An employee earning $12,500 per year supervises three employees and spends 35 hours per week on essential job duties that require discretion and independent judgment. Is this employee:

    **A.** Exempt, based on the short executive exemption test.

    **B.** Exempt, based on the short administrative exemption test.

    **C.** Nonexempt, based on the short executive exemption test.

    **D.** Nonexempt, based on the short administrative exemption test.

**32.** As of September 1, 1997, the federal minimum wage is set at:

    **A.** $5.15 per hour

    **B.** $7.16 per hour

    **C.** $5.75 per hour

    **D.** $6.75 per hour

**33.** The FLSA requires employers to pay nonexempt employees for time spent:

    **A.** At home while waiting to be called to work

    **B.** At work reading a book while waiting for an assignment

    **C.** Attending a voluntary training program

    **D.** Commuting to work

**34.** Which of the following would be considered an extrinsic reward?

    **A.** Challenging work on a new project

    **B.** A 10 percent salary increase

    **C.** A feeling of accomplishment after completing a tough assignment

    **D.** Recognition by the CEO at a company meeting

**35.** An example of a nonqualified deferred compensation plan is

    **A.** An excess deferral plan

    **B.** A target benefit plan

    **C.** A money purchase plan

    **D.** A cash balance plan

**36.** The Economic Growth and Tax Relief Reconciliation Act of 2001

    **A.** Requires pension plans to account for employee contributions separately from employer contributions.

    **B.** Allows employers to contribute a percentage of company earnings to retirement plans each year.

    **C.** Allows employees over 50 years old to make catch up contributions to retirement accounts.

    **D.** Requires employer pension contributions to be funded on a quarterly basis.

**37.** The Health Insurance Portability and Accountability Act

    **A.** Prevents HR from investigating claims issues

    **B.** Requires continuation of health benefits

    **C.** Established EPO networks

    **D.** Limited preexisting condition restrictions

**38.** A target benefit plan

    **A.** Uses actuarial formulas to calculate individual pension contribution amounts.

    **B.** Requires an actual deferral percentage test to be performed each year.

    **C.** Provides a means for employees to become owners of the company.

    **D.** Uses a fixed percentage of employee earnings to defer compensation.

**39.** "Thanks for such a great presentation! You'll always have a job with us." This is an example of

    **A.** The duty of good faith and fair dealing.

    **B.** An express contract.

    **C.** An implied contract.

    **D.** Fraudulent misrepresentation.

**40.** A lockout occurs when

    **A.** The employees shut down operations by refusing to work.

    **B.** The employer refuses to allow the union to unionize the workplace.

    **C.** The employer shuts down operations to keep employees from working.

    **D.** The employees patrol the entrance to the business.

41. Which one of the following statements is true of a hostile work environment?

    A. When a single incident of unwanted touching occurs a hostile work environment has been created.

    B. A hostile work environment may be created when an individual witnesses the ongoing harassment of a coworker.

    C. A hostile work environment can only be created by a supervisor.

    D. A grievance procedure and policy against discrimination protect employers from hostile work environment claims.

42. An effective progressive disciplinary process begins with

    A. A written warning.

    B. A verbal warning.

    C. A suspension.

    D. Coaching or counseling.

43. During the union organizing process, the bargaining unit is determined

    A. By the union organizers.

    B. Jointly, by the union and the employer.

    C. By the National Labor Relations Board.

    D. By the employees during the election.

44. The Excelsior list is

    A. A list of all employees in the bargaining unit provided by the employer to the union within 7 days of the scheduling of an election by the NLRB.

    B. A list of the employees who do not want the union to represent them.

    C. A list of the employees who have signed authorization cards for the union.

    D. A list of all employees in the bargaining unit provided by the union to the employer within 7 days of the scheduling of an election by the NLRB.

45. When an employer wants to obtain insight into employee goals and job satisfaction and provide career counseling to those in the work group, the most effective method to utilize would be

    A. An employee survey.

    B. A skip-level interview.

    C. An employee focus group.

    D. A brown-bag lunch.

46. Health and wellness programs are beneficial for employers because they:

    A. Increase productivity, reduce medical costs, and attract top-quality job candidates

    B. Provide nutrition counseling, exercise programs, and health education programs

    C. Require employees to lose weight, stop smoking, and avoid substance abuse

    D. Provide on-site opportunities for physical fitness

**47.** Which of the following statements is *not* true about substance abuse policies?

   **A.** Substance abuse policies identify who will be tested.

   **B.** Federal law requires all employers to implement substance abuse policies.

   **C.** An effective policy describes when tests will occur and what drugs will be tested.

   **D.** An effective policy describes what happens to employees who test positive.

**48.** According to the OSHA inspection priorities, which type of workplace hazard receives first priority for an inspection?

   **A.** Catastrophes and Fatal Accidents

   **B.** Programmed High-Hazard Inspections

   **C.** Imminent Danger

   **D.** Employee Complaints

**49.** When workplace conditions pose a threat to an unborn child, the company must:

   **A.** Do nothing. It is up to employees to protect their unborn children.

   **B.** Move the employee into a different job that does not pose a threat to the unborn child.

   **C.** Advise the employee of the potential threat and allow the employee to make the decision.

   **D.** Allow only sterile employees to work in jobs that pose a threat to unborn children.

**50.** The Occupational Safety and Health Act of 1970 grants employees the right to do all of the following *except*:

   **A.** Be advised of potential safety hazards.

   **B.** Speak privately to an OSHA inspector during an inspection.

   **C.** Observe the employer when measuring and monitoring workplace hazards.

   **D.** View detailed reports of all workplace accidents.

**51.** Which of the following activities does *not* contribute to ergonomic injuries?

   **A.** Awkward postures

   **B.** Extended vibrations

   **C.** Falling down stairs

   **D.** Contact stress

**52.** The OSHA consulting service

   **A.** Helps employers identify the OSHA standards that apply to their workplace.

   **B.** Fines employers for violating OSHA safety standards.

   **C.** Does not require compliance with OSHA standards.

   **D.** Is a one-time service.

# Answers to Assessment Test

1.  D.   In this case, the organization will be best served by a third-party investigator. The most important consideration in an investigation of sexual harassment is that the investigator is seen as credible and impartial. See Chapter 2 for more information.

2.  A.   Vroom explains his theory with three terms: expectancy, the individual's assessment of their ability to achieve the goal; instrumentality, whether or not the individual believes they are capable of achieving the goal; and valence, whether or not the anticipated goal is worth the effort required to achieve it. See Chapter 2 for more information.

3.  C.   Distance learning is similar to a lecture in that a presenter provides information to a group of participants but does not require active participation. See Chapter 2 for more information.

4.  B.   The purpose of a diversity initiative is to increase the effectiveness of an already diverse workforce by educating the employee population about the benefits of a diverse workforce, which include increased creativity and an enhanced ability to attract customers. See Chapter 2 for more information.

5.  C.   The concept of human relations was first introduced in the 1920s and challenged previous assumptions that people work only for economic reasons and could be motivated to increase productivity simply by increasing monetary incentives. See Chapter 2 for more information.

6.  D.   A needs analysis will provide answers to these questions as well as whether or not the HRIS will be integrated with payroll or other systems and what kinds of reports will be produced. See Chapter 2 for more information.

7.  A.   The correlation coefficient is useful in determining whether or not two factors are connected. For example, the correlation coefficient will tell you whether an increase in resignations is related to a change in location of the worksite, and if so, whether the change had a strong impact on resignations. See Chapter 2 for more information.

8.  B.   Risk management identifies areas of possible legal exposure for the organization and reduces those risks with preventive actions. A risk assessment is used to determine how likely it is that an emergency will occur. See Chapter 2 for more information.

9.  D.   Workplace privacy, conflicts of interest, and whistle-blowing are all examples of workplace ethics issues. Ethics are considered a standard of conduct and moral judgment defined by the processes that occur and the consequences of these processes. See Chapter 3 for more information.

10.  A.   To be effective, most experts agree that it is best to first do your homework, that is, learn how the legislative and political process works. In this way, you can participate effectively in the process. See Chapter 3 for more information.

11.  D.   An HR audit is an organized process designed to identify key aspects of HR in the organization such as employee morale, HR policies, programs, and procedures, and HR effectiveness. See Chapter 3 for more information.

**12.** C.    There are three types of statistical HR measurements: employee measures, such as turnover/ retention and job satisfaction; productivity measures, such as revenue per employee and OSHA incident rates; and HR activities measures, such as cost per hire and ratio of total employees to HR staff. See Chapter 3 for more information.

**13.** B.    A statement of cash flows provides information about the money that flowed through the business. It identifies whether the cash was received from customers, loans, or other sources, how much cash was spent to operate the business, and how much was reinvested in the business. See Chapter 3 for more information.

**14.** D.    Marketing is responsible for determining what new products will be produced based on market research designed to find out what products customers are willing to purchase. See Chapter 3 for more information.

**15.** C.    A PEST analysis is used to scan the political, economic, social, and technological conditions in the external environment to determine what impact those conditions will have on the success of the organization. See Chapter 3 for more information.

**16.** C.    The Delphi technique is a qualitative tool for building consensus using a consecutive round of questions that are collated and distributed for review in subsequent rounds. Participants in the process never meet, so this is an advantageous method to use when participants are geographically separated. See Chapter 4 for more information.

**17.** B.    An on-call worker is the best solution for situation in which the employer needs the same job to be done on a sKelly_82074s. This allows the employer to rely on the same person to do the job, reducing training requirements. An intern program would not be appropriate because it is a short-term training solution. Seasonal workers are generally only required at specific times of the year. Temp workers provided by agencies may not be available when needed because they may be on other assignments. See Chapter 4 for more information.

**18.** B.    Disparate impact occurs when an employment practice that seems to be fair unintentionally discriminates against members of a protected class. See Chapter 4 for more information.

**19.** D.    A simple linear regression measures one variable against another. See Chapter 4 for more information.

**20.** B.    The knowledge-of-predictor effect occurs when an interviewer is aware that a candidate has scored particularly high or low on an assessment test and allows this to affect the hiring decision. The halo effect occurs when the interviewer allows a single positive characteristic of the candidate to overshadow other considerations. Cultural noise occurs when a candidate gives answers they think the interviewer wants to hear. Stereotyping occurs when the interviewer makes assumptions about a candidate based on generalizations about the group the candidate belongs to (for example, women). See Chapter 4 for more information.

**21.** C.    The WARN Act requires employers to provide 60 days' notice when 500 employees or 33 percent of the workforce are laid off, and it requires the number be counted over a period of 90 days. Five employees a week for 3 months is a total of 65 employees (5 employees times 13 weeks) which is 33 percent of the workforce. The three exceptions are the "faltering company exception," when knowledge of a layoff will negatively impact the company's ability to obtain additional funding, the "unforeseeable business circumstance," when unexpected circumstances occur, and the "natural disaster" exception. See Chapter 4 for more information.

**22.** D.    VEVRA applies to government contractors and requires that all job openings be listed with state employment agencies *except* those that will be filled from within, are for senior-level management positions, or will last less than 3 days. See Chapter 4 for more information.

**23.** C.    Techno-structural interventions address issues of how work gets done in an organization. A high involvement organization is one in which employees at all levels are involved in making decisions about how work is accomplished. For more information, see Chapter 5.

**24.** B.    Theater style is best for lectures, films, and so on, while classroom style is best for listening to presentations. Banquet style is best for small group discussions, and U-shaped style is best for case discussions where everyone can observe each other and a trainer. For more information, see Chapter 5.

**25.** C.    Four factors are considered in determining whether or not use of published material is a fair use: the purpose of the use, the nature of the work being copied, how much of the work is copied, and what economic effect copying the material will have on the market value of the work. For more information, see Chapter 5.

**26.** A.    Inter-rater reliability seeks to reduce bias by having multiple reviewers rate an individual's performance and averaging the ratings. For more information, see Chapter 5.

**27.** D.    Organizations that are able to successfully repatriate employees after global assignments do so by carefully selecting candidates for global assignments, setting appropriate expectations before the assignment begins, and establishing a formal program to assist employees in reintegrating into the home office after a global assignment. See Chapter 5 for more information.

**28.** A.    The TQM concept reviews processes to eliminate waste, relies on teamwork, and involves all members of the organization in meeting customer needs. See Chapter 5 for more information.

**29.** C.    Learning organizations and knowledge management are examples of strategic OD interventions; TQM is an example of a techno-structural intervention; leadership development and teambuilding activities are examples of human process interventions. See Chapter 5 for more information.

**30.** B.    A continuous feedback review process is most effective because it provides immediate feedback to employees, enabling them to correct performance issues before they become major problems. See Chapter 5 for more information.

**31.** C.    To be exempt based on a short exemption test, an employee must earn at least $13,000 per year ($250 per week × 52 weeks = $13,000). See Chapter 6 for more information.

**32.** A.    The federal minimum wage was raised to $5.15 per hour on September 1, 1997. See Chapter 6 for more information.

**33.** B.    A nonexempt employee who is waiting for an assignment while at work must be paid for the time spent waiting. See Chapter 6 for more information.

**34.** D.    Extrinsic rewards are nonmonetary rewards from which self-esteem comes from others, such as formal recognition for a job well done. See Chapter 6 for more information.

**35.** A.   An excess deferral plan makes up the difference between what an executive could have contributed to a qualified plan if there had not been a limit on contributions and how much was actually contributed because of the discrimination test required by ERISA. These plans are nonqualified because they are not protected by ERISA; they are limited to a small group of executives or highly compensated employees. See Chapter 6 for more information.

**36.** C.   EGTRRA made changes to pension contribution limits and allows employees over 50 to make catch-up pension contributions. See Chapter 6 for more information.

**37.** D.   HIPAA prohibits health insurance providers from discriminating on the basis of health status and limited restrictions for preexisting conditions. See Chapter 6 for more information.

**38.** A.   A target benefit plan is a hybrid plan that has similarities to defined benefit pension plans and money purchase plans. These plans use actuarial formulas to calculate individual pension contribution amounts. See Chapter 6 for more information.

**39.** B.   An express contract can be oral or written and states what the parties to the contract agree to do. The duty of good faith and fair dealing is a common law doctrine that parties to an oral or written contract have an obligation to act in a fair and honest manner to facilitate achievement of the contract goals. An implied contract can be created by conduct and doesn't have to be stated explicitly. Fraudulent misrepresentation occurs when an employer makes false statements to entice a candidate to join the company. See Chapter 7 for more information.

**40.** C.   A lockout is an action taken by the employer to stop employees from working. A strike occurs when employees refuse to work. An employer that refuses to allow the union to conduct an organizing campaign is committing an unfair labor practice. Picketing occurs when employees patrol the entrance to the business. See Chapter 7 for more information.

**41.** B.   A coworker who witnesses the ongoing harassment of another individual may have an actionable claim of a hostile work environment. A single incident of unwanted touching, unless it is particularly offensive or intimidating, will not reach the threshold of a hostile work environment established by the courts. A hostile work environment may be created by any individuals in the workplace, including customers, vendors, or visitors, in addition to supervisors or coworkers. In the case of *Meritor Savings Bank v Vinson*, the Supreme Court held that the mere existence of a grievance procedure and anti-harassment policy does not necessarily protect an employer from hostile work environment claims. See Chapter 7 for more information.

**42.** D.   An effective progressive discipline process begins with coaching or counseling, acknowledging good performance, and providing guidance on performance that needs to be changed. Providing ongoing feedback, both positive and negative, reduces the stress level for both employees and supervisors when serious performance issues arise and must be addressed. See Chapter 7 for more information.

**43.** C.   The National Labor Relations Board (NLRB) determines which jobs will be included in the bargaining unit based on the "community of interest" shared by the requirements of the jobs. See Chapter 7 for more information.

**44.** A.   Once an election has been scheduled, the employer must provide a list, known as an Excelsior list, containing the names and address of all employees in the bargaining unit determined by the NLRB. See Chapter 7 for more information.

**45.** B.   A skip-level interview provides an opportunity for a manager's manager to obtain insight into the goals and satisfaction of employees in the work group. An employee survey is best used to gather information on various issues that can be collated and summarized. A focus group can be utilized to involve employees in the decision making process. A brown bag lunch is an effective way for senior managers to meet with small groups of employees to answer questions about the company goals and mission and to obtain feedback about operations. See Chapter 7 for more information.

**46.** A.   Employers look for benefit programs that add value to the bottom line. Health and wellness programs do this by increasing productivity and reducing costs. These programs are attractive to job candidates and enhance recruiting efforts. For more information, see Chapter 8.

**47.** B.   The Drug-Free Workplace Act of 1988 requires only federal contractors and subcontractors to establish substance abuse policies. A fair and effective policy will describe which employees will be tested, whether it is all or specific job groups. The policy should describe when tests will be done (pre-employment, randomly, upon reasonable suspicion, or according to a predetermined schedule), what drugs are included in the process, and the consequences for employees who test positive. For more information, see Chapter 8.

**48.** C.   First priority for OSHA inspections are those that will prevent injury or illness. An Imminent Danger hazard is one that has a reasonable certainty of death or serious injury occurring before normal enforcement procedures can occur. For more information, see Chapter 8.

**49.** C.   The Supreme Court determined in *Automobile Workers v Johnson Controls, Inc.* that it is the responsibility of prospective parents to protect their unborn children. While employers must provide information about potential hazards, the employer may not decide for the employee whether or not to work in a job that poses a risk to an unborn child. For more information, see Chapter 8.

**50.** D.   Employees have the right to review accident reports without information that identifies the employees involved in the accident. For more information, see Chapter 8.

**51.** C.   Ergonomic injuries are caused by repeated stress to a part of the body. A fall down the stairs is a single occurrence and therefore not an ergonomic injury. For more information, see Chapter 8.

**52.** A.   OSHA consultants provide free services to assist employers in identifying workplace hazards and the standards that apply in their workplaces. The consulting service requires employers to abate any hazards that are identified during the consultation, but does not fine them for violations. To receive a free consultation, employers must agree to advise OSHA of changes in operating processes that may require additional consultations. For more information, see Chapter 8.

# Chapter 1

# Certifying Human Resource Professionals

Human resources. Ask 10 different people what human resources is or does, and you'll get at least eight different answers. Management advisor, recruiter, employee advocate, paper-pusher, union negotiator, counselor, policy police, coach, mediator, administrative expert, corporate conscience, strategic business partner, and the dreaded "party planner"—these are just a few of the roles that those both inside and outside of the profession think we play. Some of these descriptions are based on misperceptions from nonpractitioners, others describe the roles we aspire to attain within our organizations, and some describe what we do each day. The HR body of knowledge (BOK) provides the means by which we define ourselves to the larger business community and communicates to them what roles are appropriate for the human resource function in an organization. This chapter provides you with an overview of HR certification: the growth of human resources as a profession, a little history about the certification process, a discussion of the levels of professional HR certification (there are two), and the required and recommended eligibility standards for each. You'll also learn about the HR body of knowledge and a few tips to assist you in preparing for the PHR and SPHR exams.

# The Human Resource Profession

By the end of the nineteenth century, the industrial revolution had changed the nature of work—businesses were no longer small organizations that could be managed by a single owner with a few trusted supervisors. As a result, many support functions were delegated to individuals who began to specialize in specific areas. One of these functions became known as industrial relations or personnel and evolved into what we know today as human resources. As businesses continued to become even larger entities, standards began to develop as practitioners met and shared information about the ways they did their jobs. The need for more formal training standards in various aspects of this new function became apparent, and colleges began to develop courses of study in the field. By the middle of the twentieth century, the personnel function was part of almost every business, and numerous individuals worked in the field. A small group of these individuals got together in 1948 and determined that personnel was developing into a profession and was in need of a national organization to define it and to represent and promote its interests in the larger business community. Thus, the American Society for Personnel Administration (ASPA) was born.

For the first 16 years of its existence, ASPA was a strictly volunteer organization. By 1964, membership had grown from the small group that started it in 1948 to over 3,100 members—enough to support a small staff to provide services for its members. With membership growing, the discussion quite naturally turned to the topic of defining the practice of personnel as a profession. While there are similarities in the characteristics of established professions, such as a code of ethics, a specific and unique body of knowledge, and an education specific to the profession, there are aspects to most professions that set them apart from each other, and personnel was no different. To solicit the contribution of practitioners in this process, ASPA cosponsored a conference with Cornell University's School of Industrial Relations to determine how best to define the characteristics that made personnel a profession. This conference spawned a year of consideration and debate among ASPA members.

According to the HRCI website, the culmination of this process was an agreement on five characteristics that were needed to set personnel apart as a profession. The original characteristics were only slightly different than the following characteristics currently listed by HRCI:

1.  The HR profession must be defined by a common body of knowledge which must be the subject of courses of study at educational institutions.

2.  There must be a code of ethics for the HR profession.

3.  HR as a profession must be the focus of ongoing research and development to move it forward in keeping with changing business needs.

4.  There must be a certification program for HR professionals.

5.  There must be a national professional association that represents the views of practitioners in the larger business community and in the legislative process.

Once ASPA had a clear definition of what was required for the practice of personnel to be considered a profession, the members knew what needed to be done to make this a reality: develop a body of knowledge and a certification program to evaluate the competence of practitioners.

# Development of the Human Resource Body of Knowledge

With their goal clearly set, ASPA members went about the process of developing a body of knowledge for their profession. ASPA created a task force to study and report on the issues involved and recommended a course of action. ASPA formed the ASPA Accreditation Institute (AAI) in 1975 with a mandate to define a national body of knowledge for the profession and develop a program to measure the knowledge of its practitioners.

As a first step in the process, AAI created six functional areas for the BOK:

- Employment, Placement, and Personnel Planning
- Training and Development
- Compensation and Benefits
- Health, Safety, and Security
- Employee and Labor Relations
- Personnel Research (later replaced by Management Practices)

Over time, as personnel evolved into human resources, ASPA changed its name to the *Society for Human Resource Management (SHRM)* to reflect changes in the profession. At that point, AAI became the *Human Resource Certification Institute (HRCI)* for the same reason. These associations exist today to represent and certify the profession.

HRCI ensures the continued relevance of the BOK to actual practice with periodic codification studies. The first of these occurred in 1979; subsequent studies were conducted in 1988, 1993, and 1997. These reviews enlisted the participation of thousands of human resource experts in ongoing assessments of what a human resource generalist needs to know to be fully competent.

As with all previous codification studies, HRCI began the most current review in January 2000 with the question, "What should a human resource practitioner know and be able to apply to be considered a competent HR generalist?" HRCI commissioned the Professional Examination Service (PES) to conduct a *practice analysis study* to obtain information from a variety of sources on the existing state of human resource practices as well as trends predicted for future needs of the profession. Under the guidance of PES, additional information was collected through the use of critical incident interviews and focus groups. Finally, 3,000 PHR and 3,000 SPHR certified professionals were surveyed to obtain their views on the current and future needs of the human resource profession.

The practice analysis study culminated in a major revision to the BOK announced in July 2001. The resulting six functional areas constitute the current human resource body of knowledge.

- Strategic Management
- Workforce Planning and Employment
- Human Resource Development
- Compensation and Benefits
- Employee and Labor Relations
- Occupational Health, Safety, and Security

Clearly, the nomenclature has changed over the past 30 years, yet the basic functional areas of HR have remained fairly stable. Significant changes have occurred, however, within the six functional areas, ensuring the relevance of human resource practice to the changing needs of business in the twenty-first century. A major change reflected in the current BOK is the move to ensure that HR professionals understand, and are conversant in, the language of business. By changing the emphasis to "Strategic Management" from "Management Practices," the BOK reflects the increasing need for practitioners to not only fully understand the traditional operational and administrative requirements of human resources, but to also have a broad understanding of other functional areas in business organizations. In order to be true partners actively involved in developing long-term strategies and setting business goals, human resource professionals must be able to tie traditional functions to business needs and actively contribute to achieving organization goals.

As the practice of human resources continues to evolve to meet the needs of international business operations, more emphasis is being placed on the area of global human resources. In response to this globalization, HRCI has developed a new certification, the Global Professional in Human Resources (GPHR). This exam is currently in development, and HRCI plans to offer it to candidates in Spring 2004.

Initially, the certification process was a series of exams, one for each level of certification in each of the six functional areas that was identified by the AAI task force. A few years later, HRCI added a generalist exam. The intent of the process in this early stage was to serve the needs of both specialists and generalists. Because there were two levels of certification for each functional area, the process was quite cumbersome and not a little confusing. Eventually the popularity of the generalist exam led to elimination of the specialist certifications, which left just two: Professional in Human Resources (PHR) and Senior Professional in Human Resources (SPHR). These are the certification levels in existence today.

## Defining the Functional Areas of the BOK

Once HRCI collated the information from the practice analysis study, test specifications were developed to define each functional area. While the body of knowledge is the same for both exam levels (PHR and SPHR), the functional areas in each test are weighted differently to distinguish the different experience requirements of candidates for each level. To understand how this works, let's take a look at what each functional area covers:

*Strategic Management*   Looks at the "big picture" of the organization and requires an understanding of overall business operations, basic knowledge of other functional areas in the organization, and the ability to interact and work effectively with those functions. Strategic Management ensures that traditional HR activities contribute to and support organization goals through the HR planning process, incorporating change initiatives when needed to move the organization forward and providing tools to measure HR effectiveness.

*Workforce Planning and Employment*   Covers activities related to planning for and managing entry into and exit from the organization to meet changing business needs.

*Human Resource Development*   Utilizes training, development, change, and performance management programs to ensure that individuals with the required knowledge, skills, and abilities are available when needed to accomplish organization goals.

*Compensation and Benefits*   Concerns the development, implementation, and maintenance of total compensation systems to support organization goals.

*Employee and Labor Relations*   Addresses the employment relationship in both union and nonunion environments.

*Occupational Health, Safety, and Security*   Covers the regulations and practices for ensuring a safe, secure, and healthful work environment for employees.

## Core Knowledge Requirements of the BOK

In addition to the six functional areas of the BOK, HRCI identified 18 core knowledge requirements for the HR body of knowledge, all of which have implications in all six of the functional areas. Among the core knowledge requirements are topics such as needs assessment and analysis, liability and risk analysis, and motivation concepts and applications to name just a few. I'll discuss each core knowledge topic in more detail in Chapter 2, "Core Knowledge Requirements for HR Professionals."

In the meantime, as an example, let's take a look at how one of the core requirements, "Knowledge of communication strategies," applies in each of the six functional areas:

**Strategic Management**   Building consensus among senior managers for communicating a reorganization to the workforce

**Workforce Planning and Employment**   Communicating a sexual harassment policy to new hires

**Human Resource Development**   Introducing a new performance management process to the workforce

**Compensation and Benefits**   Communicating company benefit plan changes to employees affected by the changes

**Employee and Labor Relations**   Advising management on appropriate responses to a union organizing campaign

**Occupational Health, Safety, and Security**   Introducing an emergency response plan to the workforce

As you can see, each of these scenarios requires a different strategy in order to effectively communicate necessary information to the intended audience. These core knowledge requirements can be the basis for exam questions in any of the functional areas, so it is important to not only be familiar with them in general terms but also to understand how they apply to each area.

HRCI's functional areas, test specifications, and functional area weightings are subject to change at any time and at the Human Resource Certification Institute's sole discretion. Please visit HRCI's website (www.hrci.org) for the most current information on their exams' content. On the HRCI website, you'll find the *PHR & SPHR Certification Handbook*, which is essentially HRCI's bible for PHR/SPHR certification and requirements.

Now that I've introduced the six functional areas in broad terms, let's look at what each exam is intended to measure and how the weightings reflect this in each exam.

## Certification Levels

The questions asked most often by those considering taking the step toward certification are, "Which level should I choose? Is the PHR easier than the SPHR? What is the difference?" Choosing an exam level is an individual choice—if you meet the eligibility requirements (which will be discussed in the next section), the choice is really up to you. As to whether one is easier than another, I doubt that anyone who has taken them would say that either test is easy. They are equally difficult, but in different ways. Let's take a look now at what each of the certifications are intended to measure:

**Professional in Human Resources (PHR)**   The PHR certification measures a candidate's ability to apply HR knowledge at an operational or technical level according to the HRCI website. This exam tests a candidate's ability to apply HR knowledge to handle situations occurring on a day-to-day basis. PHR candidates are skilled in implementing processes and procedures and are knowledgeable in the requirements of employment legislation for problems or situations with a narrow organizational impact. They are able to develop solutions by drawing on a variety of sources and knowledge that apply to a particular situation.

The functional areas in the PHR exam are weighted to reflect its emphasis on the operational, administrative, and tactical application of the elements of the body of knowledge. Table 1.1 shows the functional area weightings for the PHR exam.

**TABLE 1.1**   PHR Functional Area Weighting

| Functional Area | Exam Weight |
| --- | --- |
| Strategic Management | 12% |
| Workforce Planning and Employment | 26% |
| Human Resource Development | 15% |
| Compensation and Benefits | 20% |
| Employee and Labor Relations | 21% |
| Occupational Health, Safety, and Security | 6% |

In the PHR exam, then, the bulk of the questions (47 percent) are related to operational and tactical application of the responsibilities and knowledge for Workforce Planning and Employment and Employee and Labor Relations.

**Senior Professional in Human Resources (SPHR)**   The SPHR certification measures a candidate's strategic perspective and ability to pull information from a variety of sources to address issues with organization-wide impact. This exam measures the candidate's ability to apply HR knowledge and experience in developing policies that will meet the organization's long-term strategic objectives and have impact on the entire organization.

This exam measures a senior-level candidate's strategic ability to integrate HR processes into the "big picture" of an organization's needs and to develop policies to support the achievement of business goals. Table 1.2 demonstrates how the weightings for the functional areas reflect this.

**TABLE 1.2** SPHR Functional Area Weighting

| Functional Area | Exam Weight |
| --- | --- |
| Strategic Management | 26% |
| Workforce Planning and Employment | 16% |
| Human Resource Development | 13% |
| Compensation and Benefits | 16% |
| Employee and Labor Relations | 24% |
| Occupational Health, Safety, and Security | 5% |

From these weightings, you see that 50 percent of the questions on the SPHR exam are related to the senior candidate's ability to develop effective strategic plans for successful business operations (Strategic Management) and policies to guide employment relationships in the organization (Employee and Labor Relations).

The *PHR and SPHR Certification Handbook* contains the most current listing of the HRCI test specs. Because both the PHR and SPHR exams are built around them, I strongly urge those preparing for the test to review the *Handbook* and familiarize themselves with the test specs for each functional area prior to reading the related chapter.

## Eligibility Requirements

As I've mentioned, complete information on eligibility requirements for the exams is available in the *PHR and SPHR Certification Handbook*, and HRCI, of course, makes the final decision as to whether or not a candidate meets them. In this section, I will provide a broad overview of the requirements, along with some suggestions based on the experience of successful candidates.

Any individual with two years of experience in human resource management at the exempt level meets the minimum requirement for either exam. (If you are unsure what this means, see Chapter 6, "Compensation and Benefits," in which I discuss exemption status in some detail.) In order to meet the two-year experience requirements, candidates must spend 51 percent of their work time on exempt-level human resource activities. It's important to note that almost all supervisors and managers perform some HR functions as part of their daily requirements but because these activities are not usually the major function of the position and constitute less than 51 percent of their time at work, this experience most likely would not meet the requirements established by HRCI.

So, the minimum requirements are pretty simple. Let's be realistic for a moment, though. The PHR and SPHR exams do not just measure book knowledge. They measure your ability to apply that knowledge in work situations. The more experience you have in applying knowledge at work, the greater your chances of passing the test. To give candidates an idea of what is needed to be successful (as opposed to what is minimally required), HRCI has developed profiles of the ideal candidate for each of the exams. You can find these on the inside cover of the *PHR & SPHR Certification Handbook* as well as on the HRCI website at www.hrci.org/faq/faq_7.html.

**Recommendations for PHR candidates**    To summarize the ideal PHR profile, HRCI suggests that candidates have between two and four years of professional-level, generalist HR experience before they sit for the exam. PHR candidates generally report to a more senior HR professional within the organization and during the course of their daily work focus on implementation of programs and processes that have already been developed. PHR experience focuses on providing direct services to HR customers within the organization.

**Recommendations for SPHR candidates**    According to HRCI, the ideal SPHR candidate has six to eight years of increasingly responsible HR experience. An SPHR needs to be able to see the "big picture" for the entire organization, not just what works best for the human resource department. This requires the ability to anticipate the impact of policies and decisions on the achievement of organizational goals. SPHR candidates are business focused and understand that HR policies and processes must integrate with and serve the needs of the larger organization. While a PHR's decisions and activities have a more limited effect within narrow segments of the organization, decisions made by SPHR candidates will have organization-wide impact.

**Student or Recent Graduate Requirements**    HRCI has a program that allows college students who will graduate in one year or less and those who have graduated less than one year ago to take the PHR exam without having met the experience requirement. However, students or recent graduates who pass the exam may not use the PHR designation until they provide documentation of having met the two-year minimum experience requirement.

# Recertification

Up until 1996, HRCI awarded lifetime certification to individuals who successfully recertified twice. At that time the policy was changed to reflect the need for professionals to remain current with developments in the field. As a result, the lifetime certification program ended and, with the exception of those who were awarded lifetime certification prior to 1996, all PHRs and SPHRs are now required to recertify every three years.

There are a number of ways to be recertified; they fall into two basic categories: recertification by exam or professional development.

**Recertification by exam**    HR professionals may retake either exam to maintain certification at that level. Information on recertifying by exam is available in the *PHR & SPHR Certification Handbook*.

**Professional development**    To recertify on this basis, PHRs and SPHRs must complete 60 hours of professional development during the three-year period. These 60 hours may be accomplished in a variety of ways. One of the more common is through attending continuing education courses, including workshops and seminars related to HR functions. Another way to earn recertification credit is by developing and/or presenting HR courses, seminars or workshops. Recertification credit for teaching a specific course is awarded only for the first time it is taught.

On-the-job experience can also be the basis for recertification credit: the first time you perform a new task or project that adds to your mastery of the HR BOK, you may earn credits for the work if it meets criteria established by HRCI.

Professionals who take on leadership roles in HR organizations or on government boards or commissions may earn certification for those activities if they meet the criteria established by HRCI.

Finally, certified professionals receive credit for membership in SHRM and other national professional associations or societies. HRCI publishes the *PHR & SPHR Recertification Guide* to provide detailed information on the various methods of recertifying and the amount of credit that can be earned for the different activities. This guide may be downloaded at www.hrci.org, or you may request a copy by calling HRCI at (866) 898-4724.

# The Test

Now, just a little bit of information about the test.

One question asked of me frequently by candidates preparing for the exam is, "What are the questions like?" The HRCI website provides a very detailed explanation of testing theory and question development. In this section, I've summarized what I think is the most practical information for those preparing to take the exams. Those of you who are interested in the details will find more than you ever wanted to know about it on the HRCI website at www.hrci.org/faq/faq_3.html#1.

The questions in these tests are designed to measure whether candidates meet the objectives established by HRCI as the standard required for a minimally qualified human resource professional to achieve certification. The exam questions are designed to assess the depth and breadth of candidates' knowledge and their ability to apply it in practice. Questions at the basic level examine a candidate's ability to not only recall information but to comprehend it as well. These questions designed to measure knowledge and comprehension constitute the smallest percentage of questions on both the exams, but there are slightly more of them on the PHR exam. Questions at the next level, application, are more complex and require the candidate to apply their knowledge in practical situations that require the ability to differentiate which information is most relevant to the situation and will solve the problem. Questions of this type are the ones most prevalent on both the exams. Questions at the highest level of complexity, synthesis, require candidates to use their knowledge in multifaceted situations by drawing upon information from different areas of the body of knowledge to create the best possible result. They require the ability to review actions taken in a variety of situations and evaluate whether or not the best solution was implemented. This type of question appears on both the exams but is more prevalent on the SPHR.

The exam questions, which HRCI refers to as "items," are developed by two panels of volunteers, all of whom are SPHR-certified professionals trained to write test items for the exams. These panels meet twice a year to review items that each member has written between meetings.

Each volunteer generates about 50 questions annually that are then reviewed by the whole panel. Questions that make it through the item-writing panel process move to an item-review panel for additional consideration. As a question travels through either panel, one of three things can happen to it:

1. The item can be rejected as not meeting the criteria for the exam.

2. The item can be returned to the writer for additional work.

3. The item can be forwarded to the next step in the process.

When an item is accepted by the review panel, it moves on to the pretest process for inclusion as an unscored pretest question.

Each item consists of the stem, or premise, and four possible answers: one of these is the correct or best possible answer, and three others are known as distractors. There may be two answers that could be technically correct, but one of them is the best possible answer. As part of the item development process, HRCI requires that the correct answers are documented, and they take great care to ensure that the best possible answer is one that is legally defensible.

Each of the exams consists of 200 multiple-choice test questions (which are used to determine your score) and 25 pretest items (which are not scored), for a total of 225 test items. The exams are four hours long. This means that you will have 1.07 minutes to answer each question. You'll be surprised at how much time this gives you to consider your answers if you are well-prepared by your experience and have taken sufficient time to study the test specifications. As you answer practice questions in preparation for the exam, be sure to time yourself so you can get a feel for how much time it takes you to answer each question.

Test candidates often ask why the pretest questions are included on the exam, and the answer is simple: these items are included to validate them prior to inclusion on future exams as scored questions. While the 25 pretest items are not scored, you will not know which questions are scored or not while taking the exam, so it's important to treat every question as though it will be scored.

The more you know about how the questions are designed, the better able you will be to focus your study, which leads us to the next section: some tips on preparing for the exam and what to expect on test day.

If you are anything like the tens of thousands of HR professionals who have taken the certification exam since 1976, you are probably a little nervous about how you will do and what is the best way to prepare. In this section, I will provide you with some hints and tips gathered from my experiences as well as from others who have generously shared their experience in taking these exams.

## It's *Experiential* and *Federal*

The most important thing to keep in mind, and this can't be stressed enough, is that these exams are *experiential*. That means they test your ability to apply knowledge, not just the fact that you have knowledge. For this reason, memorizing facts is not all that helpful. With a few exceptions, it is far more important to understand the *concepts* behind laws and practices and how they are best applied in real life situations. Having said that, you should be aware of the requirements of different *federal* employment legislation and significant case law that has developed since the 1960s.

Another crucial factor to keep in mind is that these exams test your ability to apply knowledge of *federal* legislation, which is very often different from the requirements of your particular state. This brings us to our first bit of advice from previous test candidates:

> Do not rely on your past experiences too heavily. Just because you have done it
> that way at one company doesn't mean it is the right (or legal!) way.
> —*Becky Rasmussen, PHR, May 2003*

> Don't necessarily think of how you would do it at work. It is possible the way
> your company is doing it is wrong so you will answer the question wrong.
> Look for the most correct answer and take plenty of practice tests. The more
> you take, the more familiar you will become with test taking.
> —*Susan K. Craft, MS, PHR*

This tip applies to several situations: your state requirements may be different from the federal requirements that are the subject of the test, your company practice may not be up-to-date with current requirements, and in some cases, you may be operating on the basis of a common myth about legal requirements or HR practices that is not, in fact, accurate. One way that HRCI tests the depth of knowledge of candidates is to provide one of those commonly held myths as one of the distractors for a question. It's not really a trick question, but a candidate with minimal experience may not know the difference. As you study, think about why you do things in a particular way, how you got that information, and how sure you are that it is the most current and up-to-date. If it is current, great! You're a step ahead of the study game. If you aren't sure it's the most current, do a little research to find out if it will apply on the exam, if it's a state requirement, or if it's possibly some misinformation that you picked up somewhere along the way.

## What the Questions Look Like

As mentioned earlier, the HRCI website goes into a fair amount of detail on the technical aspects of test development. Much of that technical information won't help you in developing a study plan. However, you may find it useful to know the types of questions that the item-writing panels are trained to develop.

In the previous section, we discussed the different parts that make up a test item. Each item begins with a stem, which presents a statement or a question requiring a response. The stems will either ask a question or present an unfinished statement to be completed. Within that context, the stem can be categorized in one of the following ways:

**Purpose**   To answer these questions, you need to demonstrate that you know the objective of a particular law, regulation, or HR practice.

**Ordering**   These questions require that you know the sequence of a multipart process or practice. A question may require that you are able to identify what needs to happen before or after any step in the process.

**Recognition of error**   These questions require you to be familiar with HR practices and federal laws in order to identify practices or actions that are incorrect and to understand why they are.

**Cause and effect**   To answer a question phrased in this way, you will need to understand the consequences of a practice or action.

**Similarity**   To correctly answer these questions, you must be able to identify the common elements of two or more practices, ideas, or concepts.

**Association**   These questions require candidates to form a connection between two concepts or ideas.

**Definition**   These questions may provide a definition and require that you select the correct term, or they may provide a term and provide four possible definitions.

Finally, SPHR candidates in particular should prepare themselves for scenario-type test items. These items are preceded by a short description of a typical HR situation and are followed by two or more questions that relate back to the same scenario. These items are well suited to test concepts at the synthesis level of complexity.

> My experience was that the actual test differed from any of the prep materials or sample tests that I had seen. The exam questions were differentiated by nuance rather than clear distinctions. Studying from multiple sources helped me be better prepared for this unexpected approach.
> —*Lyman Black, SPHR, May 2003*

# Preparing for the Exam

There are a number of options available to assist candidates in preparing for the exams. One option is a self-study program that you put together for yourself based on the test specifications. Another option, depending on your location, is to attend a formal preparation course. In the last few years, informal online study groups have become popular and effective ways to prepare for the exam. Regardless of the option you choose, the most important step is to know what you already know. Then figure out what you need to learn and develop a study plan to help you learn it.

## Develop a Study Plan

While many are tempted to jump in and immediately start reading books or taking classes, the best thing you can do for yourself at the outset is to identify where you are right now and what study methods have worked for you in the past and develop a study plan for yourself.

> The study technique that worked best for me was simply making preparation for the test a priority! I outlined a realistic study schedule for myself and stuck to it as much as possible. Plus, I studied away from my everyday environment in order to avoid distractions. For me this was a local bookstore café, a table covered with notes, a latte in one hand and a pack of flashcards in the other...and it worked!
> —*Julie O'Brien, PHR, May 2003*

**Where are you right now?**   The best way to answer this question is to take the self-assessment test immediately following the Introduction to this book. This will help you to see where your strengths and weaknesses lie. Based on the assessment test and on your work experience, make a list of areas in which you will need to spend the bulk of your time studying (your weaknesses) and the areas you simply need a refresher review (your strengths).

**What study methods have worked for you in the past?**   This may be easy or hard to determine, depending on how long it's been since you took a class. Make a list of study methods that you have used successfully in the past.

**Develop a study plan.**   With your list of strengths and weaknesses and the study methods that work for you, create a study plan:

> **Develop a timeline.**   Decide how much time you need to spend on each functional area of the body of knowledge.
>
> Working back from the test date, schedule your study time according to your strengths and weaknesses. You may want to leave time close to the test date for an overall review—be reasonable with yourself! Be sure to factor in work commitments, family events, vacations, and holidays so you don't set yourself up for failure.
>
> **Get organized!**   Set up folders or a binder with dividers to collect information for each functional area so you know where to find it when you are reviewing the material.
>
> **Plan the work, then work the plan!**   Make sure you keep up with the plan you have set for yourself.

> > Keep up with the reading; do it every week, faithfully. Take notes on what you don't understand, then ask someone about them.
> >
> > *—Becky Rasmussen, PHR, May 2003*
> >
> > Make sure you don't cram; at least a week before the test, take some days off or make extra time available to study so that you're not cramming the night before.
> >
> > *—Rose Chang, PHR, December 2002*

You can use the following list to help keep you organized.

> **Did you do the following?**

> Assess your strengths and weaknesses by taking the assessment test at the beginning of this book?

> Review the HRCI test specifications?

> Identify study methods that will work for you such as self-study, working with a study partner, using a virtual (online) study group, or taking a formal preparation class?

> Identify useful study materials such as this study guide and CD contents, online HR bulletin boards, current HR books and magazines?

> Develop a study time line?

Plan to start studying three to four months before the test?

Allow more time to study weaker areas?

Allow refresh time for stronger areas?

Schedule weekly meetings with a study partner?

Set up a file or a binder with space for each functional area to store all your study materials, questions, and practice tests?

Allow time two to three weeks before the test for a final review of everything you've studied?

Simulate the test experience by finding a place to study that is free from distractions and giving yourself 1.07 minutes to answer each bonus exam question from this book? Challenge yourself further by setting a timer to see how well you do?

 Stop studying two days before the test. Rest. Relax. You've done everything you could. Now it's time to prepare mentally and physically for test day.

## Study Options

There are several study options available for exam candidates: study partners, self-study, and formal preparation courses are the most common. Whichever option you choose, be sure to review the *PHR and SPHR Certification Handbook*, specifically Appendix A, to ensure that you cover all areas of the test specifications.

**Study partners**   No matter which study option works best for you, many have found that partnering with someone else is a critical part of the process. Find one or two others who are studying, develop a group study plan, and meet each week to review the material for that week. Working with a reliable study partner makes the process more enjoyable and helps you to stay focused. The ideal study partner is one whose areas of strength coincide with your areas of weakness and vice versa. One effective technique is to prepare the material and "teach" it to your study partner. Teaching your partner one of your weaker areas results in a deeper understanding than just reading or listening to someone else talk about it.

**Online study groups**   If there is no one local for you to partner with, try an online study group. If you are a member of SHRM, you can find others interested in forming an online study group on the HRCI/Certification bulletin board at www.shrm.org/forums. There are also a number of other online communities where you may find study partners, including HR-Man at www.hr-man.com/.

> I'd advise anyone to form a study group and meet on a regular basis to read, compare notes, quiz each other, and lend moral support! Not only did I learn a lot from my study partners, I gained some wonderful professional friendships—and we ALL passed!
>
> —*Julie O'Brien, PHR, May 2003*

> Present the material yourself! Don't just listen, participate. If you teach it, you think of it much differently than if you are sitting passively and listening.
>
> —*Alicia Chatman, SPHR, May 2001*

> I set up a very small study group; three people. We met once a week until a month before the test, when we met twice a week. It was good to have someone say, "Listen to the question." This made me slow down and review the phrasing and some key words like "most," "not," "least," etc.
>
> —*Patricia Kelleher, SPHR, May 2003*

**Preparation materials**   There are several publications designed to prepare candidates for the exams. This book (of course!) is an intense, very focused overview of material you may find on the exam.

Other helpful publications include the SHRM Learning System, available online from the SHRM Store at www.shrm.org/learning/, and the Human Resource Certification Program (HRCP) available at www.hrcp.com/.

At the end of this book, Appendix B, "Resources," provides a list of additional materials that focus on specific functional areas, and there are many other excellent sources available.

> I think there was a synergistic benefit from applying several approaches rather than using just one technique or single source of information. I used several approaches to prepare: two study guides, a review course, and flash cards. I also found that my kids enjoyed quizzing me during our times driving to school, sports, etc.
>
> —*Lyman Black, SPHR, May 2003*

**Self-study**   Self-study provides you with the greatest flexibility in deciding what areas to focus on. If you go this route, developing a study plan is crucial in keeping you focused (and be sure to use Appendix A of the *PHR/SPHR Certification Guide* when you set up your plan). Equally important to this method is finding a study partner to share questions and ideas.

> Capitalize on your resources. Look to guidance from peers, bosses, consultants, subject matter experts, textbooks, white papers, and articles, and anyone/anything else you can find that will complement your knowledge. I made my own flash cards on specific topics where my knowledge was weaker. Those helped a lot, too.
>
> —*Shirley Pincus, SPHR, May 2000, Recertified June 2003*

**Formal preparation courses**   A number of organizations sponsor formal preparation courses designed specifically for the exam. These are offered by colleges and universities and by local SHRM chapters in some cases. Contact your local SHRM chapter for information on courses in your area.

## Preparation Techniques

To begin with, the best preparation for the exam is solid knowledge of human resource practices and employment law combined with broad generalist experience. Because it is experiential in nature, your ability to use HR knowledge in practical situations is the key to success. This is not a test that you can "cram" for, regardless of the materials you use.

Rewrite the book in your words! Use your experiences to explain the lesson. It will help you remember the lesson.

> —*Alicia Chatman, SPHR, May 2001*

Preparation materials can help provide an organized way of approaching the material. In many cases, you already have the information, you just need a refresher of where it came from and the reason it is appropriate for a particular situation.

> A friend of mine used the practice tests to give me oral exams on the material. This was very helpful because I was not reading the questions, just listening to them and answering them, marking of course the ones that I answered wrong to emphasize my study on that specific topic.
>
> —*Marcela Echeverria, PHR, May 2003*

> I found an "SQ3R" technique (Survey, Question, Read, Recite, Review) effective in studying the materials.
>
> —*Lyman Black, SPHR, May 2003*

Possibly the best advice to give you is this: don't rely on a single source of information in your preparation. If you have a limited budget, make use of the library to check out books about the various functional areas. If you are financially able and so inclined, take the opportunity to build your personal HR library (and don't forget to read the books while you're at it!). Take a preparation course. Form a study group. Ask questions of your peers at work. Find a mentor willing to answer your questions. Make use of online HR bulletin boards to ask questions and to observe what others ask and the responses they receive.

A word of caution about HR bulletin boards: although they can be a great source of information and provide a wide range of responses, in some cases, the answers provided are *not correct*. If you make these bulletin boards part of your preparation, make sure you verify the information you receive with other sources.

None of the people who create the preparation materials for the PHR/SPHR exams have special access to the test. The best any preparation materials can do is to provide you with a review of HRCI's test specifications. It is to your advantage to utilize as many sources of information as you can to obtain the broadest possible review of the HR body of knowledge.

Answer as many questions as possible! Whether or not they are the same format as the questions on the exam, they will assist you in recalling information, and that will benefit you during the exam. Aside from the practice questions provided with this book, a great source of questions is the *HRCI Certification Guide*, by Raymond B. Weinberg (SHRM and HRCI, 2002) (not to be confused with the *PHR/SPHR Certification Handbook*). This little book provides 125 practice questions and answers and is available from online booksellers.

> Knowing the material isn't always enough. Many people sitting for the exam have been away from test-taking for a long time. I think it helped me a lot to practice taking tests with time limits. Practice evaluating similar answers and identifying the best of the lot (not always the very best answer, but the best one presented).
>
> —*Judy Wiens, SPHR, May 2001*

HRCI now also provides a sample test online. There is a fee to take this test, but it does include questions that have been retired from HRCI's test item pool, so it will give you an idea of what to expect.

## Taking the Exam

One of the comments heard most often by candidates as they leave the test site is that the information in their preparation materials did not bear any resemblance to what was on the test. None of the questions in this book or in any other preparation materials will be exactly like the questions on the exam. The broader your preparation and experience, the greater your ability to successfully answer the exam questions.

Knowing the kinds of questions that may be asked, as described earlier in this chapter, can help you focus your study and be as prepared as possible.

One of the best pieces of advice I've heard about getting ready for test day is to stop studying two or three days before the test. By then, if you've been diligent about your study plan, you will be well prepared. The night before, get a good night's sleep. Allow yourself plenty of time to get to the test site.

> Go to bed early the night before and have a light breakfast in the morning before the test, so you are alert...unlike me who kept falling asleep during the test!
>
> —*Rose Chang, PHR, December 2002*

## On Test Day

Beginning in May 2004, the PHR/SPHR exams will be administered as a Computer Based Test (CBT) by Prometric. This provides candidates with greater flexibility in scheduling the test and has other benefits as well.

The following list provides some time-tested hints and tips for exam day gathered from many who have gone before you and were willing to share some of what they learned in the process. For the day of the exam:

- Get a good night's sleep the night before the test.

- Plan to arrive at least 15 minutes before your scheduled test time.

- Bring your ID and HRCI admission ticket, along with any other required documents.

- Bring only items you must have with you. You will not be able to take anything into the testing area except your ID.

- Don't overeat in the morning or drink a lot of caffeine before the exam.

While taking the exam:

- Read the entire question carefully; don't skim it. Taking the time to do this can make the difference between a correct and incorrect answer.

> I am a speed reader and missing one little word could change the entire question. Slow down and read every word.
>
> —*Marie Atchley, SPHR, December 1999*

- Read all of the answer choices carefully; don't skim them or select an answer before you've read them all.

- If you are unsure of the answer, eliminate as many "wrong" answers as you can to narrow down your choices. Remember: one of them is the correct one!

- Very often your "gut" instinct about the correct answer is right, so go with it.

- Don't over-analyze the questions and answers.

- Don't look for patterns in the answers. A myth has been circulating for a number of years that the longest answer was the correct one—it's just not true.

- If you don't know the answer to a question, *guess*. If you don't answer it, it will be counted as incorrect, so you have nothing to lose, and you might get it right.

> I was not surprised by the test at all. Everyone said it was hard; it was! Everyone said that it was subjective; it was! Everyone said that you will feel like you flunked; I did! (But I actually passed.)
>
> —*Patricia Kelleher, SPHR, May 2003*

## The Aftermath

The best thing about CBTs is that you will know whether or not you passed the exam when you leave the test site. If you pass, knowing immediately relieves you of the anxiety of worrying and wondering about the results for four to six weeks until they arrive in the mail. If you don't pass the test, knowing immediately will probably not make you feel any better about it, but there are a couple of consolations:

1. The time and work you put into studying has already benefited you by increasing your knowledge about your chosen profession—congratulate yourself for investing in your career.

2. While the test is important to you, put it in its proper perspective—it's only a test about HR, it's not your life. People take tests every day and not all of them pass on the first attempt.

If you plan to take the test again, review HRCI's advice on retaking the exam at `http://www.hrci.org/faq/faq_9.html`. Browse through the entire HRCI website—there is a lot of information about how the test is constructed and scored that may help you refine your study plan for better success.

# Summary

Certification for HR professionals is a process that has been evolving for more than 50 years. The HR BOK was first developed in 1975 to define the profession and provide the basis for certification. Over the years, HRCI has updated the BOK to reflect current business needs and trends to ensure its viability in business. Both the PHR and SPHR exams are based on federal legislation and case law and are experiential, meaning that in order to pass them candidates need to have exempt-level experience in the field.

Questions on the exams are developed by certified HR professionals who volunteer their time to produce 50 questions per year. The questions go through two levels of review prior to inclusion as unscored pretest questions on an exam. A question that is validated in this process goes into the pool of questions that are available for testing purposes. Questions that do not pass this rigorous process are either discarded or returned to the writer for additional work.

There are a number of methods that can be used to prepare for the exam. The most important are to use as many sources of information as possible and to study with a partner or group.

# Key Terms

Before you take the exam, be certain you are familiar with the following terms:

Compensation and Benefits

Occupational Health, Safety, and Security

Employee and Labor Relations

Society for Human Resource Management (SHRM)

Human Resource Certification Institute (HRCI)

Strategic Management

Human Resource Development

Workforce Planning and Employment

# Chapter 2

# Core Knowledge Requirements for HR Professionals

## THE HRCI CORE KNOWLEDGE REQUIREMENTS COVERED IN THIS CHAPTER ARE:

- ✓ The interrelationships among HR activities and programs across functional areas
- ✓ Needs assessment and analysis
- ✓ Third party contract management, including development of requests for proposals
- ✓ Communication strategies
- ✓ Documentation requirements
- ✓ Adult learning processes
- ✓ Motivation concepts and applications
- ✓ Training methods
- ✓ Leadership concepts and applications
- ✓ Project management concepts and applications
- ✓ Diversity concepts and applications
- ✓ Human relations concepts and applications (for example, interpersonal and organizational behavior)
- ✓ HR ethics and professional standards
- ✓ Technology and human resource information services (HRIS) to support HR activities
- ✓ Qualitative and quantitative methods and tools for analysis, interpretation, and decision-making purposes

- ✓ **Change management**
- ✓ **Liability and risk management**
- ✓ **Job analysis and job description methods**
- ✓ **Employee records management (for example, retention, disposal)**

As we discussed in Chapter 1, "Certifying Human Resource Professionals," the BOK for HR consists of six functional areas plus the core knowledge requirements. These core areas have been identified as those knowledge and skill capabilities that are essential to competency as an HR professional. Because each of these knowledge areas may have implications for practice in two or more of the HR functional areas, I am introducing the basic concepts in this chapter. These introductions are brief, designed only to provide a refresher for each of the concepts. You will see many of these topics discussed in more detail in subsequent chapters when we discuss how they apply to specific areas of practice.

# Understanding How HR Programs Relate to Each Other

It has become increasingly important for HR practitioners to understand how individual HR programs, processes, policies, and functions interact with each other. Particularly for SPHR candidates, the ability to link together various aspects of best practices and legal requirements from a variety of functional HR areas, along with being able to evaluate the impact of these activities as a whole, is crucial to exam success.

For example, let's consider the possible consequences of changing an organization's compensation strategy.

**Changing the Compensation Plan**

Wright Sisters, Inc. (WSI) manufactures garden equipment and employs about 3,000 people, most of whom work on the production line. WSI prides itself on the quality of its products and the loyalty and dedication of its workforce. For many years, WSI has been considered one of the best places to work in the community; as a result, they were able to be selective about who they hired. About six months ago, a new plant opened in the area, and WSI now faces unaccustomed competition in the labor market. Candidate quality has declined noticeably in recent months and line managers are having some problems maintaining product quality. Senior management is considering a number of options to solve the problem.

While the pay being offered by the new company is about the same as WSI's pay plan, the new plant is located in a brand new building with many amenities that WSI's building doesn't offer. Making changes to the building would require a lengthy remodeling process, and WSI's management wants to take some immediate steps to increase the quality of the candidates they are attracting. As a result, management has decided to increase the starting pay for new hires. At the same time, they are unwilling to make any changes to pay rates for current workers. As the VP of HR contemplates this decision, she foresees some problems:

- Because management is not willing to consider a change to the pay ranges even though they are increasing the starting pay, compression will become an issue within a very short period of time.

- Once word gets out that new employees are making more than employees with more seniority, the VP foresees an increase in employee relations issues, most notably morale problems among the production workers. As she is well aware, morale problems generally lead to decreases in productivity and quality.

- While WSI's workforce has remained loyal to this point, with only a very few defections to the new plant, the VP is concerned that there will be an increase in turnover when employees feel their loyalty is not appreciated.

- Management has always been very open and responsive to employee concerns, so employees have not been susceptible to union organizing efforts. The VP is concerned that this change will open the door for an organizing campaign.

- Finally, the VP is concerned about possible claims of discrimination, as much of WSI's workforce is older than the average age of applicants for these positions.

As she considers these issues, the VP begins work on a presentation for management to ensure that they understand all the implications of this change prior to its implementation: while this change may temporarily solve the recruiting issue, it could easily lead to increased costs in a number of areas.

Understanding the impact of individual programs on the HR function, as well as on the organization as a whole, is key to increasing the strategic value of HR to organizations. As you study the material in this book, keep in mind the possible impact of the various principles, theories, laws, and regulations on HR activities and programs. In this way, you'll gain a better understanding and appreciation of their role in HR.

# Needs Assessment and Analysis

*Needs assessment* and *needs analysis* are terms used interchangeably to describe methods for obtaining the information necessary to make decisions that will best accomplish an organization's goals. These methods can measure needs in any area of business; in HR they are often employed in the areas of training and development, staffing projections, and benefit planning for an organization, but they can be utilized to gather information for any program.

There are many models for needs assessment. The common elements involve the following steps:

**1.** Describe the objective.

This step answers the question, "Where do we want to be?" and looks at the various elements necessary to accomplish that objective. It is important to obtain relevant information from all the possible stakeholders to ensure a full understanding of what is needed, as well as to ensure buy-in when recommendations are put forth. The elements to consider include strategic business goals, department goals and objectives, budget constraints, available resources, and any other factors that impact the situation, whether they are people, skills, or materials—whatever is necessary to meet the objective.

**2.** Define the current situation.

This step answers the question, "Where are we now?" and looks at each element described in Step 1 to determine what is already available within the organization and create an inventory of skills, people, equipment, technology, and whatever assets are already in place.

**3.** Conduct a gap analysis.

A *gap analysis* compares the objective to the current situation and results in a list of people, actions, or items that will be needed to attain the objective described in Step 1. As part of this process, it's important to gather as much information as possible about the gaps so that they are clearly understood and to identify any constraints that may exist to inhibit closing the gaps.

**4.** Set priorities.

In a world of limited resources, you probably won't be able to immediately go out and obtain everything that is needed to fill the gaps that have been identified, so it is important to set priorities.

**5.** Investigate and develop options.

This step answers the question, "What is the most effective way to fill this gap?" Be as open-minded as possible when developing options and collect data from as many sources as are available. Involve others in brainstorming sessions as appropriate and look for ways in which similar needs have been met in your organization and elsewhere.

**6.** Evaluate options and determine budget impact.

Determine which of the possible options you've developed will be the most effective way to fill the gap. A crucial element of this step, and one that some HR professionals neglect to fully consider, is the cost element. It is important to consider both direct and indirect costs: the impact on the company's bottom line in the short term, as well as the return on investment (ROI) and long term costs and savings. Another budgetary consideration is the cost of not implementing the option: in the long run, will it cost more or less to operate without it?

**7.** Recommend solutions.

Whether you or someone higher in the organization is the final decision maker, it's important to document the reasons for selection of a particular solution.

# Third Party Contract Management

A *contract* is a legally enforceable agreement between two or more parties in which all parties benefit in some way. Generally, one party makes an offer to do or provide something of value (a product or service), and the other agrees to do or provide something in return (payment). Contracts can be formal or informal, oral or written. While an oral contract can be legally enforceable, written contracts provide more protection for the parties involved.

In a *third party contract*, some part of the transaction is provided by an entity other than those who have signed the contract. There are many examples of third party contracts in business; perhaps the best-known for HR professionals is an agreement with a temp agency in which the company agrees to pay the temp agency for services provided by an employee of the agency.

As an increasing number of HR functions are outsourced, the need for practitioners to understand the issues involved in effectively managing third party contractors becomes more important. A critical factor for a successful contractor relationship is a clear understanding of the product or service to be provided, along with clearly defined expectations for quality and service levels. This information is best communicated through a process known as a *request for proposal (RFP)*.

In many organizations the RFP process is handled by a purchasing group or is outsourced to someone who specializes in preparing them, but it's important to understand what information is needed to develop an RFP that satisfies both parties. A well-constructed RFP serves as the basis on which the product or service is obtained, a guide to ensure that the delivery meets the organization's requirements and a means of evaluation at the end of the project. While there is no standard RFP format for use in all situations, the elements for developing one are similar.

**Conduct a needs assessment**    Whether you are requesting bids for a one-time project or an ongoing outsource relationship, you must be able to describe your objectives and budget clearly so that vendors will provide an accurate and appropriate proposal.

As part of the needs assessment process, very often a client will conduct informal "pre-proposal" meetings with possible vendors. This is particularly useful when the client has little direct experience with the project or wants to learn more about the product or service in order to describe it more clearly in the RFP. This is sometimes known as "scoping" the project, and can become a more formal process with the use of a scoping document that solicits information from a variety of possible vendors before the RFP is written.

**Developing the RFP**    The format of an RFP varies with each organization. In general, the following components should be included:

1. A brief description of your organization, including information that will help the vendors provide an accurate bid, such as number of employees, locations, and so on.

2. An overview of the project summarizing your needs.

3. Administrative details about the process, including submission deadlines, how to request an extension, the format requirements for submissions, and what happens if there are errors or omissions in the RFP. Information about how the proposals will be evaluated should be included here as well (i.e., will the project be awarded to the lowest bidder or will other criteria be more important?). You should also describe any penalties for late deliveries and how you plan to handle work that comes up that is beyond the scope of the RFP.

4. A clear, complete, and detailed description of the project (also known as the scope of work, technical description, or project specifications) that contains information significant to the ability of the vendor to prepare a bid and that can be measured during the evaluation phase.

5. The name of the contact person for additional information about preparing the proposal.

**Proposal formats** As per Step 3, the RFP should provide vendors with a format to follow when submitting their proposals. This serves two purposes. First, it makes an evaluation of the proposals easier, and second, it ensures that vendors provide all the relevant information for an evaluation of the project. While the format will vary between organizations and different projects, the following elements will enhance your ability to compare and evaluate the proposals:

**Executive summary** A brief overview of the vendor's qualifications to provide the product or service needed by the client.

**Vendor qualifications** Includes references from other clients.

**Project management plan** Describes specifically how the vendor intends to supply the product or service.

**Project team** Includes personnel who will be supplied by the vendor as well as the client's employees who will be involved.

**Roles and responsibilities** Includes information about members of the project team.

**Delivery schedule** Provides a timeline and milestones for the completion of specific events.

**Pricing information** Includes how the project will be billed and whether it is based on project completion, time and materials, or completion of specific milestone events. The vendor should also provide pricing information for any requested work that is beyond the scope of the proposal.

**Evaluate the proposals** Once the proposals have been submitted, the evaluation process can begin. There are many factors to consider, including the reputation of the vendor, the qualifications and experience of the project team, the size of the company and whether or not it has the capability to complete the project, how flexible the vendor can be in terms of schedule or other issues, the proposed cost, whether the schedule submitted meets the needs of the organization, and whether the vendor's approach to the project is compatible with the organization's culture.

**Select a vendor** When the evaluation has been completed, notify the successful vendor, along with those whose proposals were not accepted.

**Negotiate the contract** Formalize the agreement and sign a contract with the successful vendor.

**Execute the agreement** Implement the project. Initially, gathering together all the members of the project team, both those who work for the vendor and those who work for the organization, is important to ensure that the project gets off to a good start. It is also important to maintain contact with the vendor during the implementation phase to ensure that it stays on track and meets your expectations.

**Evaluate the project**    Whether this is an ongoing outsource function or a one-time project, an evaluation ensures that the project continues to meet your needs and provides useful information for future projects.

# Communication Strategies

HR professionals must develop expertise in communicating information to a variety of stakeholders, from top executives to production workers, customers, and vendors. This requires the ability to determine which strategies will most successfully communicate different types of information to these various audiences.

An effective employee *communication strategy* is one that balances management's need to ensure the confidentiality of sensitive company information with the need of employees to know, understand, and feel part of what is happening with the company. An effective strategy not only communicates information, it builds employee trust in the organization in the process. Communicating meaningful information to employees engages them in the success of the business. The more employees know about the company's vision, goals, and operations, the more productive they are. Employees who feel connected to the success of the organization become good-will ambassadors, enhancing its reputation in the community and effectively recruiting qualified candidates for open positions.

Developing an effective communication strategy begins with a clear picture of the result to be accomplished by the information. This piece of information helps to answer additional questions needed for development of the strategy:

- What information will be provided?
- Who is the intended audience?
- Who will provide the information?
- Is the information time sensitive?

The answers to these questions will dictate which delivery methods are most appropriate for the organization, because an effective communication strategy employs multiple methods to deliver its message. To select the best delivery mechanisms for a particular organization and message, it is important to consider the organization's culture. The most effective strategies will be a reflection of the culture, whether it is a very formal one, or one with an informal, laid-back atmosphere. Another consideration that will guide the selection of communication methods is the employee base: is the workforce computer savvy or are employees accustomed to receiving communications in small group meetings from their managers?

An effective communication strategy includes the means for "bottom-up" messages to be delivered to management. This is a key element in building employee trust for the organization. When employees feel that their concerns are heard and addressed, they feel more invested in the organization's success. There are, of course, many communications that are most appropriately delivered "top-down" as well. Mechanisms to enhance both types of communication will contribute to the effectiveness of the overall strategy.

Because HR professionals must communicate a variety of messages to differing audiences, it is likely that multiple communication strategies will be developed to ensure that each audience receives necessary information in the way that best meets its needs.

In subsequent chapters, we will discuss communication strategies for specific employment situations.

# Documentation Requirements

Documentation requirements fall into two basic categories: collecting and maintaining required employment records, such as application forms, tax documents, and benefit records, and maintaining appropriate documentation of employee performance issues.

## Documenting Employment Actions

Traditionally, the HR department has been charged with the responsibility of ensuring that all the i's are dotted and t's are crossed when it comes to documenting employment relationships. As the *subject matter experts (SME)*, HR professionals are those most qualified to ensure the maintenance of proper documentation and to safeguard the privacy of personal employee information. The maintenance of these records is important for two basic reasons: some are required to be maintained to comply with federal, state, or local employment laws, and others provide information necessary for effective management of the organization. In some cases, the records are needed to meet both of those requirements.

Appendix C, "Employment Documents and Retention," provides a detailed list of most employment documents that must be maintained for legal purposes, along with the required retention period required by each federal law.

## Documenting Performance Issues

There are two sides to this topic. The first is the need for managers to address performance issues when they occur in order to effectively manage employee performance. All too often, line managers are reluctant to confront employees about performance issues and neglect to advise employees of any problems until either the annual performance review or when the situation becomes so untenable that the manager's only thought is immediate termination of the employee. In either situation, the employee is taken completely by surprise at the seriousness of the situation and will not have had the opportunity to rectify the problem. This side of performance management will be fully discussed in Chapter 5, "Human Resource Development."

The other side of this issue concerns documentation of the performance issue, which I will discuss now.

Most HR professionals are aware of the general disciplinary process used in nonunion companies. Documenting performance issues begins with keeping written records of each step in this process.

As experienced HR practitioners are aware, including a disciplinary process in an employee handbook can abridge the doctrine of at-will employment (to be fully discussed in Chapter 7, "Employee and Labor Relations"). This presents a dilemma: without documentation of adverse employment actions, employers are unable to defend against claims of discrimination. With a published disciplinary process, employers are vulnerable to claims of discrimination if the process is not followed in all cases. To address these conflicting issues, some employment attorneys recommend that the following process be used as a guideline for managers to follow in addressing performance issues, but that it not be published in the employee handbook.

1. Verbal warning

   While it may seem contradictory to state that a written record of a *verbal warning* should be maintained, it is not. The written record can be as simple as a contemporaneous note by the supervisor that describes the date and time of the warning, the name of the employee involved, what was discussed, and any agreements that were made about future changes in behavior or performance.

2. First written warning

   At this stage, the written record becomes more formal. In some companies, forms are provided for managers to fill in with the appropriate information. In companies without specific forms, the *first written warning* is a memo to the employee describing steps that have already been taken, exactly what the performance problem is, steps that need to be taken to avoid future warnings, and any agreements that have been made about performance changes. This document should be signed by the employee. When employees balk at signing a warning with which they disagree, the supervisor can advise them that signing does not indicate agreement, just that the warning has been discussed. If employees still will not sign, the supervisor can make a note indicating the date and time of the discussion and the fact that the employee refused to sign the document.

3. Final written warning

   A *final written warning* is similar to the first, with the addition of a statement advising the employee that continued inability or refusal to make necessary performance changes will result in further action, up to and including termination of employment.

4. Suspension

   Some companies take an additional step prior to termination and suspend employees for varying periods of time depending on the seriousness of the offense and other considerations. A *suspension* should be accompanied by a written document spelling out all the steps previously taken to resolve the issue, the reason for the suspension, and a statement that continued nonconformance may result in termination.

5. Termination

   At this stage, the employee should be well aware of the issues leading up to the *termination*. Prior to taking this step, it is advisable that HR have counsel review the existing documentation and provide guidance for the final termination letter.

Written documentation of any agreements for severance (with accompanying releases) or for compliance with the ADEA (discussed in Chapter 4, "Workforce Planning and Employment"), along with documentation of compliance with COBRA requirements (discussed in Chapter 6, "Compensation and Benefits") and state unemployment documentation (if required) are some of the additional documents that must be provided and maintained when employees are terminated.

Maintaining contemporaneous records as just described can make the difference between a summary judgment in the employer's favor and a large jury award to a former employee. This process, or one similar to it, should be familiar to all candidates for the PHR/SPHR exams; it covers most performance issues. There are other situations, however, which call for a more extensive record to back up a disciplinary action and require workplace investigations.

## Workplace Investigations

When serious accusations of wrongdoing are made by one employee against another, or when management suspects that illegal activities or serious violations of company policy are occurring, a formal *workplace investigation* must be conducted. The level of the investigation will vary depending on the seriousness of the situation, but in all cases, human resources should be involved, whether as the neutral internal investigator or as the coordinator of an investigation conducted by a third party.

One policy that should be developed and disseminated to employees is the process the company will follow in conducting a workplace investigation. The policy should explain when and why investigations will occur and identify situations that will trigger an investigation. Formulating a policy when there is not an urgent need to implement it accomplishes two purposes. First, it lets employees know the steps the company will take to investigate allegations or suspicions of wrongdoing. Second, it promotes consistency in the execution of the process when it does need to be implemented. Conducting a formal investigation, while not required for all suspected or alleged violations, demonstrates to employees and those outside of the organization that the company is serious about the policies it has published and is fair in investigating allegations of wrongdoing. Should the situation result in some form of legal action, the fact that an investigation is conducted will benefit the company in court.

Investigations are crucial for one type of allegation in particular: sexual harassment. To protect itself from liability, a company must conduct a full, complete, and impartial investigation into all allegations of sexual harassment. The following process for conducting a workplace investigation focuses on allegations of sexual harassment, but the principles can be adapted for use in other situations as needed.

1.  Take action as soon as the company becomes aware of the situation.

    A company may learn of a situation requiring an investigation in a number of ways. A manager may observe something, a witness may report a problem, or an audit may uncover financial discrepancies. In the case of sexual harassment, the need for an investigation usually comes to the attention of the company when an allegation of harassment is made by an employee. In harassment situations, the company must act rapidly to begin its investigation or risk liability for neglecting to protect the complainant in a timely manner.

The first call to make when a company becomes aware of situation requiring an investigation is often to the corporate attorney. Involving the attorney at an early stage in an investigation can benefit the company as it allows documents to be designated as attorney work products covered by attorney-client privilege. They would thus have some protection from discovery in any legal action.

2. Plan the investigation.

   Once the need for an investigation becomes apparent, the next step is to plan the investigation. At this stage, a written investigation policy is of great use in ensuring that the investigation is conducted in a manner that is consistent with previous investigations and uncovers the facts so the employer can take any necessary steps to rectify the situation.

3. Select the investigator.

   Depending upon the situation, the investigator may be an employee of the company, the corporate attorney, or a professional investigator. The key is that the investigator is someone who is credible, impartial, and trained in harassment investigations and who will be an effective witness in the event that the situation results in a lawsuit.

Use caution if you choose your corporate attorney to conduct an investigation. While this may be the appropriate choice in some cases, in the event of legal action, the investigator will likely be called as a witness. This would clearly present a conflict of interest for an attorney who represents the company in other matters.

Any investigations conducted by a third party are subject to requirements of the Fair Credit Reporting Act (FCRA) that these may be considered "investigative consumer reports" subject to FCRA rules. One of these rules requires employees to sign consent forms advising them that they may be subject to third party investigations of misconduct. The consent may be a part of paperwork that is completed by all new hires, is required of all employees when an investigation policy is implemented, or is completed at the time of an investigation. The latter option, from the company's point of view during a confidential investigation, may not be the best alternative.

4. Conduct the investigation.

   The investigator begins by interviewing the complainant and getting the complaint in writing if it has not already been written. The complaint can be either written by the employee or dictated to the investigator and signed by the employee.

   Next, all potential witnesses are interviewed to obtain as much information as possible about the allegation. The investigator should provide little or no information about the situation so as to maintain the integrity of the investigation. Witnesses should be instructed not to discuss the investigation in the workplace.

The final interview is with the alleged harasser, who is given the opportunity to respond to each and every allegation. The investigator should take steps to protect the complainant by reminding the alleged harasser that no retaliatory action will be tolerated.

When interviews are complete, any documents applicable to the situation should be collected, including a review of the files of the employees involved in the complaint, to determine if previous complaints were alleged or committed.

5.  Review and report results.

It is up to the investigator at this stage to determine whether or not any wrongdoing occurred. If wrongdoing did occur, was it simply a violation of company policy or was it unlawful? Based on the answers, an appropriate plan of action can be devised to respond to the complaint.

6.  Take action.

If the results of the investigation are that discrimination did occur, the company must take action to end it.

When the result of the investigation is that no wrongdoing occurred, the investigator should remind both the complainant and the alleged harasser that violations of company policy will not be tolerated. The accused harasser should also be reminded that retaliatory actions against the complainant will not be tolerated.

7.  Maintain records.

The records of internal investigations are subject to discovery should legal action be taken. For that reason, it is important to ensure that there are no extraneous comments or records unrelated to the investigation in the report.

8.  Follow up.

Particularly with regard to sexual harassment allegations, it is important to follow up with the complainant at regular intervals to ensure that corrective action has been taken and no retaliation has occurred. A contemporaneous written record of these follow-up meetings provides additional documentation that the company has responded to the allegation and taken steps to ensure that it has not recurred.

# Adult Learning Processes

The concept that adult learning processes were different from those of children was developed in the United States by Eduard Lindeman during the 1920s. Lindeman first promoted the idea that, for adults, the methods of learning were more important than what was being taught. His belief was that the most effective learning for adults took place in small groups where knowledge could be shared based on the life experience of the participants. Malcolm Knowles expanded on Lindeman's theories in the 1970s when he identified characteristics that set adult learning apart from the way children learn. The work of Lindeman and Knowles is the basis for the study of how adults learn known as *andragogy*. The definition of andragogy evolved as researchers sought to further define adult learning; today it has come to mean education in which the learner participates in decisions about what will be taught and how it will be delivered. This approach is in contrast to *pedagogy*, the study of how children learn, which is defined as education in which the teacher decides what will be taught and how it will be delivered.

Much of Knowles' work centered on identifying characteristics of adult learning that would make the process more productive for learners. Knowles promoted the idea that, with maturity, people grow into new ways of learning, characterized by the following five characteristics, which form the basis of andragogy today:

1.  Self-concept

    An individual's self concept moves from dependency on others to autonomy and self-direction.

2.  Experience

    An individual builds a wealth of knowledge that grows with each new experience. This information reserve can then be drawn upon for further learning.

3.  Readiness to learn

    Individuals become increasingly interested in the relevance of information to specific needs and how directly it applies to their current situations.

4.  Orientation to learning

    The ability to apply information immediately to solve current problems is increasingly important to learners.

5.  Motivation to learn

    The motivation to learn is based more on personal needs and desires than on expectations of others.

These basic characteristics of adult learners are important concepts with implications beyond traditional training and development; they will be covered further in Chapter 5. Understanding the best ways to provide information in work situations can enhance productivity and job satisfaction for the workforce.

# Motivation Concepts and Applications

From the beginning of the industrial revolution, business owners have sought the key to improving productivity. This desire prompted scientists to study the work environment, businesses, and the relationship of people to the organization. These studies led to many theories about work, some related to the physical environment or organization structures and others that looked at why people work and what motivates them. These traditional theories of motivation, discussed in the following sections, center either on the need for employees to be self-motivated or the need for managers to motivate them. They provide a basis for understanding what drives employees to perform at peak levels of productivity, which can help managers understand the reasons for lowered productivity. Each functional area of the HR body of knowledge is impacted by whether or not employees are motivated or demotivated at work. HR professionals need to understand how these concepts affect their HR programs.

## Abraham Maslow: The Hierarchy of Needs (1954)

Maslow, a behavioral scientist, developed his *hierarchy of needs* to explain how people meet their needs through work. This theory describes needs that begin with the most basic requirements for life—food, shelter, and basic physical comforts—and progresses through stages of growth as people strive to fill higher-level needs. Maslow identified five levels of needs that motivate people:

**Physiological needs**   These are the most basic needs. Individuals striving to find enough food to eat or a place to live are motivated by attaining those things. People at this level are motivated by actions that provide the basic necessities of life.

**Safety needs**   Once people have food and shelter, they look for ways to ensure that they are safe from physical and emotional harm.

**Social needs**   At this level, people are motivated by the desire for acceptance and belonging within their social group.

**Esteem needs**   At this level, people are motivated by recognition for their achievements.

**Self-actualization needs**   When people are confident that their basic needs have been met, they become motivated by opportunities to be creative and fulfill their own potential. They do not look outside themselves for these opportunities, but depend on themselves to find and act on them.

## Fredrick Herzberg: Motivation/Hygiene Theory (1959)

Herzberg's *motivation/hygiene theory* (also known as the *two-factor theory*) began with a study on job attitudes that he conducted in Pittsburgh in the 1950s. He began the study believing that the causes of job satisfaction would be the opposite of the causes of job dissatisfaction. However, his review of several thousand books and articles on job attitudes did not prove his premise; in fact, the results were so vague that it was not possible to draw any conclusions. This led Herzberg to conduct a study in which he asked the participants to identify the work experiences that resulted in positive feelings about their jobs and the ones that resulted in negative feelings.

The result, as Herzberg himself described it in an interview, was that "What makes people happy is what they do or the way they're utilized, and what makes people unhappy is the way they're treated." ("An Interview with Frederick Herzberg: Managers or Animal Trainers?" *Management Review*, 1971) Both factors can motivate workers, but they work for very different reasons. The satisfaction (motivation) factors motivate by changing the nature of the work so that people are challenged to develop their talents and fulfill their potential. The dissatisfaction (hygiene) factors motivate to the extent that they allow people to avoid unpleasant experiences. For example, as long as they continue to do the work, they continue to receive a paycheck. Hygiene factors provide only short-term benefits to employers, while the motivation factors lead to longer-term job satisfaction.

A result of Herzberg's theory is the concept of *job enrichment* in which the significance of the tasks in a job is increased to provide challenging work and growth opportunities.

## Douglas McGregor: Theory X and Theory Y (1960)

McGregor expanded on Maslow's work to describe the behavior of managers in their relationships with their employees. McGregor identified two distinct management approaches, *Theory X and Theory Y*.

Theory X managers have a world view of employees as lazy and uninterested in work and needing constant direction to complete their work. Theory X managers believe that employees do not want to take responsibility and are interested in job security above all else.

In contrast, Theory Y managers believe that, given the opportunity, people will seek out challenging work and additional responsibility if the work is satisfying.

## Clayton Alderfer: ERG Theory (1969)

The *ERG theory* developed by Alderfer builds on Maslow's work as well. Alderfer identifies three levels of needs: existence, relatedness, and growth.

**Existence**   Relates to Maslow's definition of physiological and safety needs as those that are required to maintain basic life needs.

**Relatedness**   Similar to Maslow's descriptions of social needs and the esteem we find from others.

**Growth**   Based on the self-esteem and self-actualization concepts Maslow described.

The premise for Maslow's theory was that people move sequentially through the levels one at a time. Alderfer's theory allows for the possibility that people can work on multiple levels simultaneously. It also describes the concept of frustration-regression, which occurs when an individual falls back to a lower level in frustration at the difficulty of a higher level.

## David McClelland: Acquired Needs Theory (1961)

The premise of McClelland's *acquired needs theory* is that people's motivations are based on experiences acquired throughout their lives, and that they are motivated to achieve in one of three areas:

**Achievement**   Those motivated by achievement take moderate risks to achieve their goals, respond to frequent feedback, and generally prefer to work as sole contributors or with others interested in achieving at the same level.

**Affiliation**   Individuals who need affiliation look for acceptance within the work group and need regular interaction with their coworkers or customers.

**Power**   These individuals are either looking for personal power or institutional power. Those interested in institutional power are often effective managers who are motivated by coordinating work groups to achieve organization goals.

## J. Stacy Adams: Equity Theory (1963)

The basic concept of Adams' *equity theory* is that people are constantly measuring what they put into work against what they get from work. If their perception is that it is a fair trade, they are motivated to continue contributing at the same level. When they perceive there is an imbalance and they are putting in more than they are getting back, they become demotivated and lose interest in their work, decreasing productivity and quality.

## Victor Vroom: Expectancy Theory (1964)

Vroom's *expectancy theory* maintains that people are motivated by the expectation of the reward they will receive when they succeed, and that each individual calculates the level of effort required to receive a particular reward to determine if the reward is worth the effort that is required to attain it. Vroom uses the following terms to explain this theory:

**Expectancy**   Vroom's theory starts with an individual's assessment of their capability to successfully complete the assigned work.

**Instrumentality**   If an individual believes they are capable of completing the assignment, they next assess "what's in it for me"—that is, will their effort to complete the work be the instrument for obtaining a reward for the work.

**Valence**   This is the result of the calculation made by an individual of whether the possible reward is worth the effort required to successfully complete the work.

## B. F. Skinner: Operant Conditioning (1957)

The results of Skinner's work on *behavioral reinforcement* are more commonly known as behavior modification. His basic theory is that behavior can be changed through the use of four intervention strategies:

**Positive reinforcement**   Encourages continuation of the behavior by providing a pleasant response when the behavior occurs.

**Negative reinforcement**   Encourages continuation of the behavior by removing an unpleasant response to a behavior.

**Punishment**   Discourages future occurrence of the behavior by providing an unpleasant response when the behavior occurs.

**Extinction**   Discourages the future occurrence of the behavior by ceasing to provide a reinforcement for it. For example, when a parent praises a child for doing his homework each night and the child starts doing it without being reminded, the parent may stop praising the child.

If the child then reverts to the previous behavior of forgetting to do his homework, the behavior has become extinct.

## Real World Scenario

### Operant Conditioning in Customer Service

The customer service manager at Wright Sisters, Inc., Susan Sherwood, has a problem employee, David Rogers. David can be charming and has a knack for calming down disgruntled customers on the phone. In fact, his coworkers often rely on him for assistance with unhappy customers who are difficult to please. David has worked for WSI for three years and is for the most part productive and cooperative. There are times, however, when he has snapped at coworkers, and he is often disruptive in staff meetings. Recently, Susan has observed him being rude to some customers during customer support calls. She has also noticed that coworkers have stopped giving him work that he is supposed be doing; instead they are doing it themselves to avoid dealing with him. Susan, who has been working on her MBA, just finished a course in industrial psychology and decides to give Skinner's theory of operant conditioning a try to see if it will work in a practical application. She comes up with the following interventions to use with David:

**Positive reinforcement**   At the end of each meeting in which David exhibits professional behavior, Susan will thank him publicly for his contribution during the meeting.

**Negative reinforcement**   When David behaves professionally during the day and does not create any disruptions, he will not have to meet with Susan at the end of the day.

**Punishment**   Whenever David is rude to a customer or coworker, Susan will reprimand him.

**Extinction**   Coworkers will no longer do his work for him when David becomes confrontational with them.

# Training Methods

Devising suitable delivery methods for training programs is subject to a number of factors, including what information is to be covered, who will be attending the training, the experience level of the participants, availability of technology, and others. In Chapter 5, I will go into some detail about the factors to consider in selecting the appropriate method and delivering the training. Here I will simply introduce the various training methods:

**Passive training methods**   *Passive training methods* are those in which the learner listens to and absorbs information. These methods are instructor focused and require little or no active participation from the learner.

   **Conference**   *Conferences* are generally a combination of lecture or presentation with question-and-answer sessions involving the participants.

**Lecture**   *Lectures* are used to inform and to answer questions, often in combination with other training methods such as demonstrations.

**Distance learning**   Similar to lectures, *distance learning* allows simultaneous training to occur in geographically dispersed multiple locations. Distance learning provides participants with the ability to communicate with presenters and participants in other locations.

**Active training methods**   *Active training methods* are those in which the learning experience is focused on the learner.

**Case studies**   A *case study* reproduces a realistic situation that provides learners with the opportunity to analyze the circumstances as though it was encountered in the course of business. Case studies provide learners with the opportunity to investigate, study, and analyze the situation and then discuss the possible solutions with the group. Solutions are developed and presented to fellow learners.

**Computer-based training (CBT)**   *Computer-based training* is an interactive training method that combines elements of the lecture, demonstration, one-on-one, and simulation methods, thus allowing the learner to have a real-world learning experience. Well-designed CBT programs ensure consistency of training across a company that is geographically dispersed. CBT is based on the programmed instruction method.

**Programmed instruction**   *Programmed instruction*, also referred to as self-paced training, is the forerunner of CBT. In this method, the learner progresses from lesson to lesson in a predesigned course of instruction as mastery of the objectives is attained. This method allows learners to progress at their own rate. Programmed instruction is effective for disseminating facts and concepts, refreshing previously learned skills, or expanding a learner's knowledge in a field that is already familiar.

**Self-study**   A program of *self-study* is directed entirely by the learner, who determines what, when, and where learning will occur. It may be based on a defined program and involve a trainer or mentor, but it is controlled by the learner.

**Simulation**   *Simulation training* is an interactive training method that provides the learner with opportunities to try out new skills or practice procedures in a setting that does not endanger the inexperienced trainee, coworkers, or the public.

**Vestibule**   *Vestibule training* is a form of the simulation method. It allows inexperienced workers to become familiar with and gain experience using equipment that is either hazardous or requires a level of speed that can only be attained with practice. Vestibule training is commonly used to train equipment operators in the construction industry and to help retail clerks gain speed at the checkout counter.

**Experiential Training Methods**   *Experiential training methods* provide experience in real-time situations.

**Demonstration**   The *demonstration* method of training can be used as part of an on-the-job training program or combined with a lecture program. The method involves the trainer explaining the process or operation, demonstrating it on the equipment, and then having the learner perform it under the guidance of the trainer.

**One-on-one**    In *one-on-one training*, an inexperienced worker is paired with an experienced supervisor or coworker who utilizes a variety of techniques to provide the worker with the information and hands-on experience necessary to do the job.

**Performance**    *Performance-based training (PBT)* is most often utilized to correct performance problems in highly technical or hazardous professions. The trainee is provided with opportunities to practice and demonstrate the necessary skill or knowledge until the required level of proficiency is mastered.

# Leadership Concepts and Applications

Much has been written about leaders and how they develop: are they born or made? There is little agreement in research about where leaders come from. Does the effectiveness of a leader depend on the situation? Which is more important as a function of leadership, the ability to develop structures or the ability to develop people? One thing is certain: however they do so, effective leaders are able to inspire the people around them to do their best work and influence people to follow them in achieving a common goal. In this section, I'll introduce you to some of the theories researchers have developed to explain leadership; as you will see, none of the theories are able to explain all aspects of leadership. While some theories are currently more popular than others, all of them are the subject of ongoing study as researchers continue to try to explain leadership ability.

The study of how leaders become leaders was first addressed during the nineteenth century when Thomas Carlyle suggested the "great man" theory; that is, that leaders are born with innate qualities that set them apart from other "mere mortals." It was Carlyle's premise that leadership could not be learned but was instead the result of the superior qualities of some few men. Early in the twentieth century this premise became the basis for trait theories of leadership that look to the personality, intellect, and physical traits of individuals to explain their ability to lead others.

Several drawbacks to trait theories became apparent over time. The first and most significant of these was that each researcher identified different leadership traits, which resulted in multiple lists of relevant traits. The second was that research showed there was little difference between the traits exhibited by leaders and those of followers. Traits such as courage and intelligence were found in followers as often as in leaders. Finally, trait theories did not explain how leaders were successful in different situations using very different methods. As the limitations of early explanations for leadership development became clear, researchers turned to other areas for investigation, including behavioral, situational, and contingency theories of leadership.

## Behavioral Theories

During the 1940s, researchers moved to a new area of research and focused on the ability of leadership to be taught: anyone could become a leader with the right information. This view of leadership moved the research focus from personality traits to what leaders did to inspire people to follow them. Two aspects of behavior became apparent in the research. The first was behavior that focused on the structural elements of the job, such as establishing rules and guidelines for employees. The second was behavior that considered the needs of employees, such as standing up for them and explaining decisions. Douglas McGregor's Theory X and Theory Y provide an example of a behavioral theory of leadership.

As with trait theories, there were leadership characteristics that were not explained by behavioral theories, most notably, how or why one behavioral aspect worked in one situation but not in others. This led to a new avenue for research: the impact of leadership in different situations.

## Situational Theories

Situational theories of leadership seek to explain leader effectiveness in different situations. The elements that are considered in situational theories are how the leader and followers interact and how the work is structured. There are several well-known theories that fall into this category.

**Blake-Mouton Managerial Grid, 1968**    Robert R. Blake and Jane S. Mouton developed a grid to explain the characteristics of different leadership styles. The grid considers two aspects of leadership: concern for people and concern for production, as shown in Figure 2.1.

**FIGURE 2.1**    Blake-Mouton managerial grid

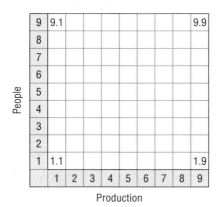

The grid uses nine levels to measure each aspect. Leaders at the lowest extreme (1,1) show no concern for either people or production. At the highest extreme (9,9), leaders show maximum concern for both production and people, and according to Blake and Mouton, are the most effective leaders.

**Path-goal theory, 1971**    The path-goal theory of leadership was developed by Robert House, a professor at the Wharton School of Business. This theory proposes that a leader can impact the behavior of a group by establishing goals and providing direction on reaching those goals.

House describes four leadership styles that may be used to accomplish this, based on the specific situation: directive, which specifies what is to be done; supportive, in which the leader provides encouragement for the group members; participative, in which the leader involves the group in the decision-making process; and achievement, in which the leader establishes a difficult goal and encourages the group to accomplish it.

**Hersey-Blanchard-1977**   Paul Hersey and Kenneth Blanchard describe leadership in terms of the maturity level of their followers. In this theory, maturity refers to both psychological maturity (or motivation), and job task maturity (or level of experience). The model provides four styles of leadership appropriate in different circumstances:

**Telling**   When followers are immature or inexperienced, the leader must be more directive by providing guidelines and defining roles for them.

**Selling**   When followers have some experience, the leader is still directing them but in a more general sense. Greater emphasis is placed on encouraging followers who have the motivation but lack sufficient experience to do the job.

**Participating**   At this level, the followers have progressed in terms of their ability but may lack the necessary motivation and require support to encourage them to act on their own.

**Delegating**   At this level, followers have both the experience and motivation to accomplish their tasks. The leader identifies the goal, and followers are accountable for producing results.

While situational theories address issues that were missing in both the trait and behavioral theories, they are criticized for being two-dimensional and not allowing for multifaceted situations that occur in the real world of business. In addition, these theories do not account for differences in culture and gender in explaining leadership.

## Contingency Theories

To address some of these criticisms, Fred E. Fiedler developed a model known as Fiedler's Contingency Theory to address the shortcomings of situational theories. Fiedler's theory begins with an assessment of the leader's style. Fiedler uses a method known as the "least preferred coworker" scale to determine this. Leaders identify the coworker, past or present, with whom they had the most difficulty working and rate this person on a scale of 1 to 8 on a series of measures such as the coworker's level of cooperation and friendliness. The result is known as the least preferred coworker (LPC) score. A high LPC score indicates that the leader has a greater concern for people than for tasks, and a low score indicates a greater concern for tasks. Fiedler proposed that the LPC score could be used to predict the situations in which a leader would have a better chance for success.

Fiedler then describes situations in terms of three aspects:

**Leader-member relations**   The relationships leaders have with members of the group are the key factor in determining the level of influence the leader has within the group.

**Task structure**   Jobs that are highly structured provide a leader with greater influence than do those that require less structure.

**Position power**   Situations in which a leader has the discretion to assign tasks or to reward or punish members of the group provide the leader with a greater chance of success.

Each of these theories provides a different perspective on leadership and helps to explain something about it. They are the basis for many of the discussions in subsequent chapters; in particular, Chapters 3, 5, and 7 consider different aspects of the interactions between employees and managers, and these theories may provide the basis for a deeper understanding of the ways in which managers and leaders are able to influence employees.

## Leadership Styles

Everyone has experienced leaders with different styles: the authoritarian leader who tells employees what to do, the democratic leader who involves employees in the process, the laissez-faire leader who abdicates responsibility and leaves employees to figure things out without guidance or support, and the coach who prepares employees to take on additional responsibility. There are different situations when all of these styles may be appropriate.

**Authoritarian or directive**   These leaders are effective in situations requiring immediate action or those that are life threatening. When productivity is the highest concern, authoritarian leadership may be the best style.

**Democratic**   These leaders are most effective in environments of highly skilled professional employees who are self-motivated and accomplish tasks on their own. When relationships in the work environment are of primary concern, this style is most effective.

**Laissez-faire**   These leaders allow group members to operate on their own. This leadership style provides no direction or guidance and can lead to chaos if members lack confidence in their abilities. For individuals who are highly motivated and can work independently, this may be an acceptable style. In general, it results in lower levels of productivity.

**Coaching**   These leaders work with group members to develop skills and abilities so they will be able to operate independently.

There are two other leadership styles to keep in mind: transactional leadership and transformational leadership.

**Transactional**   *Transactional leadership* focuses on getting the job done and seeks to do this by offering a reward in exchange for accomplishing organization goals. Transactional leaders manage by exception, either by seeking out areas where rules are not being followed and making a correction, or by taking action when the goal is not met.

**Transformation**   *Transformational leadership* focuses on the relationships in the group, building them to achieve organization goals. These leaders set the ideal for the group and act as role models, inspiring excellence within the group and stimulating new ideas and perspectives. Transformational leaders are coaches who work with individuals to develop their skills and abilities and improve their performance.

# Project Management Concepts and Applications

*Project management* describes the process of initiating, planning, executing, controlling, and closing an assignment that is temporary in nature. The assignment may involve designing a new software program, constructing a building, implementing a new marketing strategy, or any other activity that is not part of the ongoing operations of a business.

For HR professionals, the ability to manage projects is critical to success. The following list shows how HR projects can occur in any of the functional areas:

**Strategic Management**   Integrating the cultures of two organizations after a merger

**Workforce Planning and Employment**   Developing a new hire orientation program

**Human Resource Development**   Creating a career development program

**Compensation and Benefits**   Developing a stock option program

**Employee and Labor Relations**   Developing an employee handbook

**Occupational Health, Safety, and Security**   Developing an emergency response plan

Each of these activities is a short-term assignment that will result in a program that will become part of the organization operations when it is complete, but the process of designing the program is not an ongoing operation.

The Project Management Institute maintains a website with additional information about projects and how they are managed at www.pmi.org.

# Diversity Concepts and Applications

As businesses become global entities employing individuals with diverse cultural, racial, and ethnic backgrounds, understanding *workplace diversity* becomes more critical to organizational success. Aside from the fact that workplace diversity is the right thing to have, there are many business reasons to make it a priority:

**A diverse workforce is more creative**   Increasing the variety of perspectives available to an organization brings new perspectives to decision-making processes, challenging conventional wisdom and creating an atmosphere that encourages the synergy of ideas.

**A diverse workforce reflects the population**   When businesses increase the diversity of their workforces, they increase their ability to attract customers. Customers are attracted to organizations when they feel comfortable with its representatives, and employees who understand and communicate well with customers help increase the customer base for a company's products or services.

**A diverse workforce increases the candidate pool**   The Department of Labor predicts an increasing shortage of qualified candidates for available positions in the near future, with a projected shortfall of about 5 million workers by 2010. Increasing the candidate pool by including a wide diversity of applicants will be essential to fill open positions.

Workplace diversity presents challenges that organizations will look to HR professionals to address, including the difficulty associated with change and the need to do things in new ways. It is also a challenge to work with people who behave in ways to which we are not accustomed. Something as seemingly simple as differences in the amount of "personal space" that are customary in different cultures can create uncomfortable situations such as one person backing away from another to increase the space between them while the other seeks to decrease it.

Difficulties also arise for employees whose backgrounds are dissimilar to the group. They may feel uncomfortable in situations that require them to make major adjustments in order to be accepted by a group whose culture is different from their own.

The comfort level for all involved can be improved with *diversity training*, which seeks to educate all groups about the cultures, needs, and attitudes of other groups in the workforce to ensure the inclusion of all groups in workplace activities.

A *diversity initiative* seeks to increase the diversity of the organization's workforce or to increase the effectiveness of an already diverse workforce. As with any company-wide objective, top management support is a key to success of the initiative, as is a clear picture of the challenges that the initiative will address. Communicating the purpose of the initiative and providing feedback mechanisms for employees to ask questions will help to ease any fears about the changes taking place in the organization. The initiative may begin with training designed to educate employees about the need for and benefits of diversity for the organization and to explain the benefits of diversity to them as individuals. As with any HR program, an evaluation of its effectiveness should be conducted at an appropriate time.

# Human Relations

The concept of human relations covers a broad spectrum of ideas that concentrate on the importance of the human element at work. This approach, introduced in the 1920s, challenged traditional assumptions that people work only for economic reasons and that monetary incentives provided sufficient motivation for increased productivity. Traditional studies of workplace productivity were concentrated on technical and mechanical issues, such as breaking jobs down into small units of repetitive work that could be done more rapidly than jobs with greater task diversity.

The human relations approach recognized that businesses are social as well as economic systems and looked at the impact of formal (management) and informal (work group) social connections in the workplace and the impact these connections have on work processes. For the first time there was a recognition that employees are complex individuals, motivated at different times by different factors, and that increased productivity could be tied to employee job satisfaction.

The complexities of human relations and the ways in which behavior affects organizations will be discussed at length in both Chapter 3, "Strategic Management," and Chapter 5.

# HR Ethics and Professional Standards

Both the Society for Human Resource Development (SHRM) and the Human Resource Certification Institute (HRCI) have developed standards for professional behavior for the human resource profession.

The SHRM Code of Ethical and Professional Standards in Human Resource Management consists of six core principles summarized here:

**Professional responsibility**   HR professionals represent their profession to their organizations. As such, they must hold themselves accountable for their decisions and ensure their actions further the credibility of the profession.

**Professional development**   HR professionals are expected to continuously expand their knowledge of the profession and the organizations in which they work.

**Ethical leadership**   HR professionals are expected to model ethical behavior in their organizations and act as an example and guide to develop other ethical leaders.

**Fairness and justice**   HR professionals bear a responsibility to ensure that all those with whom they come in contact and all those within their organizations are treated with dignity and respect and afforded equal employment opportunities.

**Conflicts of interest**   To maintain trust within their organizations, HR professionals must avoid even the appearance of conflicts of interest and prevent situations where they appear to or actually do receive personal gain from their positions.

**Use of information**   HR professionals are privy to confidential information related to their organizations and the employees who work for those organizations. As such, HR professionals have a responsibility to protect this information from inappropriate uses.

The complete text of the SHRM Code of Ethics is available at `www.shrm.org/ethics/` `code-of-ethics.asp`.

HRCI's Model of Professional Excellence sets a high standard of professional integrity and excellence for practitioners with expectations for honesty, reliability, fairness, and cooperation at all times. The complete text is on the inside back cover of the *PHR/SPHR Certification Handbook*.

# Technology and Human Resource Information Systems

With the reams of paper generated during the course of an employment relationship, the advent of the *human resource information system (HRIS)* was a clear benefit for HR professionals. An HRIS serves two purposes: the first, as a repository of information, and the second, as an aid to effective decision making.

As a repository of information, the HRIS provides an electronic means of storing employment documents, thereby reducing the need to maintain physical files. In firms with multiple locations, both national and global, the ability for employees to access information through the company's intranet or via the World Wide Web reduces delays in payroll processing tasks and ensures instant access to the information for those with the authority and need to access it. For companies required to produce reports for the Equal Employment Opportunity Commission (EEOC) or the Office of Federal Contract Compliance Programs (OFCCP), electronic access to the data needed to compile reports has increased accuracy and reduced the time required to produce them.

As an effective decision-making tool, the HRIS provides access to a wealth of information that is needed to make strategic decisions, such as analyzing turnover trends, creating succession plans, and creating staffing projections.

## Selecting an HRIS

As with any project, the first step in selecting an HRIS is to conduct a needs analysis and identify:

- What information will be converted to the HRIS, and how is it currently maintained? Some uses for an HRIS to consider in this analysis could include:

| | |
|---|---|
| Applicant tracking | COBRA administration |
| Automated benefit administration | EEO/AA reporting |
| Tracking recruitment efforts | Administering training programs |
| Eliminating multiple data entry | Compensation administration |
| Sharing payroll information with finance department | Tracking time and attendance |
| Tracking service awards | |

- Will the system need to integrate or share data with other company systems?
- Who will have access to the information and how many levels of access will be needed (for example, view and change individual records, view and change workgroup records, view payroll information, and so on)? A typical access hierarchy could look something like this:

**Employee Access (restricted information)**

| | |
|---|---|
| Change address and family status | Change payroll tax withholding |
| View company policies | View attendance/vacation tracking |
| Bid for internal job openings | |

**HR Access (global information)**

| | |
|---|---|
| Maintain employee records | Coordinate payroll administration |
| Administer employee benefits | Administer labor relations program |

| | |
|---|---|
| Post jobs | Administer safety programs |
| Administer compensation plan | Track applicants |
| Administer FMLA leaves | Administer employee relations |
| Track attendance/vacation time | Manage recruiting |
| Track applicants | Complete EEO/AAP reports |
| Manage relocations | Administer training programs |
| **Payroll Access (restricted information)** | |
| View payroll information | Administer payroll |
| **Management Access (for restricted work groups)** | |
| View budget/forecast reports | Manage performance |
| View succession plans | Administer service awards |
| Track attendance/vacation time | View compensation |
| Manage training needs | View recruiting status |

- What kinds of reports will need to be produced based on the information?
- Will the HRIS be accessible via the intranet or the Web? If so, what security will be in place to protect the privacy of employees?

Once this information has been collected, research can begin on the availability and cost of a system that will fulfill the requirements. This analysis should include not only the cost to purchase the system, but a comparison to the cost of maintaining the current system.

## Implementing an HRIS

Once the needs assessment is completed, money for the project is included in the budget, and the vendor is ready to install the selected product, some practical considerations need to be worked into the implementation schedule. If a third party will be handling the implementation phase, your RFP should include this information. If the implementation is to be done with internal IT staff, it's important to establish a timeline that works for both departments and that allows the organization's needs to be met during this phase.

When implementation is complete and the product is running the way it is supposed to run, the new service can be rolled out to those who will be using it; if an employee self-service component is included, this means providing the necessary level of training for all employees. Utilizing some of the training methods described earlier in this chapter could mean this happens via small group trainings with demonstrations, with self-study CBT training, or by some other means that ensures those who will need to access the system are able to do so.

# Quantitative and Qualitative Analysis Methods

Making business decisions requires accurate and reliable information; without it, for example, a decision can result in excess inventory rather than increased profits because demand for the product was less than projected. Because there are no crystal balls in the board room, business leaders must rely on the judgment of experienced managers and an analysis of historical data to predict possible future trends.

There are two types of research, primary and secondary. *Primary research* is original, meaning that the researcher has performed the research. *Secondary research* is based on information that has been collected or reported by others, such as books or articles by primary researchers; industry standards; or analysis of trends within an organization.

One very formal method of primary research is known as the *scientific method*, and although it is not generally identified as such in analyzing business problems, the process is very similar to the way in which business problems are analyzed prior to making decisions. There are five steps to the scientific method. To show how they can be used in solving HR problems, I'll use a common problem as an example:

1.  Identify a problem:

    Absenteeism is too high.

2.  Create a hypothesis:

    The absentee rate is higher with new employees.

3.  Decide how to test the hypothesis:

    A correlation analysis of length of employment and attendance data will confirm or not confirm the hypothesis.

4.  Collect data to verify the hypothesis:

    Review employee attendance records.

5.  Draw conclusions/analyze the data:

    Does the correlation analysis verify or not verify the hypothesis?

If you think about how you analyze problems in your work, you will probably find that you follow a very similar process.

Making decisions about how to test a hypothesis has implications for HR, particularly with regard to employment tests. In Chapter 4, I will discuss the processes of reliability and validity, key elements of testing data. Another issue to consider is whether or not there will be a control group in your test. Using a control group tells you if the hypothesis being tested causes the result you are looking for, or the result is the same with both the group being tested and the control group.

Collecting data is an important element of the analysis process; if the proper data is not collected, any decision based on it, regardless of the method of analysis used, will not be an accurate decision. So how do you find reliable data to use in analyzing HR problems? Here are some ways:

**Personnel records**   Personnel records provide information that can be used for analyzing trends. For the absentee example, personnel records tell you how long each employee has worked for the company as well as how often the employee is absent from work.

**Observations**   The hypothesis for my absentee example could have been based on observations: a manager noticed that several new employees were frequently absent.

**Interviews**   Interviews provide direct information about problems. The HR department can interview some new employees to find out how often they are absent and why. Interviews can provide more information than records, but their relevance depends on the frankness of the person being interviewed and their willingness to share information. In addition, they are time consuming and may not be cost effective for that reason.

**Focus groups**   Focus groups are often used to find out how people feel about products or advertisements. They can also be effective methods for gathering information for HR analysis, but again, they are subject to the willingness of participants to open up. In a focus group, this may be limited by the presence of coworkers or supervisors.

**Questionnaires**   Questionnaires can be an effective means of gathering information from large groups of geographically dispersed employees, but they are limited in the types of data that can be collected.

Once data has been collected, there are two basic categories of data analysis tools: quantitative analysis methods based on mathematical models and qualitative analysis methods based on the best judgment of experienced managers. Both methods are inexact, and to minimize errors it is advisable to use several different tools during any analysis.

## Quantitative Analysis

*Quantitative analysis* is based on a mathematical model for measuring historical data. Some quantitative analyses commonly used to analyze HR and other business data include the following:

**Correlation**   A *correlation* measures two variables to determine if there is a relationship between them. For example, if the HR department posts a quarterly reminder for employees of the referral bonus that is paid for new hires, a correlation analysis could be used to determine if there is an increase in referrals in the weeks after the reminder.

**Correlation coefficient**   The *correlation coefficient* describes the relationship between two variables and is stated as a number between $-1.0$ and $+1.0$.

For example, say the HR department wants to find out what factors contribute to absenteeism in the company. One of the factors they decide to analyze is length of time at the company, so one hypothesis they might use is "The absentee rate is higher with new employees."

To analyze this, they would collect two numbers for each employee: how many months employed and how many days absent. The numbers are then plotted on a graph for analysis.

If this hypothesis is correct, they would expect to see a *negative* correlation coefficient, that is, the shorter amount of time employed, the higher the absentee rate would be. This would be reflected by a negative number, for example, –.2. Figure 2.2 shows how this looks.

**FIGURE 2.2**    Negative correlation

A *positive* correlation coefficient would tell HR that the opposite is true, that the absentee rate is actually higher when employees have longer tenure with the company. This would be reflected by a positive number, for example, +.8. Figure 2.3 shows what this would look like.

**FIGURE 2.3**    Positive correlation

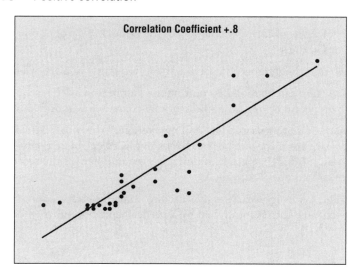

If there were no correlation at all, that is, if length of employment had nothing to do with absenteeism, the correlation coefficient would be 0.0, as shown by Figure 2.4.

**FIGURE 2.4**   No correlation

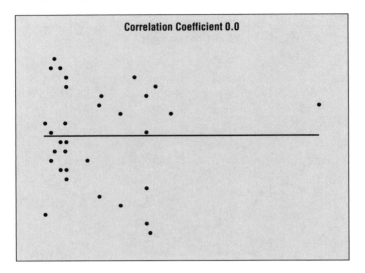

The steeper the trend line (the higher the absolute number), the greater the connection between the two variables. In the absentee example, the positive correlation (+.8) reflects a stronger connection between a longer amount of time with the company and more absences than the example of negative correlation (–.2).

**Measures of central tendency**   Often referred to as the "average," there are several measures that can be used in analyzing data:

**Mean average**   The *mean average* is the sum of the values in a set of numbers, divided by the number of values in the set.

**Mode**   The *mode* is the number that occurs most frequently in a set of numbers.

**Median**   The *median* can be found by putting the numbers in a set in sequential order. The median is at the physical center, so half the numbers are below it and half are above it.

**Moving average**   Sometimes called a "rolling average," the *moving average* is used to calculate an average for a specific period, for example, to calculate the average number of new hires each month for the past 12 months. As the number for the most recent month is added, the oldest number is dropped.

**Weighted average**   A *weighted average* is used to compensate for data that may be out of date; the more current data is multiplied by a predetermined number to better reflect the current situation.

**Weighted moving average**   The *weighted moving average* calculation assigns more weight to current data with the use of a predetermined number as well as dropping the oldest data when new data is added.

## Qualitative Analysis

*Qualitative analysis* tools are subjective judgments. These judgments may be very informal; for example, an experienced sales manager may be able to predict by the end of the first month of a quarter quite accurately whether or not the sales goal will be met.

In Chapter 4, I will discuss some other qualitative assessment tools, including the Delphi technique and the nominal group technique.

# Change Management

*Change management* is another concept that will be more fully developed in Chapter 5. Its reason for inclusion as a core knowledge requirement is simple: change is everywhere. Processes change constantly to meet changing business needs. People change jobs. Economies change. Government regulations change. All of these changes and many others must be addressed with HR programs that are flexible enough to take in the changes while continuing to serve the needs of people within the organization.

Major changes in an organization occur as the result of mergers or acquisitions. When these occur, two organizations, two sets of processes, two cultures, and two groups of people doing similar jobs must acclimate to each other to ensure the success of the business. The process is stressful for employees because, almost inevitably, some people will lose their jobs as the organization eliminates redundancy from its operations. Maintaining morale and productivity during this process often presents a monumental challenge for organizations and HR professionals.

A key element of managing change is ensuring that employees receive current information as soon as possible. While management is often tempted to "wait until we have all the answers," the absence of information creates added stress and apprehension that hinders the acceptance of change by employees. Keeping employees abreast of a situation in flux, even by telling them that all decisions have not been made yet, builds trust that they will not be left in the dark about what is happening.

In general, people resist change for many reasons, some of which can be explained by the motivational theories discussed earlier in this chapter. Change removes the underlying sense of safety and impacts the social structures people create around them within organizations. This makes it difficult for them to accept change, particularly when there is a lack of certainty about the future. Balancing the organization's need to continually adapt to changes in the business environment with the employee's need for clarity and direction presents challenges for every functional area of human resources.

# Liability and Risk Management

Liability is a legal term that refers to a duty or responsibility owed by one party to another. A *liability* can result from an agreement or a contract or can be created through a tort. A *tort* is another legal term that describes an action that injures someone. Torts are not related to laws or contracts but can result in legal action: the party who has been injured is able to sue the wrongdoer and collect damages for the injury that has been done.

As will be discussed in Chapter 7, liability for wrongful actions in employment relationships costs businesses millions of dollars in judgments for many different types of torts, from wrongful termination to sexual harassment and discrimination. HR professionals are uniquely qualified to make sure that managers understand the legal exposure that may result from making adverse employment decisions without first understanding the possible consequences, including the costs of defending a lawsuit. This process is known as *risk management*, or the process of identifying risks and taking steps to ensure that those risks are minimized.

One way to minimize risks is through insurance coverage, and an important policy for businesses to maintain is *employment practices liability insurance (EPLI)*. EPLI protects employers against lawsuits brought by current or former employees. During the application process, an insurance company evaluates the employer's human resource policies and any lawsuits or claims filed by employees or former employees. These factors, along with considerations of the employer's operations and size, are used to determine whether or not an EPLI policy may be issued and the amount of the premium to be paid. Managing risk involves taking steps to reduce the legal exposure created by poorly written policies or unlawful practices in an organization. This can be done by assessing the risk:

1. Identify possible exposures to legal action (for example, inconsistent policy application).

2. Audit the organization's employment practices. Educate managers on the possible risks that could result from unlawful employment actions.

3. Develop a plan to reduce the risks, and obtain top management support for the process.

4. Analyze the costs of purchasing insurance versus self-insuring, and recommend a course of action.

5. If losses related to employment issues have occurred in the past, develop a way to present a plan for reducing the costs of these losses to top management.

Once a risk assessment is completed, there are three possible ways to reduce the risk: the organization can obtain insurance, decide to self-insure, or mitigate the risk by replacing equipment or providing training to reduce possible hazards to employees.

# Job Analysis and Job Description Methods

Job analysis and job descriptions provide the foundation for much of what happens within the employment relationship.

As managers find that they need additional employees to meet the goals and objectives for their work groups, they must begin by defining what the new employee will do by describing the tasks, processes, or functions that will be part of the new employee's responsibilities. This is known as *job analysis*. The document containing this information is known as the *job description*.

## Job Analysis

To define a job, information must be collected that describes the work that will be done. It is important to keep in mind that the analysis focuses on the *job*, not the *person*. There are several ways to collect information during the job analysis process:

- Interview the incumbent if available.
- Interview the supervisor or a group of coworkers.
- Complete a structured or an open-ended questionnaire.
- Complete a task inventory.
- Observe incumbents and make notes.
- Utilize work logs kept by incumbents.

Regardless of the method used, the following information must be included:

- The relationships that the incumbent will have, including supervisory, coworkers within the work group, coworkers in other departments of the company, any external relationships with vendors or customers, and the level of interaction that will take place in these relationships.
- Exemption status, based on the job duties and responsibilities. In Chapter 6, I will discuss how exemption status is determined.
- A description of the essential functions of the job is required to comply with the Americans with Disabilities Act (ADA), which will be discussed in Chapter 4. Each function should describe the level of complexity, how often each task is performed, how much time is spent on each area, any equipment that is used, and the skills that will be needed to complete the work.
- A description of the nonessential job functions including the same information listed above.
- A description of the work environment, including any hazardous equipment or locations that will impact the employee. If stairs or ladders must be utilized, or the job will require work in confined spaces, this must be included as well.
- Any tools or equipment that will be used and how much time will be spent on it each day. This includes use of the computer, telephone, production equipment, and any hazardous equipment or tools that will be used, and protective gear or uniforms that will be required.
- Any physical requirements must be described to comply with the ADA. The physical requirements must be related to the essential job functions.
- Required qualifications should be described. The requirements must be related to the essential job functions, again, to comply with the ADA.

## Job Descriptions

The job description compiles all the information collected during the job analysis into a document that is used for multiple purposes in the organization, beginning with the hiring process:

- Based on the job description, the recruiter screens applicants to ensure that their *knowledge, skills, and abilities (KSAs)* are appropriate for the position.

- The applicants for the position use the job description to find out what they will be required to do if the position is offered to them.

- The job description is the basis for performance management and appraisal.

- The job description is the basis for determining the appropriate level of pay for the work that is done.

- The job description includes the essential job functions and provides a guideline for employees who request reasonable accommodation for disabilities.

## Employee Records Management

Not surprisingly, mounds of paperwork are generated in the employment process: resumes, applications, references, government forms, and performance evaluations are just a few of the many documents created for each employee. HR practitioners need to be aware of the record retention requirements for these various documents.

Appendix C provides a list of employment documents and retention requirements. As with all government regulations, it is important to keep in mind that whenever there is a conflict between the state, local, and federal requirements, the most burdensome requirement is the one that must be met. Keep in mind that the requirements I've included here are federal, and retention requirements for your state may be different.

# Summary

This chapter provided an overview of the core HR knowledge requirements, which have implications in all of the HR functional areas and are the basis for understanding responsibilities in those areas.

Each of these requirements is the subject of many books, articles, and seminars, and some are even the basis for entire professional associations or certification programs in their own right. If, after reading this chapter, you feel the need for additional information about any of these topics, the Internet or your local library will provide additional resources to enhance your knowledge. Appendix B, "Resources," at the end of this study guide also provides some resources that may be helpful.

Keep in mind that it's most important to understand the concepts introduced in this chapter and the way they apply to other areas of the body of knowledge.

# Exam Essentials

**Be able to describe how HR programs interact.**   It is important to understand the ways programs or policies developed for one functional area impact others. For example, the compensation policy will affect the quality of candidates attracted by the company, turnover rates, the ability of the company to maintain union-free status, and employee job satisfaction.

**Be able to describe the needs assessment and analysis process.**   Needs assessment and analysis refers to a process used to obtain information about what a business needs to meet its goals. There are seven steps in a needs assessment: describing the objective, defining the current situation, conducting a gap analysis, setting priorities, developing options, determining the costs, and recommending the solution.

**Understand the uses of a third party contract.**   Third party contracts are used for outsourced functions in the HR department. Choosing a third party contractor begins with a needs assessment to determine how best to serve the needs of the organization. The RFP process provides an organized way to select the best option for the needs of the business.

**Be able to describe communication strategies.**   To ensure that the right information is provided to employees when they need it and that there is a mechanism for senior management to hear from employees, a communication strategy must be developed based on what information is needed, who needs to hear it, who will provide it, and when it will be delivered.

**Understand the key elements involved in planning and conducting an effective workplace investigation.**   Workplace investigations can be relatively informal or formal depending on the organization and the circumstances. Third party investigations come under the jurisdiction of the Federal Credit Reporting Act (FCRA). All investigations should be conducted by an investigator who is seen as credible and impartial and begin with a plan for the investigation. The outcome should be based on facts obtained through interviews and documentary evidence.

**Understand the basic concepts associated with andragogy (adult learning theory).**   Andragogy, also known as adult learning theory, is built on concepts that say adults are autonomous, self-directed, goal-oriented, relevancy-oriented, and practical, and that they need respect. Also, adults build new knowledge on a foundation of life experiences. Adult participants react either positively or negatively to training as a result of the presence or absence of these characteristics.

**Be able to recognize and describe various motivation theories.**   Motivational theories help HR professionals and managers understand why employees behave the way they do and develop programs that result in highly motivated, productive workers.

**Understand how training methods are used.**   Passive training methods are instructor-focused and require little participation by the learner. Active training methods are learner-focused and require learner participation. Experiential training methods provide experience in real-world situations.

**Understand the uses for qualitative and quantitative analysis methods.**   Quantitative analysis is based on mathematical models, such as correlation and measures of central tendency. Qualitative analysis is based on more subjective judgments based on secondary research.

**Be able to describe the benefits of workplace diversity.**   A diverse workforce is more creative and better reflects the customer population. Increasing diversity in the work force provides access to more qualified candidates; this is important due to the projected shortfall of qualified workers over the next five years.

**Understand the HR Code of Ethics.**   The HR Code of Ethics developed by SHRM requires HR professionals to maintain standards of professional responsibility and development, provide ethical leadership in their organizations, ensure fairness and justice within their organizations, avoid the appearance of conflicts of interest, and use confidential information appropriately.

**Understand the difference between job analysis and job descriptions.**   Job analysis is the process used to identify and determine duties associated with a particular job; job descriptions are the end product. Typically, job descriptions document a job's major functions or duties, skill and physical requirements, and working conditions.

# Key Terms

Before you take the exam, be certain you are familiar with the following terms:

| | |
|---|---|
| acquired needs theory | employment practices liability insurance (EPLI) |
| active training methods | equity theory |
| andragogy | ERG theory |
| behavioral reinforcement | expectancy theory |
| case study | experiential training methods |
| change management | final written warning |
| communication strategy | first written warning |
| computer-based training | gap analysis |
| conferences | hierarchy of needs |
| contract | human resource information system (HRIS) |
| correlation | job analysis |
| correlation coefficient | job description |
| demonstration | job enrichment |
| distance learning | knowledge, skills, and abilities (KSAs) |
| diversity initiative | lectures |
| diversity training | liability |

mean average

median

mode

motivation/hygiene theory

moving average

needs analysis

needs assessment

one-on-one training

passive training methods

pedagogy

performance-based training (PBT)

primary research

programmed instruction

project management

qualitative analysis

quantitative analysis

request for proposal (RFP)

risk management

scientific method

secondary research

self-study

simulation training

subject matter experts (SME)

suspension

termination

Theory X and Theory Y

third party contract

tort

two-factor theory

verbal warning

vestibule training

weighted average

weighted moving average

workplace diversity

workplace investigation

# Review Questions

1. A department manager advises you that the productivity of his data entry operators is unsatisfactory and asks you to develop a training program to improve their data entry skills. What is your first step?

   **A.** Conduct a needs assessment.

   **B.** Develop a lesson plan.

   **C.** Talk to other managers to validate the situation.

   **D.** Conduct a needs analysis.

2. According to the FCRA, employees must be notified of

   **A.** All workplace investigations

   **B.** Investigations that include an employee's financial and other credit information

   **C.** Third party investigations

   **D.** Employer efforts to obtain previous employment data

3. Training methods that are focused on the learner are known as:

   **A.** Experiential

   **B.** Active

   **C.** Passive

   **D.** Vestibule

4. Maslow's hierarchy of needs does *not* include the following need:

   **A.** Social

   **B.** Safety

   **C.** Growth

   **D.** Self-actualization

5. A female employee comes to you and complains that she is being sexually harassed by her supervisor, but she tells you not to tell anyone because she is afraid he will retaliate against her. What do you do?

   **A.** Take no action since she told you in confidence.

   **B.** Suspend the supervisor pending an investigation.

   **C.** Ask her coworkers if they have noticed anything unusual.

   **D.** Begin the investigative process.

**6.** What is the purpose of a diversity initiative?

   **A.** To educate all employees about other groups in the workforce

   **B.** To educate all employees about the benefits of diversity

   **C.** To increase organizational creativity

   **D.** To increase the comfort level of employees

**7.** Which of the following is *not* an appropriate use of an HRIS?

   **A.** Tracking applicant data for the EEO-1

   **B.** Tracking time and attendance

   **C.** Tracking employee expense reports

   **D.** Maintaining employee records

**8.** The middle value when values are arranged in order from high to low, is the

   **A.** Mean

   **B.** Median

   **C.** Mode

   **D.** Moving average

**9.** A basic principle behind job analysis is that

   **A.** The analysis focuses on the job, not the person.

   **B.** The analysis focuses on the person doing the job, not the job.

   **C.** The analysis is limited to task inventories and questionnaires.

   **D.** The required qualifications should include everything the manager would like the employee to have.

**10.** After conducting a risk assessment, what should you do to reduce risks?

   **A.** Identify policies that are applied inconsistently throughout the organization.

   **B.** Obtain employment practices liability insurance.

   **C.** Develop a plan to reduce the risks.

   **D.** Present management with a plan for reducing the risks.

# Answers to Review Questions

1. **A.** A needs assessment is conducted to determine what is required to solve a problem, including whether or not training is the appropriate intervention. If, for example, network crashes are the cause of the low productivity, training will not solve the problem.

2. **C.** The Fair Credit Reporting Act (FCRA) considers a report resulting from an investigation by any third party as an "investigative consumer report" subject to the requirements of the act.

3. **B.** Active training methods such as case studies, CBT, and programmed instruction are focused on the learner.

4. **C.** Maslow's hierarchy of needs is a theory developed to explain what motivates workers. The levels are physiological, safety, social, esteem, and self-actualization. Growth is a need level identified by Alderfer in the ERG theory, which is based on Maslow's work.

5. **D.** During the course of the investigation, the alleged harasser will be told that retaliation will not be tolerated by the company. Once an employee complains of sexual harassment, even if they do so in confidence and do not want an investigation, the company is legally obligated to conduct the investigation. Based only on a single complaint, suspending the supervisor without an investigation is not appropriate. Likewise, asking her coworkers if they have noticed anything unusual should only be done as part of an investigation and with instructions to not discuss the situation with others.

6. **B.** A diversity initiative is designed to increase diversity in an organization. Diversity training educates employees about the cultural and social differences in other cultures and is designed to increase the comfort level of employees. A benefit of diversity is increased organizational creativity.

7. **C.** Data for employee expense reports is maintained by the accounting department.

8. **B.** Median is defined as the middle value when values are arranged from high to low. Half the numbers are higher than the median; half are lower.

9. **A.** The correct focus of a job analysis is the job itself, not the incumbent in the job. An analysis may utilize a number of sources in addition to task inventories and questionnaires, including interviews, observation, and supervisory input. The required qualifications should be related to the essential functions of the job to avoid complaints of discrimination.

10. **B.** As part of the risk assessment, inconsistent policies have been identified, a plan for reducing risk has been developed, and management has reviewed the plan for reducing risks. After the assessment is complete, the company may decide to purchase insurance, self-insure, or mitigate the risk by making operational changes.

# Chapter

# 3

# Strategic Management

## THE HRCI TEST SPECIFICATIONS FROM THE STRATEGIC MANAGEMENT FUNCTIONAL AREA COVERED IN THIS CHAPTER INCLUDE:

✓ Interpret information related to the organization's operations from internal sources, including financial/accounting, marketing, operations, information technology, and individual employees, in order to participate in strategic planning and policy making.

✓ Interpret information related to the general business environment, industry practices and developments, and technological developments from external sources (for example, publications, government documents, media, and trade organizations), in order to participate in strategic planning and policy making.

✓ Participate as a partner in the organization's strategic planning process.

✓ Establish strategic relationships with individuals in the organization, to influence organizational decision-making.

✓ Establish relationships/alliances with key individuals in the community and in professional capacities to assist in meeting the organization's strategic needs.

✓ Evaluate HR's contribution to organizational effectiveness, including assessment, design, implementation, and evaluation of activities with respect to strategic and organizational measurement in HR objectives (refers to participation in change management).

✓ Provide direction and guidance during changes in organizational processes, operations, planning, intervention, leadership training, and culture that balances the expectations and needs of the organization, its employees, and other stakeholders (including customers) (refers to participation in change management).

- ✓ Develop and shape organizational policy related to the organization's management of its human resources.

- ✓ Cultivate leadership and ethical values in self and others through modeling and teaching.

- ✓ Provide information for the organizational budgeting process, including budget development and review.

- ✓ Monitor legislative environment for proposed changes in law and take appropriate action to support, modify, or stop the proposed action (for example, write to a member of Congress, provide expert testimony at a public hearing, lobby legislators).

The current business environment, with its emphasis on the ability to compete in global markets and respond to rapidly changing conditions, requires more of its managers than ever before. They must seek and develop competitive advantage in their marketplaces and continuously innovate new processes, products, and services to meet the constant challenges presented by a global business environment. As each challenge is met, successful managers are already forecasting the next challenge on the horizon, looking for an advantageous market position. This ongoing process of innovation, advantage, value creation, and reassessment is known as strategic management. HR professionals seeking certification must understand what strategic management means, how the strategic management process impacts HR policies and practices, and how HR can add value in the organization's quest for market advantages.

To lay the groundwork for our discussion of strategic management, I begin this chapter with an overview of organizations: their structures, functions, leadership and management, and how the human resource function fits into them. I will discuss the strategic planning process and investigate how HR policies are developed to meet organization needs. Because a major factor in business operations is constant change, I will look at managing change in organizations and discuss the roles of HR and management in that process. This chapter will examine ethics and how HR can influence ethical standards in organizations. I'll take a look at corporate responsibility to the community, and finally, examine the legislative and regulatory environment and how HR practitioners can influence changes in that arena.

In addition to the responsibilities for strategic management just listed, HRCI expects PHR/SPHR candidates to have basic knowledge of the concepts in this functional area, as well as core knowledge requirements covered in Chapter 2, "Core Knowledge Requirements for HR Professionals" that have an impact on strategic management.

Be sure to review Appendix A of the *PHR/SPHR Certification Handbook* for the most current test specifications in this functional area. The handbook includes a detailed list of the basic knowledge requirements for this functional area in addition to the test specifications listed at the beginning of this chapter.

# Organizations and Structures

Since ancient times, people have formed groups to achieve goals that they were unable to achieve on their own. Whether it was for protection, shelter, food, or profit, organizing gave people the means to achieve more than they could by acting alone. With the advent of the Industrial Revolution in the late eighteenth century, organizations grew larger and more complex as the goals to be achieved became more complex. As the production of goods moved from a single worker creating an entire product to multiple workers completing pieces of a single product, the need for control over the production process became greater. The modern organization evolved to coordinate the many different activities that are needed to produce the goods or services necessary to achieve the organization's goals.

This section describes three aspects of organizations that must be considered by HR professionals in developing plans and programs: structures, functions, and life cycles.

# Organization Structures

Businesses in the United States are organized in one of four basic structures: sole proprietorships, partnerships, corporations, or limited liability companies.

## Sole Proprietorships

This business structure is the most basic and easy to organize. The owner is a single (sole) person who is the final authority for all decisions in the business. Any profits earned by the business belong to the owner, and the owner has unlimited, personal liability for all business decisions and activities.

## Partnerships

A partnership is owned by two or more people who share final authority for all business decisions and are jointly liable for the actions of the business. Partners are liable not only for their own individual actions, but for the actions taken by their other partner(s) as well. The profits of the business are split according to the ownership share established at the beginning of the partnership (most often equal shares, but ownership can be any arrangement agreed upon by the partners). There are several types of partnership arrangements:

**In a general partnership (GP)**    The partners share responsibility for managing the business based on the partnership agreement.

**In a limited partnership (LP)**    Or a limited liability partnership (LLP), most of the partners are involved only as investors and have little input into daily operations of the business. These forms are commonly used for medical clinics, accounting practices, law firms, and other service businesses.

**A joint venture (JV)**    Is similar to a GP but is formed to manage a specific project or for a limited time frame.

## Corporations

Corporations are entities defined by four characteristics:

1. Liability is limited to assets owned by the corporation.
2. The life of the corporation can extend beyond the life of its original owner/founder.
3. There is a central management structure.
4. Ownership may be transferred freely by selling stock.

Corporations sell stock to raise the funds necessary to operate the business. Owners of the stock, known as stockholders or shareholders, are free to sell the stock they own to other investors at any time. These stockholders can be individuals or other entities, and for the most part are not involved in the daily operation of the business. They elect a Board of Directors to represent their interests with the senior management team in making decisions about the strategic direction of the company. Because corporate liability is limited to the assets owned by the corporation, stockholder/owner liability is generally limited to the amount of stock owned by individual investors; there are exceptions for corporate officers who may be held personally liable for any wrongdoing or negligence.

Corporations are legal entities and may incur debts, sign contracts, and be sued in the same way that individuals may be. This is the most common form of business for large enterprises in the United States.

## Limited Liability Company

A limited liability company (LLC) is a cross between a general partnership and a corporation and provides its owners with the liability protection of a corporation with fewer operating restrictions. An LLC exists for a finite period of time defined at the time it is organized, and it can be extended by a vote of the owner/members when it expires. An LLC may have only two of the four characteristics of a corporation; otherwise, the entity must become a corporation.

# Organization Functions

Regardless of its legal form, every business has some common components: production and operations, sales and marketing, finance and accounting, information technology and, of course, the people who make everything happen. Whether the business is simple or complex, has one employee or hundreds of thousands, these components are all necessary for success.

## Production and Operations

The terms "production" and "operations" are, in many cases, used interchangeably. When used separately, *production* generally refers to the process by which businesses create the product or service they offer to customers. Traditionally, this meant manufactured goods, but with the growth of service and information businesses, it has come to include services as well.

*Operations* encompasses all of the activities necessary to produce the goods or services of the business, these can include such activities as:

**Product design** Working in conjunction with the marketing function (see the "Sales and Marketing" section) on new product development and the redesign of old products, operations designs and builds the product or service. Marketing provides the information it gathers from customers about their needs and then works with production staff to ensure that the product will meet those needs.

**Capacity** Determining how much of a product or service is able to be produced with the available materials, labor, and equipment (known as inputs) as well as what changes in inputs are required by fluctuating customer demands.

**Production layout**  The way in which the goods or service will be produced, for example, the design of an assembly line or, in the case of a service, the process to be used in providing it, such as a model plan or protocol for a financial audit.

**Scheduling**  Making sure that the products or services are available at times of peak customer demand.

**Quality management**  Ensuring that the product or service meets acceptable standards.

**Inventory management**  Operations managers must balance two conflicting needs related to inventory: the cost of maintaining a large inventory and the need to satisfy customers by filling orders promptly. *Just-in-time (JIT) inventory* management systems attempt to do this by purchasing smaller amounts of supplies more frequently to reduce inventories and ensure a steady supply of products for distribution.

**Technology**  Increasing the use of technology can improve product quality and the amounts that are produced.

**Facility location**  Evaluating the best places to locate production facilities involves many considerations: the cost of labor, distribution systems, and government regulations, to name a few.

**Cost control**  As with all business functions, operations must produce products that meet the quality standards set by the organization at the lowest possible cost.

## Sales and Marketing

Sales and marketing are closely related activities involved with creating a demand for the company's products and moving them from the company to the customer.

*Sales* includes all the functions involved in transferring the product or service from the business to the customer.

*Marketing* incorporates all the functions necessary to promote and distribute products in the marketplace, provides support for the sales staff, conducts research to design products that customers will be interested in purchasing, and determines the appropriate pricing for the product. Marketing begins with an identification of the target market for the organization's product or service. Once that has been identified, decisions about the 4 P's of marketing (product, price, place, and promotion) can be made:

**Product**  This can be a physical product or a service or in some cases both. Product development includes making decisions about what the product will do, how it will look, what kind of customer service is needed, whether a warranty or guarantee is appropriate, and how the product will be packaged to attract customers.

**Price**  Setting the correct price point for a product is an important marketing function. The price must attract the customer, compete with other similar products and return a profit. Pricing looks not only at the "list price" but at any discounts or allowances that will be offered.

**Placement**  Also referred to as distribution, this is where decisions are made about where the customer will find the product. Having an in-depth description of the target customer is helpful in this step: how does the customer shop? Is it on the Internet? At the mall? By phone? These and similar questions must be answered to appropriately place the product.

**Promotion**    Advertising, public relations, personal selling, and providing incentives for customers to buy, such as discounts, rebates, or contests are some of the techniques used to market products and services.

## Finance and Accounting

Finance and accounting are also closely related functions and include all the activities related to the movement of money into and out of the organization.

The *finance* function is responsible for obtaining credit to meet the organization's needs, granting credit to customers, investing and managing cash for maximum return on investment, and establishing banking relationships for the organization.

Financial analysts work with all functions of the organization in a variety of ways. For operations, the analyst can provide models to predict the number of employees needed at different production levels, along with the budget impact of those different levels. Working with operations and marketing personnel, analysts compile cost data, profit margins, and pricing information to provide accurate profitability forecasts at different sales volumes and pricing levels. HR practitioners may work with analysts to project needed staffing levels or benefit costs for budget planning purposes.

*Accounting* activities include the recording of financial transactions within an organization, including product sales and the costs related to creating the product as well as overhead expenses, money owed to the company by customers, and money the company owes to its suppliers.

The accounting function creates reports to summarize the results of business activity, including the balance sheet, income statement, and statement of cash flows. All accounting reports are produced at the end of accounting periods, which are generally monthly, quarterly, and annually. The annual reporting period can be defined as any 12-month period and does not necessarily coincide with a calendar year (January through December). An annual reporting period that is different from a calendar year is known as a *fiscal year*. Many companies, for example, have fiscal years that begin on July 1 and end on June 30 of the following calendar year.

The *balance sheet* is a picture of the financial condition of the organization on a specific day, usually the last day of the accounting period. Information on the balance sheet includes the company's assets, liabilities, and equity. This report is known as a balance sheet because the total of the liabilities and the equity must equal the total of the assets as represented by the balance sheet formula:

**Assets = Liabilities + Equity**

The *income statement*, sometimes referred to as the *profit and loss statement (P&L)* provides information about financial results of operations during the reporting period. The report tells you how much revenue was produced from various sources, how much it cost to produce the goods or services, what the overhead expenses were, and what the profit or loss for the period was.

The *statement of cash flows* provides important facts about the money that flowed through the business during the accounting period: where it came from and what it was used for. This statement shows how much cash was a result of sales, how much was spent to produce the products that were sold, how much money was borrowed or came in as a result of new capital investments, and how much was invested in assets.

HR professionals need to understand some basic accounting terminology and be able to read and understand financial reports in order to be effective strategic partners in their organizations. Table 3.1 provides definitions for some common accounting terms.

**TABLE 3.1** Common Accounting Terms

| Term | Definition/Description |
|---|---|
| Accounts receivable | Money owed to the business by customers |
| Accounts payable | Money owed by the business to its suppliers |
| Accrued expense | Expenses, such as vacation leave, that have been incurred but not yet paid |
| Asset | Tangible or intangible items of value owned by the business |
| Audited financial statements | Financial statements that have been examined by an independent auditor (not affiliated with the company) to determine if they fairly represent the financial condition of the business |
| Budget | A projection of revenue and expenses used to control actual expenses |
| Cost of goods sold | Money spent on supplies and labor to produce goods or services |
| Equity | Value of the business to owners after all liabilities have been paid |
| Expense | Money spent to operate the business |
| GAAP (Generally Accepted Accounting Principles) | Standards established by the Financial Accounting Standards Board (FASB) for recording financial transactions |
| Gross profit | Sales revenue less cost of goods sold |
| Liability | Money owed by the business to others, such as lenders, the government (for payroll taxes withheld), or to employees (for unused vacation time) |
| Net profit | Gross profit less operating expenses |
| Profit | Money earned by the business after all expenses have been paid |
| Retained earnings | Net profits that are not distributed to owners but remain in the business as equity |
| Revenue | Money received from customers for products or services |

## Information Technology

*Information technology (IT)* is the area of the business responsible for managing systems such as voice mail, computer networks, software, websites, and the Internet and the data collected by these systems. As technology has become more prevalent and sophisticated, the use of IT systems has expanded from the original data storage and retrieval function. For example, the ability of new systems to increase the accuracy of scheduling requirements for operations managers by providing real-time sales and inventory tracking makes the IT function a strategic advantage in organizations. As a result, IT plays a growing role in the strategic management of organizations.

## People/Employees

Whether it is a one-person operation or a company employing hundreds of thousands of employees throughout the world, the people who do the work *are* the business. With appropriate and effective human resource policies, employees are satisfied, productive good-will ambassadors for the company. Conversely, low productivity, higher costs, and poor customer service are by-products of ineffective HR policies. In Chapter 5, "Human Resource Development," we will discuss ways in which management practices and organization culture impact employee behavior and productivity.

# Organization Life Cycles

As organizations are established and grow, they move through four distinct phases: startup, growth, maturity, and decline. Organizations approach each of these stages with different expectations and needs.

**Startup**   During the startup phase, the organization leaders struggle to obtain funding so the organization can survive. Because employees hired during this phase must wear many different hats, there is little time for training, so they are usually fully qualified for their positions, and base pay is very often below the market rate. At this stage, outsourcing can be a cost effective alternative for specialized functions that do not require a full-time employee. There are generally few layers of management, which allows employees to work closely with the founders and leaders.

**Growth**   In the growth phase, the founder is not able to manage the organization alone and additional management personnel are brought into the company. This can lead to morale issues as employees who once had access to organization leaders lose the daily contact common in the startup phase. As the organization becomes more successful, funds are available to provide competitive compensation and benefits to attract and retain qualified employees. From an operation standpoint, the growth phase presents challenges when it exceeds the ability of the infrastructure to handle it, sometimes necessitating the outsourcing of some functions to meet needs.

Not all organizations are able to make it through the growth phase and collapse under the weight of their good fortune or are acquired by larger entities with the infrastructure to support operations.

**Maturity**   At the maturity phase, the organization has enough resources to provide planning and standardize policies and procedures. In this stage, it is possible to become bureaucratic and unwieldy, making it difficult for the company to change direction as rapidly as may be necessary to remain competitive. From an HR standpoint, the relative stability of this phase means that it is possible to hire less experienced personnel and provide them with training and development so that they are able to take on additional responsibilities. The compensation and benefits for executives are often enhanced during this stage.

**Decline**    A declining organization is characterized by inefficiency and bureaucracy. In order to remain viable, the leaders may implement workforce reductions, close facilities, and take other cost-cutting measures. The organization's products may be outdated and unable to compete, resulting in a downward sales trend.

Organizations in the declining phase of the life cycle will need to reinvigorate themselves in order to survive. This may happen with the development of new product lines or with redesign of current products to bring them up to current competitive standards. When this does not occur, the organization may be acquired by a competitor or may cease to exist altogether.

From this discussion, you know that all organizations are made up of similar components. Why, then, do some organizations succeed while others either stumble along at a mediocre level or fail completely? The difference lies in how well the organization is able to position itself to take advantage of market opportunities and avoid the pitfalls present in the business environment. The strategic planning process provides a framework within which organizations are able to do this.

# Strategic Planning

In recent years, American businesses have made increasing use of a process known as *strategic planning*. Broadly defined, strategic planning is a systematic way of setting the direction for an organization and developing strategies, tactics, and operational plans to ensure its success. Strategic planning is a dynamic process: it's not something an organization does one time to produce an attractively bound booklet that sits on the shelf gathering dust. By its very nature, strategic planning requires that organizations constantly revisit the plan to make sure it is still viable in the face of changes within the organization and in the marketplace. The strategic planning process answers four essential questions:

- Where are we now?
- Where do we want to be?
- How will we get there?
- How will we know when we arrive?

Because strategic planning has been a popular topic for business writers, consultants, and academicians during the past decade, there are a number of planning models from which to choose. The specific model selected for use in an organization will depend upon the structure and culture of that organization (both of which are discussed later in this chapter). The elements of all the models fall into four very broad categories: environmental scanning, strategy formulation, strategy implementation, and strategy evaluation.

For purposes of the PHR/SPHR exam, candidates should be aware of how all of these elements contribute to the strategic planning process. Figure 3.1 illustrates a typical strategic planning process.

**FIGURE 3.1**   Elements of the strategic planning process

 The steps are described here in a logical sequence. In real life, the process may not occur in a straight line progression; if new information that will affect results is uncovered at any stage, previous steps may be revisited so the information can be incorporated into the plans and goals.

## Planning to Plan

Very often, a strategic planning initiative is led by a consultant experienced in the process. This is helpful for many reasons, not least of which is that during the course of determining the future of the organization, disagreements about the long-term direction of the company may surface, and these are more readily resolved with a neutral third party who is better able to facilitate a resolution and move the process forward. When a consultant is used, the preplanning process is generally part of the service they provide.

The "preplan" will include decisions about who will be invited to participate and at what stages in the process, a time frame for completing the plan, and determination of the tools to be utilized in collecting data for the plan. Spending this additional time at the beginning of the process could prevent costly errors or omissions from being made and can assist in making the resulting strategic plan more accurate and meaningful.

The result of this stage should be an agreement about the process to be followed, a list of those who will be involved at various stages in the process and the type of information they will be asked to provide, the time line for completing the plan, and a list of the planning tools to be utilized in gathering information to be used by the executive management team.

Let's begin our discussion by defining the terms that will be used to discuss the strategic planning process.

A *strategy* uses the strengths of a business to its competitive advantage in the marketplace. A *goal* describes the direction the business will take and what it will achieve. Goals are set at the corporate and business unit level of the organization.

An *objective* is a specific description of the practical steps that will be taken to achieve the business goals. Objectives are set at the functional level of the organization.

## Environmental Scan

In order to effectively determine the future direction of a company, it's necessary to know what is going on within the organization, in the industry, and the marketplace and what technology developments will mean for operations. Beginning the strategic planning process with this information can help to focus management on a plan that will avoid pitfalls and take advantage of existing opportunities.

An *environmental scan* provides the framework for collecting information about factors that are relevant to the planning process. There are two elements to the scanning process: internal assessment and external assessment, and there are a number of planning tools available for use in collecting the information. Conducting a comprehensive environmental scan can be a challenge; there is a great deal of information available from many sources, and finding the information that is relevant to the specific business can be time consuming. In addition to the information available from industry associations, government agencies, and trade organizations, customers and suppliers are excellent sources of information relevant to a specific business. Many business-focused cable television channels present in-depth program segments on pertinent topics such as unemployment and inflation (among others), and business publications also provide in-depth examination of some topics. There is a wealth of information available—the challenge comes in finding what is most appropriate for your specific organization's needs.

## Environmental Scanning Tools

There are a number of tools available for use in the scanning process. Let's take a look at some of the more common tools.

**Statistical models**    As you learned in Chapter 2, "Core Knowledge Requirements for HR Professionals," there are a number of quantitative analysis models that can be used to identify trends. These are useful internally (to analyze turnover rates, for example) and externally (to analyze customer buying habits).

**SWOT analysis**    A *SWOT analysis* looks at the strengths, weaknesses, opportunities, and threats that are facing the organization. Strengths and weaknesses are internal factors that can be controlled by the organization; opportunities and threats are external factors that may impact an organization's plans.

> **Strengths**    Strengths are internal factors that will support the organization's plans. These can include people (perhaps your workforce is highly trained in a unique skill not available to other businesses in your market), machinery and equipment (a recent upgrade of manufacturing equipment that allows you to produce more high quality products at a lower cost), technology (a state-of-the-art order processing system), and other factors that give the organization an edge in the marketplace.

> **Weaknesses**    Weaknesses are also internal factors, but these represent obstacles to the organization. Weaknesses can include workforce issues such as poorly trained workers, old machinery or equipment that is inefficient and costly to operate, outdated technology, and any other factors that make it difficult for the organization to achieve its goals.

> **Opportunities**    Opportunities are external factors that will aid the organization in the marketplace. These can include a wide variety of factors such as economic upswings, demand for the product, a competitor whose product quality has declined, and other factors that I will discuss more fully in the next section.

> **Threats**    External factors that the organization must overcome or turn to an advantage are threats to its ability to achieve success. These can include strong product competition, economic problems, low unemployment rates, and other factors that make it more difficult for the organization.

**PEST analysis**    A *PEST analysis* (also sometimes referred to as a STEP analysis, depending on how the words are arranged) scans the external environment to identify opportunities and threats as part of the SWOT analysis. PEST is an acronym for political, economic, social, and technological factors. I'll discuss PEST in more detail in just a minute.

**Porter's 5 Factors**    This analytical tool was created by Michael E. Porter, PhD, a professor at Harvard Business School who has written extensively on business planning and strategy. In his book, *Competitive Strategy: Techniques for Analyzing Industries and Competitors* first published in 1980 by Free Press, he described five forces that are found in all industries. These forces include new competitors, suppliers, buyers, alternative products available to consumers, and the type and level of competition in the industry. The importance of these factors in strategic planning will be more fully discussed later.

## Internal Assessment

When preparing a strategic plan, senior management must have a firm grasp of the talent and material currently available within the organization. Some of the areas to be included in an assessment of strengths and weaknesses could include the following:

| | |
|---|---|
| Credibility of executive team | Market penetration |
| Strength of management team | Customer service reputation |
| Organization culture | Market share |
| Workforce diversity | Customer loyalty |
| Current product quality | Level of sales |
| Time to market | Employee loyalty |
| State of technology | Turnover rate |

The areas to be reviewed will depend to a certain extent on the nature of the business but should include an assessment of performance in every function of the business.

There are a number of ways to collect this information: questionnaires, qualitative analyses, focus groups, surveys (of customers, suppliers, and employees), stakeholder interviews, and other information collection techniques as discussed in Chapter 2.

## External Assessment

Scanning the external environment presents more challenges than does an internal assessment because the vast amounts of information available must be sought in a wide variety of locations. The tools discussed in the "Environmental Scanning Tools" section, PEST analysis and Porter 5 Factor analysis, can assist in narrowing down what kind of information needs to be collected. The PEST analysis provides a guide for collecting information related to the general business environment:

### Political

The political environment includes such things as increased government regulations and events that influence them, such as massive business frauds. A recent example of this is the impact of the Sarbanes-Oxley Act of 2002 enacted by Congress in response to the Enron and WorldCom scandals. Less spectacular but equally important considerations for business planning purposes include changes in employment regulations such as the changes to overtime regulations proposed by the Department of Labor during the George W. Bush administration.

For multinational corporations, consideration must be given to political situations in each country of operation, including the stability of the government in some countries, restrictive trade policies, and the friendliness of the government to foreign investment.

All countries and businesses are now faced as well with the threat of terrorism that has negatively impacted sales in the travel industry; products related to security, on the other hand, have a wider market in this situation.

## Economic

The most obvious example of economic concerns has to do with the strength of the economy—can customers afford the organization's products? The unemployment rate is a key factor here, along with interest rates, inflation, and changes in fiscal policy.

For investment and expansion purposes, the stock market impacts the ability of a business to raise capital, and the price of real estate can add to the cost of purchasing or leasing new facilities. The strength of the dollar and the rate of inflation must both be considered when creating a long-term strategy.

## Social

The demographics of the target market must be considered in long term planning as well. If an organization's products are targeted at young adults, for example, and that population is static or decreasing, the organization must either change its products or find new markets for them. For multinational corporations, analyzing the social factors of widely diverse markets around the world can prove challenging, but it is essential to ensure that the long-term planning will result in a strategy that increases the success of the business.

## Technology

The rate of change in technology varies in different industries, as does the cost of purchasing new technology. Technology affects the level of automation in an organization, and that impacts the overall cost of products. From cell phones to hand-held computers and robotics on production lines, advances in technology impact how work is done and must be considered in the environmental scanning process.

## Porter's 5 Factor Analysis

While the PEST analysis provides a guide for scanning the general business environment, Porter's 5 Factor analysis hones in on issues specific to the industry in which the organization operates. It is critical to understand these industry-specific factors and address them during the planning process. Some questions to ask in analyzing these factors include:

**How likely is it that new competition will enter the market?**    A market with great demand for a product that is inexpensive to produce and requires little initial investment will encourage new competition. This puts pressure on the organization to maintain a competitive price or to differentiate its product on some basis to maintain market share.

**How reliant is the organization on its suppliers?**    When an organization produces a product requiring a unique part that can only be obtained from one supplier, the organization may find itself at the mercy of the supplier should it decide to raise the price of the part, discontinue it, or change it substantially.

**How diverse is the organization's customer base?**    A company reliant on one or only a few customers may find itself being pressured to lower prices, particularly if the product is easy to obtain from other sources.

**Are comparable replacement products available to customers at a reasonable cost?**    A serious threat to the organization's customer base will be present if a product is generic and similar products made by competitors are easy to obtain at a similar or lower price.

**What is the level of competition in the marketplace?**    The level of competition in the market will, to a certain extent, limit the strategies available to an organization wishing to enter that market. A market dominated by one or two large competitors holding the bulk of the market share presents quite a different challenge than a new, untapped market with a few small competitors.

There is a more detailed discussion of Porter's 5 Factors at `www.quickmba.com/strategy /porter.shtml`.

The results of the internal and external scans are used to forecast future business circumstances so that the organization's strategic plan can take advantage of the strengths and opportunities presented by the marketplace while reducing the negative impact of its weaknesses and external threats. The forecasting process is particularly crucial when organizations are in the midst of rapid change. For example, the forecast allows management to be proactive by redesigning products that will comply with regulations that are being proposed by federal or state governments so that they are available when the regulations take effect.

During the planning process, management must consider *long-range plans* that set the organization's direction for three to five years, *midrange plans* that can be accomplished in one to three years and *short-range plans* that will be achieved within six to twelve months. These plans are developed during the next planning phase, strategy formulation.

## Strategy Formulation

Having scanned both the internal and external environments and gathered data relevant to the strategic planning process, the executive team is ready to create the vision, mission, and core value statements, which will serve as a long-term guide for the organization. Once these long-term guidelines have been established, corporate goals are developed to provide direction during the implementation phase.

**Vision statement**    A vision statement should inspire the organization, describe what will carry it into the future, and how the future company will look. In a very concise way, it should communicate what the company does, who they do it for, and what long-range success will look like.

**Mission statement**    The mission statement gets a bit more specific, describing how the organization will achieve the vision. Effective mission statements describe the company, what it does, where it is going and how it is different from other organizations. The message of the mission statements should be directed at the employees in the organization, and it should tell them where the company is headed in the mid- to long-range.

**Corporate values statement**    A corporate value statement is a way for the executive team to communicate what they believe about the organization to the workforce. The values chosen for this purpose should be those that will be true regardless of changes in product lines or business processes. A question to ask in selecting an organization's values is whether or not the value would hold true if the organization changed its focus entirely and began doing business in a completely different way. Values such as integrity, excellence, teamwork, customer service, and mutual respect should remain constant regardless of changes in business operations.

These beliefs about the organization are usually reflected in the organization's culture. When identifying corporate values, it is important to look not only at what the management team would like to see in the way of behaviors in the organization, but also to look at the values being demonstrated in the course of business each day. When there are discrepancies between the stated, formal values and the informal values demonstrated by the workforce, the strategic plan can include goals designed to align the two.

Once the vision and mission statements have defined why the organization exists, corporate goals are needed to describe how the organization will get there in the mid- to long-range. Effective corporate goals follow the SMART model:

**Specific**   The goal should be descriptive enough to guide business unit managers in developing action plans that will accomplish the goal.

**Measurable**   A goal must include some way of knowing when it has been met.

**Action-Oriented**   Goals must describe the actions that will be taken.

**Realistic**   The goal must be high enough to challenge the organization but not so high that it is unachievable.

**Time-Based**   Goals must include a time frame for completion.

## Strategy Implementation

The strategy implementation phase further defines the corporate goals for implementation at the business unit and functional levels of the organization. It is at this stage that most of the short-range goals are developed.

**Develop tactical goals**   While the strategic goal broadly defines direction, the tactical goal describes what will be accomplished to achieve the strategy.

**Develop action plans**   The action plan breaks the tactical goal down into steps to be taken by an individual, team, or operating group to accomplish the tactical goal.

 **Real World Scenario**

**Wright Sisters, Inc. Strategic Plan**

As you recall from Chapter 2, Wright Sisters, Inc. (WSI) is a company with 3,000 employees that has been recently challenged by the appearance of a new manufacturing plant in the small midwestern city where they are located. The unexpected impact of this seemingly small change in the external environment has made senior management and the board of directors realize how unprepared they are to respond rapidly to changes in the environment. They've decided to be proactive and implement a strategic planning process to discover what other unexpected changes could be lurking in their future.

Over the years, there have been many changes in the market for their products, both technological and demographic. Because WSI has always maintained strong relationships with the hardware stores who distribute their products, they've been able to stay abreast of these changes and meet the changing needs of their customer base.

As a result of the strategic planning process, the WSI board has settled on the following statement of their vision for the company:

"Bringing the joy of gardening to new generations of gardeners."

In order to accomplish this vision, WSI has developed a mission to guide its operations over the next five years:

"We are the home-gardening source. The quality of our products allows busy families to enjoy gardening together. Our gardening education programs grow 'gardeners for life' by teaching adults and children to make gardening easier and more enjoyable."

Based on its history and its vision and mission statements, the board created a corporate value statement to set expectations for how employees and managers interact:

"WSI values integrity and excellence in its products and its people. We treat ourselves, our customers, and our suppliers with dignity and respect. We believe in and encourage new ideas to make our products better and help our business grow, and we acknowledge and reward those who present these ideas. We are accountable for our actions and, when mistakes occur, we focus on preventing future errors and moving forward. We are passionate about achieving our goals, and we are passionate about gardening."

One result of the environmental scan was that the WSI board learned that one of its underutilized strengths is the popularity of a gardening column written by one of its founders, Lydia Wright, "Ask Lydia." Because of this, they have decided to capitalize on Lydia Wright's knowledge of and passion for gardening. To do this, they have developed the following corporate goal:

"Within three years, create a nationally recognized gardening education program based on the 'Ask Lydia' columns."

In order to accomplish this midrange goal, the marketing department has developed a short-range tactical goal and action plan:

Tactical goal: "Increase the number of newspapers in which 'Ask Lydia' appears by 25 by the end of the fiscal year."

Action plan:

1.   Identify newspapers to target.

2.   Create sales pitch.

3.   Contact editors.

**4.** Draw up contracts.

**5.** Submit weekly columns.

With the goals in place, the marketing department is now able to develop a budget and implement the plan.

**Develop budget**    When the action plans are developed, it is possible to determine how many and what kind of resources will be required to implement the plan. Whether the plan requires additional employees, funds to outsource elements of the plan, new technology, or new equipment, these elements determine how much cash the organization will need to commit to achieve the goal. There are two basic ways to create a budget; the first is based on historical budget information and the second is known as *zero-based budgeting*.

**Budgets based on historic information**    A budget based on historic information bases the current budget on the prior year's budget. Past budgets and expenditures are reviewed and the new budget is based on the historical trends. In some cases, the amounts in the budget are increased by a flat percentage rate, based on inflation or anticipated salary increases. This method assumes that operationally, nothing will change from the last budget.

**Zero-based budgeting (ZBB)**    The concept behind ZBB is very simple: assume you are starting from scratch and determine what is needed to achieve the goals. How many people will be required? How much will you need to spend on outsourcing? What will be the cost of new technology or equipment? Unlike the top-down process, ZBB requires that the need for each expenditure be justified in terms of the new goals and action plans.

As part of a zero-based budget planning process, HR will examine all the programs offered to employees to determine if they are still adding value to the organization. Programs that no longer add value should be dropped and replaced with those that do add value; or, if cost cutting is required, they should be dropped and not replaced.

Regardless of the way in which the budget is developed, it can be created from the top down, from the bottom up, or with a combination approach.

**Top-down budgeting**    The top-down budget is created by senior management and imposed on the organization. Managers with operating responsibility have little input on how much money they will have to achieve their goals. This process is advantageous to senior management because they have complete control of how and where the money is spent. The disadvantage is that those creating the budget are generally far removed from actual operations and may not have full knowledge of what will be needed to achieve the goals they establish. This method often results in political battles as mid- and lower-level managers lobby senior management for additional funds for their particular departments.

**Bottom-up budgeting**    The bottom-up budget includes all managers with budget responsibility in the budget creation process. Managers with direct operating responsibility for achieving goals develop a budget based on their knowledge of operating costs and provide the information to senior managers who have a view of the big picture for the organization. The advantages of this process include operating managers who are committed to the budget when they have a voice in its development. Disadvantages include the amount of time required, the lack of awareness of the organization's big picture on the part of operating managers, and initial budget requests that may be unrealistic.

**Parallel budgeting**   A parallel budget includes elements of both the top-down and bottom-up approaches: senior management provides broad guidelines for operating managers to follow in creating the budgets for their individual departments. This approach gives operating managers a context for developing individual budgets that are more realistic.

**Execute the action plans**   At this point, the plans are put into action and the work begins.

## Strategy Evaluation

Evaluating the strategy tells you how well you are doing toward achieving your goals. This stage is important because if the action plans are not working, or if conditions in the marketplace change, the organization must be prepared to respond immediately and adjust the tactical goals and action plans. In some cases, the corporate goal may need to be revisited and adjusted to adapt to the change in conditions. One method of evaluation is the balanced scorecard discussed in the next section.

# Management

As organizations developed and grew ever larger, the need for controlling large numbers of workers in geographically diverse locations presented a challenge for business owners, who responded by creating bureaucracies to ensure that operations were conducted in accordance with the direction set by senior management. These bureaucracies, developed by American businessmen in the mid-nineteenth century, enabled the dominance of American products throughout the world for 100 years and were emulated by businesses in other countries. As long as the demand for products was greater than the number of products available, this model, in which business dictated what it would produce to the customer, worked extremely well.

When business conditions changed and customers became more demanding, this "one size fits all" approach was not as successful. Japanese manufacturers gave customers an alternative, and the customers responded by purchasing their products. American businesses, due to their large bureaucratic methods, were slow to respond. The need for constant innovation to satisfy changing customer needs was a difficult transition, and continues to affect American business.

It is up to management to ensure that strategies and plans developed to meet customer needs are implemented and accomplished. To do this, managers utilize four basic management functions: planning, organizing, directing, and controlling. These functions take the resources of the organization and ensure that they achieve corporate goals. The planning function has been covered extensively; let's talk briefly now about the other functions.

# Organizing

Managers are responsible for providing a structure within which employees are able to complete their work. Many factors must be considered, including what work needs to be done, how employees interact and with whom, the decision-making process in the organization, and how work is delegated. Issues to be considered in developing an organization structure are whether the management is centralized or decentralized, the nature of the functions, and the span of control for each manager.

A *centralized organization* is one in which the decision-making authority is concentrated at higher levels in the organization; while in a *decentralized organization*, the decision-making authority is delegated to lower levels.

Business functions are classified as either *line functions*, such as operations and sales, which make decisions about operating needs, and *staff functions*, such as human resources and finance, which do not make operating decisions, but do advise line managers.

Finally, *span of control* refers to the number of employees that one manager can directly supervise. Depending on the nature and complexity of the task, this number varies, with managers responsible for very complex tasks requiring closer supervision able to supervise fewer employees than managers responsible for less complex tasks.

There are five basic organization structures: functional, product-based, geographical, divisional, and matrix. Each is appropriate for different situations. A sixth structure, the seamless organization, is emerging as technology provides more flexibility in defining working relationships.

## Functional Structure

This is represented by the traditional pyramid-shape organization chart with which most people are familiar. It is a hierarchical structure in which communication moves from the top down and from the bottom up. These structures are more formal and rigid than some other structures and are appropriate for businesses with a single product line where specialization is an advantage. In this structure, each functional area reports to the CEO. Functional organizations are generally very centralized.

## Product-Based Structure

A product-based organization structure is organized by product line and is appropriate when the company has well-defined product lines that are clearly separate from each other. In this structure, each product line reports to the CEO; these structures lend themselves to either centralized or decentralized decision-making processes.

## Geographic Structure

In a geographic structure, executives of regional areas are responsible for all the business functions in their assigned region and the regional executives report to the CEO. Structuring an organization in this way is appropriate when there are common requirements in the region that are different from the requirements in other regions. Geographic structures are very decentralized, with most decisions being made at the local level.

### Divisional Structure

A divisional structure has characteristics similar to that of the geographic structure, but the divisions may be based on criteria other than geography, such as the market or industry. Like the geographic structure, divisional structures are characterized by decentralized decision making.

### Matrix Structure

In a matrix structure, employees report to two managers. Generally, one manager is responsible for a product line and the other has functional responsibility. For example, the VP of marketing and the production manager for a specific product would both supervise the marketing coordinator who is creating collateral for the product. A matrix organization is advantageous because it encourages communication and cooperation; it is, however, difficult to communicate and manage and can create confusion for employees receiving conflicting directions.

### Seamless Organization

The seamless organization is one in which the traditional hierarchies do not exist—it is a horizontal organization connected by networks instead of separated by the boundaries that characterize other organization structures. The purpose of this structure is to enhance communication and creativity. Seamless organizations would not be possible without the technology that allows employees to connect with each other via e-mail and the Internet from anywhere in the world. This technology enables employees to meet with coworkers who have specialized knowledge without the expense of traveling.

## Directing

Managers must establish relationships with the employees they supervise to encourage and support them in accomplishing their goals. Management style contributes to the development of these relationships. In Chapter 2, we discussed different management styles in detail in the section "Leadership Styles."

## Controlling

The control function is the one by which managers ensure that the strategies, tactics, and plans developed during the planning process are implemented. As discussed earlier in "Strategy Evaluation," this is an ongoing process. In addition to the evaluations of individual goals and action plans described in that section, management must have a "big picture" view of overall progress.

One way of getting the big picture is by utilizing the *balanced scorecard*, a strategic management system developed by Robert Kaplan, PhD and David Norton, PhD. Their concept was that because traditional business measurements focused only on financial results, other key elements that impacted business success were not included in strategic management decisions. To address this shortcoming, the balanced scorecard concept tracks information in four key areas: financial results, customer results, key internal processes, and how people are hired and trained to achieve organization goals.

The balanced scorecard accomplishes this by tying objectives to specific measures of performance and setting targets for meeting the objectives. The purpose of the scorecard process is to tie all business functions into specific plans for achieving goals and to provide a means of measuring how each objective contributed or failed to contribute to organization-wide goals.

The Balanced Scorecard Institute provides a complete discussion of the concept at www.balancedscorecard.org/basics/bsc1.html.

# The Human Resource Role

The role of human resources in organizations is characterized by change. Not long ago, HR practitioners were expected to contribute to the organization in an advisory capacity, providing services to employees and others and controlling employment policies and procedures in their organizations. As advisors, we were asked to provide information and guidance for managers to deal with employee issues. As service providers, HR professionals were required to answer questions and provide information for a wide range of constituents, from government agencies to candidates for employment and senior management. In the control role, HR was expected to enforce policies and ensure compliance with federal, state, and local employment regulations and laws.

Today, while the roles are still in flux, they have begun to evolve into strategic, administrative, and operational roles.

Strategically, HR professionals contribute to decisions that build on employee strengths to meet corporate goals. Establishing recruiting and retention plans to attract the best-qualified employees and keep them in the organization is a key contribution that HR is uniquely qualified to make. Developing performance management systems to motivate employees and providing continuous development opportunities are other areas that provide strategic advantage to organizations. Managing change and leading or participating in reengineering or restructuring programs to ensure the retention of key employees furthers the organization's ability to meet its goals.

Administratively, HR manages compliance issues related to government regulations, maintains records of benefits, and ensures the confidentiality of employee information.

Operationally, HR professionals manage the employee relations and recruiting functions that require daily attention to maintain a productive work environment.

## HR Audits

HR audits are conducted to assess the status of HR programs, policies, and practices within an organization. Often commissioned by an HR manager or director who has recently joined a company, audits identify areas that may be out of compliance with legal requirements, are in need of updating due to strategic changes within the organization, and define elements that are working well. This tool provides a roadmap for upgrading service levels, streamlining administrative activities, and identifying possible targets for outsourcing. Audits can be conducted by a member of the HR department or outsourced to a consultant.

An experienced HR professional is capable of identifying the elements that should be audited and monitoring the process. A complete audit will include a review of policies and practices in all of the functional areas of HR, including hiring, compensation, benefits, training and development programs, records management, and compliance with changing legal requirements. HR audits can use a variety of methods to obtain the information needed for an assessment, including checklists or questionnaires, surveys of employees and managers, and interviews.

## HR Planning

During the strategic planning process, HR, along with all other business functions, must develop tactical goals and action plans designed to meet the needs of the organization. HR professionals must base their planning on corporate strategy and goals and work with managers of other functional areas to ensure that recruiting and hiring goals meet the needs created by the tactical goals and action plans of those functional areas. The planning process for HR needs is described more fully in Chapter 4, "Workforce Planning and Employment"; the information needed for the strategic plan is developed during that process.

HR should also provide measures related to workforce issues, productivity, and HR activities for the strategic plan, some of which are listed here:

- Job satisfaction
- Organizational commitment and involvement
- Turnover and retention
- Absenteeism and sick leave use and frequency
- Grievance rates
- Terminations as a percent of population

Some measures of productivity are:

- Revenue and/or cost per employee
- Units produced per employee
- OSHA incident rates
- Time to fill vacancies
- Workers' compensation cost per employee

Finally, some measures of HR activities are:

- HR expenses as a percent of operating expenses
- Ratio of total employees to HR staff
- Compensation as a ratio of company operating expenses
- Training cost per employee
- Cost per hire
- HR department expenses per employee

- Retiree benefit cost per retiree
- Yield ratios (the ratio of offers made to offers accepted)

The data collected from these measures can be examined over a period of time to identify and measure trends that indicate problems on the horizon and allow HR to be proactive in addressing those issues. This information is important not only as part of the internal scanning process, it provides ongoing controls for HR during the strategy evaluation phase of the strategic planning process.

## Change Management

It is a fact of life in American business that change will happen. Much of the time, it is unpleasant for at least some of those affected. Effectively managing change in an organization is integral to attracting and retaining employees for the long haul. In the change process, HR must balance the needs of the organization, the employees, and other stakeholders, including shareholders. While intellectually, many people understand the need for these changes, how they are personally affected has a direct impact on employee morale and productivity. Because the change process involves both organization structures (covered in this chapter) and individual behavior (covered in Chapter 5), I struggled with where to discuss the details of change and how organization structures can be used to both make the changes and ease the process. The discussion of methods and structures and how they can be used to effect organizational change occurs in Chapter 5, along with the discussion of the impact of changes on individuals in the organization. This section provides a brief look at the types of change that have the most significant effect on workforce populations today: reengineering, restructuring, and downsizing.

**Reengineering**    Involves looking at the entire organization and simplifying processes and eliminating unnecessary processes with the goal of increasing customer satisfaction through improvements in efficiency.

**Restructuring**    Looks at individual units in the organization to reduce costs and increase production.

**Downsizing**    Reduces the size of the workforce to save money and improve company profits.

Even employees who remain in the company after a change occurs are affected by it, and a key contribution to be made by HR during change is to be sure that the decision makers understand the difficulties that employees will face during and after the change and put programs into place that mitigate the negative effects of the change as much as possible. Steps to take to reduce employee anxiety include the following:

- Keep employees in the loop about the actual situation.
- If there are actions employees can take to remedy the situation, tell them what they can do.
- When talking to employees, be honest and truthful. Don't hide the facts.

The way companies handle change will be remembered, particularly if the organization has a habit of being brutal in its change processes. This can affect the ability of the organization to attract the quality of employees it wants in the future.

# Corporate Ethics and Social Responsibility

As discussed at the beginning of this chapter, a corporation is a legal entity that has rights and obligations. While a corporation itself cannot make decisions, those at top levels in the organization must make decisions on behalf of its owners. They have a *fiduciary responsibility* or obligation to act in the best interests of the shareholders by making decisions that benefit the organization over decisions that benefit them personally. Recent events have demonstrated that this responsibility is sometimes ignored.

Corporations are citizens of the communities in which they live and as such have responsibilities to their fellow citizens. This social responsibility ranges from making appropriate decisions about pollutants that are released into the environment to working with and training disadvantaged individuals to become productive members of society. In this section, we will explore some of the issues in both of these areas.

## Ethics

Since the Enron scandal erupted in December 2001, the issue of business ethics has come to the forefront of discussions about the behavior of corporate executives, auditors, attorneys, and board members. Subsequent revelations about possible accounting irregularities at other multinational corporations such as AOL, WorldCom, and Global Crossing make it clear that this was not simply a case of one company that ran amok, but it was a pervasive problem at top levels of major corporations. These scandals led to passage of the Sarbanes-Oxley Act of 2002, which made many of the practices that occurred in these companies illegal and provided penalties for violations. Some of the changes made by Sarbanes-Oxley include:

- Established the Public Company Accounting Oversight Board and required all public accounting firms to register with the board, which will conduct periodic inspections to ensure their compliance with audit standards.

- Established new standards to ensure the independence of auditors relative to the businesses they audit, including restrictions on nonaudit related services such as bookkeeping, management, human resource consulting, or other similar services; rotation of audit partner assignments at least every five years; and a requirement that the audit report and recommendations to the management team be delivered directly to the audit committee of the board of directors.

- Established standards for corporate responsibility, holding the chief executive of a public company accountable for the fairness and accuracy of financial reports filed with the Securities and Exchange Commission (SEC).

- Required CEOs and CFOs to reimburse the company for incentive- or equity-based compensation in the event of a material restatement of financial reports to the SEC caused by misconduct.

- Prohibited insider trading of stock during pension fund blackout periods when employees are not able to trade the stock in their pension accounts.

- Established ethical requirements for senior financial officers.

- Took steps to ensure the fairness, accuracy, and independence of stock analysis.
- Established criminal penalties for management officials who defraud shareholders, destroy documents, or obstruct justice.

Ethical behavior begins at top levels in the organization. The Board of Directors must demand it of the executive team, and the executive team must model it for all others in the organization. It would seem that this should be a pretty simple thing to do; after all, at the end of the day, ethical behavior occurs when, as Spike Lee said, people "do the right thing." Because the values people hold are different depending on the culture they grew up in, their family background and their personal experiences, the right thing can mean different things to different people. That is why the executive team must set the standard of behavior, communicate it, model it, and enforce it if they are serious about maintaining an ethical workplace.

# Code of Ethics

A corporate values statement can begin to set the stage for ethical behavior, but a code of conduct or code of ethics is really necessary to inform people in the organization about what behavior is expected and what is unacceptable. A code of ethics should cover topics such as those discussed in the following sections.

## Confidentiality

In most companies, confidential information can be found in every department: marketing plans, new product development, financial statements, personal employee information, and e-mail accounts can all contain highly confidential information. HR professionals work every day with confidential employee information and are sometimes pressured to share this information for one reason or another. The inappropriate use of information collected during the employment process, information about an employee's age, medical condition, or credit history may not be used in making employment decisions. HR professionals and other employees with access to confidential information have a duty to maintain its confidentiality.

## Conflicts of Interest

As mentioned at the beginning of this section, employees must put the interests of the organization before their own. Any time an employee stands to gain personally from an action taken by the employer, there is a conflict of interest (except, of course, for payment of the employee's salary). At a minimum, these situations must be disclosed to the employer, or the employee should remove themselves from the situation. The ethics statement should make it clear that even the appearance or perception of a conflict of interest is damaging to the company and should be avoided.

## Fairness

Actions taken by employers have the ability to significantly impact the lives of their employees. Whether decisions are being made about hiring or layoffs, or accusations of malfeasance or inappropriate behavior are being made, employers have an obligation to treat employees fairly in all their actions. Employees who have the power to make decisions such as selecting suppliers or evaluating employee performance have an equal responsibility to handle these decisions fairly.

A real test of an organization's fairness occurs when an employee makes a complaint to a federal agency, claiming that illegal activity has occurred. A person who does this is known as a whistle-blower. Some federal statutes, such as the Occupational Safety and Health Act, Railroad Safety Act, Safe Drinking Water Act, and Toxic Substances Control Act provide protection for employees who "blow the whistle" on their employers. Even so, it is a true ethical test to see how the whistle-blower who continues to work for the company is treated in the workplace once the complaint has been made.

 **Real World Scenario**

**Whistle-Blowing in the Wake of the Enron Scandal**

In the wake of the Enron scandal, and particularly during the month when congressional hearings into the bankrupt corporation's activities were televised each day, the Securities and Exchange Commission saw a marked increase in complaints, from an average of 365 per day in 2001 to 525 per day for the month of January 2002. On February 27, 2002, Katie Fairbank of the *Dallas Morning News* also reported an increase in whistle-blower complaints at the Department of Justice, from 33 in 1987 to 483 in 1999.

Sherron Watkins, who is credited with blowing the whistle on the Enron accounting practices that eventually led to its bankruptcy in December 2001, may have inspired the increased reports. Ms. Watkins followed a path typical of whistle-blowers by meeting with Enron CEO Ken Lay long before she went to the regulators. Her desire was to advise him of the wrongdoing so he could put an end to it. That unfortunately did not happen, and the company filed for bankruptcy a few months after their meeting.

While some whistle-blowers have statutory protection from retaliation, courts are divided on just what whistle-blowing activity is protected; those who go to regulators are often unable to work in their chosen profession after taking the action.

One whistle-blower who paid the price for his actions is Dr. Jeffrey Wigand, a former tobacco executive who was fired by Brown & Williamson Tobacco Corporation in 1993 after the company refused to remove a known carcinogen from their cigarette products. After his termination, Dr. Wigand testified against tobacco companies in civil lawsuits and appeared in an interview on the television show *60 Minutes*; his former employers launched a campaign to discredit him. Dr. Wigand was a key witness in the lawsuit brought by 46 states against tobacco companies that was settled when they agreed to pay $206 billion to reimburse the states for medical expenses that were related to smoking.

## Gifts

An ethics policy should address the issue of gift exchanges with customers, vendors, and employees. The ethics policy should describe under what circumstances gifts are acceptable and define limitations on the amounts if they are to be allowed. When the receipt of a gift unfairly influences a business decision, it becomes unethical and should be refused.

For companies operating outside the United States, this can be a difficult issue because in some cultures exchanging business gifts is a standard and expected practice, and the failure to do so can be seen as an insult. The Foreign Corrupt Practices Act of 1977 was enacted by Congress in response to revelations by multinational corporations of the bribes that were paid to obtain business in some foreign countries. The act prohibits the payment of bribes and requires accounting practices that preclude the use of covert bank accounts that could be used to make these payments.

## Honesty

The code of ethics should set an expectation of honesty in the workplace. As with all other aspects of an ethics code, the executive team must model honesty in the representations they make to employees, customers, suppliers, and all other stakeholders in order for the message to be taken seriously within the company.

## Insider Information

While insider information is most commonly associated with trading securities on the stock exchange, it can also apply to other areas. Inside information is any information that an employee has access to or comes into contact with that is not available to the general public. Using this information in the stock exchanges is illegal and can result in criminal prosecution and civil penalties.

The prohibitions against using inside information apply to an employee who overhears the information as much as they apply to decision makers in the organization. Federal law requires that those with access to inside information may not act on it until the information is made public.

## Integrity

Integrity is defined as a firm adherence to a code of moral values. Integrity is demonstrated when an individual does the right thing, even when that "thing" is unpopular.

## Personal Use of Company Assets

A code of ethics should clearly state what the employer considers to be an appropriate and acceptable use of company assets. In some organizations, the receipt of any personal telephone calls or e-mails is considered inappropriate, while in other companies a limited number is acceptable.

## Workplace Privacy

Some employers feel the need to install surveillance cameras in work areas. This happens for a variety of reasons. For a retail store open late at night, it provides a measure of security for employees. Concerns about productivity or pilferage can spur an employer to install a surveillance camera. Whatever the reason, the employer must balance the need to manage the workforce with the employee's expectation of privacy.

Advances in technology have also made it possible for employers to monitor Internet, e-mail, and voice mail usage, and this is seen as an invasion of privacy by some employees. Employers who plan to monitor employee communication and Internet usage should develop and distribute a policy clearly stating what information is subject to monitoring and under what conditions.

The code of ethics should include a statement about the use of surveillance and monitoring.

As important as a code of ethics is, it is equally important to be aware of situations where conflicting needs and desires make doing the right thing less clear cut. As those responsible for maintaining the confidentiality of personal employee information, HR professionals make ethical decisions on a regular basis and are in a position to model ethical behavior in the way they respond to inappropriate requests for information.

## Ethics Officers

Businesses serious about establishing meaningful ethics programs have appointed ethics officers or facilitators whose responsibility is to ensure the adherence of the organization to the ethical standards set by the executive team. These officers advise employees at all levels in an organization on ethical issues and manage programs designed to allow confidential reporting of ethical concerns by employees, customers, shareholders, or others and investigate allegations of wrongdoing. Ethics officers provide periodic reports for the executive team to keep them apprised of ethical issues in the organization.

# Lawmaking and Regulatory Processes

The human resource profession can play a key rule in the development of legislation and regulations affecting the employment relationship between an organization and its employees. HR professionals should be aware of the ways in which they, as individual citizens and as business leaders, can affect these processes. Because the PHR/SPHR exam is based on federal laws, this section will discuss how proposed legislation or regulation is handled by the federal government. A similar process is followed by state and local governments, and involvement at any level of government can benefit business organizations.

## Legislative Process

The federal legislative process begins when someone has an idea. This idea can come from a senator or congressman, an individual, business, church, or professional association. If the idea comes from someone other than a member of congress (MOC), it must be presented to a congressman or senator to begin the process of becoming a law.

1. When an MOC agrees to sponsor a bill and presents it to the full body of the House or the Senate, it is assigned to a committee to be studied.

2. The committee first determines the likelihood that the bill will be able to pass a vote in the full body; if the determination is made that it is not likely to pass, no further action is taken and the bill effectively dies in the committee.

3. Bills that are deemed likely to pass a vote of the full body are studied by a subcommittee, and hearings are conducted to hear from government representatives, subject matter experts, and citizens with points of view for or against the bill.

4. Once the bill has been studied, the subcommittee may make changes in a process known as "marking up" the bill. The subcommittee then votes on whether or not to return the bill to the full committee with a recommendation for further action. A bill that is not reported back to the committee dies in the subcommittee.

5. Bills that are returned to the full committee may be subjected to further study, or the committee may vote to accept the subcommittee recommendations and "order the bill reported" to the full body.

6. When the committee votes to report a bill to the full body, a written report of the findings and recommendations of the committee is prepared, including dissenting views of members who voted against the bill.

7. Bills that are reported out of committee are placed on the "legislative calendar" and scheduled for a vote by the full body.

8. Members of the full body are able to present their views about passage of the bill prior to a vote. During the debate period, members may offer amendments that will take effect if the bill is passed.

9. When debate is completed, a vote is conducted.

10. If the full body passes the bill, it must go to the other body and usually begin the process again; in some cases the other body may vote to pass the bill as it was presented. During the review process, the second body may vote it down, table it, or change the bill. Bills that are rejected or tabled at this stage are considered dead and will not become laws.

11. If the bill passes the second body, any major differences between the two bills are reconciled in a conference committee. If the conference committee cannot agree on the form of the bill, it will die and not become a law. If the committee recommends a conference report incorporating the changes, both houses of Congress must vote to approve the conference report before the bill is forwarded to the president for signature.

12. When the president receives the bill, he has three choices: he may sign it into law, veto it, or fail to sign it. If the bill is vetoed, Congress may override the veto by a two-thirds vote of a quorum in each house, in which case the bill will become a law in spite of the veto.

    If the president simply fails to sign a bill, one of two things will happen. When Congress is in session, a bill that remains unsigned for 10 days will become law without the president's signature. When Congress adjourns before the 10-day period is up, the bill will not become law. This is known as a pocket veto.

## Administrative Law

In addition to the laws passed by Congress and signed by the president, HR professionals should be aware of the process by which administrative law is developed. There are three types of administrative law that impact employment relationships: agency rules and regulations, agency orders, and executive orders.

Much of the legislation passed by Congress empowers and requires federal agencies to develop enforcement regulations. An example of this is the Occupational Safety and Health Act of 1970, in which Congress established the Occupational Safety and Health Administration and required that it develop regulations to improve the safety of American workplaces. In developing these regulations, the agencies follow an established process.

First, they develop rules or regulations and publish them in the *Federal Register* (which is the official daily publication for rules, proposals, and notices of federal agencies and the Office of the President) and give the public an opportunity to comment on the proposals. Once the comment period has been completed, the agency publishes final rules that take effect no less than 30 days after the date of public notice.

Some federal agencies, such as the National Labor Relations Board (NLRB) and the Equal Employment Opportunity Commission (EEOC) have the power to order compliance with federal laws in courts known as Administrative Law Courts. The orders issued by Administrative Law Judges (ALJ) in these cases have the effect of law and many of these decisions are published in the *Federal Register* as well.

The final type of administrative law with which HR professionals should be familiar is the executive order (EO). EOs are issued by the President of the United States and become law after they have been published in the *Federal Register* for 30 days.

## Lobbying

*Lobbying* is an activity in which anyone can participate when they wish to influence new laws and regulations. HR professionals can contribute as individuals or as part of the HR profession. The Society for Human Resource Management (SHRM) has legislative affairs committees (LAC) on the national and local levels that monitor and provide information on proposed changes to employment-related legislation and regulation in addition to coordinating lobbying efforts.

HR professionals who wish to influence the legislative or regulatory processes should first make sure they fully understand the topic and are able to provide sound justifications for the position they take. It is also important to gather as much support as possible—legislators are more likely to be responsive when there are a large number of voters who feel the same way. To be an effective lobbyist, it is also important to find a senator or congressman who will guide you through the process and introduce you to other legislators.

There are many avenues for contacting elected officials or regulators. The House of Representatives has a website, `www.house.gov` that provides information about contacting congressmen; the Senate has a similar site at `www.senate.gov`.

HR professionals who wish to stay abreast of legislative activity can find information on pending legislation in many places. In addition to the LACs mentioned previously, information about pending legislation is available at the House and Senate sites just mentioned and on the SHRM website at `www.shrm.org`.

# Summary

Strategic management occurs as the result of a planning process that reviews internal and external factors affecting the ability of an organization to successfully achieve its goals. This process requires that all business functions provide their expertise in both the planning and implementation of goals, objectives, and action plans.

The strategic planning process begins by gathering information from internal and external sources using the SWOT technique to identify internal strengths and weaknesses and external opportunities and threats. As a result of the scanning, long-range, midrange and short-range forecasts can be made to provide the information necessary for developing the vision, mission, and goals for the organization, which are needed by functional area managers to set tactical goals and action plans for their business units.

As HR moves into the twenty-first century, its role is changing into one that is more strategic and involved with planning the future direction of the organization. As a result, it is crucial for HR professionals to have a working knowledge of other functional areas of the business in order to provide the operational and administrative support necessary to attract and retain qualified employees in each area.

As change becomes increasingly prevalent in business, HR plays a role in advising management and counseling employees to reduce the stress of the change process in the organization.

HR professionals are expected to act ethically and handle their organizational responsibilities with care and respect. Employees rely on HR personnel to carry out their responsibilities in a professional manner, assuming a moral responsibility to preserve the integrity and personal nature of employee information they handle. The organization relies on HR to protect its best interests by maintaining a high standard and adhering to a professional code of ethics.

Through active involvement in the development of legislation at the federal, state, and local levels, HR professionals can influence the course of proposed laws and regulations thus providing a benefit to their employers, their employees, and the profession.

# Exam Essentials

**Understand different business functions.** HR professionals must understand the purpose of different business functions and how they interact with each other and with HR. Understanding the unique needs of production and operations, sales and marketing, finance, accounting, and information technology and how each contributes to the organization's success allows HR to be more effective in providing services to the organization.

**Understand the strategic planning process.** The strategic planning process consists of four broad elements: scanning the environment; formulating the corporate strategy with the vision, mission, values, and corporate goals; implementing the strategy with tactical goals, action plans, and budgets to accomplish organization goals; and evaluating the strategy to ensure that it can be adjusted to accommodate changes in the organization or the external environment.

**Be able to describe the environmental scanning process.**    An environmental scan uses a SWOT analysis to assess the strengths, weaknesses, opportunities, and threats that must be considered in the strategic plan. A PEST analysis is a way of looking at the external environment to assess the political, economic, social, and technological factors that will affect the organization. Porter's 5 Factors (new competitors, suppliers, customers, availability of replacement products, and level of market competition) provide additional insight into the external environment and how it will affect the organization's goals.

**Be able to explain different management structures and how they impact the organization.** Many factors are considered when deciding on a management structure for the organization, including the nature of the business, geographic diversity, and organization culture. The most effective structure is one that allows the organization to respond rapidly to changes in the environment.

**Understand the importance of change management and HR's role in managing change.** Change is a fact of life in organizations; reengineering, restructuring, and downsizing occur often as a result of strategic decisions and changes in the marketplace. HR can develop programs that provide a means for communication, both top-down and bottom-up, to ease the process and reduce stress in the work environment.

**Understand the budgeting process.**    Budgets may be created from the top down, the bottom up, or some combination of the two methods. The process for creating them is generally based on historic data or on a zero-based budgeting process.

**Understand HR's role in the organization.**    The role of HR is evolving into one that provides strategic, administrative, and operational services for the organization.

**Be able to describe the steps involved in the legislative process.**    A bill can originate in the House of Representatives or in the Senate. A bill is referred to a committee for consideration and then, if it's reported out of committee, is ready for full floor consideration. After all debate is concluded, the bill is ready for final passage. It must pass both bodies in the same form before it can be presented to the president for signature. The president may sign the bill, veto it, and return it to Congress; let it become law without signature; or at the end of a session, pocket veto it.

# Key Terms

Before you take the exam, be certain you are familiar with the following terms:

| | |
|---|---|
| accounting | decentralized organization |
| balance sheet | environmental scan |
| balanced scorecard | fiduciary responsibility |
| centralized organization | finance |

fiscal year

goal

income statement

information technology (IT)

just-in-time (JIT) inventory

line functions

lobbying

marketing

objective

operations

PEST analysis

production

profit and loss statement (P&L)

sales

span of control

staff functions

statement of cash flows

strategic planning

strategy

SWOT analysis

# Review Questions

1. The first element in the strategic planning process is
   **A.** Formulate the strategy.
   **B.** Evaluate the strategy.
   **C.** Scan the environment.
   **D.** Implement the strategy.

2. Which of the following is *not* part of a SWOT analysis?
   **A.** Technology
   **B.** Strength
   **C.** Opportunity
   **D.** Weakness

3. A statement that describes what an organization does that is different from others is a:
   **A.** Value statement
   **B.** Corporate goal
   **C.** Vision statement
   **D.** Mission statement

4. When a zero-based budget process is used,
   **A.** All proposed expenditures are based on historic trends and adjusted for inflation.
   **B.** All proposed expenditures are controlled by senior management.
   **C.** All proposed expenditures are based on goals and action plans.
   **D.** All proposed expenditures are based on costs provided by operating managers.

5. Improvements in technology have had their greatest effect on
   **A.** Employee morale
   **B.** Productivity
   **C.** Cost of living
   **D.** Management's span of control

6. The balanced scorecard concept does NOT
   **A.** Tie objectives to specific performance measures.
   **B.** Eliminate unnecessary processes to increase customer satisfaction.
   **C.** Measure how objectives contribute to organization goals.
   **D.** Set targets for meeting objectives.

7. Which of the following is an appropriate use for an HR audit?

   **A.** To determine which employees no longer have the skills needed by the organization.

   **B.** To determine the employee productivity and turnover rates.

   **C.** To determine whether the employee handbook is in compliance with current government regulations.

   **D.** To determine the timeline for changes that are necessary in the HR department.

8. The four P's summarize the marketing function. Which of the following is not one of the P's?

   **A.** Perception

   **B.** Price

   **C.** Placement

   **D.** Promotion

9. Which of the following is one of the elements of a SMART goal?

   **A.** Action-oriented

   **B.** Strength

   **C.** Technology

   **D.** Threat

10. An organization that wants to maximize the speed and flexibility with which it is able to operate would be most likely to choose which of the following structures?

   **A.** Functional

   **B.** Seamless

   **C.** Matrix

   **D.** Geographic

# Answers to Review Questions

1. **C.** Most strategic planning models are composed of four-steps: environmental scanning, strategy formulation, strategy implementation, and evaluation.

2. **A.** A SWOT analysis looks at the organization's strengths, weaknesses, opportunities, and threats.

3. **D.** The mission statement describes who the organization is, what it does, where it is going, and how it is different from others.

4. **C.** In a zero-based budgeting process, prior year budget amounts are zeroed out and all expenditures must be justified in terms of how they will accomplish the current goals and action plans for the unit.

5. **B.** The greatest effect of technology is increased worker productivity. In spite of a reduction in total work hours during the first quarter of 2003, technology improvements resulted in an overall increase in productivity.

6. **B.** The balanced scorecard ties objectives to performance measurements, sets targets, and measures how the objectives contribute to organization goals.

7. **C.** An HR audit examines HR policies and procedures for compliance and to determine whether or not the department is successfully meeting the organization needs.

8. **A.** The four P's of marketing are product, price, placement, and promotion, which summarize the responsibilities of the marketing team.

9. **A.** A SMART goal is specific, measurable, action-oriented, realistic, and time-based.

10. **B.** A seamless organization maximizes the speed and flexibility of its operations by removing barriers found in traditional structures. The cross-functional work teams that are part of a seamless organization are able to solve problems more rapidly because information is shared readily and decision-making authority is distributed to different levels in the organization.

# Chapter

# 4

# Workforce Planning and Employment

**THE HRCI TEST SPECIFICATIONS FROM THE WORKFORCE PLANNING AND EMPLOYMENT FUNCTIONAL AREA COVERED IN THIS CHAPTER INCLUDE:**

✓ Identify staffing requirements to meet the goals and objectives of the organization.

✓ Conduct job analyses to write job descriptions and develop job competencies.

✓ Identify and document the essential job functions for positions.

✓ Establish hiring criteria based on the competencies needed.

✓ Assess internal workforce, labor market, and recruitment agencies to determine the availability of qualified applicants.

✓ Identify internal and external recruitment methods and implement them within the context of the organization's goals and objectives.

✓ Develop strategies to market the organization to potential applicants.

✓ Establish selection procedures, including interviewing, testing, and reference and background checking.

✓ Implement selection procedures, including interviewing, testing, and reference and background checking.

✓ Develop and/or extend employment offers.

✓ Perform or administer post-offer employment activities (for example, employment agreements, completion of I-9 verification form, relocation agreements, and medical examinations).

✓ Facilitate and/or administer the process by which non-US citizens can legally work in the United States.

✓ Design, facilitate, and/or conduct the orientation process, including review of performance standards for new hires and transfers.

✓ Evaluate selection and employment processes for effectiveness and implement changes if indicated (for example, employee retention).

✓ Develop a succession planning process.

✓ Develop and implement the organizational exit process, including unemployment insurance claim responses (includes severance, turnover, and outplacement).

✓ Develop, implement, manage, and evaluate affirmative action program(s), as may be required.

This functional area of the Human Resource BOK covers activities related to planning for and managing entry into and exit from the organization to meet changing business needs. The chapter is organized around the key functions of workforce management: planning, staffing, and exiting the organization. The workforce planning process is key to bringing people with the appropriate skills into the organization when they are needed; employment is the process by which HR professionals work with line management to locate, hire, and integrate new employees into the organization. These processes are not limited to simply hiring new people; they include ensuring that talented individuals in the organization are identified, developed, and retained so that they are available to move into positions of greater responsibility as organization needs evolve. In this chapter, I will review the PHR and SPHR responsibility and knowledge requirements for Workforce Planning and Employment (WFP). This functional area discusses the impact of federal legislation, regulation, and case law on these activities.

In order to be fully prepared for the PHR/SPHR exam, candidates must be well versed in the basic knowledge for this functional area as well as some of the core knowledge requirements covered in Chapter 1, "Certifying Human Resource Professionals," that pertain to WFP. The *HRCI Certification Guide* described in the introduction to this book provides a detailed list of WFP knowledge requirements and should be reviewed prior to studying this area of the BOK. The core knowledge requirements significant to this functional area include the development of RFPs, knowledge of communication strategies, quantitative and qualitative analysis tools, job analysis and description methods, and the interrelationship between HR activities and other business units.

Let's begin our review with the federal laws and regulations that govern employment relationships.

# Employment Legislation

There is extensive federal legislation, regulation, and case law that impacts most employment relationships in the United States. The legislation governs all aspects of employment: recruiting, job advertisements, testing, hiring, training and apprenticeship programs, benefits, leaves, compensation, transfers, promotion, and terminations. Before you can move on to implementing workforce plans, you need to know and understand the legislation presented in this section.

While several pieces of civil rights legislation were enacted between 1866 and 1963, the Civil Rights Act of 1964 is regarded as the milestone for modern equal employment opportunity. This sweeping legislation impacted many areas of American life, and Title VII of the act was dedicated to providing equal employment opportunities for all Americans. Title VII has been amended several times to expand coverage to specific areas not covered in the act of 1964.

## Title VII of the Civil Rights Act of 1964

Title VII of the Civil Rights Act of 1964 introduced the concepts of *protected classes* and *unlawful employment practices* to American business. Title VII created the *Equal Employment Opportunity Commission (EEOC)* with a mandate to promote equal employment opportunity, educate employers, provide technical assistance, and study and report on its activities to Congress and the American people. The EEOC is the enforcement agency for Title VII and other discrimination legislation. The act identified five protected classes: race, color, religion, national origin, and sex, and defined unlawful employment practices including:

- Discriminatory recruiting, selection, or hiring actions
- Discriminatory compensation or benefit practices
- Discriminatory access to training or apprenticeship programs
- Discriminatory practices in any other terms or conditions of employment

Legitimate seniority, merit, and piece-rate payment systems are allowable under Title VII as long as they do not intentionally discriminate against protected classes.

Title VII allowed for limited exceptions to its requirements, some of which are listed below:

- *Bona fide occupational qualifications (BFOQ)* occur when religion, sex, or national origin is "reasonably necessary to the normal operation" of the business.
- Educational institutions were not originally subject to Title VII.
- Religious organizations may give preference to members of that religion.
- A potential employee who is unable to obtain, or loses, a national security clearance required for the position is not protected.
- Indian reservations may give preference to Indian applicants and employees living on or near the reservation.

Visit www.eeoc.gov/laws/vii.html to view the full text of Title VII.

## Amendments to Title VII of the Civil Rights Act of 1964

Title VII was amended in 1972, 1978, and 1991 to clarify and expand its coverage.

### Equal Employment Opportunity Act of 1972

Created in 1972, the Equal Employment Opportunity Act (EEOA) is an amendment to Title VII and addresses the issue of *disparate impact*, which was introduced by the *Griggs v Duke Power* case in 1971. Disparate impact occurs when an employment practice, which appears to be fair, unintentionally discriminates against members of a protected class. The EEOA provides that if a business can show job-related business necessity for employment actions, the burden of proof for discrimination is on the complainant. It also provides that, when individuals allege multiple discriminatory acts, they must show that each practice is in itself discriminatory unless it can be shown that the employer's decision-making process cannot be separated, in which case the individual may challenge the decision-making process itself.

The EEOA of 1972 also provided litigation authority to the EEOC in the event that an acceptable conciliation agreement cannot be reached. In those cases, the EEOC is empowered to sue nongovernment entities, including employers, unions, and employment agencies.

The EEOA extended coverage of Title VII to entities that had been excluded in 1968, including:

- Educational institutions
- State and local governments
- The federal government

In addition, the EEOA reduced the number of employees needed to subject an employer to coverage by Title VII from 25 to 15.

The EEOA also provided administrative guidance for the processing of complaints by providing that employers be notified within 10 days of receipt of a charge by the EEOC and that findings be issued within 120 days of the charge being filed. The EEOC was empowered to sue employers, unions, and employment agencies in the event that an acceptable conciliation agreement could not be reached within 30 days of notice to the employer. Finally, the EEOA protected whistleblowers from retaliatory employment actions.

The EEOA also increased the period of time an individual has to file discrimination complaints. The following list details the time frames for filing:

- In states without EEO enforcement agencies, an individual must file a charge with the EEOC within 180 days of the incident.
- In states with EEO enforcement agencies, a charge must be filed within 300 days of the incident or, if the charge was initially filed with the state enforcement agency, within 30 days after receiving written notice from the state that the investigation was terminated.
- If the EEOC does not file a civil suit or enter into a conciliation agreement within 180 days of the initial charge, the complaining individual is notified and may file a civil suit within 90 days of receiving that notification.
- Once an individual has filed a charge with the EEOC, there is a 60-day waiting period before the individual may request a right-to-sue letter. This request will end the EEOC investigation and requires the individual to file a civil action within 90 days or lose the right to pursue this claim in the future.

Visit `www.eeoc.gov/35th/thelaw/eeo_1972.html` to view the full text of the EEOA of 1972.

## Pregnancy Discrimination Act of 1978

Congress amended Title VII in 1978 to clarify that discrimination against women who are pregnant is an unlawful employment practice. The act specified that pregnancy be treated the same way as any other short-term disability, with the same benefits provided for other short-term disabilities.

## Civil Rights Act of 1991

In 1991, the CRA amended Title VII, the Age Discrimination in Employment Act (ADEA), and the Americans with Disabilities Act (ADA) to provide additional relief for victims of intentional discrimination and harassment, codify the concept of disparate impact, and address Supreme Court rulings over the previous few years that had weakened equal employment opportunity laws.

The CRA made the following changes to Title VII:

- Allowed for compensatory and punitive damages on a sliding scale based on company size as shown in Table 4.1

- Provided that any party to a civil suit in which punitive or compensatory damages are sought may demand a jury trial

- Expanded Title VII to include congressional employees and some senior political appointees

- Required that the individual alleging an unlawful employment practice is in use prove that it results in disparate impact to members of a protected class

- Provided that job-relatedness and reasonable business necessity are defenses to disparate impact, and that if a business can show that the practice does not result in disparate impact, it need not show the practice to be a business necessity

- Provided that business necessity is not a defense against an intentional discriminatory employment practice

- Established that if discrimination was a motivating factor in an employment practice it was unlawful, even if other factors contributed to the practice

- Allowed that if the business would have made the same employment decision whether or not an impermissible motivating factor was present, that there would be no damages awarded

- Expanded coverage to include foreign operations of American businesses unless compliance would constitute violation of the laws of the host country

Visit www.eeoc.gov/35th/thelaw/cra_1991.html to view the full text of the EEOA of 1972.

**TABLE 4.1**     CRA Limits for Total Punitive and Compensatory Damages

| Number of Employees* | Maximum Damage Award |
| --- | --- |
| 14–100 | $50,000 |
| 101–200 | $100,000 |
| 201–500 | $200,000 |
| 501 + | $300,000 |

*Number of employees in each of 20 or more weeks in the current or preceding calendar year.

# Executive Orders

*Executive orders* (EOs) are presidential proclamations which, when published in the Federal Register, become law after 30 days. Executive orders have been used to ensure equal employment opportunities are afforded by federal agencies and private businesses who contract or subcontract with those agencies. Executive orders relating to equal employment issues are enforced by the Department of Labor through the *Office of Federal Contract Compliance Programs (OFCCP)*.

**Executive Order 11246**   This executive order, put forth in 1965, prohibits employment discrimination on the basis of race, creed, color, or national origin and requires affirmative steps be taken in advertising jobs, recruiting, employment, training, promotion, compensation, and terminating employees.

**Executive Order 11375**   Created in 1967, EO 11375 amended 11246 and expanded coverage for protected classes to include discrimination on the basis of sex.

**Executive Order 11478**   This order, written in 1969, again expanded the scope of EO 11246 by adding handicapped individuals and those over age 40 to the list of protected classes.

**Executive Order 12138**   In 1979, with the passing of EO 12138, the National Women's Business Enterprise policy was created. This EO also required federal contractors and subcontractors to take affirmative steps to promote and support women's business enterprises.

**Executive Order 13087**   This EO from 1998 expanded coverage to include sexual orientation.

**Executive Order 13152**   Added "status as a parent" to the list of protected classes first identified in EO 11246. This EO, written in 2000, protects those who must care for an "individual who is under the age of 18 or who is 18 or older but is incapable of self-care because of a physical or mental disability" from employment discrimination. The order broadly defines a parent as a biological, adoptive, foster or step-parent, legal custodian, one who is acting as a parent, or one actively seeking legal custody or adoption of a child.

There are two levels of compliance required by these orders. The first level, which prohibits employment discrimination and requires contractors to take affirmative action in employment actions, applies to contracts totaling $10,000 or more in a 12-month period.

The second level of compliance, for contractors with 50 or more employees who have contracts of $50,000 or more, requires that a written *Affirmative Action Plan (AAP)* be developed within 120 days from the origination of the contract with the *Department of Labor (DOL)*, OFCCP, the agency charged with enforcing the act. The components of an AAP are determined by the OFCCP, and in a revision effective on December 13, 2000, include the items stated in Table 4.2.

**TABLE 4.2**   Components of an Affirmative Action Plan

| AAP Component | Description |
| --- | --- |
| Organizational profile | Organizational display (traditional organization chart) or workforce analysis (listing of job titles from lowest to highest paid) |
| Job group analysis | Places job titles with similar duties and responsibilities into groups for analysis |
| Placement of incumbents in job groups | Percentages of minorities and women in each job group |
| Determination of availability | Reports demographic data on the labor pool for each job group |
| Comparison of incumbency to availability | Compares protected classes employed in each job group with availability of protected classes in the labor pool |

**TABLE 4.2**    Components of an Affirmative Action Plan *(continued)*

| AAP Component | Description |
| --- | --- |
| Placement goals | Sets reasonable goals to address under representation of protected classes in the workforce |
| Designation of the person responsible for implementation within the business | Assigns responsibility for achieving placement goals in the AAP to a person with access to the executive team in the business |
| Identification of problem areas | Requires analysis of employment processes to determine where barriers to equal opportunity exist |
| Action-oriented programs | Requires modification of current employment practices to remove barriers to opportunity |
| Periodic internal audits | Requires periodic review of employment activity with management and reports to executives on actions taken to improve results |

# Age Discrimination in Employment Act (ADEA) of 1972

According to the preamble, the purpose of the Age Discrimination in Employment Act (ADEA) is to "promote employment of older persons based on their ability rather than age; to prohibit arbitrary age discrimination in employment; to help employers and workers find ways of meeting problems arising from the impact of age on employment."

The ADEA prohibits discrimination against persons 40 years of age or older in employment activities including hiring, job assignments, training, promotion, compensation, benefits, terminating or any other privileges, terms, or conditions of employment. The act applies to private businesses, unions, employment agencies, and state and local governments with more than 20 employees. As with Title VII, the ADEA provides for exceptions to the act such as:

- BFOQs that are reasonably necessary to business operations
- The hiring of firefighters or police officers by state or local governments
- Retirement of employees age 65 or older who have been in executive postions for at least two years and are eligible for retirement benefits of at least $44,000 per year
- Retirement of tenured employees of institutions of higher education at age 70
- Discharge or discipline for just cause

The act also provided that any waiver of rights must be written in an understandable manner and refer specifically to the waiver requirements contained in the ADEA. Any waiver of rights is valid only if valuable consideration, usually some form of payment, is exchanged and must include the following elements:

- Advice to consult with an attorney before signing the agreement

- A period of not less than 21 days to review and consider the agreement
- A period of no less than 7 days during which the agreement may be revoked

Additional requirements are needed for waivers made in connection with exit incentives or other termination programs, such as a reduction in force or lay off. In addition to the preceding requirements, the waiver must provide protected individuals with no less than 45 days to consider the agreement and:

- A list of the eligibility factors for the group or individuals affected by the employment action
- A list of the job titles and ages of all individuals participating in the program as well as those who were not selected for the program

Individuals who feel they have been subjected to an unlawful employment practice must file charges with the EEOC, which has federal enforcement responsibilty for the ADEA, or with the state equal employment agency (if one exists for the location in which the incident occurred). Timely filing of charges is essential for complainants, since the EEOC will not investigate charges that are not made according to the following guidelines:

- In states without EEO enforcement agencies, an individual must file a charge with the EEOC within 180 days of the incident.
- In states with EEO enforcement agencies, a charge must be filed within 300 days of the incident or, if the charge was initially filed with the state enforcement agency, within 30 days after receiving written notice from the state that the investigation was terminated.
- If the EEOC does not file a civil suit or enter into a conciliation agreement within 180 days of the initial charge, the complaining individual is notified and may file a civil suit within 90 days of receiving that notification.
- Once an individual has filed a charge with the EEOC, there is a 60-day waiting period before a civil action may be filed by the individual.

Visit www.eeoc.gov/laws/adea.html to view the full text of the ADEA.

# Rehabilitation Act of 1973, Sections 501, 503, and 505

The Rehabilitation Act of 1973 was enacted to expand the opportunities available for persons with physical or mental disabilities. The employment clauses of the act apply to agencies of the federal government and federal contractors with contracts of $10,000 or more during a 12-month period. Section 501 addresses employment discrimination, while section 505 details the remedies available for those who have been subjected to unlawful employment practices. The EEOC has enforcement responsibility for Section 501. Under section 503, individuals with disabilities who feel a federal contractor has violated the requirements of the Rehabilitation Act may also file complaints with the OFCCP.

# Vietnam Era Veterans' Readjustment Assistance Act (VEVRA) of 1974

Equal employment opportunity and affirmative action protection for veterans who served during the Vietnam war are provided by the Vietnam Era Veterans' Readjustment Assistance

Act (VEVRA), which applies to federal contractors or subcontractors with contracts of $25,000 or more. The act requires that contractors list all openings with state employment agencies unless they are for senior-level management positions, positions that will be filled from within, or positions lasting three days or less. The state employment agencies are required to give priority to Vietnam-era veterans when providing referrals to these openings.

A Vietnam-era veteran is one who meets specific criteria related to having served on active duty between August 5, 1964 and May 7, 1975. The act provides additional protections for special disabled veterans who have disabilities rated at 10, 20, 30 percent or more who are entitled to compensation from the Department of Veterans Affairs.

 You can view the DOL compliance requirements for additional details at www.dol.gov/esa/regs/compliance/ofccp/fsvevraa.htm.

## Americans with Disabilities Act of 1990

The Americans with Disabilities Act (ADA) of 1990 was based in large part on the Rehabilitation Act of 1973, and it extended protected class status to qualified persons with disabilities. Employment discrimination is covered by Title I of the act and identifies entities covered by the act as employment agencies, labor unions, joint labor-management committees, and employers with 15 or more employees for each working day in each of 20 weeks in the current or previous calendar year. Excluded from coverage are the federal government and 501(c) private membership clubs. The act prohibits discrimination in job application procedures; the hiring, advancement, or discharge of employees; employee compensation; job training; and other terms, conditions, and privileges of employment.

The ADA requires covered entities to make *reasonable accommodation* to develop employment opportunities for qualified persons with disabilities in two areas:

1. Facilities should be accessible to persons with disabilities.

2. Position requirements may be adjusted to accommodate qualified persons with disabilities.

The ADA allows that accommodations that constitute an *undue hardship* to the business are not required and defines undue hardships as those which place an excessive burden on the employer. The act identifies the factors to be considered in determining whether an accommodation is an undue hardship by looking at the cost, the financial resources of the organization, the size of the organization, and other similar factors.

# Conducting a Staffing Needs Assessment

Planning for the future staffing needs of an organization requires an analysis of many factors: prospects for future product sales, new product development, anticipated customer demand, competition (both global and local), changes in government regulations, economic conditions, and other factors discovered during the environmental scanning process discussed in Chapter 3, "Strategic Management." Management uses the results of these analyses to develop the organization's strategic plan. From this overall organization plan, unit and functional strategies and goals and objectives are developed for individual business units or functional areas of the business. Reviewing these plans with line managers provides HR with the information needed to conduct a staffing needs assessment to ensure that individuals with the appropriate *knowledge, skills, and abilities (KSAs)* are available in the numbers they are needed by the organization and when the business needs them.

To determine how many people will be needed to do the work required to meet organization goals, you must first determine which KSAs are required. Once you have identified the KSAs, there are a variety of planning tools available to determine the numbers of jobs you will need to fill. Figure 4.1 illustrates a typical workforce planning model. The process begins with a review of the strategic plan, followed by a needs assessment that identifies two key pieces of information: the work that needs to be done and how many people are needed to do it. With that information available, it is possible to determine if there are individuals already in the organization who have the necessary skills to do the work. If there are not, HR can determine the most effective way to supply the organization with individuals who have the necessary skills at the time they are needed to accomplish the organization goals.

**FIGURE  4.1**    The Workforce Planning model

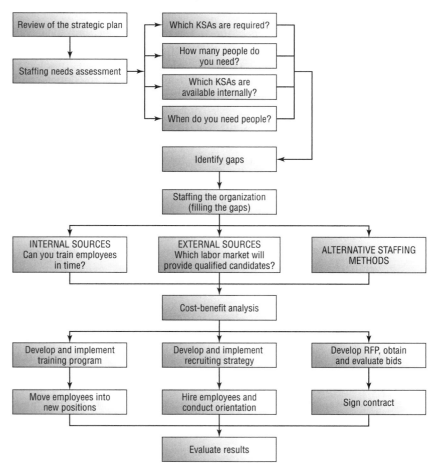

A *staffing needs assessment* determines the numbers and types of jobs needed to successfully achieve business goals and is the cornerstone of the workforce planning process. Two factors need to be assessed in this process: which KSAs are needed to achieve future goals and which KSAs are available within the organization to meet those goals. Comparing the answers to these questions identifies the gaps that will need to be filled and allows for analysis of the best way to fill those needs, whether internally or externally or by utilizing alternative staffing methods.

## Which KSAs Are Required?

In Chapter 2, "Core Knowledge Requirements for HR Professionals," I presented the various job analysis methods utilized in identifying what needs to be done to accomplish the organization's goals. Job analysis provides the data needed to identify the specific jobs for the workforce planning process. An effective analysis results in three essential planning tools:

- Job competencies
- Job descriptions
- Job specifications

*Job competencies* are broad statements of the factors needed to successfully accomplish the organization's goals. These can be based on the characteristics for success in specific functional areas, leadership characteristics, or the ability to successfully interact across business units and functional areas. *Core competencies* describe the characteristics that are valued by an organization as unique to its vision, mission, and method of operating.

Job descriptions provide a list of specific tasks, duties, and responsibilities that must be accomplished to meet the organization's goals. The description also includes information on reporting relationships, exemption status, and authority to act that defines where the job fits into the organization. This information is particularly critical in the hiring process to ensure that the job applicant fully understands what is required to perform successfully.

The job description must differentiate between essential and nonessential job functions. *Essential job functions* are those that comprise the competencies, duties, and responsibilities that are the reason for the job's existence. *Nonessential job functions* are those that are not necessary to fulfill the organization's needs for that specific position but which have been included in a particular job for a variety of reasons, including convenience for the organization.

---

 **Real World Scenario**

**Essential Job Functions for a Marketing Coordinator**

The director of marketing needs to track the response rate for various marketing pieces and comes to HR for assistance in developing a description for this new position. There are several different types of collateral that need to be tracked: the direct mail collateral, brochures distributed at trade fairs, and the online information request page. The director wants to move some other duties into this position to reduce the burden on other members of the department who are currently working overtime to meet all the department needs. These other duties include running errands for the department, such as delivering copy to the print shop across town, picking up supplies needed to meet deadlines, and ensuring that the trade show booth is maintained in good condition.

The reason the job exists is to track the response rate for the marketing collateral. If those duties were not required, the director would not be adding the position to the marketing team. These are the essential functions of the position. The other duties, running errands and maintaining the trade show booth, could be done by any position in the department, and are only being moved into this position for convenience. These are the nonessential job functions.

*Job specifications* are the KSAs necessary for successful performance of the essential job functions. To be legally compliant, specifications must:

- Be related to essential job functions
- Describe reasonable requirements for successful performance
- Contain physical requirements necessary to complete the job functions

# How Many People Do You Need?

There are a number of different tools available for use in the needs assessment process, and they fall into two basic categories: qualitative tools and quantitative tools. There are benefits and drawbacks to both types of analysis; reliance on a single method can result in forecasts that do not accurately predict future needs. Because forecasting is an inexact science, it is advisable to make use of several different tools during the workforce planning process to minimize errors.

## Qualitative Assessment Tools

*Qualitative assessment tools* are subjective evaluations of general observations and information and include various types of judgmental forecasts. These tools can be as simple as an estimate made by a knowledgeable executive or as involved as formalized brainstorming using a Delphi or nominal group technique.

The *Delphi technique* obtains input from a group of individuals who provide their expertise in succeeding rounds of questions about an issue or problem. After each round, the results are collated, prioritized, and returned to the participants in the form of additional questions for further analysis until a consensus is reached. An important factor of the Delphi technique is that the participants never meet, but provide their input in written form. There are several benefits to this technique, including the fact that it is a viable alternative when participants are geographically separated and that it encourages a wide variety of ideas that might otherwise not be considered.

The *nominal group technique* is a structured meeting format designed to elicit participation from all members of the group in order to arrive at the best possible solution to the problem at hand. The process requires a facilitator and begins with a period of time for individuals to think about and write down all their ideas about the issue. After that, each participant presents one idea, which is recorded by the facilitator for later discussion. When all of the ideas have been presented, the process of prioritizing and consensus building takes place, until a resolution has

been agreed upon. There is a detailed explanation of this process available at www.institute
.virginia.edu/services/csa/nominal.htm.

## Quantitative Assessment Tools

*Quantitative assessment tools* are objective measures of historical data that is analyzed using a
variety of statistical measures. Several of these measures provide useful data for workforce planning:

**Turnover analysis**   The analysis of turnover provides key information to forecast the need
for new employees to replace those who move out of their current positions. Turnover can be
calculated for any period of time, but it is generally measured on a monthly or annual basis. The
formula for determining the turnover rate is:

$$\frac{\text{\# of Employees on 1st Day of Period} + \text{\# of Employees on Last Day of Period}}{\text{Total of Employees During the Period}}$$

$$\frac{\text{Total Employees During the Period}}{2} = \text{Average \# of Employees}$$

$$\text{Turnover Rate} = \frac{\text{Number of Employee Terminations During the Period}}{\text{Average Number of Employees During the Period}}$$

**Times series forecasts**   There are several *time series forecasts* that can be used to measure historic
staffing levels and provide a basis from which expected future needs can be calculated:

   **Trend analyses**   *Trend analyses* compare the changes in a single variable over time, and,
   over a period of years, generally move upward or downward. Trend analysis can reveal
   information on *seasonal staffing requirements*, which are periods of time within a one-year
   period that regularly vary from the general trend. *Cycles*, periods of time during which a
   pattern of performance (growing, peaking, declining, and plateauing at the lower level),
   also become apparent in a trend analysis.

   **Simple linear regression**   *Simple linear regression* measures the relationship between one
   variable (for example, staffing) against another variable (such as production output) and
   allows prediction of one variable from the other. For example, measuring the number of units
   produced against the number of employees producing the units over a period of years would
   allow the analyst to forecast the number of employees needed to meet an increase in demand.

   **Multiple linear regression**   *Multiple linear regression* measures the relationship between
   several variables to forecast another. An application of this model in workforce planning
   would be to determine if there is a relationship between lower staffing levels, absenteeism,
   and production output.

**Simulation models**   Simulation models allow several possible plans to be tested in abstract
form. For example, an organization that wants to know the predicted results of different staffing alternatives can use a simulation model to determine which is the most cost effective.

**Ratios**   Ratios provide a benchmark based on the historic relationship of one variable to
another. For example, the average HR staffing ratio has been 1:100 for a number of years. As

the organization workforce increases or decreases, this ratio can provide an estimate of the number of staff required to provide services for the general employee population.

Choosing appropriate assessment tools provides the HR professional with a forecast of both the numbers and types of jobs that will be needed to accomplish organization goals. The next step is to determine where to find individuals with the appropriate knowledge, skills, and abilities to fill those jobs.

## Which KSAs Are Available Internally?

Now that you have job descriptions and specifications that define exactly who you need to place in these positions, you can find out which, if any, of the KSAs are already available to you internally. There are a variety of tools you can use to determine this.

First, you can develop, implement, and utilize a *skills inventory*. This HR management tool collects and stores a wealth of information that would otherwise be obtained only after many hours of research by HR staff. An effective skills inventory will collect information on special skills or knowledge, performance appraisals, fluency in foreign languages, educational qualifications, previous experience in or outside of the company, credentials or licenses that may be required, and any continuing education the employee has obtained through training classes, seminars, or educational institutions. When made a part of an automated HRIS system, obtaining a report with detailed information about your internal talent pool can be accomplished in minutes.

You might also choose to develop, implement, and utilize a *replacement chart*. This tool is useful at all levels of the organization and helps HR and line managers identify staffing needs by categorizing current employees in one of four categories:

**Ready for promotion**  Employees in this category demonstrate the KSAs to assume additional responsibilities and are ready to move forward in the organization.

**Develop for future promotion**  This group of employees are proficient in their current positions, and, with additional training opportunities and experience, will be ready to move forward in the organization.

**Satisfactory in current position**  These employees are proficient in their current positions but do not demonstrate the KSAs or interest to assume greater responsibility in the organization.

**Replace**  Employees are placed in this category for a variety of reasons, such as transfer or promotion, impending retirement, short-term disability, or unsatisfactory performance.

Finally, you can develop, implement, and utilize a *succession plan*. A well thought-out succession plan identifies individuals within the organization who have the talent and ability to move into management and executive positions in one to five years. Once these individuals are identified, individual development plans are created to ensure that they are mentored and have opportunities to obtain education, training, and experience in areas that will enhance their ability to move into senior positions when the organization needs them.

## When Do You Need People?

Answering this question in the needs assessment enables HR to be proactive by providing alternatives to management in the way the need for people is met by the organization. By looking to the future, HR can analyze, evaluate, and recommend solutions that best meet the long-term needs of the organization. For example, planning staffing needs one to two years in the future allows time for training and development activities to prepare internal candidates to assume roles with greater responsibility. A longer view also allows time to build recruiting relationships with candidates possessing specialized skills to enhance the chances of hiring them when the organization needs them.

## Identify the Gap

At this point, you know which KSAs will be needed for the future and have developed job competencies, descriptions, and specifications to assist you in filling those needs. You know how many people you need to meet the organization's future needs and who is available internally to fill those needs, and you've identified the gap between the two. You are ready to determine the best way to meet those needs.

This next step is governed by federal, state, and local legislation enacted over the years to address issues of discrimination in the workplace and to ensure equal employment opportunities are available to all qualified candidates. Before I discuss filling the gap that exists between the organization's needs and its current workforce capabilities, let's review the relevant employment legislation, regulation, and court cases that impact how candidates are selected.

# Staffing the Organization

The first issue to consider is that of locating candidates who are best qualified to fill your positions. There are a number of factors involved in this decision, and the answers relate to characteristics of each position. The labor market can be viewed in many different ways depending upon specific job requirements and most often falls into one of three broad categories: geographic, technical or professional skills, and level of education. The geographic labor market can be local, regional, national, or international and can contain individuals with a wide variety of technical and professional skills and levels of education. Where you search for candidates depends upon your analysis of the availability of the specific KSAs in the various labor markets. Where you look for candidates impacts the cost of the recruiting effort as well as how much you must pay to attract the right candidate.

You've identified the jobs you need to fill, when they are needed, where they are located, and the KSAs needed for successful performance. You've written the job competencies and job descriptions and developed job-related specifications so that you can recruit qualified candidates. You've reviewed your internal demographics to determine if your past recruiting efforts have resulted in a diverse workforce or whether you need to explore alternative ways to promote diversity within the organization. Armed with this information, you can begin the process of finding qualified candidates for the positions you need to meet the organization's strategic goals. The question now becomes where to find the appropriate people to fill the gaps, and what the cost will be to bring them into the organization. There are three choices here: internal transfers or promotion, external hires, or alternative staffing. Are there sufficient skills within the organization that can be redirected to the new requirements through transfers or promotions? Is it best to bring in full-time employees, or better to use temps or some other staffing alternative? Let's take a brief look at these alternatives and discuss the strategic implications of each source.

## Internal Candidates

Earlier in this chapter I looked at ways to identify internal candidates who possess the KSAs needed for future operations and are ready for transfer or promotion into new positions. There are a number of advantages to filling jobs internally or "promoting from within." Management has an opportunity to evaluate candidates over an extended period of time to determine their suitability for advancement, and the possibility of future promotion can encourage employees to maintain a high level of performance. Providing advancement opportunities for employees communicates that the organization values and rewards their contributions. When promotion from within is an organization policy, most hiring is done at the entry level, which allows employees to become acclimated to the organization culture and operating procedures early in their careers, leading to greater success when they move into positions with greater responsibility.

Of course, there are disadvantages associated with relying solely on promotion from within to fill positions of increasing responsibility. First, there is the danger that employees with little experience outside the organization will have a myopic view of the industry. Second, while the morale of those promoted will be high, employees who have been passed over or lost out on promotions may have lower morale and be less motivated in performing their jobs. When several people are being groomed for promotion, the competition can lead to a breakdown in team work and jockeying for political position. If the organization lacks diversity in its workforce, over-reliance on promoting from within can perpetuate the imbalance. Finally, reduced recruiting costs will be offset by an increase in training costs to prepare employees for supervisory or management positions. Once the organization has decided to fill positions internally, there are several methods for communicating information about the openings to employees. When replacement and succession plans are in place, conversations with potential candidates can take place over a period of time, often during performance reviews and goal setting sessions. When multiple candidates are available for transfers or promotions, there are two methods for communicating them to the employee population. The first, *job posting*, is an internal job announcement that provides basic information about the opening, including the title; a brief description of the competencies, duties, responsibilities, and specifications; the salary range; and the application procedure.

A system offering *job bidding* opportunities to employees provides a means by which interested employees express interest in a position before it is available. This gives the supervisor and HR department an opportunity to review the job qualifications with the employee, provide training opportunities, let the employee gain additional experience if needed to meet the position requirements and add the employee's name to the replacement or succession plan as appropriate.

## External Candidates

At some point you will need to look outside the organization for new employees; even if you have a policy of promotion from within, entry-level positions will need to be filled as employees are promoted or transferred. There are, of course, advantages and disadvantages to bringing new people into the organization.

One advantage is that experienced professionals bring new ideas into the organization and can revitalize operations. Another is that it is usually easier and more cost-effective to hire individuals with highly specialized skills than it is to develop them within the organization. Looking outside the organization to fill positions provides opportunities to increase the diversity of the workforce as well.

There are several disadvantages to looking outside the organization. First, current employees who have been passed over for promotion will very likely have lower morale. Second, it is always difficult to know how someone from outside the organization will fit in once they start working. Finally, the new hire is an unknown—until the person actually starts doing the job, it's very difficult to know what their performance level will be.

## Alternative Staffing Methods

To expand the pool of available candidates who possess the desired skills, it's often wise to consider alternative staffing methods. There are a wide range of alternatives that can provide varying levels of flexibility to the organization. Particularly when staffing needs require highly specialized skills or during a tight labor market, these methods can provide access to highly qualified candidates who might otherwise be unavailable to the organization.

Due to advances in technology, *telecommuting*, which allows employees to work at home and connect to the office electronically, has become a viable solution for employees who do not wish to commute or who have other reasons to work at home. Aside from the benefits telecommuting employees enjoy, reducing the number of employees required to be at the office each day can allow employers to reduce overhead costs as well as contribute to reductions in commute traffic congestion.

*Job sharing* is an alternative which allows two people with complementary skills to share the duties and responsibilities of a full-time position.

*Part-time employees* are those who work less than a regular work week. They can be a cost-effective solution for organizations needing particular skills on an ongoing but not full-time basis.

*Internship programs* are usually designed to give students opportunities to gain experience in their chosen fields prior to graduation. Successful programs provide meaningful work experiences for the students and offer a variety of learning opportunities, including opportunities to meet with senior executives. The student gains a valuable learning experience, and the organization benefits by developing low-cost access to employees and the chance to observe the intern's performance prior to making an offer for full-time employment.

The temporary worker category covers a wide-range of flexible staffing options. The traditional "*temp*" is employed by an agency that screens and tests candidates prior to sending them to a work site for variable periods of time, from short, one-day assignments to assignments lasting for long periods of time. *Temp-to-perm* arrangements allow organizations to observe and evaluate a worker's performance prior to making an offer of full-time employment. *On-call workers* are employed by the organization, available on short notice and called to work only when they are needed. *Payrolling* allows the organization to refer individuals they want to hire to an agency. The agency hires them to work for the organization and provides payroll and tax services for either a fixed fee or percentage of the salary, which is generally less than a traditional temp agency fee. *Seasonal workers* are hired only at times of the year when the workload increases, such as the Christmas shopping season, or when it is time to harvest agricultural products.

There are two types of contract workers. *Independent contractors* are self-employed individuals who work on a project or fee basis with multiple customers or clients. Both federal and state governments have guidelines to determine the difference between an independent contractor and an employee. Misclassifying an employee as an independent contractor can result in substantial penalties to the employer, so it is important to ensure that the guidelines are followed. *Contract workers* are employed by brokers or agencies that act as the employer of record, providing payroll, marketing, and other services to the worker, including negotiating the contract with the client on the worker's behalf.

A *professional employer organization (PEO)* operates as the organization's HR department. The PEO becomes the employer of record and then leases the employees back to the organization. PEOs provide full service HR, payroll, and benefit services and can provide a cost-effective solution that enables smaller companies to offer benefits comparable to those offered by much larger organizations.

*Outsourcing* moves an entire function out of the organization to be handled by a company specializing in the function. This solution can be beneficial by allowing the organization to focus on its basic business operations.

## Cost-Benefit Analysis

How do you decide which staffing method best suits your business needs? Each method has advantages and disadvantages, costs and benefits. To build a business case for the best solution requires a cost-benefit analysis. A *cost-benefit analysis* compares the cost of each alternative to the benefits that will be realized if that course is chosen, forecasts the net impact on the bottom line, and recommends the preferred course of action. An effective cost-benefit analysis begins with a statement of the purpose for the analysis. In this case, the purpose is to staff the organization to achieve the goals established in the strategic plan. For each alternative being considered, the direct and indirect costs are detailed and the benefits are identified and quantified. A comparison of the short- and long-term benefits to the organization for each alternative is then done, along with a recommendation for the suggested course of action.

## Recruiting Applicants

Once it's been decided that the appropriate method for filling positions is to bring them in from outside, a number of factors must be considered. Particularly when the skills needed by the organization are in short supply in the labor market, the organization must find ways to effectively publicize its openings to appropriate candidates. Defining the employer's brand identity sets the stage for many aspects of the recruiting process. Each organization has a brand identity in the marketplace, whether or not it has been consciously developed. The reputation established with employees, current and former, along with the way the organization presents itself in the general marketplace contribute to the brand. Because the information is out there, HR can take a leading role in defining the brand so that it is an accurate reflection of where the company wants to be and can be utilized in the recruiting process.

## Employer Branding

Simply developing a catchy PR campaign is not enough to make an effective employer brand. For a brand to be useful in attracting high quality employees to the organization, it must first match the reality of working in the organization and describe what is unique about it. Building an employer brand begins with identifying unique elements of the organization culture. What values are important to the company? How are employees treated? Is the company on the leading edge in its industry? Is risk taking encouraged or frowned upon? Are employees involved in the decision-making process? Is performance management fair? Do employees receive regular feedback? How does the company respond to economic downturns? These are some of the considerations that become part of the brand. An accurate brand message gives candidates an idea of what it would be like to work in the organization and positively impacts retention. If the employer has differentiated its organization as an employer of choice with a clearly defined message about the benefits of working there, then attracting the quality of candidates desired by the organization becomes less difficult. It is critical, however, that the "official" brand message is an accurate reflection of the organization. To ensure that this is the case, an employee survey can be conducted to find out if current employees perceive the organization the way the brand portrays it. If there is a discrepancy, the organization can choose whether to adjust the brand message or make operational changes that address the differences between employee perceptions and the branding message.

An effective employer brand that accurately portrays the organization culture benefits the organization in any economic climate. During times of economic growth when high quality employees are in great demand, the brand both attracts and retains qualified employees. In an economic downturn, the brand becomes a vehicle for fostering communication and improving morale.

## Recruiting Strategies

Development of a recruiting strategy can be considered in two ways. The first encompasses the entire workforce planning process, tying recruiting efforts to the strategic plan, working with line managers to develop job requirements, establishing an advertising budget, and determining whether or not internal or external sources will be utilized to fill positions. That overall strategy is the subject of this chapter. This section concerns development of a recruiting strategy for particular jobs or groups of jobs. In that sense, there are a number of factors to consider.

During the process of creating the job competencies, descriptions and specifications, HR works with line managers to ensure that the job requirements are accurately presented. In the recruiting process, HR works with line managers to create a candidate profile so that applicants who go through the selection process fit the requirements of the position. In developing this profile, line managers often want to describe an "ideal candidate" who possibly even exceeds the requirements of the position. It's up to HR to work with line managers in developing candidate profiles that are realistic, given the working conditions and salary range offered for the position. At this time, it's also effective to work with the line manager to develop alternatives to the candidate profile, possibly substituting years of experience for education requirements, or lowering experience requirements if the experience is in the same industry. This expands the pool of available candidates and increases the chances of success in the recruiting process.

With the job description and candidate profile in hand, HR is able to determine the best sources for qualified candidates. As discussed at the beginning of this section, there are a number of factors to consider when making this decision. Choosing appropriate sources for candidates depends upon how available the specific KSAs are in various labor markets, along with workforce diversity issues that need to be addressed in the hiring process. In general terms, where you recruit for candidates depends in large part upon the scarcity of the KSAs you need to hire—the scarcer the KSAs, the larger the labor market to reach and the greater the recruiting budget.

## Recruiting Methods

There are a variety of recruiting methods to be considered in finding new employees. The appropriate method depends upon the type of employee needed by the organization in a particular situation. This means that a number of methods may be utilized in a single organization at any given time:

**Media sources**    Up until the advent of Internet job boards, the most prevalent means for recruiting was newspaper advertising; for many jobs it is still the preferred method. Advertising jobs on the radio is used quite less often than newspaper ads, but it can be effective if a company is trying to fill a large number of positions in a short period of time. Television advertising is rarely used to advertise individual positions; when used it is most often by agencies who accomplish a dual purpose with the ads—attracting candidates and soliciting clients.

**Internet job boards**    Advertising open positions on the Internet has become quite prevalent in recent years, particularly for positions in high technology companies. Its popularity as a recruiting source is growing because it is often more cost effective than traditional media advertising. A downside for employers who use this method is that some job seekers are indiscriminate when responding to posted jobs, which results in a large number of resumes from unqualified applicants that must be sorted through to find appropriate candidates.

**Company Websites**    Most companies with a web presence have a "career" or "opportunities" page on their websites where current openings are posted. When combined with recruiting software that requires applicants to enter their own information into the recruiting database, this recruiting method can greatly reduce the time spent wading through resumes from applicants who do not qualify for positions.

**Colleges and universities**    Colleges and universities are a good source for entry-level hires in areas such as accounting, engineering, or human resources. An effective college recruiting program capitalizes on school ties by sending alumni to the campus as recruiters. Recruiters are carefully chosen for their enthusiasm about the students as well as for the company. Key factors for recruiting success are delivering informative presentations about the organization and being honest about the job opportunities currently available in the organization.

College recruiting has become a reliable source for locating minority applicants in recent years.

**Job fairs**    Job fairs are events designed to bring employers and job seekers together in a single location. This format gives employers a chance to meet many potential job applicants in a short period of time. Including line managers and other employees with HR reps in the booth staff gives job seekers an opportunity to find out about the organization without going through an interview process.

**Alumni employees**    Building and maintaining professional relationships with former employees who left in good standing and on good terms can be a cost-effective, worthwhile source for re-recruiting. Particularly if they enjoyed their experience in the organization, they may be enticed to return if an appropriate opportunity presents itself, and they can be good sources for referrals.

**Previous applicants**   Often during the recruiting process, a recruiter may remember a candidate who was not the best fit for one position but left an impression as someone who would be good elsewhere in the organization. Maintaining professional contact with such individuals can pay off when an appropriate position becomes available.

**Vendors and suppliers**   Individuals who provide goods or services to the company are often aware of potential candidates for openings. Particularly when there has been a long-term relationship, the vendor is aware of the organization's culture and needs and may prove to be a good source for applicants.

**Labor unions**   In union environments, the union hiring hall can be a good source for qualified employees.

**Professional associations**   Relationships developed in connection with attendance at professional association functions or conferences often provide leads for qualified applicants. In addition, many associations provide job posting opportunities on websites or sell job advertisements in their publications.

**Employment agencies**   Each state has an agency dedicated to providing services to job seekers, including job counseling and training opportunities. There is no charge for employers to list job openings with the agency, which then screens, tests, and refers appropriate candidates.

Contingent employment agencies generally focus on jobs in a specific profession or job category, such as accounting professionals or administrative employees. Fees paid by the employer only when a candidate is hired are usually based on a percentage of the first year's salary and vary widely with different agencies. The fee is often negotiable.

Retained employment agencies are often referred to as headhunting firms or executive search firms. When these agencies are engaged by an organization, a fee for recruiting services is paid whether or not any of the candidates are hired. Retained firms are generally used for executive-level positions and specialize in sourcing candidates from the passive labor market (those not actively seeking work).

**Walk-in candidates**   Candidates may come into the business in person to fill out applications and apply for jobs.

# Screening Applicants

The result of the recruiting phase of the employment process should be resumes and application forms from job seekers hoping to be selected for the position. Screening these hopeful candidates to find those who best meet the needs of the position begins with establishing procedures that ensure equal employment opportunities.

## Uniform Guidelines on Employee Selection Procedures

The Uniform Guidelines on Employee Selection Procedures (known as the Guidelines) were jointly developed by the EEOC, the Civil Service Commission (CSC), the OFCCP, and the

Department of Justice (DOJ) to assist employers in complying with requirements of Title VII, EO 11246 (as amended), and other federal equal employment opportunity legislation. Specifically exempted from the Guidelines are requirements under the ADEA and the Rehabilitation Act. The Guidelines state that any selection tool that has an adverse impact against a protected class is discriminatory unless the employer can show that the tool is both job related and a valid predictor of success in the position. The Guidelines direct that if employers have access to more than one selection tool, the tool that has the least adverse impact is the one to be used. Records are to be kept by sex, race, and ethnic group (Black, American Indian, Asian, Hispanic, and Caucasian) and used for appropriate EEO reporting purposes.

One report required by the Guidelines is a determination of whether or not selection procedures have an adverse impact on one or more protected groups. An *adverse impact* occurs when the selection rate for a protected class is less than 4/5ths or 80 percent of the selection rate for the group with the highest selection rate. Figure 4.2 illustrates an adverse impact calculation.

**FIGURE 4.2**    Calculating adverse impact

| Group | Applicants | Hired | Selection Rate | 4/5 of Highest Rate |
|---|---|---|---|---|
| Males | 255 | 48 | 19% | 15% |
| Females | 395 | 52 | 13% | |
| Total | 650 | 100 | | |

In this example, the company advertised 100 openings. Applications were received from 255 males and 395 females for the position. Adverse impact is calculated as follows:

1.  For each group, divide the number of applicants hired by the total number of applicants:

    Males: 48/255 = 19%

    Females: 52/395 = 13%

2.  Multiply the highest selection rate by 80%:

    Males: 19% × 80% = 15%

3.  Compare the selection for the other group(s) to determine if adverse impact has occurred:

    Females: 13%

    Males: 15%

In this example, female applicants were adversely impacted by the selection process.

## Employment Applications

The first information received by a recruiter from an applicant is very often a resume. While resumes can be informative documents, they generally present information about the applicant in the most favorable light and do not always contain all of the information necessary to determine if the applicant is qualified for the position. For that reason, having all applicants complete an employment application is a good practice.

Because application forms are considered employment tests by the EEOC, employers must be certain that the information requested on them is both job related and a valid predictor of success in the position. There are four basic types of application forms to consider using; one will suit the needs of the specific position:

**Short form employment application**   As its name implies, the short form application is less extensive than other application forms; the term "short" is relative—it describes application forms that range from one to five pages. Short form applications are often used by employees who are applying for transfers or promotions and are useful for prescreening candidates or for positions with minimal skill requirements.

**Long form employment application**   The long form application provides space for additional information related to the job requirements, such as advanced degrees and longer employment histories.

**Job-specific employment application**   If the organization hires a substantial number of employees for positions with similar requirements, the application form can be designed to gather specific information related to the position or profession. This type of form would be appropriate for teaching, scientific, or similar professions.

**Weighted employment application**   The weighted application form was developed to assist recruiters in evaluating candidate qualifications. The form is developed using the job description; aspects of the job that are more important for success are given higher weights than other, less critical requirements. Weighted applications tend to reduce bias in the screening process, but they are expensive to maintain as they must be redesigned whenever job requirements change.

## Communicating with Applicants

HR departments are often criticized for ignoring job applicants. While a large volume of applications makes it difficult to personally contact each person who expresses interest in a position, many companies use an "auto respond" e-mail to acknowledge receipt of electronic resumes and applications and let candidates know that they will be contacted if selected for the interview process. Mail or in-person applications can be similarly acknowledged with preprinted post cards carrying the same message.

Recruiters need to stay in contact with candidates who move forward in the process until they have been removed from consideration and then a final, respectful communication that they are no longer being considered is appropriate. These communications can be made in writing, but candidates who have made it to the final round of interviews deserve a personal call. This allows job seekers to move forward and leaves them with a favorable impression of the HR department and the organization.

## Screening Interviews

After reviewing the application forms and choosing those that meet the job specifications and candidate profile, the recruiter conducts screening interviews to decide which candidates will be forwarded to the hiring manager. The purpose of these interviews is to both discover facts about the candidate and provide information about the position. The recruiter can assess the interest of the candidate in the position and begin the process of determining which candidates are the best fit for the position. Screening interviews are relatively short, lasting from 15 to 30 minutes.

# Testing

The use of pre-employment tests has become more prevalent in recent years. These tests take many forms and have a variety of purposes. The key issue to keep in mind with regard to employment tests is the requirement that they must be job related and, should they be challenged by an EEOC complaint, defensible as valid predictors of success in the position.

 **Real World Scenario**

## The Courts Address Employment Tests

Once Title VII was enacted, employees who felt they had been subjected to unlawful employment discrimination were able to initiate lawsuits to resolve their grievances. Pre-employment testing practices were the subject of a number of cases, the most prominent of which are described here.

**1971: *Griggs v Duke Power Co.*** Duke Power Company, located in North Carolina, employed 95 workers in its Dan River Steam Station in 1964. There were five departments at the plant: Labor, Coal Handling, Operations, Maintenance, and Laboratory and Test. The Labor department was the lowest paid department in the company; in fact, the highest paying job in the department paid less than the lowest paying job in the other four. In 1955, the company began to require that employees in all departments except Labor have a high school diploma, but prior to that time employees could be hired into any of the departments without one. On July 2, 1965, the effective date of Title VII, Duke added a requirement that all new employees must pass two aptitude tests, and that an employee wishing to transfer from Labor to another department needed a high school diploma.

Willie Griggs was one of 14 black employees working in the Labor department at the plant. There were no black employees in any of the other departments. Mr. Griggs filed a class action lawsuit on behalf of himself and 12 of the black employees, alleging that the requirement for a high school diploma and satisfactory scores on the aptitude tests discriminated against them. The district court that first heard the case dismissed it. The court of appeals found that Griggs had not shown that there was a discriminatory purpose to the requirements and that a discriminatory purpose was required to show discrimination. The Supreme Court granted *certiorari* (agreed to review the case) and heard oral arguments in December 1970.

Because a number of the white employees who did not have high school diplomas had been hired prior to the requirements for the diploma or the aptitude tests, and those employees performed well on the job, it was clear that the requirements did not predict job performance, and Duke Power did not dispute this fact. The Supreme Court found that "good intent or absence of discriminatory intent" in the face of a job requirement that adversely impacts a protected class is not a sufficient defense against discrimination. The job requirement must be shown to be job related in order to be lawful, and it is up to the employer to prove this.

The HR significance of *Griggs v Duke Power Co.* is that discrimination does not need to be intentional to exist. It is up to employers to prove that job requirements are related to the job.

**1975: *Albemarle Paper v Moody***   In 1966, a group of current and former black employees at the company's paper mill in Roanoke Rapids, North Carolina, filed a lawsuit against both their employer, Albemarle Paper, and the union representing them with the company. The group asked the court for an injunction against "any policy, practice, custom, or usage" at the plant that was in violation of Title VII. When the case dragged on for several years, a demand for back pay was added to the injunction request in 1970. One of the policies in question was the employment testing practice used by Albemarle Paper. The district court denied the claim for back pay and refused to consider the testing procedure, saying that the tests had been validated.

The court of appeals reversed the ruling, finding that the absence of bad faith was not sufficient grounds to deny back pay, and that the validation process had four serious flaws:

1.   It had not been used consistently.

2.   It had compared test scores to the subjective rankings of supervisors, which could not be tied to job-related performance criteria.

3.   The tests were validated against the most senior jobs and not entry-level positions.

4.   The validation study used only experienced white employees, not the new job applicants who were mostly nonwhite.

The HR significance of *Albemarle Paper v Moody* is that test validation must be in accordance with the Uniform Guidelines for Employee Selection Procedures. Subjective supervisor rankings are not sufficient for criterion validation; the criteria must be able to be tied to the job requirements.

**1975: *Washington v Davis***   In 1970, two applicants for the police department in Washington, D.C. filed suit against the city, claiming that the written personnel test given to applicants had an adverse impact on black applicants. The Supreme Court upheld the district court's finding that the test was a valid predictor of successful performance in the police training program.

The HR significance of *Washington v Davis* is that tests that have an adverse impact on a protected class are lawful if they are valid predictors of success on the job.

**Aptitude tests**   These tests are designed to measure an individual's knowledge and ability to apply skills in various areas, such as mathematics, typing, language, and reasoning. Properly constructed aptitude tests have been shown to be valid predictors of job success.

**Cognitive Ability Test (CAT)**   CATs measure an individual's ability to analyze and solve problems and draw conclusions from a set of facts. They also measure an individual's potential for learning, thinking, and remembering.

**Personality test**   Personality or psychometric tests assess how a candidate will "fit" into a specific job. If, for example, an employer uses a personality test that has shown particular characteristics to be valid predictors of success in sales positions and an applicant does not reflect those characteristics when tested, the test would indicate an area to be explored with the candidate prior to making the hiring decision.

**Integrity tests**   Also known as honesty tests, integrity tests assess a candidate's work ethic, attitudes toward theft and drug and alcohol use, and similar traits. According to the EEOC, professionally developed integrity tests do not create an adverse impact for protected classes as long as the tests are administered equally to all candidates.

**Psychomotor assessment tests**   A psychomotor assessment tests an individual's coordination and manual dexterity.

**Physical assessment tests**   Physical assessment tests are used to determine whether or not candidates are physically capable of performing specific job duties. The tests generally require that tasks be completed within a predetermined period of time and most often simulate activities that regularly occur on the job. A common physical assessment test is one that is given to potential firefighters to ensure that they are capable of lifting and carrying heavy weights for predetermined periods of time in a variety of circumstances.

As previously discussed, a key requirement for selection tools is that they be both related to specific job requirements and valid predictors of successful job performance. To determine whether or not a specific employment test meets those criteria, employers must ensure that tests are both reliable and valid.

## Reliability

Reliability measures whether or not a test or other measurement produces consistent results so that, over time, the scores will not vary greatly. Test reliability is enhanced by several factors, including wording instructions and test questions clearly. Providing optimal conditions for administering the test contributes to its reliability, as does making sure it is long enough to accurately test the candidate's knowledge.

## Validity

*Validity* considers the characteristics being measured by a test and whether or not the test is measuring the characteristic accurately.

**Content validity**   Content validity is the simplest of the three validation measures. Job analysis is a key element of the content validity process, which confirms that a selection procedure samples significant parts of the job being tested. For example, a driving test given to a delivery person who would drive a truck 80 percent of the time if hired for the job is a test with content validity.

**Construct validity**   Construct validity determines whether a test measures the connection between candidate characteristics and successful performance on the job. According to the DOL, construct validity is not only a more complex validation technique, it has not been widely used in employment testing. While it is an acceptable method for validation, its use in employment testing is still the subject of research and, therefore, care should be taken to ensure that its use meets DOL validation standards.

**Criterion validity**   A criterion is a trait or work behavior that is predicted by a test. Criterion validity is established when the test or measure either predicts or correlates the behavior.

> **Predictive validity**   Compares the test scores of a test given at the beginning of a job, before new employees have experience. When the employees have had some experience (for example, six months or one year) with the job, the manager evaluates their performance. The original

test scores are then measured against the criterion (the evaluation ratings) and the test is validated if they are similar.

**Concurrent validity**    The process for determining concurrent validity is similar to that of determining predictive validity. The difference is that the criterion measurement occurs at the same time the test is given and not at a later time.

---

 **Real World Scenario**

**Validity in Action**

What does all this validity stuff have to do with HR? As I discussed earlier, the courts look to validation studies to determine whether or not specific job requirements are discriminatory against protected classes. A professionally developed validation test serves as proof in court that the employment requirement is a valid predictor of successful performance on the job. Following are some ways that companies can use forms of validity in various situations.

Imagine a company needs to hire a business analyst who will spend 95 percent of their time analyzing sales trends and predicting future sales. The company would want to administer a test that measures a candidate's ability to reason. In this case, a test that measures a candidate's ability to reason would have *construct validity*.

In another example, an accounting firm that has had significant turnover in its entry-level accounting positions in the last few years wants to put some measures in place that will result in new hires who have a better chance at success in their positions. As a result, the HR director commissioned a test to measure analytical ability to use in the hiring process. The firm recently hired 100 recent college graduates with accounting degrees as entry-level accountants, none of whom has ever worked in the accounting field. On their first day of work, all 100 accountants took the new test. Six months later, the accountants were evaluated by their supervisors, and the results of the evaluation ratings (the criterion) were compared to the test results. The accountants who were highly rated by their supervisors had high scores on the test, and those who scored poorly on the test had lower evaluation ratings. The test has *predictive validity*.

Here's an example to illustrate the use of concurrent validity. The owner of CADServ, a computer aided design service bureau, recently won a large contract for design work with a nationally known developer. The project will require that CADServ hire at least 20 more CAD operators within a few months. The owner would like to bring in some entry-level operators but needs to be sure they will be successful on the job. The owner contracts with a testing firm to administer an abstract reasoning test to the candidates but wants to be sure it will be accurate. The owner decides to have the 30 CAD operators who already work at CADServ take the test. The test is given around the same time as the annual review cycle, and when the test results come in, they are very similar to the ratings received by the employees—those who received high test scores also received high performance ratings. The test has *concurrent validity*, and CADServ will use it in the hiring process for the new operators.

To read an excellent (and easy-to-understand) explanation of testing, assessment, reliability, and validation, go to www.uniformguidelines.com/testassess.pdf.

# Selecting Candidates

Once HR has screened the applicants for a position and narrowed the candidate pool to those who meet the requirements of both the job specifications and candidate profile, the process of selecting the best candidate for the position begins. In-depth interviews of the candidates are conducted by hiring managers and others who know what the successful candidate will need to do in the position. The selection process may include other elements, such as a realistic job preview, an in-box test, or participation in an assessment center process (all discussed later in the chapter). In-depth interviews, however, are the cornerstone of the selection process, used in virtually all hiring decisions.

## Developing an Interview Strategy

The purpose of an interview strategy is twofold: First, it ensures that everyone on the interview team is aware of the position requirements and candidate profile. Second, when several interviewers will be interviewing the candidates for a position, it ensures that everyone is using the same criteria to evaluate candidates. During the strategy development phase, you must decide the appropriate type of interview for the position.

### Types of Interviews

There are several types of interviews that can be conducted. Not all of them are appropriate for every situation, and it is up to HR to counsel the hiring manager on what will work best in each situation.

**Behavioral interviews**    These interviews are based on the premise that past behavior predicts future behavior and asks candidates to describe how they have handled specific situations in previous jobs. The candidate is expected to be able to describe the situation or problem, the actions they took to resolve it, and what outcome resulted. Interviewers skilled in this type of questioning are able to drill down into the answers to determine the depth of experience the candidate has.

**Directive interviews**    As the name implies, a directive interview is very much controlled and guided by the interviewer with a predetermined set of questions asked of all candidates.

**Nondirective interviews**    In this interview style, the interviewer asks broad questions and allows the candidate to guide the conversation. This interview style may produce a great deal of information relating to the candidate's qualifications, but it is difficult to ensure consistency in questions for all candidates, and that can become a problem when evaluating them.

**Patterned interviews**    A patterned interview is structured to cover specific areas related to the job requirements. The interviewer will cover each area with all candidates, but may ask different questions of them.

**Panel interviews**    In a panel interview, several interviewers interview the candidate at the same time.

**Structured interviews**    For a structured interview, questions are prepared in advance and asked of all candidates.

**Stress interviews** There are some positions in which employees encounter highly stressful situations on a regular basis, such as airline pilots, law enforcement officers, or astronauts. A stress interview subjects candidates to an intimidating situation to demonstrate how the candidate will handle stress in the position.

## Question Guidelines

Equal opportunity legislation and regulations described earlier in this chapter require that questions asked of candidates during the selection process be constructed to obtain only job-related information. There are some topics that may never be a consideration in a selection decision, such as race. Others, such as age are BFOQs that may be asked in a nondiscriminatory manner (for example, state laws may require that a bartender be at least 21 to serve alcoholic beverages). Table 4.3 illustrates appropriate and inappropriate ways to obtain job-related information in an interview.

**TABLE 4.3** Sample Illegal and Legal Interview Questions

| Sample Illegal Questions | Sample Legal Questions |
|---|---|
| **Affiliations** | |
| What clubs or social organizations do you belong to? | Do you belong to any professional or trade associations or other organizations you think are relevant to this job? |
| Do you go to church? | |
| **Age** | |
| How old are you? | Are you over the age of 18? |
| When did you graduate from high school? | Can you, after employment, provide proof of age? |
| **Arrest Record** | |
| Have you ever been arrested? | Have you ever been convicted of _____? (Name a crime that is plausibly related to the job in question.) |
| **Disabilities** | |
| Do you have any disabilities? | After reviewing the job description, are you able to perform all the essential functions of the job? |
| Have you had any recent or past illnesses or operations? If yes, list them and give dates when these occurred. | Can you demonstrate how you would perform the following job-related functions? |

**TABLE  4.3**    Sample Illegal and Legal Interview Questions *(continued)*

| Sample Illegal Questions | Sample Legal Questions |
| --- | --- |
| **Disabilities** | |
| How's your family's health? | Any job offer will be made contingent upon a medical exam. Are you willing to undergo one if we offer you a job? |
| When did you lose your vision/arm/hearing? How did it happen? | |
| **Marital/Family Status** | |
| What is your marital status? | Are you willing to relocate?* |
| With whom do you live? | This job requires frequent travel. Are you willing and able to travel when needed?* |
| What was your maiden name? | Is there anything that will prevent you from meeting work schedules?* |
| Do you plan to have a family? When? How many children will you have? | |
| What are your child-care arrangements? | |
| **Military** | |
| Were you honorably discharged? | In what branch of the armed services did you serve? |
| What type of discharge did you receive? | What type of training or education did you receive in the military? |
| **National Origin/Citizenship** | |
| Are you a U.S. citizen? | Are you authorized to work in the United States? |
| Where were you/your parents born? | What language(s) do you read/speak/write fluently? (Acceptable if related to essential functions.) |
| What is your race? | |
| What language did you speak in your home when you were growing up? | |

**TABLE 4.3**   Sample Illegal and Legal Interview Questions *(continued)*

| Sample Illegal Questions | Sample Legal Questions |
|---|---|
| **Personal** | |
| How tall are you? | This job requires the ability to lift a 50-pound weight and carry it 100 yards. Are you able to do that? |
| How much do you weigh? | This job will require work on the weekends. Are you able to do so? |
| Would working on weekends conflict with your religious beliefs? | |

*Acceptable if asked of every candidate.

## Interviewer Bias

Any interviewer may bring preconceived ideas or biases into an interview situation; these can have an unintended impact on the hiring decision. Once interviewers are aware of the different types of interview bias that can occur, listed next, it is possible to reduce the impact on the selection process.

**Average/central tendency**   The *average bias* becomes apparent when the interviewer has difficulty deciding which candidate is best and rates them all about the same.

**Contrast**   The *contrast* effect occurs when an interviewer compares candidates to each other, or compares all candidates to a single candidate. If one candidate is particularly weak, others may appear to be more qualified than they really are.

**Cultural noise**   *Cultural noise* occurs when candidates answer questions based on information they think will get them the job—what they think the interviewer wants to hear. For example, a candidate who has been an individual contributor may tell an interviewer that they prefer working as part of a team.

**First impression**   This bias can work either for or against a candidate, depending on the interviewer's first impression. A candidate who is very nervous and stutters during the first few minutes of the interview may be viewed as less qualified even if during the remainder of the interview they are poised and well spoken.

**Gut feeling**   The *gut feeling bias* occurs when the interviewer relies on an intuitive feeling that the candidate is a good (or bad) fit for the position without looking at whether or not the individual's qualifications meet the criteria established by the job specifications and candidate profile.

**Halo effect**   The *halo effect* occurs when the interviewer evaluates a candidate positively based on a single characteristic. For example, a candidate's self-confident attitude may overshadow a lack of experience in a particular requirement.

**Harshness/horn effect**    *Harshness*, or the *horn effect*, occurs when the interviewer evaluates a candidate negatively based on a single characteristic.

**Knowledge-of-predictor**    *Knowledge-of-predictor* bias occurs when the interviewer is aware that a candidate scored particularly high (or low) on an assessment test that has been shown to be a valid predictor of performance.

**Leniency**    *Leniency bias* occurs when an interviewer tends to go easy on a candidate and give a higher rating than is warranted, justifying it with an explanation.

**Negative emphasis**    The *negative emphasis bias* occurs when the interviewer allows a small amount of negative information to outweigh positive information.

**Nonverbal bias**    *Nonverbal bias* occurs when an interviewer is influenced by body language. For example, a candidate who frowns when answering questions could be rated negatively even though the answers were correct.

**Question inconsistency**    *Question inconsistency* occurs when an interviewer asks different questions of each candidate. While this is acceptable to a certain extent in order to delve more deeply into each candidate's qualifications, there is no baseline for comparison if there are no questions that were asked of all candidates.

**Recency**    The *recency* bias occurs when the interviewer recalls the most recently interviewed candidate more clearly than earlier candidates.

**Similar-to-me**    The *similar-to-me bias* occurs when the candidate has interests or other characteristics that are the same as those of the interviewer and cause the interviewer to overlook negative aspects about the candidate. For example, an interviewer who played college football may select a candidate who did so even though the candidate's qualifications are not the best for the position.

**Stereotyping**    The *stereotyping* bias occurs when the interviewer assumes a candidate has specific traits because they are a member of a group. For example, an interviewer may assume that a woman would not be able to successfully perform in a job that required frequent lifting of packages weighing 50 pounds.

## Conducting Effective Interviews

Job interviews are stressful situations for interviewers and candidates alike. The interviewer has a very short period of time to determine whether or not the candidate is the best choice for the position, and the candidate wants to make a good impression with the ultimate goal of obtaining a job offer. To reduce the stress and improve the chances of obtaining the information needed to make the best hiring decision, preparing for the interview is essential. HR can assist interviewers in this process by providing advice on structuring an effective interview.

**Selecting the interview team**    HR's role in selecting the interview team is to work with the line manager to ensure that everyone who needs to be involved in the interview process is involved. In a team environment, it may be appropriate for all members of the team to participate in the interview process; in other situations, employees from other business units who have frequent contact with the person in the position may be invited to participate in the process, along with employees who are knowledgeable about the work to be done.

**Preinterview strategy meeting**   Conducting a preinterview strategy meeting with the interview team provides an opportunity for the hiring manager to share what will be required of the successful candidate and to ensure that all interviewers are on the same page for the interviews. Topics for discussion can include the job description, specifications, and competencies. At this time, a discussion of the type of interview to be conducted and of common interview biases is also appropriate. This is a good opportunity for HR to share best interview practices with interviewers, such as not making notes on the application form or resume, and a review of appropriate, legal interview questions.

**Candidate evaluation forms**   During the preinterview strategy discussion, HR can review the candidate evaluation form with the interview team. This form provides consistency in the interview process by providing interviewers with a list of topics to be covered during the interview. The form is useful in rating candidates on job requirements and acts as a reminder of what to discuss during the candidate evaluation phase of the selection process.

**The interview**   Interviewers should prepare to meet the candidates by reading the application forms or resumes and making notes of any items that need explanation. During the interview, the candidate should be treated with dignity and respect, beginning with starting the interview on time and giving full attention to the candidate during the course of the interview. Setting the candidate at ease in the first few minutes will set the stage for a productive and informative interview. Providing a clear explanation of the organization's mission, values, and culture; the position; and what will be expected of the successful candidate early in the interview gives prospective employees a context in which to answer questions. Listening carefully to the candidate's answers, taking notes as appropriate, and following up on points that need clarification indicate a genuine interest in what is being said and encourage an open and honest exchange. Be honest with the candidate about the workplace environment, and give them time to ask their own questions. End the interview with an explanation of the next steps in the process.

**Post-interview evaluation**   When everyone on the interview team has met with all of the candidates, a final meeting takes place. During this meeting, the interviewers review the candidate evaluation forms and share their thoughts on each candidate.

## Other Selection Procedures

There are a variety of additional selection techniques available for evaluating candidates.

### Realistic Job Preview

A *realistic job preview (RJP)*, designed to give candidates an accurate picture of a typical day on the job, provides an opportunity for them to self-select out if the job is not what they expected it would be. This increases the chances for success on the job, thereby reducing turnover. Depending on the type of job, the RJP can take many forms, including observing a current employee doing the job (as in a call center environment, for example), a simulated experience of the job, or a video presentation about the organization, work environment, and coworkers. A tour of the workplace is another way to provide candidates with an idea of what it would be like to work in the organization. These techniques, either singly or in some combination, can provide candidates with realistic expectations of the job and the organization.

## Assessment Centers

Assessment centers are characterized by multiple tests designed to measure different aspects of the job. Generally used to assess candidates for management potential and decision-making skills, they have been demonstrated to be valid predictors of success on the job. Used extensively by state and local governments and large organizations for assessing internal candidates for promotion, their use is limited due to the high cost of conducting them. Typical assessments include interviews, testing and problem-solving skills, in-basket tests, leaderless group discussions, and role-playing exercises.

## Reference Checks

Reference checks provide insight into previous educational and employment experiences, and, depending on the type of job, may include a check of the candidate's financial records. Prior to checking references, it is advisable to have written permission from the candidate.

---

### The Privacy Act of 1974

The Privacy Act of 1974 was an attempt by Congress to regulate the amount and type of information collected by federal agencies and the methods by which it was stored in an effort to protect the personal privacy of individuals about whom the information had been collected. The Act requires written authorization from an individual prior to releasing information to another person. The Act does not currently apply to private employers.

First, the Act provides individuals the right to know what kind of information is being collected about them, how it is used and maintained, and whether it is disseminated. The Act prevents this information from being used for purposes other than that for which it was collected, and it allows individuals to obtain copies of the information, review it, and request amendments to inaccurate information. The Act requires the government to ensure that information collected is not misused. Except under specific circumstances covered by the Privacy Act, such as law enforcement or national security needs, the information collected by one agency may not be shared with another. Damages for violation of these requirements may be sought in federal district court, and if found by the judge to be warranted, are subject to reimbursement of attorney's fees and litigation costs, as well as a fine for actual damages incurred by the individual of up to $1,000 paid by the federal government.

---

An organization may ask for several types of references from potential employees. Some kinds of references you may consider include the following:

**Employment references**  To make an informed decision about a potential employee, employers should obtain all the information they can from previous employers. Information that should be collected during the reference checking process includes previous employment history, dates, job titles, and type of work performed. Many employers are reluctant to provide more information than this for privacy reasons, but as long as the information is factual and given in good faith, most states consider it "qualifiedly privileged," which protects the employer from legal action. It is desirable to obtain additional information about the employee's work habits and interpersonal skills and find out if the employee is eligible for rehire.

**Educational references**   Depending upon the position applied for and the length of time since graduation, some employers request high school, college, and post-graduate transcripts to verify the accuracy of information presented during the selection process.

**Financial references**   Financial references are generally only used when candidates will be handling large sums of cash. As with all other selection tools, a financial reference must be shown to be job related and a valid predictor of success in the position. When required, financial references, generally provided by credit reporting agencies, are subject to requirements of the federal Fair Credit Reporting Act (FCRA).

---

### The Fair Credit Reporting Act of 1970

The FCRA was first enacted in 1970 and has been amended several times since then. The FCRA is enforced by the Federal Trade Commission (FTC) and requires certain actions be taken by employers prior to the use of credit reports in employment decisions.

First, a clear and conspicuous disclosure that a consumer report may be obtained for employment purposes must be made in writing to the candidate before the report is acquired.

Second, the candidate must provide written authorization to the employer to obtain the report.

Third, before the employer can take an adverse action based in whole or in part on the credit report, the employer must either provide the candidate with a copy of the report and a copy of the FTC notice, "A Summary of Your Rights Under the Fair Credit Reporting Act," or, if the application was made by mail, telephone, computer, or similar means, the employer must notify the candidate within three business days that adverse action has been taken based in whole or in part based on the credit report; provide the name, address, and telephone number of the reporting agency; and indicate that the agency did not take the adverse action and cannot provide the reasons for the action to the consumer. The employer must provide the candidate with a copy of the report within three days of a request from the candidate for a copy of the report, along with a copy of the FTC notice just described.

The FCRA may be viewed in its entirety at www.ftc.gov/os/statutes/fcra.htm#603.

---

**Negligent hiring**   Negligent hiring occurs when an employer knew or should have known about an applicant's prior history that endangered customers, employees, vendors, or others with whom the employee comes in contact. Employers can prevent negligent hiring lawsuits by carefully checking the references and running background checks for all candidates. Once an employer finds out about such a history, the employer is obligated to safeguard others who come in contact with the individual during the work day by taking whatever action is necessary to maintain a safe work environment.

**Polygraph tests**   The use of polygraph tests in the employment process is limited by the Employee Polygraph Protection Act (EPPA).

---

**The Employee Polygraph Protection Act of 1988**

The EPPA prohibits private employers from using polygraph tests in making employment decisions except under very limited conditions. The act applies to private employers but not federal, state, or local governments, and is administered by the Wage and Hour Division of the Department of Labor. Violations of its provisions may result in fines of up to $10,000 against an employer.

The EPPA allows polygraph tests to be administered to employees of federal contractors or subcontractors with national defense, national security, or FBI contracts; to prospective employees of armored car or security services; and to prospective employees who would have access to the manufacture, storage, distribution, or sale of pharmaceutical products. The act also allows the use of polygraph tests during an ongoing investigation of an economic loss to the employer if an employee had access to the property in question. Under these limited circumstances, polygraph tests may be administered by individuals licensed by the state in which the test takes place.

See `http://www4.law.cornell.edu/uscode/29/2006.html` to view the complete text of the Employee Polygraph Protection Act.

---

**Medical examinations**   Medical examinations may only be required after a job offer has been extended to the candidate. As with all other assessment tools, medical examinations are allowable if their purpose is both job related and required of all candidates. These exams are used to ensure that the employee will be fully capable of performing the requirements of the job, and in some cases, may be part of an employer's health and safety program.

Drug tests are considered medical tests and are, therefore, subject to the above requirements. Drug testing is covered in more detail in Chapter 8, "Occupational Health, Safety, and Security."

# Hiring the New Employee

The post-interview strategy meeting has been concluded, the references have been checked, and results of the pre-employment tests are in. It's been a difficult decision for the hiring manager, but the decision has been made and its time to extend an offer. After discussion with HR, the hiring manager contacts the successful candidate and extends a verbal offer.

## Making the Employment Offer

The offer letter should be prepared immediately upon acceptance of the verbal offer by the candidate. The standard offer letter should be reviewed by the corporate attorney to ensure that its provisions do not compromise the organization and that it contains the terms of the offer as well as any contingencies that apply, such as a medical exam. The salary offer should be stated in an hourly or monthly amount. The offer should state clearly that the organization is an at-will employer and that only the terms and conditions of the offer contained in the offer letter are valid. Finally, there should be a reasonable time frame for returning a signed acceptance of the offer.

Care should be taken to ensure that any promises of benefits or special conditions agreed upon by the hiring manager are included in the offer letter so that there is no ambiguity about the complete offer.

**Relocation packages**   In some circumstances, employers may be willing to pay the costs of relocating an employee or an applicant. When that occurs, HR may manage the process. Elements of relocation packages that can be negotiated include a company-paid trip for the spouse and family to see the area and look for a new home, assistance with selling the old and/or purchasing the new home, payment of moving expenses, assisting the spouse in a job search in the new area, and guaranteeing the sale price of the old house if it doesn't sell.

Relocation is an activity that lends itself to outsourcing, and there are many professionals who will manage the entire process for the organization and the family. This can be a cost-effective solution that saves time for in-house staff.

## Employment Contracts

An employment contract binds both parties to the agreements contained in the contract. Contracts are generally reserved for senior-level managers and can cover a wide range of topics. Any areas of the employment relationship not specifically covered in the contract are subject to common law. Some standard clauses seen in employment contracts can include the following:

**Terms and conditions of employment**   This clause covers the start date and duration of the contract and, if the contract is for a set period of time, includes any automatic extension agreements.

**Scope of duties**   The general and specific duties and responsibilities are covered by this clause. The duties can be part of the contract or the job description may be incorporated into the agreement as an addendum. Expectations for performance are included here as well.

**Compensation**   The compensation package is described in this clause, which includes the base salary, any bonus and incentive agreements, auto allowance, and company car agreements.

**Benefits and expense reimbursements**   Items covered by this clause include disability and health insurance benefits and retirement plans. The extent and conditions for expense reimbursements are also described here.

**Nondisclosure of proprietary information**   Requirements for the maintenance of confidentiality with regard to proprietary information are included here, along with noncompete language and requirements for the return of company property when the employment relationship ends.

**Nonsolicitation agreement**   This clause sets forth agreements that limit the employee's ability to solicit customers, vendors, and employees during the course of the contract and for an agreed-upon period of time after the contract ends.

**Advice of counsel**   A clause advising the employee to seek legal counsel prior to signing the contract is often included.

**Disability or death**   The employer can include a clause that states what happens to the agreement in the event of the disability or death of the employee.

**Termination clause**   The termination clause sets forth conditions that would lead to a termination for cause, such as inability to perform, neglecting the duties of the position, misconduct, violations of company policy, or other egregious acts.

**Change of control**    A change of control clause protects the employee's job and compensation in the event of a reorganization, acquisition, or merger, for a specified period of time.

## Immigration Status

Prior to 1965, the last major legislation regarding immigration was the Immigration and Nationality Act (INA) of 1952. The INA remains the major federal immigration law, and subsequents acts are amendments to it. In 1986, legislation was enacted to reform the immigration process and attempt to control illegal immigration; in 1990, additional legislation addressed issues related to legal immigrants.

**Immigration and Nationality Act (INA) of 1952 and Amendments of 1965**    The purpose of the INA was to simplify the multiple laws that previously governed U.S. immigration policy. Immigration quotas continued to be set on the basis of national origin.

Following the trend of equal opportunity established by the Civil Rights Act of 1964, the 1965 amendment eliminated national origin, race, and ancestry as bars to immigration and changed the allocation of immigrant visas to a first-come, first served basis. The amendment also established seven immigration categories with the goals of reunifying families and giving preference to those with specialty skills that were needed in the U.S.

**Immigration Reform and Control Act (IRCA) of 1986**    The Immigration Reform and Control Act (IRCA) was enacted in 1986 to address illegal immigration into the United States. The law applied to businesses with four or more employees and made it illegal to knowingly hire or continue to employ individuals who were not legally authorized to work in the United States. Unfair immigration-related employment practices were defined as discrimination on the basis of national origin or citizenship status.

Employers were required to complete Form I-9 for all new hires within the first three days of employment and to review documents provided by the employee that establish identity or employment authorization or both from lists of acceptable documents on the I-9 form. IRCA requires employers to maintain I-9 files for three years from the date of hire or one year after the date of termination, whichever is later, and allows, but does not require, employers to copy documents presented for employment eligibility for purposes of complying with these requirements. The Act also provides that employers complying in good faith with these requirements have an affirmative defense to inadvertently hiring an unauthorized alien. Substantial fines for violations of both the hiring and recordkeeping requirements were provided in the law. Failure to maintain acceptable records of I-9s is subject to fines of not less than $100 nor more than $1,000 for each employee without a completed form available upon request to an authorized agent of the Immigration and Naturalization Service (INS). The following table outlines the fines for hiring violations under the IRCA.

| Violation | Amount of Fine |
|-----------|----------------|
| First | Not less than $250 or more than $2,000 for each unauthorized employee |
| Second | Not less than $2,000 or more than $5,000 for each unauthorized employee |
| Third | Not less than $5,000 or more than $10,000 for each unauthorized employee |

In addition to the fines listed, employers who knowingly hire unauthorized workers are subject to fines of $3,000 per employee and/or six months imprisonment.

Visit www.immigration.gov/lpBin/lpext.dll/inserts/publaw/publaw-146?f= templates&fn=document-frame.htm#publaw-p199603 to view the full text of IRCA.

**Immigration Act of 1990**   The Immigration Act of 1990 made several changes to IRCA, including adding the requirement that a prevailing wage be paid to H-1B immigrants to ensure that U.S. citizens did not lose jobs to lower-paid immigrant workers. The act also restricted to 65,000 annually the number of immigrants allowed under the H-1B category and created additional categories for employment visas as shown next.

| VISA | CLASSIFICATION |
|------|----------------|
| **Visas for Temporary Workers** | |
| H-1B | Specialty occupations, DOD workers, fashion models |
| H-1C | Nurses going to work for up to three years in health professional shortage areas |
| H-2A | Temporary agricultural worker |
| H-2B | Temporary worker: skilled and unskilled |
| H-3 | Trainee |
| J-1 | Visas for exchange visitors |
| **Visas for Intra-company transfers** | |
| L-1A | Executive, managerial |
| L-1B | Specialized knowledge |
| L-2 | Spouse or child of L-1 |
| **Visas for Workers with Extraordinary Abilities** | |
| O-1 | Extraordinary ability in sciences, arts, education, business, or athletics |
| **Visas for Athletes and Entertainers** | |
| P-1 | Individual or team athletes |
| P-1 | Entertainment groups |
| P-2 | Artists and entertainers in reciprocal exchange programs |
| P-3 | Artists and entertainers in culturally unique programs |

## Visas for Religious Workers

R-1                      Religious workers

## Visas for NAFTA Workers

TN                      Trade visas for Canadians and Mexicans

Visit www.immigration.gov/lpBin/lpext.dll/inserts/publaw/publaw-2724?f=templates&fn=document-frame.htm#publaw-pl101649 to view the full text of the Immigration Act of 1990.

**Illegal Immigration Reform and Immigrant Responsibility Act (IIRIRA) of 1996**   This act reduced the number and types of documents allowable to prove identity, employment eligibility, or both in the hiring process and established pilot programs for verification of employment eligibility. Table 4.4 shows the documents currently approved to prove employment eligibility. Documents in List A are proof of both identity and employment eligibility, while those in List B prove only identity, and List C proves employment eligibility.

**TABLE 4.4**   Documents to Establish Identity and Employment Eligibility

| List A | List B | List C |
| --- | --- | --- |
| Documents that Establish Both Identity and Employment Eligibility | Documents that Establish Identity | Documents that Establish Employment Eligibility |
| **U.S. passport (unexpired or expired)** | **Driver's license or ID card issued by a state or outlying possession of the United States provided it contains a photograph or information such as name, date of birth, gender, height, eye color, and address** | **U.S. social security card issued by the Social Security Administration (*other than a card stating it is not valid for employment*)** |
| Certificate of U.S. citizenship (*INS Form N-560 or N-561*) | ID card issued by federal, state, or local government agencies or entities, provided it contains a photograph or information such as name, date of birth, gender, height, eye color, and address | Certification of Birth Abroad issued by the Department of State (*Form FS-545 or Form DS-1350*) |
| Certificate of Naturalization | School ID card with a photograph | Original or certified copy of a birth certificate issued by a state, county, municipal authority, or outlying possession of the United States bearing an official seal |

**TABLE 4.4** Documents to Establish Identity and Employment Eligibility *(continued)*

| List A | List B | List C |
|---|---|---|
| Unexpired foreign passport with I-551 stamp or attached INS Form I-94 indicating unexpired employment authorization | Voter registration card | Native American tribal document |
| Permanent Resident card or Alien Registration Receipt card with photograph (*INS Form I-151 or I-551*) | U.S. military card or draft record | U.S. citizen ID card (*INS Form I-197*) |
| Unexpired Temporary Resident card (*INS Form I-688*) | Military Dependent ID card | ID card for use of resident citizen in the United States |
| Unexpired Employment Authorization card (*INS Form I-688A*) | U.S. Coast Guard Merchant Mariner card | Unexpired employment authorization document issued by the INS (*other than those listed under List A*) |
| Unexpired Reentry permit (*INS Form I-327*) | Native American tribal document | |
| Unexpired Refugee Travel document (*INS Form I-571*) | Driver's license issued by a Canadian government authority (additional documents are authorized for persons under 18) | |
| Unexpired Employment Authorization document issued by the INS which contains a photograph (*INS Form I-688B*) | | |

## New Hire Orientation

New hire orientation programs provide an introduction to the organization for new employees. In many organizations, daily events move so quickly that new hires are sometimes left to fend for themselves without understanding what it is they are supposed to do or how to get help when they need it. An effective orientation program is structured to ensure that new employees have someone to turn to for assistance. Scheduled follow-ups at regular intervals provide opportunities for HR to provide support as needed.

In many organizations, HR provides the organization's orientation with information about the company's mission, goals, and values and answers general questions. If a buddy program is in existence at the organization, the buddy greets the new employee during this time as well. The hiring manager provides a department orientation with specifics about the position, sets expectations, and ensures the new hire knows where to go for assistance when it is needed.

Extending orientation over a period of several months ensures that the employee has support on an ongoing basis and enhances the chances of longevity in the organization.

# Exiting the Organization

Organization exits happen in one of two ways: the employee either chooses to leave of their own volition (resignations and retirements), or they are asked to leave in one way or another (termination, downsizing, or layoff). Organization exits are stressful. Even when the employee has chosen to leave and is going on good terms, issues arise for the organization in replacing the employee or allocating duties to remaining coworkers. Coworkers can be affected by the change as well, so developing an exit process that reduces the stress and builds a smooth transition will pay off in many ways. Most significant for HR is the positive message it sends to employees who remain in the organization.

## Voluntary Exits

Employees voluntarily exit the organization by either resigning or retiring. *Resignations* occur when an employee decides to leave the organization and pursue other interests. For HR, resignations present few legal issues, but they do require decisions about replacement or reassignment of work that may lead to promotions or transfers of other employees, all of which affect the Workforce Planning process. Resignations require HR to ensure that any loans or advances are repaid to the organization or arrangements are made for that to happen. In addition, COBRA and HIPAA notices must be provided for departing employees. (COBRA and HIPAA requirements are covered in detail in Chapter 6, "Compensation and Benefits.")

*Planned retirements* occur when an employee decides to stop working full time and pursue other interests. HR can provide preretirement counseling to prepare employees for the transition from the structure provided by full-time work to unstructured time for pursuing other activities in leading a full and rewarding life. Employee Assistance Programs (EAPs) are excellent sources for this type of counseling and assistance. (EAPs are covered in detail in Chapter 8.)

Before an employee leaves the company, the HR department should conduct an *exit interview*. An effective exit interview provides an opportunity for employees to communicate information to the organization about why they decided to leave, what improvements the organization could make to enhance the employment experience, and any specific issues that need to be addressed. If the employee is one who has been a significant contributor and whom the organization would consider rehiring in the future, this would be the time to leave the door open for that possibility. Ideally, exit interviews are conducted by a third party so that employees feel free to be candid. There are a number of organizations that provide this service, most often as a telephone or online interview.

# Involuntary Exits

Involuntary exits occur as the result of either performance problems or changing business needs. Performance problems and terminations resulting from those issues are discussed in Chapter 2. In this chapter, I will discuss issues related to *downsizing*, which occurs as businesses change strategic direction or react to economic situations. There are a number of issues to consider in this process, beginning with legal notice requirements.

## Worker Adjustment and Retraining Notification Act of 1988 (WARN)

The WARN Act was passed by Congress in 1988 to provide some protection for workers in the event of mass layoffs or plant closings by requiring 60 days advance notice be given to either the individual workers or their union representatives. The intent of Congress was to provide time for workers to obtain new employment or training before the loss of their jobs. The WARN Act is administered by the Department of Labor and enforced through the federal courts.

Employers with 100 or more full-time employees or those with 100 or more full- *and* part-time employees who work in the aggregate 4000 hours or more per week are subject to the provisions of the WARN Act. The employee count includes those who are on temporary leave or layoff with a reasonable expectation of recall.

The WARN Act established that a *mass layoff* occurs when either 500 employees are laid off or 33 percent of the workforce and at least 50 employees are laid off. A *plant closing* occurs when 50 or more full-time employees lose their jobs because a single facility shuts down, either permanently or temporarily. In cases where the employer staggers the workforce reduction over a period of time, care must be taken that appropriate notice is given if the total reductions within a 90-day period trigger the notice requirement.

The WARN Act also established rules on notice. For instance, notice is required to be given to all affected employees or their representatives, the chief elected official of the local government, and the state dislocated worker unit. Notice requirements vary according to which group they are being sent to, but they must contain specific information about the reasons for the closure, whether the action is permanent or temporary, the address of the affected business unit, the name of a company official to contact for further information, the expected date of closure or layoff, and whether or not bumping rights exist.

The WARN Act provides for three situations in which the 60-day notice is not required, but the burden is on the employer to show that the reasons are legitimate and not an attempt to thwart the intent of the Act.

1. The "faltering company" exception applies only to plant closures in situations where the company is actively seeking additional funding and has a reasonable expectation that it will be forthcoming in an amount sufficient to preclude the layoff or closure, and that giving the notice would negatively impact the ability of the company to obtain the funding.

2. The "unforeseeable business circumstance" exception applies to plant closings and mass layoffs and occurs when circumstances take a sudden and unexpected negative change that could not have reasonably been predicted.

3. The "natural disaster" exception applies to both plant closings and mass layoffs occurring as the result of a natural disaster.

Once the organization has determined whether or not compliance with WARN Act requirements is necessary, decisions regarding a *reduction in force (RIF)* can be made. Also commonly referred to as a *layoff*, planning and conducting a RIF is stressful for managers, who must decide which employees will be asked to leave the organization, and even more so for employees, who usually figure out that layoffs are coming long before the management announcement. Maintaining productivity in a workforce that is waiting to find out whether or not they will have jobs is a challenging prospect. During these times, honest communication with employees is essential, and you should provide as much information as possible before actual layoff decisions are complete. Once the layoff has occurred, open and honest communication is still essential, as remaining employees struggle with feelings of anger that their coworkers had to leave the company, "survivor guilt" because they are still employed, and dissatisfaction that they are now asked to take on the work of the employees who left the company.

## Making Layoff Decisions

As managers struggle with decisions about who will go and who will stay, the focus of those decisions must be on what is necessary for the business. Documenting the business reason for the decision with clear and unambiguous reasoning is essential in case the decision is challenged on the basis of disparate impact or other equal opportunity requirements.

 **Real World Scenario**

### *Taxman v Board of Education of Piscataway* (1993)

In 1989, the Piscataway Board of Education found it necessary for budgetary reasons to reduce the faculty. Based on state law, the board was required to conduct the layoffs based on seniority. There were two teachers with the least seniority, Sharon Taxman and Debra Williams. Both had been hired on the same day in 1980, had equivalent educational qualifications and had received equally outstanding evaluations. In essence, the board felt they were both equally qualified to be retained. In making previous layoff decisions in similar cases when there were no differences in qualifications, the board had drawn lots to determine which teacher to lay off. In this case, however, there was one difference between the teachers that the board considered: Taxman was white and Williams was black. The board decided that it was in the interest of the school to demonstrate the importance of diversity in the workplace and decided to retain Williams because she was black.

There was no evidence of past discrimination that needed to be rectified based on the Affirmative Action Plan; in fact, blacks were employed in the school district at about twice the rate of the applicable labor pool. Sharon Taxman sued the school board for racial discrimination in violation of Title VII. The federal district court that heard the case found in favor of Taxman, and the school board appealed to the Third Circuit Court of Appeals, which also found in favor of Taxman. The school board then appealed to the U.S. Supreme Court, but agreed to settle the case before the Supreme Court hearing.

Managers often look to layoffs as a way to remove low performers. If this is the route taken, documentation of the method used to determine who these employees are is necessary. Performance appraisals are often utilized in this way.

**Severance**   Offering a severance package to departing employee helps to ease the shock of unemployment. Severance packages must be consistent, based on a rationale that ensures equity to all departing employees. Severance amounts can be based on seniority or employee classes, or some combination of the two.

**Outplacement**   Providing outplacement counseling for employees can be a great assistance in finding new jobs or in coping with the change in circumstances. Continuing the EAP for a finite period of time for laid off workers is another way to assist them in coming to terms with the termination.

**Unemployment insurance**   If the RIF or layoff meets WARN notice thresholds, the state unemployment office will be aware of the pending layoff. Whether or not that is the case, HR should ensure that employees are clear about their eligibility for unemployment and how to apply for it. Most states provide pamphlets explaining the requirements that are distributed at the time of the layoff.

### Conducting the Layoff Meeting

During the layoff meeting, managers should communicate the message unambiguously and with compassion. If the layoff decision is a permanent one, employees should be advised that they will not be called back to work; if there is a possibility for rehire, they should be advised of the time frame in which that will occur. Employees should be given adequate time to gather personal items prior to leaving but should not be allowed to hang around indefinitely, as this is hard on employees who will be staying with the organization. Once the termination meetings have been conducted, it is important that management meet with the remaining employees to answer questions and provide reassurance.

# Measuring Effectiveness

As HR professionals become more focused on the strategic impact of HR decisions to the bottom line, it is essential to demonstrate the effectiveness of programs in business terms that are meaningful to senior management. This can be accomplished by quantifying the results of HR programs and proposals. There are a number of commonly-used metrics for employment activities, including the following:

- Cost-benefit analysis
- Return on investment
- Costs-per-hire (including direct and indirect costs)
- Time to fill
- Time to hire
- Selection ratios
- Offer-to-acceptance rate

Employment is one area of HR that is fairly easy to quantify. Using these measures to demonstrate the results of current programs or to project the effectiveness of proposals for new programs communicates to senior management that HR not only understands business needs but provides cost-effective programs that support strategic plans.

Jac Fitz-enz has written an excellent resource for measuring HR effectiveness titled *How to Measure Human Resources Management*. This book provides a number of measures and how to use them effectively.

# International Workforce Planning and Employment

As the globalization of business increases, more American companies find themselves employing all or part of their workforce in positions overseas. In addition to the planning steps discussed previously, there are a number of additional factors to consider for an international workforce, beginning with determining in what labor market the company will recruit its employees. There are three possible areas:

- The home or parent country is the domicile of the company, where its corporate headquarters are located. Employees who originate from the home country are known as *expatriates*, or *parent-country nationals (PCNs)*.

- The host country is the country wherein the corporation is operating, or is planning to operate, a business unit. Employees originating from the host country are known as *host-country nationals (HCNs)*. While this may seem to be a solution with few problems, there can be many unexpected issues to resolve, including those related to compensation and cultural differences.

- Employees from any country other than the home or host country are known as *third-country nationals (TCNs)*. Experienced third-country nationals who are familiar with the organization culture and business practices are most often utilized to set up a new business unit in a neighboring country. This can be an advantageous situation for the business because it is less expensive than relocating an expatriate.

It is important to understand the international staffing strategies that can be used in building the global workforce. There are four basic strategies used by multinational corporations in making these decisions.

The *ethnocentric* approach is one in which all of the key management positions are filled by expatriates. The benefits of an ethnocentric approach include the ability of the organization to maintain control of its business units and ensure that business is conducted in accordance with corporate mandates. Communication with the home office is made easier because the expatriate is familiar with the organization's culture and business practices. International assignments also provide opportunities to develop individuals who are part of the succession plans for senior management roles. This approach is often taken during the startup phase of a business unit to ensure that organization standards are maintained, or when there is a real or perceived lack of management talent available in the host country labor market. While this approach encourages a cohesive culture throughout the organization, it focuses on the home country/parent organization and doesn't take into consideration local customs and business practices. This can lead to misunderstandings and create ill will between the local government and the company.

A *polycentric* approach fills corporate positions in the home country with expatriates, while management positions in the host country are filled by home country nationals. This approach can have a positive impact by showing commitment to the host country and generating goodwill for the business, but it does not afford upward mobility for top managers in the host country. The business benefits, because it is less expensive to hire local employees—even at top dollar—than it is to fill international positions with expatriates. However, it can also limit communication between business units in the different locations and result in animosity between the home and host country business units due to differences in cultural practices and compensation levels between countries.

A *regiocentric* approach takes a somewhat larger operational view than does the polycentric, covering a trade region such as the European Union and having managers move between business units in different countries in the region.

The *geocentric* approach seeks to place the best-qualified person into each position, regardless of their country of origin. As a result, the business builds an international management team whose members are able to move into and address issues in any geographic area. Once the company has decided which approach best suits its strategic goals and culture, there are many complex issues to be addressed by HR. There are a myriad of laws, customs, and local practices to be dealt with that often conflict with home-country practices, and it is important to understand the impact of these issues when evaluating international workforce needs.

Expatriate issues in workforce planning fall into three main categories.

**Cost**   The cost of sending an employee to work in a foreign country can be substantial, up to twice the annual salary. After you factor in family moving costs, costs required to minimize the cultural adjustment of the employee and their family, adjustments in pay (to keep the employee's salary "whole" and retain their equity within the company, it is often necessary to subsidize schooling costs, taxes, and housing costs).

**Foreign business practices**   The way business is done in foreign countries can be significantly different from the way business is done in the United States. Candidates for expatriate jobs must receive training on the culture and practices of the country to which they will be assigned to be successful in their positions and to avoid unintentionally insulting those with whom they are working. It is important as well to provide training on laws governing U.S. business practices in foreign countries, particularly the Foreign Corrupt Practices Act (FCPA), which prohibits American businesses from proffering bribes in order to obtain contracts or encourage foreign bureaucrats to get things done in a timely fashion.

**Cultural acclimation**   Cultural acclimation can be difficult for not only the employee, but also for the employee's spouse and children, and often results in the resignation of the employee or insistence on transfer back to the home country. Another issue is that, while women are accepted in business leadership positions in this country, cultural difficulties can be encountered in other countries with fewer women in the workforce. This issue alone can become a huge conflict, with equal employment opportunity requirements to provide equal access to training and upward mobility at odds with the ability to do business in a country unaccustomed to dealing with women in powerful positions.

Finally, *inpatriates* may be brought to the home office for a period of time for training and to become accustomed to the culture and practices of the organization before returning to their countries of origin for work assignments as host-country nationals.

# Summary

When strategically tied to the organization's vision, mission, and goals, planning for workforce needs is a key element for success. HR professionals must provide expertise for management in deciding whether to aggressively develop current employees for future growth in the organization, hire candidates from the outside, or use alternative staffing methods to accomplish the work that needs to be done. Understanding the implications of each approach allows HR to guide management in making decisions that best suit the organization's needs, culture, and values.

Identifying candidates who have not only the best KSAs for the job, but whose personal goals, ambitions, and qualities complement the needs of the organization requires HR professionals to be keenly aware of its strategic direction. Providing opportunities to all qualified candidates opens up the labor pool available to the organization and includes candidates with a great deal to offer who might not have been considered in the past.

An effective hiring process begins with using sources that produce a pool of candidates with diverse backgrounds who have the required KSAs, continues with screening the candidates with a fair and equitable process designed to find the best match for the organization, and concludes by welcoming them with orientation programs that assist them to be productive members of the team. Having an effective organizational exit process in place eases the transition for the employees who remain with the company as well as for those who are leaving. When downsizing decisions are made fairly and equitably, voluntary exits are treated with respect, and terminations for poor performance are handled with due process, remaining employees respond with greater loyalty and commitment to organization goals.

HR professionals can show that they understand the fundamental needs of business by making recommendations and decisions based on quantifiable measures. Being able to show, for example, how much a bad hiring decision costs the organization in terms of the direct and indirect costs of hiring, training, and replacing employees demonstrates to management that effective HR management has a positive effect on the bottom line.

# Exam Essentials

**Be able to conduct a staffing needs assessment.** A staffing needs assessment is used to determine which KSAs are needed to meet future strategic goals and where training efforts (if filling jobs internally) or recruiting efforts (if hiring from the outside) should be focused.

**Be able to develop a succession plan.** A succession plan identifies high performing individuals within the company who have the capability to take on positions at the senior and executive management levels. Once the individuals have been identified, they are coached, mentored, and provided with training opportunities to prepare them for greater responsibility.

**Understand the Affirmative Action Plan process.**   An AAP is required to be filed by companies with federal contracts of $50,000 or more per year and 50 employees. The plan identifies how many incumbents in different job classifications are members of protected classes and compares that information to the availability of protected classes in the labor market.

**Be able to develop job requirements from a job analysis.**   Job analysis provides the information necessary to develop the job competencies, job descriptions, and test specifications necessary to both identify what needs to be done on a daily basis and recruit effectively for the best candidate to fill the position.

**Be able to identify recruitment methods.**   Depending on the level of experience and skill being sought, there are a variety of methods to consider in the recruiting process. HR professionals must understand which methods will produce the candidates who are most appropriate to fill positions at different levels.

**Be able to establish and implement selection procedures.**   Effective selection procedures help ensure that candidates selected for the organization meet all the job requirements and are the best fit for the position. Interviewing, testing, realistic job previews and assessment centers help organizations determine if the candidate is the right fit for the job. Reference checks ensure that the candidate has performed successfully in previous positions.

**Understand the implications of federal immigration policy.**   Immigration laws were designed to protect American workers while encouraging the immigration of highly educated and skilled workers for jobs requiring high-level KSAs. Employers may only hire non-citizens when they can demonstrate that no American citizens with the necessary qualifications are available. When non-citizens are hired, they must be paid the prevailing wage for the position.

**Be able to conduct post-hire activities.**   HR activities conducted during the post-hire phase have implications for the long-term success of new hires. It is important to understand the ramifications of employment offers and ensure that the new employee has all the necessary information to be successful. An effective orientation will make new employees feel welcome, introduce them to the company and provide information on company policies.

**Be able to create the organization exit process.**   HR professionals must develop fair and equitable processes for downsizing and laying off employees, and be aware of legal notice requirements that must be followed when applicable. Resignations and retirements require that HR conduct exit interviews and create processes that provide for timely replacement of exiting employees.

# Key Terms

Before you take the exam, be certain you are familiar with the following terms:

| | |
|---|---|
| adverse impact | Bona Fide Occupational Qualifications (BFOQ) |
| Affirmative Action Plan (AAP) | certiorari |
| average bias | concurrent validity |

construct validity

contract workers

contrast bias

core competencies

cost-benefit analysis

cultural noise

cycles

Delphi technique

Department of Labor (DOL)

disparate impact

downsizing

Equal Employment Opportunity Commission (EEOC)

essential job functions

ethnocentric

Executive Orders

exit interview

expatriates

geocentric

gut feeling bias

halo effect

harshness

horn effect

host-country nationals (HCNs)

independent contractors

inpatriates

internship programs

job bidding

job competencies

job posting

job sharing

job specifications

knowledge, skills, and abilities (KSAs)

knowledge-of-predictor

layoff

leniency bias

mass layoff

multiple linear regression

negative emphasis bias

nominal group technique

nonessential job functions

nonverbal bias

Office of Federal Contract Compliance Programs (OFCCP)

on-call workers

outsourcing

parent-country nationals (PCNs)

part-time employees

payrolling

planned retirements

plant closing

polycentric

predictive validity

professional employer organization (PEO)

protected classes

qualitative assessment tools

quantitative assessment tools

question inconsistency

realistic job preview (RJP)

reasonable accommodation

recency

reduction in force (RIF)

regiocentric

replacement chart

resignations

seasonal staffing requirements

seasonal workers

similar-to-me bias

simple linear regression

skills inventory

staffing needs assessment

stereotyping

succession plan

telecommuting

temp

temp-to-perm

third-country nationals (TCNs)

time series forecasts

trend analyses

undue hardship

unlawful employment practices

validity

# Review Questions

1.  The marketing director needs to hire a replacement for the marketing coordinator, who is being promoted. The position has changed quite a bit since the last time the job was advertised, and the director is looking to HR to assist in redefining the job requirements so that the recruiting process can begin. Which of the following would *not* be used in determining the job requirements?

    **A.** Job competencies

    **B.** Job description

    **C.** Job specifications

    **D.** Candidate profile

2.  Which of the following is NOT a BFOQ?

    **A.** A synagogue hiring a new rabbi requires that the rabbi be Jewish.

    **B.** A lingerie catalog hires only female models.

    **C.** A retail store in a predominantly Asian neighborhood advertises for Asian clerks.

    **D.** A swimming club requires that the men's changing room attendant be male.

3.  The court case which identified adverse impact as an unlawful employment practice was

    **A.** *Griggs v Duke Power Co*

    **B.** *Albemarle Paper v Moody*

    **C.** *Washington v Davis*

    **D.** *Taxman v School Board of Piscataway*

4.  To determine the numbers and types of jobs necessary to realize business goals, HR must assess the KSAs available within the organization during a staffing needs analysis. What other factor is necessary to complete the assessment?

    **A.** The KSAs needed to achieve future goals

    **B.** The tasks, duties, and responsibilities for the work

    **C.** The KSAs available in the local labor market

    **D.** The organization's core competencies

5.  An organization has decided to utilize the nominal group technique to determine how to cut costs without laying off any employees. The second step in the process is to

    **A.** Prioritize and build consensus

    **B.** Consent to a solution

    **C.** Think about and write down ideas

    **D.** Present ideas one at a time for later discussion

6.  Please refer to the following table for this question. A company advertised for 100 sales representative positions. They received 650 applications and hired the 100 employees as follows:

| Group | Applicants | Hired |
|---|---|---|
| Black | 140 | 23 |
| Asian | 120 | 21 |
| Hispanic | 145 | 19 |
| Caucasian | 230 | 35 |
| Native American | 15 | 2 |
| Total | 650 | 100 |

Which group has the highest selection rate?

A.  Black

B.  Asian

C.  Caucasian

D.  Native American

7.  Please refer to the following table for this question. A company advertised for 100 sales representative positions. They received 650 applications and hired the 100 employees as follows:

| Group | Applicants | Hired |
|---|---|---|
| Black | 140 | 23 |
| Asian | 120 | 21 |
| Hispanic | 145 | 19 |
| Caucasian | 230 | 35 |
| Native American | 15 | 2 |
| Total | 650 | 100 |

In which groups has adverse impact occurred?

A.  Hispanic and Caucasian

B.  Caucasian and Black

C.  Hispanic and Native American

D.  Native American and Black

8.  An affirmative action plan must be completed by employers who meet which criteria?

A.  Private employers with 25 or more employees

B.  Government contractors and subcontractors with contracts of $10,000 or more in a 12-month period

C.  Government contractors with contracts of $2500 or more in a 12-month period

D.  Government contractors with 50 or more employees and contracts of $50,000 or more each year

9.  When a reduction in force occurs, the ADEA allows that protected employees may waive their rights under some circumstances. In order for the waiver to be valid, the employee must be allowed how long to review and consider the agreement?

    **A.** 7 days

    **B.** 21 days

    **C.** 45 days

    **D.** 180 days

10. Which of the following is *not* required by the IRCA?

    **A.** That an I-9 form be completed for all new hires within 3 days of hire

    **B.** That employers comply with the IRCA in good faith

    **C.** That I-9 forms be maintained for all employees

    **D.** That copies of documents presented for employment eligibility be maintained

# Answers to Review Questions

1. **D.**   The candidate profile is developed after the job requirements have been determined, beginning with the job description and developing the competencies (broad requirements of the position) and the specifications necessary for successful performance.

2. **C.**   According to the EEOC, there are no circumstances where race or color are a BFOQ.

3. **A.**   *Griggs* identified adverse impact, that discrimination need not be intentional to exist; *Albemarle Paper* extended the concept to require that tests must be validated in accordance with the EEOC Uniform Guidelines for Employee Selection Procedures; *Washington* determined that employment tests resulting in adverse impact are acceptable if they predict future success on the job; *Taxman* found that employment decisions made on the basis of race are discriminatory.

4. **A.**   A staffing needs analysis begins with an assessment of the KSAs needed to achieve future goals along with those that are currently available within the organization.

5. **D.**   The steps in a nominal group technique are to begin with a period of time for reflection and write down ideas. Each participant then describes one idea for later discussion. The group prioritizes the ideas and builds consensus for actions and, finally, the group resolves the issue.

6. **B.**   To calculate the selection rate, divide the number of applicants hired by the total number of applicants:

| | |
|---|---|
| Black | 23/140 = 16% |
| Asian | 21/120 = 18% |
| Hispanic | 19/145 = 13% |
| Caucasian | 35/230 = 15% |
| Native American | 2/15 = 13% |

7. **C.**   To determine whether adverse impact has occurred, multiply the highest selection rate, which is Asian at 18%, by 4/5 or 80%. (18% × .80 = 14%) Only two groups fall below 14%, Hispanic and Native American, both at 13%.

| Group | Applicants | Hired | Selection Rate | 4/5 of Highest Rate |
|---|---|---|---|---|
| Black | 140 | 23 | 16% | |
| Asian | 120 | 21 | 18% | 14% |
| Hispanic | 145 | 19 | 13% | |
| Caucasian | 230 | 35 | 15% | |
| Native American | 15 | 2 | 13% | |
| Total | 650 | 100 | | |

**8.** D. Government contractors with 50 or more employees and $50,000 or more each year must complete Affirmative Action Plans.

**9.** C. ADEA waivers are valid *during* a reduction in force only if the employee has 45 days to consider the agreement and 7 days to revoke it. Terminations that are not part of a reduction in force require only 21 days for consideration. An employee has 180 days to file a charge with the EEOC in states that do not have their own EEO enforcement agency.

**10.** D. The IRCA allows, but does not require, employers to make copies of documents presented for employment eligibility.

# Chapter 5

# Human Resource Development

**THE HRCI TEST SPECIFICATIONS FROM THE HUMAN RESOURCE DEVELOPMENT FUNCTIONAL AREA COVERED IN THIS CHAPTER INCLUDE:**

- ✓ Conduct needs analyses to identify and establish priorities regarding human resource development activities
- ✓ Develop training programs
- ✓ Implement training programs
- ✓ Evaluate training programs
- ✓ Develop programs to assess employees' potential for growth and development in the organization
- ✓ Implement programs to assess employees' potential for growth and development in the organization
- ✓ Evaluate programs to assess employees' potential for growth and development in the organization
- ✓ Develop change management programs and activities
- ✓ Implement change management programs and activities
- ✓ Evaluate change management programs and activities
- ✓ Develop performance management programs and procedures
- ✓ Implement performance management programs and procedures
- ✓ Evaluate performance management programs and procedures
- ✓ Develop programs to meet the unique needs of particular employees (for example, work-family programs, diversity programs, outplacement programs, repatriation programs, and fast-track programs)

- ✓ **Implement programs to meet the unique needs of particular employees (for example, work-family programs, diversity programs, outplacement programs, repatriation programs, and fast-track programs)**
- ✓ **Evaluate programs to meet the unique needs of particular employees (for example, work-family programs, diversity programs, outplacement programs, repatriation programs, and fast-track programs)**

Human Resource Development (HRD) is the functional area of human resources that seeks to affect the behavior of employees so the organization can achieve its goals. In this chapter, HRD is explored within the context of *organization development (OD)*. The two are inextricably linked, for an organization cannot exist or change without people. Organization development is a systematic method of examining an organization's technology, processes, structure, and human resources and developing action strategies to improve the way it achieves its goals. These action strategies are known as *organization development (OD) interventions* and may be directed toward structures, processes, technology, individuals, groups of individuals, or entire organizations. For purposes of discussion in this chapter, I discuss activities that focus on organization-wide changes to structure, process, and technology in the OD section, and I discuss the activities focused on individuals and groups of individuals in the HRD section.

Chapter 3, "Strategic Management," examined the structural, procedural, and technological aspects of an organization's systems and discussed the vision, mission, and value statements that result from the strategic planning process. Building on what you know about strategic management, this chapter looks at the ways organizations implement the changes necessary to accomplish their missions and the strategies they use to align their employees with the vision, mission, and goals developed by their leaders.

This chapter begins with a review of several different approaches to the human element of organization development and the ways these approaches positively impact organizational culture and climate. It's followed by a review of techniques for developing employees, managers, and leaders and a systems model for use in developing training programs. Finally, we will look at HR programs that serve the special needs of different employee groups and how these programs are guided by the organizational culture and climate.

 Be sure to review the HRCI knowledge requirements for HRD as you begin this chapter. Several sections in Chapter 2, "Core Knowledge Requirements," have particular relevance here; a review of the discussions on needs assessment, communication strategies, adult learning processes, motivation concepts, and applications and training methods will enhance your review of the material in this chapter.

# Organization Development

HRD does not occur in a vacuum; it occurs within the context of how the organization sees itself, how it conducts business, and how it views its employees. Every organization makes determinations about these things, whether consciously, as part of an OD process, or unconsciously, as a result of the way its leaders operate on a day-to-day basis. Effective organizations are those in which values and beliefs are shared at all levels and reflected in the behavior of individuals throughout the organization. This sharing of values and beliefs and the behavior related to them is known as the *organization culture*. The culture of an organization, combined with the styles of leadership and management in the organization and the level of bureaucracy, creates an *organizational climate* that will either inspire and motivate employees to achieve the corporate mission, or inhibit employee motivation and enthusiasm for their jobs, thereby limiting the success of the organization. Organizational culture and climate determine the level of employee involvement in the decision making process and provide the unwritten ground rules upon which decisions can be based in the absence of relevant policies.

While it is possible for businesses to earn a profit without considering the needs of their employees (and some do), the results of job satisfaction surveys consistently show that employees are motivated by a variety of factors that can be influenced by culture and climate. Challenging work and respect are very often of greater importance to employees than the amount of money they earn in determining their level of satisfaction, commitment, and productivity. While it is important to keep in mind that businesses exist to earn a profit, not to merely provide a satisfying work experience for employees, organizations that are able to create atmospheres including trust, respect, and challenging work are generally rewarded with higher rates of productivity than are organizations focused only on cost reduction and efficiency. The OD process provides a method for developing strategies to accomplish this.

When the culture and climate tend to inhibit goal achievement instead, an OD intervention can be implemented to correct the problem. In their text *Organization Development and Change* (South-Western College Pub, 7th edition, January 2001), Thomas Cummings and Christopher Worley identify four categories of interventions: strategic, techno-structural, human process, and human resource management. As is evident by the category names, interventions can remove obstacles in strategy, technology, structure, process, and management. In this section, I will concentrate on interventions and strategies in each category that relate to human resource development and the ways they can influence the organization culture and climate.

## Strategic Interventions

Strategic OD interventions are often utilized to implement changes made to the vision, mission, and values of the organization during a strategic planning process as discussed in Chapter 3. These interventions are designed to align various elements within the organization with the new direction or focus established by the leaders. Some examples of strategic OD interventions are change management, knowledge management, and learning organizations.

### Change Management

The result of any OD process is a change in the way things are done in an organization. Whether it is new technology, a more efficient process, or a different reporting structure, the resulting change will have to be implemented by people—and no matter how difficult it is to create the new operating plans, implementing them successfully will be even more difficult because the people in the organization must be motivated and committed to making the changes work.

## Change Process Theory

An early model of *change process theory*, developed by a social psychologist named Kurt Lewin, described three stages for change:

**Unfreezing** This stage creates the motivation for change by identifying and communicating the need for the change. In this stage it is important to create a vision for the outcome of the change and a sense of urgency for getting to the new outcome.

**Moving** During this stage, resistance is examined and managed and the organization is aligned with the change. Communication remains an integral part of the process.

**Refreezing** In the final stage of the theory, the change becomes the new norm for the organization, the outcome is evaluated, and additional changes occur to adjust the actual outcomes to those that are desired.

Human resource professionals can use change process theory to aid employees through a stressful work change. Let's take a look at some other ways HR can help employees deal with change.

## Tools for Successful Change

People dislike change for a variety of reasons: change moves them out of the "comfort zone" to which they have become accustomed and they may be fearful of the unknown. The politics of the organization may make change undesirable in one group or another, and employees may perceive that they will lose status or control. Changes fail most often because the people who are expected to implement them are not prepared to do so. Organizations can take steps to ensure the success of change initiatives, including the following:

**Prepare for change** The only constant in the current business environment is change. Organizations must be aware of situations developing within the industry or geographic areas in which they operate so that they can be ahead of the curve in developing strategies that will effectively handle changes in the environment.

**Communicate** To enhance the likelihood of a successful implementation, leaders must communicate with employees well in advance of any planned implementation. Soliciting ideas from those who are closest to operations may provide insight into better solutions and increase buy-in when it is time to implement the change. Communication at every stage of the process will enable employees to get used to the idea of the change gradually, increase the level of acceptance, and build commitment for the process.

**Develop a plan** A comprehensive plan that clearly defines the goals of the change, addresses all of its implications, and includes tools for evaluating its success is essential. Scheduling training for employees who may need to upgrade skills, integrating processes from different areas of the organization, upgrading equipment, and developing a plan to address resistance to the change and reduce stress will increase the chances for successful implementation.

**Have a sponsor** The CEO or another senior executive who is committed to and enthusiastic about the change must be able to inspire employees to commit to the implementation.

**Motivate direct supervisors** Employees want to know how their supervisors feel about changes and will be influenced by what the supervisors say about the change.

**Recruit unofficial leaders**   Every organization has unofficial leaders who are able to influence coworkers; obtaining their commitment to the change will influence others.

**Implement**   Put the change into action. Ensure that employees have the tools needed to successfully implement the change, whether that is new equipment, facilities, training, or support.

**Evaluate**   Compare results to the evaluation criteria developed during the planning stage to determine whether or not the change was successfully implemented.

HR professionals are in a unique position to act as change agents during this process. A *change agent* must be able to balance the needs of various stakeholders in the process, listen to their concerns, and move them toward acceptance of and commitment to the change.

## Knowledge Management

Increasingly, organizations are realizing how important it is to manage the knowledge acquired by individual employees. Given the increasing mobility of the workforce, much of the knowledge that an individual acquires over time in an organization disappears when that person leaves the organization. Finding a way to retain that knowledge in a database that is accessible by others in the organization turns information into useful knowledge needed for improving processes and increasing profits.

An application of knowledge management (KM) is exemplified by the intelligence services of the United States. As has been well-reported since September 11, 2001, the Federal Bureau of Investigation (FBI), National Security Agency (NSA), and Central Intelligence Agency (CIA) all had pieces of information about the hijackers. Even within the FBI, field offices in different parts of the country had bits of information that, taken together, could have provided some warning of what was being planned. Had a knowledge management process to collect and collate these different pieces of information been in place, it may have been possible to prevent the attacks.

An example of an effective knowledge management program with which many people have had some experience is customer relationship management (CRM). For example, you may have experienced the frustration of calling a customer support or help line and having to repeat all the details of a problem with a product to each new customer service representative (CSR) who comes on the line. An effective KM process has each CSR enter facts about customer problems into a database so that, when the customer calls back, the next CSR to answer the call knows everything that has already transpired between the customer and the company. The customer does not need to repeat information, and the CSR can avoid going back to step one in the problem solving process.

## Learning Organizations

*Learning organizations* are innovative environments in which knowledge is originated, obtained, and freely shared in response to environmental changes that affect the ability of the organization to compete. The atmosphere in a learning organization is one in which employees are able to solve problems by experimenting with new methods that have been observed outside the organization or that have been experienced in other parts of the organization.

Peter Senge, author of *The Fifth Discipline* (Doubleday/Currency, 1990), identifies five disciplines, or guiding principles, that enable organizations to increase their ability to realize desired results, cultivate new ways of thinking, expand on individual ideas, and encourage continuous lifelong learning within the organization. These disciplines include the following:

**Systems thinking**   *Systems thinking* describes the ability of individuals and organizations to recognize patterns and project how changes will impact on them.

**Personal mastery**   *Personal mastery* describes a high level of expertise in an individual's chosen field and a commitment to lifelong learning.

**Mental models**   *Mental models* refer to the deep-seated beliefs that color perceptions and have an effect on how individuals see the world around them and react to it.

**Building a shared vision**   Stretching beyond the corporate vision statement and building a *shared vision* encourages the organization to plan for a future that inspires commitment on the part of all individuals in the organization.

**Team learning**   *Team learning*, as defined by Senge, refers to the ability of a team to share and build upon their ideas without holding anything back.

# Techno-Structural Interventions

OD interventions that fall into the techno-structural category address issues of how work gets done in the organization by examining the level of employee involvement and redesigning work processes. *Total quality management (TQM)*, a process that focuses all resources within the organization on providing value for customers, is an example of a techno-structural intervention. Another intervention that is used in this category is a high involvement organization.

## Total Quality Management (TQM)

TQM is a long-term intervention requiring employees at all levels within an organization to focus on providing products that meet customer needs. A successful TQM implementation requires the commitment of top management to lead the process. Because TQM is focused on customer needs, market research and product development are key components of the system. Processes are reviewed to eliminate wasted time as well as materials that either do not contribute or are obstacles to producing the end product. Teamwork is an essential function in a TQM environment; all members involved in the product or service, from front-line workers to suppliers and sales managers, must work together to solve problems for customers.

There have been a number of leaders in the quality movement; four of them who have made significant contributions are introduced here with a brief description of their contributions:

**W. Edwards Deming**   The quality movement originated in the 1940s with the work of W. Edwards Deming, who proposed that quality is defined by the consumer. Deming developed a 14-point plan that placed the burden for quality on management because they are able to control the systems within the organization. While American business was initially cool to the quality concept, Deming's theories were warmly received in Japan during the 1950s. In 1951, the Japanese named their quality award, the Deming Prize, after him.

**Joseph M. Juran**   Another early proponent of the quality movement was Joseph M. Juran who, like Deming, believed that quality begins with defining customer needs. Unlike Deming, Juran proposed that once customer needs were identified, they would be translated into the "language" of the business in order to deliver a product or service that met the needs of both customers and the business. He developed the Juran Trilogy, which identified three phases in the process: quality planning, quality control, and quality improvements.

**Dr. Kaoru Ishikawa**    Dr. Kaoru Ishikawa made significant contributions to the quality movement: he provided a collection of analytical tools to use in the workplace and developed the cause and effect diagram that bears his name. The following list explains some of these tools and provides examples.

**Check sheets**    *Check sheets* are the simplest analysis tools, requiring only a list of items that might be expected to occur. In an HR setting, a check sheet might be used to keep track of the reasons people resign from their positions. Figure 5.1 is an example of a check sheet used for that purpose. When an item occurs, a check or tick mark is placed next to it on the list. The data collected with a check sheet may be graphically represented in a histogram so that it is easier to analyze.

**FIGURE  5.1**    Sample check sheet

| Reason | Number of Occurrences | Total |
|---|---|---|
| Lack of advancement | ℍℍ | 5 |
| Lack of recognition | ℍℍ ℍℍ \\\\ | 14 |
| Long commute | \ | 1 |
| Low pay | \\ | 2 |
| Poor supervision | ℍℍ ℍℍ ℍℍ \ | 16 |
| | | |
| | | 38 |

**Histograms**    *Histograms* provide a way of looking at random occurrences to find out if there is a pattern. Using the data from the previous check sheet, a histogram provides a visual image of the reasons for resignations as illustrated by Figure 5.2.

**FIGURE  5.2**    Sample histogram

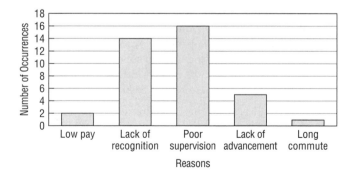

**Pareto chart**    The *Pareto chart* provides a graphical representation of the 80/20 rule: 80 percent of the problems are caused by 20 percent of the reasons, a principle established by an Italian economist named Vilfredo Pareto. The Pareto chart points out which areas of concern will provide the greatest return when corrected. The difference between a Pareto chart and a histogram is that the Pareto chart arranges the data in descending order and includes a cumulative percentage on the right side of the chart. Figure 5.3 uses the Pareto chart to identify the most significant causes of resignations. In this case, poor supervision and a lack of recognition cause 80 percent of the resignations.

**FIGURE 5.3** Pareto chart

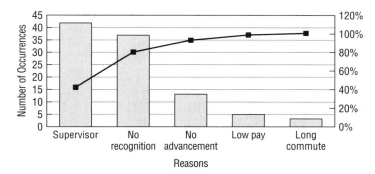

**Cause and effect diagram** A *cause and effect diagram* aids in organizing information during brainstorming sessions. This quality analysis tool is also known as the Ishikawa diagram or fishbone diagram. In Figure 5.4, I use it to analyze what PHR/SPHR candidates can do to maximize their chances for success on the exam.

**FIGURE 5.4** Cause and effect diagram

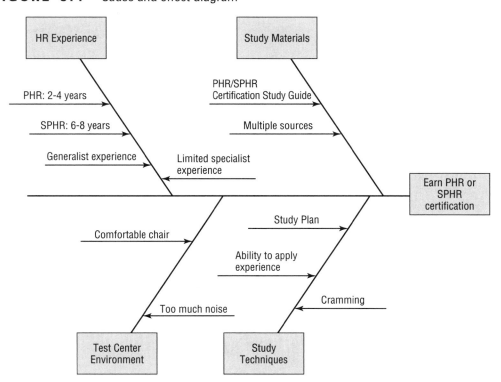

**Stratification**  *Stratification charts* show the individual components of a problem in addition to the total or summary. This aids in identifying possible strategies for correcting problems. Figure 5.5 is an example of a stratification chart. In our resignation example, the shorter bars represent components of each category, the taller bar is the total amount. For example, the poor supervision reasons could be broken down into categories for poor management skills and the inability to delegate. This kind of chart aids in the development of appropriate programs to solve the individual problems that make up a whole.

**FIGURE 5.5**  Stratification chart

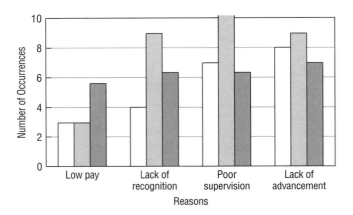

**Scatter charts**  See Chapter 2 for more information on scatter charts and the concept of correlation.

**Process control charts**  *Process control charts* provide a graphical representation of elements that are out of the acceptable range by setting parameters above and below the range. This tool is most effective for determining variances in production processes over time. While this tool is generally used in a production context, to help you understand how it works, let's look at how it could be applied in an HR context.  Let's say your department has established that open positions will be filled within 30 days from the date of notification to the HR department with a five-day grace period. The sample process control chart in Figure 5.6 shows you that two positions were out of the normal range: one took less than 25 days and the other took more than 35 days. Both of these are considered to be "out of control" and warrant investigation to determine what caused the variance.

**FIGURE 5.6**  Process control chart

**Philip B. Crosby**    Philip B. Crosby's approach to quality, unlike that of Deming and Juran, focused on management as the key to quality. His approach is based on strategic planning as the means to accomplish a high level of quality. Crosby advanced four absolutes of quality:

**Conformance to requirements**    Crosby believed that once management clearly described what was required, quality could be determined by whether or not the product met the standard.

**Prevention**    "Do it right the first time" is a phrase Crosby associated with this absolute.

**Performance standards**    "Zero defects" is another term Crosby came up with to describe the quality standard that should be met.

**Measurement**    In Crosby's view, quality should be measured by the additional cost of not producing zero-defect products the first time.

Although TQM originated in manufacturing environments, its concepts translate easily to service and other industries. For example, a public accounting firm can establish standards and then develop checklists and templates for accountants to follow when providing client services. By emphasizing the importance of accuracy and measuring how many corrections must be made, the firm can quantify the work of its accountants to ensure that it is up to the standards it established.

## High Involvement Organizations

In *high involvement organizations*, employees are involved in designing their own work processes, empowered to take the actions necessary to complete their work, and accountable for the results. Jobs in these organizations are broadly defined within self-directed work teams. These organizations are characterized by flat hierarchies in which continuous feedback is provided and information flows between and among work teams.

As discussed in the introduction to this chapter, OD strategies address organization-wide issues while HRD strategies concentrate on individuals or groups within the organization. The next two sections provide a review of HRD strategies that are used to improve the ability of an organization to achieve its goals by developing its employees.

# Human Process Interventions

Human process interventions are directed at developing competencies at the individual level within the organization. Common interventions in this area include teambuilding activities, leadership and management development, supervisory training, conflict resolution, management by objective programs, and developing an understanding of emotional intelligence and the impact it can have on organizational success.

## Teambuilding Activities

In order for a team to function effectively, the members must know the goals they are working toward and what is expected of them as team members. Teambuilding exercises build relationships within the team to communicate expectations and to involve team members in developing creative and effective ways of accomplishing their goals. Teambuilding activities run the gamut from expensive events staged by consultants, such as wilderness adventures, to games devised by managers in their individual work groups. The goal of any teambuilding activity is to put team members in unusual situations in which they must rely on each other to solve a problem. These activities are fun and effective methods for starting the process, but to be fully effective they must be reinforced when team members are back in the normal routine.

## Leadership Development

Chapter 2 reviewed various leadership theories used to explain how a leader becomes a leader. However that happens, effective leaders are crucial to the success of organizations. They are responsible for inspiring everyone in the organization to achieve the goals they set, and those who do this well are rewarded with a motivated and committed workforce. Leaders must be creative individuals who are able to project future needs and aim the organization in a direction that will be successful for the long term. They must be able to inspire trust and confidence and challenge others to put forth their best efforts.

Leaders must also be able to balance the needs of the various constituencies in the organization from the Board of Directors, who represent the owners; to the management team who are responsible for implementing the goals; to employees, who are on the front line of the organization working with customers to achieve organization goals.

A *leadership development* program seeks out employees who show promise as potential leaders. Some of the elements of such programs include the following:

**Leadership training**   Leadership training programs can be a combination of classroom training in specific areas, sponsorship of an advanced degree program such as an MBA, and hands-on training with a mentor or coach. It may mean time spent in company operations outside the country, in different divisions within the country, or in different functional areas. Leaders who are exposed to various facets of the organization are better able to understand the various needs and challenges of these areas and thus are more effective in the leadership role.

**Mentoring programs**   In a business context, a mentor is generally an experienced individual who acts as a teacher, guide, counselor, or facilitator and provides personalized feedback and guidance to a more junior colleague. In many cases, a mentor is someone who takes an interest in an employee's career and acts as a sponsor for them, providing a sounding board for issues and decisions. Traditionally, the mentor relationship is based more on an informal personal interest than on a formal program. *Mentoring programs* formalize this concept and ensure that the benefits of mentoring are available to a diverse group of employees who demonstrate leadership potential.

Formal mentors are those approved by an organization to take on protégés after being screened to ensure that only those who are best suited for mentor relationships enter the program. Mentors in formal programs receive training to develop skills in mentoring, and both mentors and mentees receive training to ensure everyone understands what to expect from the relationship.

A relatively new feature of mentoring is the *reverse mentor*. These are young individuals who help older coworkers understand technology and the culture of the "younger generation."

**Fast track programs**   Unlike a mentoring program, a *fast track program* provides specific training opportunities to individuals who have been identified as having high potential for leadership.

These programs generally ensure that fast-tracked employees are given priority for assignments designed to broaden their experience and leadership ability.

**Coaching programs**    A coach is typically a specialist who becomes involved, often at the organization's expense, to develop an employee in a particular area; for example, to hone leadership skills, or to improve communications skills. Some coaches can offer guidance in many areas. However, ultimately, they differ from mentors in that they focus on skills rather than development.

 **Real World Scenario**

**Process Council and Facilitators**

When organizations get employees involved with team building, leadership, and process improvement, the result can improve organizational processes as well as morale.

One San Francisco Bay Area organization has given the responsibility of process updating and building to a Process Council. Process Council members are specifically chosen for their leadership abilities, experience at the organization, and knowledge of how the organization operates as a whole. When a process issue is identified, the Process Council decides whether a team is needed to tackle the problem. With the help of upper management, the Process Council recommends team members and a team leader and facilitator and provides the leader with a charter outlining the council's expectations for the team. The Process Council meets quarterly to discuss process issues, appoint new teams, and discuss teams in progress.

The organization appoints several facilitators to help the Process Council teams meet their goals. Facilitators are chosen for their leadership abilities, their work with various employees across the organization, and their energetic personalities. Facilitators are specifically trained to provide a safe, objective environment in which team members can discuss the process issue at hand without judgment or criticism. Facilitators guide team members by asking pointed questions, politely interrupting "timer robbers" (those who talk incessantly with no relevance to the team goal), and keep members on track to solve the issue in a timely manner.

The Process Council and facilitators have tackled several cross-departmental problems and have even been involved with two reorganizations that occurred as a result of Process Council team decisions. Because facilitators and Process Council members are also employees at the organization who will be affected by Process Council team results, they have a vested interest in team success. They are also trained to tackle day-to-day problems that may not need a team discussion.

## Management Development

Chapter 2 described the various styles of management in some detail, from the authoritarian Theory X to the opposite participative management styles. Each organization develops a preferred management style, very often based on the style of its leader. A *management development* program seeks to upgrade skills such as motivating employees, delegating work, managing time and productivity, setting goals, planning and communicating effectively. Management skills are different from leadership skills. While leaders must inspire, managers must keep people on track; while leaders must innovate, managers must implement. Managers must be able to motivate employees, understand that not all are motivated for the same reasons, and be able to adjust their techniques to encourage each individual to excel.

## Supervisory Training

*Supervisory training* usually involves topics related to interactions with employees, such as progressive discipline, performance appraisals, workplace safety, interviewing, and training. In addition, supervisors need to be trained on employment laws such as the ADA and FMLA so that they understand the exposure to the organization for dealing inappropriately with issues related to those and other employment laws.

## Employee Development

During the discussion of staffing plan development in Chapter 4, "Workforce Planning and Employment," I introduced the concepts of succession and replacement planning. These concepts identify employees who are capable of moving into positions of greater responsibility in the organization. While succession plans are geared for management and executive level positions, replacement planning can be used effectively at all levels in the organization.

## Conflict Resolution

Conflict occurs whenever people work together; it can affect relationships between individuals or groups and cover a wide range of intensity levels. *Conflict resolution* is a process of developing strategies for resolving issues and maintaining or rebuilding effective working relationships. These interventions can be conducted by a direct supervisor or manager, an HR professional, or in some cases, a consultant who specializes in this process. The nature and intensity of the conflict will determine which solution will be most effective in a specific case.

## Management by Objectives

A *management by objectives (MBO)* intervention aligns individuals with organization goals and measures the successful attainment of objectives as well as the quality and/or quantity of performance. Because it is an effective way of tying results to goals, MBO is often used as a performance appraisal tool. Its application and acceptance results, at least in part, from its philosophy that rewarding people for what they accomplish is important. The MBO process is built on the concepts of mutual involvement in setting performance goals, ongoing communications during the performance period (usually a year), and measurement and reward for accomplishments at the end of the period. The process identifies and clarifies expectations and provides for a broad assessment of individual performance. It usually begins in the first quarter of each fiscal year when the supervisor and the employee agree upon a few significant business objectives, such as sales volume, new business development, completion of specific projects, or achievement of other specific goals. You'll recall from Chapter 3 that utilizing the SMART goal process will result in goals that clearly communicate what is expected.

The use of an MBO process to tie individual goals to corporate goals and objectives has value but must consider the rapid pace of change in the current business environment and use goals that are broad enough to be meaningful for the entire review period.

## Emotional Intelligence

*Emotional intelligence (EI or EQ)* describes how people deal with their feelings and how they perceive and interact with others. On an individual level, understanding yourself and why you react to others in the way you do increases your ability to work well with others in general. In an organizational setting, individuals who understand how their feelings impact their thought processes can increase their ability to collaborate with coworkers and influence relationships within the organization.

An EI intervention seeks to improve individual interactions and increase individual effectiveness. Individuals who are able to influence and motivate others are able to move the organization more rapidly toward successful accomplishment of its goals. While EI is not particularly necessary in organizations characterized by strictly authoritarian management methods, it is a necessary component for business environments seeking to manage with more facilitative models. EI competencies, while not a substitute for technical expertise, are essential in growing and developing successful organizations.

# Human Resource Management Interventions

OD interventions in the human resource management category focus on individuals within the organization. Some examples of these types of interventions include:

- Designing jobs that increase employee satisfaction.
- Developing hiring and selection procedures that attract people with the KSAs needed by the organization (as discussed in Chapter 4).
- Developing reward systems (discussed in Chapter 6, "Compensation and Benefits") that provide incentives for employees to exceed expectations.
- Developing performance management systems that develop individuals for future needs in the organization.
- Developing diversity programs that blend employees from various backgrounds into cohesive work units for the organization.

Two examples of human resource management interventions are performance management systems and diversity programs. The former focuses on developing individuals into productive members of an organization by providing performance feedback; the latter focuses on promoting understanding of individual diversity within the workforce.

## Performance Management Systems

*Performance management* is an ongoing process of providing feedback for employees about their performance to develop them into increasingly productive contributors to the organization. This process ensures that employees are on the right track for completion of their goals, that individual goals are aligned with organization goals, and that employees receive the support they need to be successful. The performance management process provides for an employee's professional development within the context of organizational needs.

Effective performance management must be based on an agreement between the manager or supervisor and the employee about what the job requires. This information comes from the organization's strategic plan, the manager's goals and objectives, and the employee's essential job functions as contained in an accurate job description. With these elements, the parties can develop individual goals and objectives and agree upon the standards of performance to be used in measuring results.

One important aspect of performance management is the *performance appraisal*, *performance evaluation*, or *performance review* process. These three terms are used interchangeably to describe the process of reviewing how well employees perform their duties during a specified review period. There are three factors in the appraisal process that are important to understand: the timing of review cycles, the methods used, and the elements included in an appraisal process.

## Timing Appraisals

Performance appraisals can be conducted either on employee anniversary dates or during an organization-wide focal review period. In organizations that time reviews to coincide with employee anniversary dates, managers conduct individual reviews throughout the year. The advantage to this process is that there are fewer reviews to conduct at one time; disadvantages occur when awarding salary increases and when utilizing comparative appraisal methods. Managers who do not plan adequately for salary increases may find that increases for high performers toward the end of the year are lower than increases awarded earlier in the year. It is also difficult to use comparative appraisal methods when appraisals occur on individual employee anniversary dates because the manager will need to consider the performance of employees not up for review at the same time.

During a *focal review period*, all employees in the organization are reviewed at the same time. This is more difficult for managers, as well as for HR, due to the sheer volume of reviews that must be completed. On the other hand, the focal process provides managers with an opportunity to allocate salary increases to appropriately reflect individual performance levels. Comparative appraisal methods are more easily conducted during a focal review as well.

## Performance Appraisal Methods

Employee performance appraisal may be based on quantitative data, such as whether or not specific goals were accomplished, or on more qualitative factors. There is currently much discussion in the HR field about the effectiveness of traditional performance appraisal processes. Some HR texts suggest that appraisal systems be abolished and replaced with more effective methods of providing feedback and developing employees. However, there are a number of methods that have been developed for use in evaluating employee performance; all of them can be placed in one of four basic categories: comparison, rating, essay, and behavioral.

**Comparison methods**   Comparison appraisal methods compare the performance of individuals or employees to each other. The most common methods of comparison are ranking, paired comparison, and forced ranking.

**Ranking**   In the *ranking* method, employees are listed in order from the highest to the lowest performer. This method works well for small groups of employees but becomes increasingly difficult as the size of the group increases.

**Paired comparison**   In the *paired comparison* method, all employees in the group are compared to one employee at a time. For example, if there are three employees in the work group, Susan, Jack, and Rachel, Susan's performance is compared to Jack's and Rachel's, Jack's performance is compared to Susan's and Rachel's and finally, Rachel's performance is compared to Susan's and Jack's.

**Forced ranking**   Also known as *forced distribution* or *forced choice*, *forced ranking* requires managers to rank employees according to the bell curve, rating a small group of employees at the high end, a small group at the low end, and the bulk of the employees in the average range. This appraisal tool can be utilized as part of any of the appraisal methods to reduce the effects of the leniency or harshness biases discussed in detail in Chapter 4.

**Rating methods**   Common rating methods for performance appraisal include the use of rating scales and checklists.

**Rating scales**   Rating scales may be numeric, with ratings of 1 through 5 to differentiate levels of performance, or may use phrases such as "exceeds expectations," "meets expectations," or "does not meet expectations." Rating scales attempt to quantify what is a very subjective process, but because of the different ways in which the descriptors are interpreted by raters, these scales are not as objective as they may appear at first glance.

**Checklists**   A performance checklist is a list of statements, phrases, or words that describe levels of performance. For example, "always finishes work on time." The reviewer checks off those that best describe the employee. The various descriptions may be weighted and used to calculate a rating score.

**Narrative methods**   Narrative methods of appraisal require managers to describe the employee's performance. These include critical incident, essay, and field reviews.

**Critical incident**   The *critical incident review* process requires that during the review period supervisors make notes for each employee of successful and unsuccessful performance issues. At the time of the review, the supervisor is able to review these critical incidents and present them to employees in a written narrative.

**Essay**   An *essay review* requires the reviewer to write a short description of each employee's performance during the year. This format provides maximum flexibility for managers to cover areas they feel are most important to improving employee performance.

**Field review**   A *field review appraisal* may be conducted by someone other than the supervisor. This can be an HR practitioner or someone from outside the organization.

**Behavioral methods**   The best-known behavioral review method is the *behaviorally anchored rating scale (BARS)*. The BARS method uses the job description to create dimensions that represent the most important requirements of the job. For each dimension, anchor statements are created to represent varying levels of performance behaviors that describe rating numbers on a scale. For example, a job dimension for a receptionist might be greeting customers. The anchors for measuring the behaviors associated with this job dimension could be:

5.      Greeted customers warmly and made them feel welcome.

4.      Was pleasant to the customers and answered their questions.

3.   Was courteous to the customer.

4.   Finished a phone call before greeting the customer.

5.   Was rude to the customer when they approached the desk.

**Continuous feedback**   The most effective review process is a *continuous feedback program* that addresses basic employee/employer needs on an ongoing basis throughout the review period. This provides employees with the support they need to be successful in their work, eliminates surprises when projects are completed and submitted, and reduces the stress related to providing feedback only once a year, or only when things go wrong.

Regardless of the review method utilized in an organization, raters should be aware of the various biases that can impact the fairness of a review. It is also important to keep in mind that the same bias and errors described in Chapter 4's discussion of interviewer bias, such as the halo/horn effect, leniency, harshness and similar-to-me errors, can influence a review. Supervisors should be cognizant of this when preparing the review. When bias is a concern, organizations can use a process known as inter-rater reliability, which uses multiple raters to reduce the possibility of rating errors due to bias. The scores of all raters are averaged, with the goal of providing a review that is as free from bias as possible.

## Elements of Performance Appraisals

Performance appraisals are stressful for both supervisors and employees. Continuous feedback reduces the level of stress involved because the process becomes a regular part of daily routine instead of an annual review of mistakes made during the year. Regardless of the type of appraisal that is conducted, however, there are several elements that should be included as part of an effective annual review:

**Supervisor assessment**   The supervisor's assessment begins with a review of the goals and objectives set at the beginning of the review cycle and whether or not the anticipated results were achieved. The supervisor must then evaluate whether any deficiencies were due to inadequate performance by the employee or whether they were the result of circumstances outside the employee's control, such as a change in the organization's direction. The supervisor must then develop a plan to address the discrepancies.

**Employee self-assessment**   Because this process is meant to be a two-way conversation, employees should be asked to assess their own performance at this time. Giving employees advance notice of the scheduled review meeting allows time for reflection about their past performance as well as goals they may have for the future and areas of professional development that are of interest to them.

**Assessment from others**   It is important for supervisors to obtain feedback from those with whom the employee has contact each day to find out if there are areas of concern or outstanding performance of which the supervisor may not be aware. When this is part of the formal review process, it is known as a 360° review and includes feedback from coworkers, internal and external customers, vendors, and subordinates.

**Goal setting**   A key component of the review is planning for the future using changes to the strategic plan and the supervisor's goals and objectives to help plan the employee's goals.

**Development goals**   As part of the review, supervisors can provide training opportunities for employees to address any areas of deficiency or to prepare them for the next level.

Performance management is not a once-a-year proposition—for maximum effectiveness, it must be an ongoing process that enables a manager to intervene in the early stages if an employee is getting off track.

## Diversity Programs

Discussed in more detail in Chapter 2, diversity programs are designed to ensure that all members of the organization are treated equitably and to facilitate understanding between employees with widely divergent cultural backgrounds. Diversity programs can be used as a human resource management intervention to help individuals feel more connected within the company and promote understanding and tolerance among employees.

# Training Programs

Training is an effective tool for improving productivity and increasing operational efficiency, but it is not the answer to every organizational problem. Training can solve problems that are related to employee skills or knowledge about a specific process, but it cannot solve problems caused by structural or system issues. Before developing a training program, it's important to find out what is causing the problem and if training is the appropriate solution.

For example, if customer service representatives (CSRs) are expected to handle an average of 20 calls per hour and they are handling an average of 12, it is important to find out why. One possibility is that the CSRs are not familiar enough with the products to answer the questions easily, so they must look up answers in the manual. Another possibility is that the call volume has tripled since the call center phone system was installed and it can no longer handle the load so it is frequently offline. The first possibility can be resolved with training, but the second cannot.

Training may take place at one of three levels: organizational, task, or individual.

**Organizational**   *Organizational level training* may encompass the entire organization or a single division or department. At this level, training is focused on preparing for future needs. From an HRD viewpoint, analysis of organizational effectiveness can be an indicator of the need for a training intervention. A high number of accidents, a change in strategic direction or addition of a new product line, as well as employee satisfaction and productivity measures are all indicators that training is needed at this level.

**Task**    *Task level training* involves processes performed in a single job category. The need for training at this level may be indicated by low productivity for a single process or poor quality results.

**Individual**    *Individual level training* involves a review of performance by individual employees and can be indicated by poor performance reviews or requests for assistance by the employee.

While development programs address long-term organizational needs, training programs are designed to address short-term needs. Training activities are more technical in nature and include such topics as new-hire orientation, safety, and skill development, among others. The design and development of training programs follows an instructional design model known as the *ADDIE model*. ADDIE is an acronym that describes the five elements of instructional design:

- Analysis
- Design
- Development
- Implementation
- Evaluation

The ADDIE model is discussed here in the context of training at the task level, but the principles of the model can be used to develop training programs at the organizational or individual levels as well.

## Analysis

The basic process for analyzing training needs is very similar to the generic needs analysis process described in Chapter 2. The following process addresses issues unique to assessing training needs.

Training needs are often identified by managers who notice a problem in their departments and determine that training is needed to correct it. This determination may be based on a drop in the production rate, installation of new machinery or equipment, or the addition of a new line of business. Once the need for training has been identified, HRD performs a needs analysis to determine whether or not training will solve the problem and, if it will, to propose possible solutions.

Following is a sample needs assessment for analyzing training needs.

1. Identify goal.

    The needs assessment begins by identifying the desired outcome. In the preceding example, the Customer Service Manager determined that the CSRs should handle an average of 20 calls per hour, which is the desired outcome. The desired outcome forms the basis for several other steps in the analysis process, including what data is collected, the identification of instructional goals, and development of solutions.

2. Gather and analyze data.

    Once you know the desired outcome, you can begin to collect relevant information that will be used to determine the cause of the problem. Information may be gathered in a number of ways from a variety of sources:

    **Review documents**    There are many types of documents that can be used to gather information about training needs. These include measures of organizational effectiveness such as production records and records of customer complaints, a review of the human resource succession plan to determine what training is needed to prepare individuals for future needs based on skills inventories and performance appraisal forms, and an analysis of the organizational climate based on HR metrics such as turnover rates and the results of exit interviews.

**Ask people**   There are many methods for gathering information from people, including observations; interviews with employees, supervisors, or subject matter experts (SMEs); attitude surveys; questionnaires; focus groups; or advisory committees. In Chapter 7, "Employee and Labor Relations," these techniques are discussed in more detail.

**Test employees**   Some options for testing employee knowledge to determine if training is needed include assessment centers, knowledge tests to measure what people know, and practical tests to determine if they know how to apply what they know.

**Analyze jobs**   In some cases, it may be necessary to conduct a full job analysis to determine where training is needed.

When the data has been gathered and analyzed, a determination can be made as to whether or not training is the appropriate solution. If it is, the needs analysis continues; if not, HRD can report the results of the analysis to the requesting manager with a recommendation for an appropriate solution.

3. Identify the performance gap.

   Once all the data has been gathered, it is possible to compare where the organization is to where it wants to be. At this stage, the HRD professional begins to have a sense of the type of training that will be required.

4. Identify instructional goals.

   The performance gap is the starting point for identifying the corrections that need to be put into place.

5. Propose solutions.

   At this stage in the needs assessment, all possible means for filling the gap should be identified and considered to find the solution that best meets the organization's needs.

6. Evaluate options and estimate budget impact and training time line.

   Once a comprehensive list of possible solutions is available, it is possible to conduct a cost-benefit analysis (described in Chapter 4) to estimate the cost of implementing each of them and the benefits that will result from the training. It is important to include both direct and indirect costs associated with the program in the estimated budget. This includes the cost of the trainer, facility, preparation of materials, use of equipment, transportation, meals and lodging costs, wages and salaries of the participants for the time they spend training and in traveling to the training, and the cost of lost production time due to the training and incidental office support costs. It is also important to consider potential savings, increased productivity, reduced errors, better quality, and other similar gains that will result from the training and, finally, what it will cost the organization if the training does not occur.

At the same time, an estimate of the time required to implement the solution can be made.

The result of the needs assessment should be a proposal that describes the desired outcome, the current situation, and the gap between the two. The proposal should include as many alternative solutions as is feasible, with an estimate of the cost and time needed to implement each of them and HRD's proposed solution.

During the assessment phase, a key consideration will be whether the program will be created internally, if a prepackaged program will be used, or whether the process will be outsourced. These decisions are based on a variety of factors unique to every organization and include the size of the organization, training expertise and availability of in-house staff, the uniqueness of the subject matter, and availability of prepackaged programs on the topic. For example, sexual harassment training may be best conducted by a trainer specializing in the subject matter who is able to answer in-depth questions about technical aspects and "what-if" scenarios. Conversely, a training program that is specific to a proprietary manufacturing process may be better developed in house.

## Design

During the design phase of a training project, the program begins to take shape. The data gathered during the needs analysis phase will be useful in this stage as well.

1. Compile a task inventory.

   To complete the design process, the trainer must know what tasks are a part of the job in question. A task inventory lists all tasks included in the job. Each should contain an action verb, an object, and a function. The inventory can be compiled from the information collected during the needs assessment process, or additional information can be acquired during the design phase. The inventory may also be gleaned from a job description if it was written as a result of a job analysis.

2. Identify the target audience.

   Knowing who will be attending the training will be of great use in designing a program that will keep the audience interested. Preparing a training program about proper completion of expense reports for a group of middle managers from the accounting department will look very different from the same presentation to the sales force.

   In identifying the audience, it is important to keep in mind the three learning styles that impact an individual's ability to learn: visual, auditory, or kinesthetic. *Visual learners* retain information better when they can see or read it. *Auditory learners* retain information more easily when they hear it, and *kinesthetic learners* retain information best when they are able to have a hands-on experience during training.

3. Develop training objectives.

   Keeping in mind the target audience, and with the task inventory in hand, the trainer can develop the training objectives for the course.

   A training objective is a statement that describes a measurable outcome of the training. Objectives help the HRD professional focus the development process and during training let the employee know what they will learn. They are also useful during the evaluation phase of training.

Effective training objectives are precise descriptions of what is to be accomplished in normal job circumstances. For example, a training program for carpenters may include a session on building walls that are straight. The objective begins with a description of a normal job situation, uses an action verb to describe a measurable behavior, describes the conditions under which the behavior will occur, and finally describes the criteria that will be used to measure the results. An objective that includes all these elements could be something like this:

"Given the necessary materials and tools, build a wall that is perfectly plumb." This objective leaves no doubt about what is to be accomplished and includes the basis for determining whether or not the training was successful.

4. Develop the course content.

Using the training objectives that management has developed, the trainer can begin to design the course, identifying what material should be included to best prepare the attendees to take the information back to their jobs and begin using it immediately.

An important consideration for this aspect of training design is the learning curve associated with various subjects. A *learning curve* is a graphical representation of the rate of learning over time. Let's look at some examples of various learning curves:

**Negatively accelerating learning curve**   A *negatively accelerating learning curve* is characterized by rapid increases in learning at the beginning that taper off as the learner becomes more familiar with the process or task. Negative learning curves are representative of routine tasks, for example, operating a cash register. Figure 5.7 provides an example of this learning curve.

**FIGURE 5.7**   Negatively accelerating learning curve

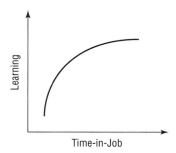

Positively accelerating learning curve**   A *positively accelerating learning curve* is characterized by a slow start in learning that increases as the learner masters different aspects of the process or task. Positive learning curves are representative of tasks that are complex, such as a junior accountant learning to use an accounting software program. The accountant must first know basic accounting practices in order to become proficient in using the program. Figure 5.8 shows a positive learning curve.

**FIGURE 5.8**    Positively accelerating learning curve

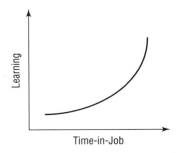

S-shaped learning curve   The *S-shaped learning curve* is a combination of positive and neg-ative learning curves. It begins with a slow learning process that accelerates over time and then slows down again. This learning pattern can be found in software conversion projects. The system users must understand how the new system works before they are able to become as proficient at it as they were with the older system. Figure 5.9 is an example of an S-shaped learning curve.

**FIGURE 5.9**    S-shaped learning curve

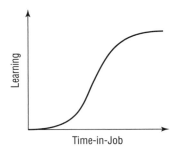

Plateau curve   A *plateau learning curve* begins with a rapid increase in knowledge that levels off after a period of time, and no additional progress occurs for an extended period of time. A plateau curve might occur when an employee performs a task irregularly, not often enough to become proficient. Figure 5.10 shows a plateau learning curve.

**FIGURE 5.10**    Plateau learning curve

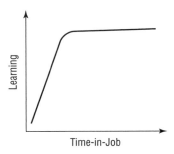

**5.** Develop evaluation criteria.

Now is the time to develop the evaluation criteria for the program. The initial evaluation will be based on whether or not the trainees are able to perform the task described by the objective within the parameters that it sets forth. The real evaluation of training effectiveness is whether or not the trainees are able to maintain the level of proficiency that was developed during the training.

# Development

During the training development phase, the program design is translated into the presentation format. The program developer creates a strategy for the presentation, deciding on the materials that will be used and the learning activities that will be included, and creating tests for participants. The trainer may conduct a pilot presentation during this phase to "work out the kinks" and, if necessary, will revise the program based on the results of the pilot.

One of the activities occurring during the development phase of the training process is the collection of appropriate training materials. It is often tempting to use work created by others, particularly if the material is perfectly suited to the topic of training. Two federal laws protect the rights of writers, artists, and inventors with regard to unauthorized use of their original works: the Copyright Act of 1976 and the U.S. Patent Act.

## Copyright Act of 1976

The use of musical, literary, and other original works without permission of the owner of the copyright is prohibited under most circumstances. The copyright owner is, for the most part, the author of the work. There are two exceptions to this. The first is that an employer who hires employees to create original works as part of their normal job duties is the owner of the copyright because the employer paid for the work to be done. The second exception is that the copyright for work created by a freelance author, artist, or musician who has been commissioned to create the work by someone else is owned by the person who commissioned the work. These exceptions are known as work-for hire exceptions.

For trainers who want to use the work of others during training sessions, there are two circumstances that do not require permission. The first is related to works that are in the *public domain*. Copyrights protect original works for the life of the author plus 70 years; after that, the works may be used without permission. Works for hire are protected for the shorter of 95 years from the first year of publication or 120 years from the year of creation.

Other works in the public domain include those produced as part of the job duties of federal officials and those for which copyright protection has expired. Some works published without notice of copyright before January 1, 1978, or those published between then and March 1, 1989, are also considered to be in the public domain.

The second circumstance for use of published works without permission is known as fair use. The act specifies that use of a work for the purposes of criticism, commentary, news reporting, teaching (including multiple copies for classroom use, scholarship or research) is not an infringement depending upon four factors:

**1.** The purpose and character of the use: is it to be used for a profit or nonprofit educational purpose?

**2.** The nature of the work itself.

3.  How much of the work (1 copy or 50?) or what portion (one paragraph or an entire chapter?) of the work will be used?

4.  What effect will the use of the material have on the potential market value of the copyrighted work?

## U.S. Patent Act

A *patent* allows inventors exclusive rights to the benefits of an invention for a defined period of time. Patent laws in the United States define three types of patents:

**Design patents**   *Design patents* protect new, original, and ornamental designs of manufactured items. Design patents are limited to 14 years.

**Utility patents**   *Utility patents* protect the invention of new and useful processes, machines, manufacture or composition of matter, and new and useful improvements to the same. Utility patents are limited to 20 years.

**Plant patents**   *Plant patents* protect the invention or discovery of asexually reproduced varieties of plants for 20 years.

## Training Materials

Aside from considerations related to the use of copyrighted material, training materials developed in the development phase should be appropriate to the subject matter and the needs of the participants. Some types of materials to consider include:

**Leader guide**   When more than one trainer will be presenting the training sessions, a leader guide is developed to ensure consistency in the presentations. These guides may provide notes to assist the trainer in presenting the material, timing information, and questions for use in facilitating discussion during the session. The guide provides a basic road map for the presentation.

**Manuals**   Manuals can provide a reference for participants when they return to their jobs to assist in reinforcing the information covered during the training session. In addition to an agenda or schedule, they can contain handouts and copies of slides for note-taking purposes as participants follow along during the presentation.

**Handouts**   Handouts may be used in place of a manual or included with the manual. For presentations that do not require a manual because they are relatively straightforward, a handout can help keep participants focused and provide a place to take notes. In addition, handouts can provide additional information that is not covered during the presentation but that is related to the presentation. When the material being covered is technical in nature, a handout can make it easier for participants to follow along and provide a reference for use when they return to their jobs.

# Implementation

Implementation is the phase of training where all the preceding work comes together for the presentation. The process begins with selection of the facility and trainers or facilitators. The trainers and facilitator set up a program schedule and notify participants of the training.

They also create the agenda. At this time, trainers confirm that they have the proper training for implementation (if they don't, they must be trained).

**Facility**   The facility selected for the training will depend on the type of training to be conducted, the number of participants and the amount budgeted for the program. While individual level training may best be conducted at the employee's work station, conducting training for larger groups of people is best done away from the distractions of the workstation. If the size of the group is small (or the room large enough), a conference room at the work site may provide an adequate training facility. It may be necessary for a variety of reasons to conduct the training offsite. While the cost will be greater to rent a room, the reduction of distractions may result in a more effective training experience with longer lasting results.

The amount of space needed for the training depends largely on what training activities will take place. Passive training that requires little more of participants than listening requires the least amount of space. More space is required for situations in which participants will be taking notes or practicing work activities. Table 5.1 describes some common seating styles for trainings and the type of trainings for which each is most appropriate:

**TABLE 5.1**   Types of Seating Styles

| Seating Style | Type of Training |
| --- | --- |
| Theater style | Lectures, films, and video presentations |
| Classroom style | Listening to presentations and taking notes |
| Banquet style | Small group discussions and group interaction |
| Chevron style | Interacting with a presenter and other trainees |
| Conference style | Group discussions among members of equal status |
| U-shaped style | Case discussions where everyone can observe each other and a trainer |

**Trainers**   Trainers may be selected based on their mastery of the subject matter or for their ability and skill in training. This decision will be based largely on the nature of the training being conducted.

**Schedule**   The training schedule is affected by many factors, including the feasibility of shutting down operations entirely for the length of the training session, and whether it is more cost effective to conduct multiple sessions in order to maintain operations.

# Evaluation

Training evaluation occurs after the training takes place and is based on criteria established in the assessment phase. The ultimate goal of the training is to improve performance on the job.

This is known as *transfer of training*, and occurs when learning occurs away from the regular work environment and must then be applied to the real job situation. It is obviously important that the investment made in training employees provide a return in increased productivity, quality, or safety (whatever the subject of the training) on the job. A failure of training to transfer to the job can occur when the new skill is not applied in the work environment so that it is reinforced. A technique that can overcome this problem is the development of an action plan to be implemented after training. This approach requires trainees to visualize and describe how they plan to apply the training when they are back on the job so they are more like to use their new skills. An effective evaluation will include provisions for measuring job performance for a period of time after the training has been completed to ensure that the new skills have been transferred to the job.

A common model for training evaluation was developed by Donald Kirkpatrick. He proposed four levels of evaluation for training programs: reaction, learning, behavior, and results. Measurements at each level are based on the objectives developed during the design phase.

**Reaction**   The *reaction evaluation method* measures the initial reaction of the participants. This is most commonly determined by a survey that is completed by participants at the end of the training. While this level of evaluation does not measure the organization impact, it does provide feedback for the trainer in terms of the presentation of the information.

**Learning**   The *learning evaluation method* uses a test to measure whether or not the participants learned the information that was presented. While this level of evaluation provides more information about the effectiveness of the training, it still does not provide feedback about the application of the information on the job.

**Behavior**   The *behavior evaluation method* measures job performance between six weeks and six months after the training. This follow-up evaluation can be based on observations, interviews, tests, or surveys and tells the trainer if the new skills were successfully transferred to the job.

**Results**   The *results evaluation method* provides the feedback most meaningful to the business: did the training have an impact on business results? The measurement compares an objective statement, such as, "This training will reduce product defects by 20 percent in 12 months," to the actual product results at the end of the 12-month period to determine its success.

# Unique Training Needs

As the workplace becomes more diverse and demographics change, HRD programs must be available to address the unique needs of various employees.

## Work-Family

The need for employers to consider the impact of family issues on an employee's performance has been increasing in the United States, due to pressure from an increasing number of dual-income families, an aging population, and government regulations. Employers respond to this in different ways. At one end of the spectrum are employers who comply with legal requirements but do not provide any additional leeway for employees who must deal with family issues. At the other end of the spectrum are companies like SAS, a software company in North Carolina that provides onsite childcare, an eldercare information and referral program, wellness programs, recreation and fitness facilities, and other benefits designed to assist employees in managing the balance between their work and the rest of their lives.

## Outplacement Services

*Outplacement* services are utilized to transition employees who are leaving the company, most often as the result of a downsizing or layoff. These services assist employees with updating resumes, preparing for interviews and the search process for a new job. Outplacement services are often provided in a group seminar setting for individuals who have been terminated.

Executive outplacement may occur as the result of a merger or acquisition and may include additional benefits, such as headhunting services and one-on-one counseling.

## Repatriation

As businesses become more globally oriented, issues of expatriating and repatriating employees will continue to grow. Issues of expatriate training were discussed in Chapter 4, but of equal concern to employees returning from expatriate assignments is how their careers will be impacted after having been away from the home office for an extended period.

As with all issues related to employee relations, it is crucial that appropriate expectations be set before employees begin their expatriate assignment, including the issue of what types of assignments will be available to them when they return to the home office. As business conditions at the home office change, the expatriate should be kept advised of any possible changes to the expectations for return assignments. Employees who expect to return to a position of equal or greater authority, responsibility, and pay but find themselves in a position they see as a demotion are understandably demotivated and provide a negative report to their coworkers of their experience. A formal repatriation program that includes a component of career planning services can assist employees in making the transition back to the home office. Returning expatriates can be a valuable resource for others entering expatriate assignments, and ensuring that the experience is a positive one will add value to the organization. For many companies, repatriation management and career planning are keys to developing global leadership in the long term.

Managing the repatriation process effectively includes time to debrief the repatriate personally, to assist in managing the transition back to the home country and professionally, to add to the knowledge base for the organization and increase its effectiveness in the global marketplace. The manager responsible for the repatriate plays a key role in the integration process by reacquainting the repatriate with corporate policies and politics.

With formal repatriation management and career planning strategies in place, companies will more effectively manage assignees' career expectations upon repatriation, retain their valuable international experience, and, as a result, maximize the return on investment for both the individual assignee and the organization as a whole.

# Summary

Human resource development (HRD) is tied closely to organization development (OD). HRD is more often tied to organizational "software" issues of change management, leadership and management development and performance management, while OD is generally utilized to address the "hardware" issues of the organization: developing its strategy, technology, and structure.

HRD/OD interventions address organizational challenges with such programs as learning organizations, total quality management, and management by objectives that are designed to align the workforce with the leaders and the organization strategy. These programs must be selected to fit in with the culture and strategy of the organization to be successful.

Development programs prepare talented individuals to accept positions of greater responsibility and authority in the organization and aid the retention of individuals who are key to its long-term success.

Training is an important aspect of HRD. The ADDIE model is used to develop training programs that address the needs of the organization and of individuals within the organization.

Finally, HRD programs that address the unique needs of some employees can be implemented to increase goodwill and attract and retain quality employees.

# Exam Essentials

**Understand and be able to describe the ADDIE model.**   The ADDIE model is an instruction design tool used in creating training programs and stands for Analysis, Design, Development, Implementation, and Evaluation.

**Be able to conduct a training needs analysis.**   A training needs analysis begins with an identification of the goal, the current level of training, and the performance gap. The analysis then identifies instructional goals, proposes solutions, estimates their budget impact, and recommends the preferred solution.

**Understand the connection between change management and OD.**   OD *is* change management. It seeks to address issues that prevent organizations from becoming fully effective and introduces interventions to align the workforce with the organization strategy.

**Be able to identify the five characteristics of a learning organization.**   The following five characteristics of a learning organization distinguish it from other organizations: systems thinking, personal mastery, mental models, building a shared vision, and team learning.

**Be able to identify the four types of training evaluation.**   The four types of evaluation are reaction, which measures immediate feedback; learning, which measures what was learned through testing; behavior, which measures job performance six months or more after training; and results, which measures whether or not the training had a positive impact on the bottom line.

# Key Terms

Before you take the exam, be certain you are familiar with the following terms:

ADDIE model

auditory learners

behavior evaluation method

behaviorally anchored rating scale (BARS)

cause and effect diagram

change agent

change process theory

check sheets

conflict resolution

continuous feedback program

critical incident review

design patents

Emotional intelligence (EI or EQ)

essay review

fast track program

field review appraisal

focal review period

forced choice

forced distribution

forced ranking

high involvement organizations

histograms

individual level training

kinesthetic learners

leadership development

learning curve

learning evaluation method

learning organizations

management by objectives (MBO)

management development

mental models

mentoring programs

negatively accelerating learning curve

organization culture

organization development (OD)

organization development (OD) interventions

organizational climate

organizational level training

outplacement

paired comparison

Pareto chart

patent

performance appraisal

performance evaluation

performance management

performance review

personal mastery

plant patents

plateau learning curve

positively accelerating learning curve

process control charts

public domain

ranking

reaction evaluation method

results evaluation method

reverse mentor

shared vision

s-shaped learning curve

stratification charts

supervisory training

systems thinking

task level training

team learning

Total Quality Management (TQM)

transfer of training

utility patents

visual learners

# Review Questions

1. _____ is one of several learning organization characteristics.

   **A.** An assessment center

   **B.** Massed practice

   **C.** Systems thinking

   **D.** Programmed instruction

2. Leadership and management styles, shared values and beliefs, and how the members of an organization behave is known as:

   **A.** Organization climate

   **B.** Organization culture

   **C.** Organization development

   **D.** Total Quality Management

3. In the evaluation phase, the _____ evaluation method focuses on how well the training resulted in learning new skills and competencies.

   **A.** Reaction

   **B.** Learning

   **C.** Behavior

   **D.** Results

4. Which of the following factors can adversely affect transfer of training?

   **A.** The trainer's expertise

   **B.** A lack of job reinforcement

   **C.** The subject of the training

   **D.** None of the above

5. A _____ learning curve begins slowly, with smaller learning increments but increases in pace and with larger increments as learning continues.

   **A.** positively accelerating

   **B.** negatively accelerating

   **C.** S-shaped

   **D.** plateau

6. The most common reason for the failure of organizational change initiatives is that

   **A.** The strategic plan was not communicated to employees.

   **B.** Organization leaders did not support the change.

   **C.** There was no training system in place.

   **D.** Employees were not prepared for the change.

7. The best quality tool to use for gathering information about a specific problem is:

    **A.** A Pareto chart

    **B.** An Ishikawa diagram

    **C.** A stratification chart

    **D.** A histogram

8. Which employee growth and assessment program is characterized by performance objectives?

    **A.** Behavioral-based performance assessment

    **B.** Skills-based performance assessment

    **C.** Management by objectives (MBO)

    **D.** Continuous feedback program

9. Which performance appraisal method would be used most effectively in a large, geographically dispersed organization with many similar jobs?

    **A.** critical incident

    **B.** forced ranking

    **C.** behaviorally anchored rating system

    **D.** field review

10. Mentoring involves someone

    **A.** Who monitors an employee's performance in doing their job.

    **B.** Whose goal is to develop an employee in a particular area.

    **C.** Who takes a personal interest in an individual's career and who guides and sponsors the individual.

    **D.** Who provides training in areas of interest to an employee.

# Answers to Review Questions

1. **C.**  Systems thinking refers to the characteristic of a learning organization that uses a variety of information-gathering techniques to acquire knowledge of new technology, determine its value, and convert this knowledge into new and improved practices and procedures.

2. **A.**  The culture of an organization is based on shared values and beliefs and the way in which members of the organization behave. In addition, the culture is affected by the style of its leaders and managers.

3. **B.**  The learning evaluation method focuses on how well the training resulted in learning new skills. The reaction evaluation method focuses on participant reactions. The behavior evaluation method measures on-the-job behavior changes as a result of training, and the results evaluation methods measures on organizational results. Of the four methods, the results evaluation method is considered the most valuable for the organization.

4. **B.**  A lack of job reinforcement can adversely affect transfer of training. Other adverse impacts are the result of interference from the immediate work environment and a nonsupportive organizational climate. The other choices may affect learning but would have little or no effect on transfer of training.

5. **A.**  The positively accelerating learning curve begins with smaller increments but increases in pace and size as learning continues. The negatively accelerating curve begins with larger increments that decrease as learning continues. The S-shaped learning curve is a combination of the positively and negatively accelerating learning curves, while a plateau occurs when no learning seems to take place.

6. **D.**  The most common reason for the failure of change initiatives is that people were not prepared for the change and given time to assimilate the reasons for the change. While a change in strategic direction is the basis for organization changes, failing to communicate it in and of itself will not lead to failure of a change initiative. Leaders who do not support change do have an influence on employees, but that factor alone is not the most common reason for failure.

7. **B.**  An Ishikawa diagram is an effective tool for organizing information about a problem when brainstorming with a group. The other tools are useful in analyzing data about production problems.

8. **C.**  The first three choices are all employee growth and assessment programs. Behavioral-based performance assessment focuses on behaviors, while skills-based performance assessment focuses on skills. MBO programs measure the successful attainment of objectives. The continuous feedback program is a performance management program.

9. **C.**  The BARS system is used most effectively in organizations with a number of jobs with similar duties. Because it is expensive and time-consuming to implement, an organization must have enough resources available to develop the program.

10. **C.**  A mentor is someone who takes a personal interest in an employee's career and who guides and sponsors them. While a supervisor may be a mentor, mentors are usually individuals who are outside the chain of command and may even be someone outside the organization.

# Chapter

# 6

# Compensation and Benefits

---

## THE HRCI TEST SPECIFICATIONS FROM THE COMPENSATION AND BENEFITS FUNCTIONAL AREA COVERED IN THIS CHAPTER INCLUDE:

- ✓ Ensure the compliance of compensation and benefits with applicable federal, state, and local laws.
- ✓ Analyze, develop, implement, and maintain compensation policies and a pay structure consistent with the organization's strategic objectives.
- ✓ Analyze and evaluate pay rates based on internal worth and external market conditions.
- ✓ Develop/select and implement a payroll system.
- ✓ Administer payroll functions.
- ✓ Evaluate compensation policies to ensure that they are positioning the organization internally and externally according to the organization's strategic objectives.
- ✓ Conduct a benefit plan needs assessment and determine/select the plans to be offered, considering the organization's strategic objectives.
- ✓ Implement and administer benefit plans.
- ✓ Evaluate benefits program to ensure that it is positioning the organization internally and externally according to the organization's strategic objectives.
- ✓ Analyze, select, implement, maintain, and administer executive compensation, stock purchase, stock options, and incentive, and bonus programs.
- ✓ Analyze, develop, select, maintain, and implement expatriate and foreign national compensation and benefit programs.
- ✓ Communicate the compensation and benefits plan and policies to the workforce.

Understanding compensation and benefit programs and their impact on the strategic objectives of an organization is a basic component of human resources. For those taking the PHR/SPHR exams, knowledge of federal employment laws governing compensation and benefits is essential. It is important to keep in mind that these federal laws and regulations may differ from state and local requirements, so be certain you understand the differences between them for the exams. Because this area of human resources is closely tied to the accounting function, understanding accounting practices as they relate to payroll, compensation calculations, and benefit reporting is required. Exam candidates must understand how to develop and implement fair pay practices utilizing job evaluation methods to price jobs and set pay structures for the organization. HR professionals must also be conversant with executive compensation needs and programs and understand noncash compensation methods.

An important component of any compensation program is the benefit plan. PHR/SPHR candidates should understand how to conduct a needs analysis and use it to propose and implement a program that meets the needs of the organization with a full range of benefits including medical and life insurance programs, educational reimbursements, fitness programs, and other programs to meet employee needs.

Finally, with the continuing globalization of business organizations, PHR/SPHR candidates need a basic understanding of international compensation and benefit laws as they apply to expatriates, host-country nationals, and third-country nationals, including mandated benefit programs.

This chapter provides a review of compensation and benefit practices and the impact they have on strategic organization goals.

# Compensation

At a high level, compensation can be described as an exchange of payment for the services provided by employees. In today's competitive economy, the total compensation package is vital to attracting, retaining, and motivating employees, and is therefore an extremely important component of any organization's human resource program.

The organization's culture drives its compensation philosophy and policies. Deciding how best to compensate employees for the work they do is based on various factors including internal value (the importance of jobs relative to each other), external value (economic factors, such as supply and demand) and the individual employee's knowledge, skills, and abilities (KSAs) demonstrated on the job.

I'll discuss these concepts in the coming sections. Let's start with establishing a definition for total compensation, the backbone of the organization's compensation programs.

# Total Compensation

*Total compensation* includes cash compensation, equity, benefits, and perquisites as well as other, nonmonetary rewards. Total compensation is the entire package—the items that attract employees to an organization and motivate and retain them. Let's take a look at the things that make up monetary and nonmonetary compensation.

**Monetary compensation**   Monetary compensation includes any costs the organization incurs for the benefit of employees, such as 401(k) matching, medical care premiums, pension plans, and paid time off. Other kinds of rewards include benefits that support the organization's culture such as stock options, Employee Stock Ownership Programs (ESOPs), and incentive plans.

**Nonmonetary compensation**   It is important to recognize that just as monetary rewards are critical to offering a competitive total compensation program, so are nonmonetary rewards. This chapter focuses primarily on tangible rewards, but providing an environment that supports nonmonetary intrinsic and extrinsic rewards is a very important part of the total compensation package.

An *intrinsic reward* is one that encourages individual employee self esteem, such as satisfaction from challenging and exciting assignments. An *extrinsic reward* is one in which esteem is achieved from others, such as fulfillment from working with a talented team of peers. The supervisor and employee relationship, recognition of accomplishments, and teamwork are a few examples of nonmonetary rewards. Nonmonetary rewards also include nontraditional benefits such as telecommuting, employee training, on-site child-care, and flex time. The motivational theories discussed in Chapter 2, "Core Knowledge Requirements for HR Professionals," help explain how these nonmonetary rewards can be used effectively in organizations. Theories such as Maslow's hierarchy of needs and McClelland's acquired needs theory help clarify how the individual's drive to achieve nonmonetary rewards such as belonging, esteem, and self actualization can be impacted with these reward systems.

Determining what constitutes total compensation for your organization is a major part of its compensation philosophy. Let's discuss this in greater detail next.

# Compensation Philosophy

*Compensation philosophy* is a high-level mission statement that guides the development and implementation of compensation programs to attract, motivate, and retain employees. The human resource department will typically partner with executive management in the development and approval of the organization's compensation philosophy.

Compensation philosophy can be deliberately created or revised or it can be the result of compensation programs developed and implemented over a period of time. When creating a compensation philosophy for a new organization, the HR management team can facilitate the process by gathering input from and building consensus with key stakeholders such as members of the executive team and, in organizations governed by a board of directors, involving board members in the process as well. Organizations that do not proactively define a compensation philosophy may have one that has developed over time as a result of compensation programs and decisions.

The challenge in developing a compensation philosophy comes from balancing the conditions that impact the organization. These can be split into two categories, internal and external conditions.

## Internal Conditions

Internal conditions include the organization's willingness and ability to pay. Financial constraints may prevent the organization from following through with a generous bonus program, for example. Cost-sensitive industries and competing priorities will impact the ability to introduce new programs and maintain existing ones.

Corporate culture, which I'll discuss in a moment, combined with the types of products and services offered, determines a "pecking order" for certain positions: businesses consciously or unconsciously identify the jobs that are the most valuable. Differentiating jobs is an important aspect of the compensation philosophy. For example, implementing an incentive program for the entire organization may not be feasible due to cost. In that case, the organization might choose to include jobs with the highest impact on the organization's success in an incentive program while jobs with less impact would be ineligible.

Another internal condition that impacts compensation philosophy is the organizational structure. Organizations that answer to a parent company or corporate headquarters will have additional constraints to consider when making compensation decisions, such as the need for conformance to the compensation philosophy of the parent corporation.

## External Conditions

Depending on external conditions, management must decide if the organization's *pay structure* will lead, match, or lag the market. If the organization's pay philosophy is to lead the market, it will pay above the market rate. If an organization wants (or finds it necessary for financial reasons) to lag, it will pay below the market rate. If an organization wants to pay the market rate, it will match the average market rate. This strategy is a key element in the organization's pay philosophy because it determines the development of salary structures, merit budgets, bonus programs, benefit programs, and other compensation programs.

Next, I will discuss corporate culture and its impact on compensation philosophy.

## Corporate Culture

You'll recall from Chapter 5, "Human Resource Development," that *corporate culture* is rooted in the values and beliefs advocated by an organization's leadership and the ways in which members of the organization behave. The compensation philosophy selected by the organization should reflect these factors. The philosophy determines whether pay is based on merit/performance or on seniority and how the total compensation package is divided among base salary, variable pay, equity pay, and benefits. To a certain degree, the culture of the organization dictates how these questions are answered.

**Performance-based philosophy**    Organizations with a *performance-based philosophy* uses compensation to shape a key component of the corporate culture, employee behavior, by rewarding performance or behavior that moves the organization closer to achievement of the goals established by its leaders.

In a performance-based culture, compensation programs have what is known as line of sight. *Line of sight* occurs when employees know that their performance, good or bad, impacts their pay. This provides an increased consciousness for associating behavior with a reward. If employees have the awareness that their performance impacts their rewards, both monetary and nonmonetary, a high performance culture can be created.

**Entitlement philosophy**    An *entitlement philosophy* rewards employee longevity. When pay is based on seniority, performance will be secondary to time with the company or time on the job. Rewarding seniority creates loyalty to the company and, ideally, benefits such as pension plans, stock options, and vacation accrual can reinforce the importance of seniority. I'll discuss seniority in more detail shortly.

An effective compensation philosophy complements the corporate culture, provides rewards for those who contribute to the achievement of organizational goals, and addresses internal and external conditions. The next section looks at various factors that must be considered when developing a compensation philosophy.

# Factors That Influence Compensation

Organizations must be aware of a variety of external factors when developing programs and administering compensation including economics, the labor market, competition in the marketplace, and other pressures such as those related to tax and accounting requirements and government legislation and regulations.

## Economic Factors

The ability of an organization to find qualified employees is affected by a number of economic factors at the local, national, and global levels including economic growth, inflation, interest rates, unemployment, and the comparative cost of living. These factors impact the *cost of labor*, or the cost to attract and retain individuals with the skills needed by the organization to achieve its goals. Organizations recruiting employees with a particular skill set create a competitive environment for individuals with those skills that results in an increase in the cost of labor. For example, when two large companies in a metropolitan area are hiring large numbers of experienced manufacturing technicians, the supply of individuals with this skill set is in demand and the availability of qualified individuals decreases. This combination of increased demand and decreased availability raises the competitive compensation rate for this skill set, thereby increasing the cost of labor.

With the increasingly competitive global economy, many industries are constantly assessing how to increase quality, accelerate time to market, and improve productivity. This increased intensity has resulted in a creative approach to organizing and redesigning work which, in turn, affects the skill sets needed by the organization and the cost to employ individuals with those skills.

## Labor Market

Organizations may need to revise their compensation programs to meet the demands of changing labor markets. The *labor market* is comprised of any sources from which an organization recruits new employees; a single organization may find itself recruiting from several different labor markets depending on the availability of skills for different positions. Ultimately, the combination of supply and demand for a certain skill set in the labor market impacts what the employers competing for those skills must pay to individuals who possess them. For example, during the unprecedented growth of the late '90s, intense competition for software engineering skills led to upwardly spiraling levels of compensation for individuals who possessed those skills. Because the U.S. labor market was not producing enough college graduates to meet the demand for qualified candidates, the labor market expanded to include candidates from other countries. This resulted in an increase in the annual immigration quota for the year 2000 to meet the demand of U.S. based companies for employees with these technical skills.

Labor markets vary by region and industry. In urban areas, there is a greater pool of candidates with a wider set of skills from which to select. Because there are more businesses in urban areas competing for this pool of candidates, urban environments may be more competitive, leading to an increase in the cost of labor. As a result, the cost of labor for a single skill set may vary widely between the areas in which an organization operates. To offset these differences, many companies utilize regional pay structures to reflect the market conditions of the different areas in which they have business locations. For example, a company that is headquartered in the southeast may have a different pay structure for their regional office in the Silicon Valley in California to reflect the higher cost of labor in that area.

Experts say the way people look at pay has changed because of the increased mobility of the workforce, the shift from a manufacturing economy to a knowledge-based economy, and the economic downturn. During the technology boom of the late '90s, job hopping and generous compensation packages were prevalent. Organizations recruited at a national level and were willing to relocate candidates because the labor market was so competitive. When the technology bubble burst and the unemployment rate increased, organizations were able to recruit for many positions locally, reducing the cost of labor. HR professionals must stay in contact with a changing labor market and ensure compensation programs achieve the desired objectives to maintain a competitive edge in the labor market.

## Market Competition

Competition in the marketplace places financial pressure on the organization and challenges its ability to attract and retain qualified employees. Increased competition creates pressure to do everything faster, better, and cheaper. These added pressures place a strain on the employee population. In a climate epitomized by strong competition between organizations, accompanied by a decrease in demand, issues related to the financial health of an organization will likely surface. Some of the repercussions of these pressures for employees can include wage freezes, which may result in skipping a merit review process; eliminating promotions; and/or not paying incentives. In a strong economy, increased competition can mean growth for the organization due to increasing demand resulting in increased financial rewards for employees. HR professionals must be aware of the implications of changes in the competitive environment to ensure that the programs they propose are in line with these pressures.

## Tax and Accounting

The Internal Revenue Service (IRS) affects compensation and benefits issues through its enforcement of federal tax legislation, such as social security and Medicare taxes, pension regulation, and enforcement of rules about some benefit programs (these will be discussed later in this chapter in the "Benefits" section). When an organization wants to make changes to compensation or benefit programs it may want to find out how the IRS will view the changes for tax purposes before it makes them. In that situation, it may be beneficial to request a *private letter ruling* from the IRS before the changes are made. These rulings apply only to the specific taxpayer and circumstances included in the request and are used to find out what the tax implications of a complex or unusual financial transaction will be.

Under the Securities Exchange Act of 1934, Congress gave statutory authority for establishing reporting standards for publicly held companies to the Securities and Exchange Commission (SEC). In 1939, the American Institute of Certified Public Accountants (AICPA) established a committee to develop accounting standards and reports for the private sector. This committee developed generally accepted accounting principles (GAAP) for use by accounting professionals. In 1972, an independent body, the *Financial Accounting Standards Board (FASB)*, was created by the AICPA to take over responsibility for setting accounting standards. FASB standards are officially recognized by the SEC as the authority for accounting practices. These standards are essential to the efficient functioning of the economy because investors, creditors, auditors, and others rely on credible, transparent, and comparable financial information. One FASB standard that is relevant to HR professionals is the requirement that the value of stock options be recognized as an expense.

You can find additional information about IRS requirements, FASB and its requirements, and the SEC at www.irs.gov, www.fasb.org and www.sec.gov, respectively.

## Legislation Governing Compensation

The industrial revolution led to advances in manufacturing technology and created challenging environments for workers in the United States. This led to the creation of a number of laws designed to protect workers from unfair pay practices and other abuses by employers. The next few sections provide an overview of federal legislation that relates to compensation issues.

### Davis Bacon Act (1931)

The Davis Bacon Act was the first federal legislation to regulate minimum wages. This act required that construction contractors and their subcontractors pay at least the prevailing wage for the local area in which they are operating if they receive federal funds. Employers with federal construction contracts of $2,000 or more must adhere to the Davis Bacon Act.

### Walsh Healy Public Contracts Act (1936)

The Walsh Healy Public Contracts Act requires government contractors with contracts exceeding $10,000 (for other than construction work) to pay their employees the prevailing wage for their local area as established by the Secretary of Labor.

### Service Contract Act (1965)

The Service Contract Act of 1965 requires any federal service contractor with a contract exceeding $2,500 to pay its employees the prevailing wage and fringe benefits for the geographic area in which it operates, provide safe and sanitary working conditions, and notify employees of the minimum allowable wage for each job classification, as well as the equivalent federal employee classification and wage rate for similar jobs.

The Service Contract Act expands the requirements of the Davis Bacon and Walsh Healy Acts to contractors providing services to the federal government, such as garbage removal, custodial services, food and lodging, and maintenance and operation of electronic equipment. Federal contractors already subject to the requirements of Davis Bacon, Walsh Healy, or laws covering other federal contracts, such as public utility services or transportation of people or freight, are exempt from the Service Contract Act.

The full text of the Service Contract Act is available at www.arnet.gov/far /current/html/Subpart_22_10.html.

### Fair Labor Standards Act (1938)

The Fair Labor Standards Act (FLSA), was the first federal regulation for employee compensation in private enterprises. Enacted in 1938, today FLSA remains a major influence on basic compensation issues for businesses in the United States and is administered by the Wage and Hour Division of the Department of Labor, Employment Standards Administration. FLSA regulations apply to workers who are not already covered by another law. For example, railroads and airlines are subject to wage and hour requirements of the Railway Labor Act so the FLSA does not apply to their employees.

There are two categories of employers subject to the requirements of the FLSA: enterprise and individual coverage. *Enterprise coverage* applies to businesses employing at least two employees with at least $500,000 in annual sales or employers who are hospitals, schools, or government agencies. *Individual coverage* applies to companies whose daily work involves interstate commerce. The FLSA defines interstate commerce so broadly that it includes those who have regular contact by telephone with out-of-state customers, vendors, or suppliers; on that basis, it includes virtually all employees in the United States.

The FLSA established requirements in five areas relevant to the PHR/SPHR exams:

1. It introduced a minimum wage for all covered employees.

2. It identified the circumstances in which overtime payments are required and set the overtime rate at one and one half times the regular hourly wage.

3. It identified the criteria for determining what jobs are exempt from FLSA requirements.

4. It placed limitations on working conditions for children to protect them from exploitation.

5. It identified the information employers must keep about employees and related payroll transactions.

**Exemption status**    The FLSA covers all employees except those identified in the law as *exempt* from the regulations. All other employees are considered *nonexempt* and must be paid in accordance with FLSA requirements.

Positions may be exempt from one or all of the FLSA requirements (minimum wage, overtime, or child labor). For example, police officers and firefighters employed by small departments of less than five employees are exempt from overtime requirements, but not exempt from the minimum wage requirement. On the other hand, newspaper delivery jobs are exempt from the minimum wage, overtime, and child labor requirements. A complete list of current FLSA exemptions can be viewed at www.dol.gov/elaws/esa/flsa/screen75.asp.

The determination of exemption status is often misunderstood by both employers and employees. Employers often think that they will save money by designating jobs as exempt and paying incumbent employees a salary. Employees often see the designation of a job as exempt as a measure of status within the company. Neither of these perceptions is accurate, and jobs that do not meet the legal exemption requirements can have costly consequences for employers.

One result of the economic downturn of the early 2000's was an increase in complaints filed by laid off employees claiming that they were misclassified as exempt and that their former employers owed them overtime payments. These, and other employee complaints about wage payments, are investigated by state or federal agencies. If they are found to be accurate, employers are required to pay retroactive overtime pay and penalties to the affected employees. The investigation of a complaint by a single employee at an organization can trigger a government audit of the employer's general pay practices and exemption classification of its other employees and may result in additional overtime payments and penalties to other employees if they are found to be misclassified. To avoid theses consequences, HR professionals should ensure that the classification of positions in their organizations meet FLSA requirements. For purposes of the PHR/SPHR exams, candidates should be familiar with exemption requirements for the more commonly used exemptions—those for white collar jobs (executive, administrative, professional, and outside sales) and computer professionals.

To assist employers in properly classifying positions, the DOL regulations include exemption tests to determine if a job meets those requirements and is therefore exempt from FLSA regulations. The DOL provides both a long and short test for each of the four white collar classifications identified in the FLSA. The long test is used for salaried jobs paying between $155 and $250 a week, while the short test may be used for salaried positions paying more than $250 a week. In both cases, the job duties must meet the requirements detailed in the regulations which are, as a general rule, relatively high-level, requiring judgment and discretion.

   **Executive exemption**    The short test for exemption as an executive requires that the job pay at least $250.00 per week. In addition, the primary duties of the position must be related to the management of an organization or one of its operating units, and require the supervision of two or more full-time employees.

Jobs paying between $155 and $250 per week may meet executive exemption requirements based on the long test if, in addition to the previous requirements, they also:

- Have the authority to hire, fire, promote, and evaluate employees or to provide input regarding those actions that carries substantial weight.

- Regularly exercise discretion when making decisions.

- Do not spend more than 20 percent (40 percent in retail or service establishments) of their time on duties that are unrelated to the management duties of the position.

**Administrative exemption**   The administrative exemption applies to positions in business organizations and in educational institutions. The administrative exemption short test requires that the job pay a salary of at least $250.00 per week and that the duties consist of nonmanual or office work related to management policies or general business operations, or to the administration of educational programs.

Administrative positions which pay salaries between $155 and $250 per week may be classified as exempt if, in addition to the previous requirements, they also:

- Use discretion and independent judgment on a regular basis.

- Regularly assist a proprietor, executive, or administrator of the organization.

- Perform work which requires specialized knowledge, training, or experience under only general supervision.

- Do not spend more than 20 percent (40 percent in retail or service establishments) of their time on duties that are unrelated to the office or nonmanual work previously described.

**Professional exemption**   The professional exemption may be used for four types of positions:

1. Those that require knowledge acquired by a prolonged course of specialized intellectual instruction.

2. Those that involve original, creative work in a recognized artistic field.

3. Those that involve teaching or otherwise imparting knowledge in a school system or other educational institution.

4. Those that require the theoretical and practical application of highly-specialized computer system analysis, programming, or software engineering.

The professional exemption short test may be used for salaried jobs paying at least $250.00 per week with duties previously listed in number 1, 3, or 4, if those duties require consistent use of discretion and judgment, or in number 2 if the work requires invention, imagination, or talent in its performance.

Professional jobs paying between $170 and $250 per week may qualify as exempt, if in addition to the previous requirements, they also:

- Require the consistent use of discretion and judgment.

- Are predominantly intellectual and varied and produce unique results.

- Do not spend more than 20 percent of time on duties that are nonessential and unrelated to the work previously described in numbers 1–4.

Computer systems analysts, computer programmers, software engineers or other similar technical professionals who earn more than $6\frac{1}{2}$ times the minimum wage (currently $27.63 per hour) are exempt from FLSA requirements.

**Outside sales exemption**    Unlike the other white collar exemptions, there is no salary requirement for outsides sales personnel. DOL regulations identify outside sales jobs as those regularly performed away from the employer's place of business for the sole purpose of selling the company's product or services. To be classified as exempt, duties that are nonessential or unrelated to the job may not make up more than 20 percent of time worked during the week. The regulations state specifically that duties "incidental to or in conjunction with" the sales duties, such as making deliveries or collecting payments, are not considered nonexempt work.

**Minimum wage**    The FLSA sets the federal minimum wage, which at the time of this writing is $5.15 per hour. Some states have set the minimum wage at a higher rate than the federal government; when this is the case, the state requirement supersedes the federal minimum wage. Nonexempt employees must be paid at least the minimum wage for all compensable time.

**Overtime**    Regulations established by the FLSA require nonexempt employees to be paid *overtime*, which is defined as one and one half times their regular wage rate, for all compensable time worked that exceeds 40 hours in a work week (also commonly known as *time-and-a-half*).

While double-time, or two times regular pay, is not required by the FLSA, it may be required by some states or may be part of a labor agreement. Candidates for the PHR/SPHR exams must be aware of the difference between the federal requirements that will appear on the test and state requirements or other practices that are more stringent.

While the FLSA does not require payment of overtime for exempt employees, it also does not prohibit overtime payments for them. Employers who choose to compensate exempt employees for hours worked above the regular work week are free to do so without risking the loss of exemption status. As long as overtime payments are in addition to the regular salary, exemption status is not affected. Exempt overtime can be paid at straight time, time and a half, or as a bonus.

Public employers may compensate employees with what is known as *compensatory time off*, or *comp time*, instead of cash payment for overtime worked. For example, a road maintenance worker employed by a city government may work 20 hours of overtime during a snow storm. Instead of being paid time and a half for the overtime hours, the employee may receive 30 hours of additional paid time off (1.5 times 20 hours) to be used just as paid vacation or sick leave.

In order to accurately calculate overtime payments, it is necessary to understand the difference between *compensable time*, hours that must be paid to nonexempt employees, and noncompensable time. The FLSA definition of compensable hours includes time for work that is "suffered or permitted" by the employer. For example, a nonexempt employee who continues to work on an assignment after the end of the business day to finish a project or make corrections must be paid for that time. In addition, employers are required to pay for time involved in preparing or in cleaning up, such as the time involved in dressing in protective clothing. FLSA requires payment in some other circumstances, which are described next:

**Waiting time**    Time spent by nonexempt employees waiting for work is compensable if it meets the FLSA definition of "engaged to wait," which means that employees have been asked to wait for an assignment. For example, a marketing director may ask an assistant to wait for the conclusion of a meeting in order to prepare a PowerPoint presentation needed for a client meeting early the next morning. If the assistant reads a book while waiting for the meeting to end, that time is still compensable.

Time that is spent by an employee who is "waiting to be engaged" is not compensable. For example, time spent by an employee who arrives at work 15 minutes early and reads the newspaper until the beginning of a shift is not considered to be compensable.

**On-call time**    Employees who are required to remain at the work site while waiting for an assignment are entitled to on-call pay. For example, medical interns required to remain at the hospital are entitled to payment for all hours spent at the hospital waiting for patients to arrive. The FLSA does not require employees who are on-call away from the work site to be paid for time they spend waiting to be called. These employees may be required to provide the employer with contact information. If, however, the employer places other constraints on the employee's activities, the time could be considered compensable.

**Rest and meal periods**    While rest and meal periods are not required by the FLSA, if they are provided, that time is subject to its requirements. Commonly referred to as "breaks," short periods of rest lasting less than 20 minutes are considered compensable time. Meal periods lasting 30 minutes or longer are not compensable time unless the employee is required to continue working while eating. For example, a receptionist who is required to remain at the desk during lunch to answer the telephone must be paid for that time.

**Lectures, meetings, and training programs**    Nonexempt employees are not required to be paid to attend training events when all four of the following conditions are met: the event must be outside normal work hours, it must be voluntary, it may not be job related, and no other work is performed during the event.

**Child labor**    The FLSA states that a child must be at least 16 years old to work in most nonfarm jobs and 18 to work in nonfarm jobs that have been identified as hazardous either in the law or by the Secretary of Labor.

Children 14 and 15 years of age can work in nonfarming, nonmining, and nonhazardous jobs outside of school hours if they work the following hours:

- No more than 3 hours a day or 18 hours in a work week
- No more than 8 hours on a nonschool day or 40 hours in a nonschool work week

During the school year, youths can work between 7:00 A.M. and 7:00 P.M. During the summer months, June 1 through Labor Day, the work day can be extended to 9:00 P.M.

**Record keeping**    There are two common methods for reporting time worked: *positive time reporting*, in which employees record the actual hours they are at work along with vacation, sick, or other time off, and *exception reporting*, in which only changes to the regular work schedule are recorded, such as vacation, sick, or personal time. While the DOL regulations accept either method, in general, the positive time method is best for nonexempt employees because it leaves no doubt as to actual hours worked by the employee, and protects both the employee and the employer if there is ever a question about overtime payments due. Exception reporting is more appropriate for exempt employees because their pay is not based on hours worked.

The FLSA does not prevent employers from tracking the work time of exempt employees. These records may be used for billing customers, reviewing performance, or for other administrative purposes, but they may not be used to reduce pay based on the quality or quantity of work produced. Reducing the salary invalidates the exemption status and subjects the employee to all requirements of the FLSA.

Records required by the FLSA are usually maintained by the payroll department. These requirements are discussed in the section "Payroll Systems and Administration."

 For more information on the FLSA, visit the Department of Labor website at www.DOL.gov.

FLSA can be complicated, and compliance is critical to protecting both the organization and the employee population.

## FLSA Amendments

The FLSA has been amended numerous times since 1938, most often to raise the minimum wage to a level consistent with changes in economic conditions.

I will discuss two significant federal amendments that have been added to the FLSA since 1938. The first, the Portal to Portal Act, is about paying for time that is part of an employee's primary responsibilities and duties. The second amendment is the Equal Pay Act.

**Portal to Portal Act (1947)**    The Portal to Portal Act clarified what was considered to be compensable work time and established that employers are not required to pay for employee commute time. This act requires employers to pay nonexempt employees who perform regular work duties before or after their regular hours, or for working during their lunch period.

**Equal Pay Act (EPA) (1963)**    The Equal Pay Act, the first anti-discrimination act to protect women, prohibits discrimination on the basis of sex. Equal pay for equal work applies to jobs with similar working conditions, skill, effort, and responsibilities. The Equal Pay Act applies to employers and employees covered by FLSA, and is administered and enforced by the Equal Employment Opportunity Commission (EEOC). The EPA allows differences in pay when they are based on a bona-fide seniority system, a merit system, a system that measures quantity or quality of production, or any other system that fairly measures factors other than sex. Prior to the EPA, the comparable worth standard was used by the U.S. government to make compensation decisions. When Congress passed the EPA, it deliberately rejected the comparable worth standard in favor of the equal pay standard.

You can view the text of the EPA at www.eeoc.gov/laws/epa.html.

In March 2003, the Department of Labor published proposed changes to its regulations governing overtime and exemption rules. The changes were designed to modernize the FLSA to reflect the current business environment. The proposed changes included eliminating overtime pay for any worker earning more than $65,000 per year and raising the exemption salary threshold from $155 per week to $425. As might be expected regarding a major change such as this, there is some debate in Congress over whether or not these changes should be implemented. In October 2003, the House of Representatives approved a procedural motion intended to prevent the DOL from implementing the changes. While the DOL does not require Congressional approval to do so, there is some doubt as to whether or not they will be implemented. PHR/SPHR candidates should follow the status of the proposal and be aware of any changes that do occur.

## Types of Compensation Programs

Before discussing various types of compensation programs, it is important to understand *base pay*, the cornerstone of compensation. Whether paid as a salary or as an hourly wage, base pay is the amount of compensation that the employer and the employee agree will be paid for the performance of particular job duties. Base pay is closely correlated to the company's compensation philosophy as it reflects the internal value of jobs while striving to recognize their external market value.

Human resource managers take a variety of factors into consideration when making base pay determinations: the KSAs employees brings to their jobs, previous earnings, and internal equity are all part of the decision-making process. Once an employee is hired, changes in base pay may be based on various factors, including performance in the job, seniority, or increased skills.

Base pay is typically evaluated on an annual basis, through a merit- or seniority-based process, which I'll discuss in detail in this section. When employees take on new roles and responsibilities, base pay can increase through the promotion process. Other changes in base pay can occur as result of a demotion or a change in job duties.

When determining a new hire's base pay, length and type of previous experience are key factors to consider. Years of experience in a certain profession, a certain industry, or total experience may be relevant to the job. Type of experience may also be relevant to a certain position. How well the new hire will perform in the job is an unknown variable, and will be taken into account once the employee begins work.

The company's compensation philosophy will drive the type of compensation program that is used. Let's discuss the various compensation programs in more detail.

### Performance-Based Compensation

*Performance-based pay* programs, which may include merit increases or promotions, are based on how well individual employees perform against the company's process for measuring performance (as discussed in Chapter 5). The performance ratings earned by employees determine the eligible range of increase for the review period. Differentiating pay based on performance means that employees in the same classification or salary range will have base salaries that vary from one another. When utilizing a performance-based compensation system, it is important to ensure that accurate records are kept with regard to the reasons for disparity in salaries between employees in the same positions. This documentation will be useful in defending against claims of unfair pay practices should they occur.

*Merit pay* is an adjustment to an employee's base pay based on demonstrated performance. When the connection between performance and the amount of increase is unclear, employees can begin to view merit increases as cost of living adjustments. Many organizations struggle with merit programs as they often create an atmosphere of entitlement.

Merit programs are often aligned with an organization's performance management system. When this is the case, an annual performance rating is the key determining factor for the employee's merit increase. Merit reviews may be conducted on an employee's anniversary date, or during a focal review period when all employees are reviewed for merit increases.

Merit matrices are commonly used by managers as a tool for planning merit increases. Merit matrices combine a performance rating with the employee's position in the salary range to recommend the amount of increase. The matrix shown in Table 6.1 demonstrates that in addition to differentiating employees based on performance, it is important to also differentiate based on their positions in the salary range. For example, employees at the midpoint of the salary range are considered to be fully trained and able to perform all job duties. Employees on the low end of the salary range who are moving up the learning curve quickly may warrant a higher merit increase than the employee at the midpoint or maximum of the salary range.

**TABLE 6.1**    Merit Increase Matrix, Assuming 5 Percent Annual Merit Budget

| Performance/Position in Range | Minimum | Midpoint | Maximum |
|---|---|---|---|
| Exceed Expectations | Merit 8–10 percent | Merit 6–8 percent | Merit 3–6 percent |
| Meet Expectations | Merit 5–7 percent | Merit 4–6 percent | Merit 0 percent |
| Does Not Meet Expectations | Merit 0 percent | Merit 0 percent | Merit 0 percent |

In addition to performance ratings, some organizations may strongly consider skill sets as determining factors for merit increases. Additional merit dollars may be awarded to employees who possess skills that are critical to the organization's success. Some organizations may provide additional compensation for the development and acquisition of new skills. An example of this can commonly be found in manufacturing environments, where an entry-level operator who acquires additional skills for the position receives additional compensation for these skills. Considering an employee's skill can be an important factor when making performance-based compensation decisions.

There are several things to consider before giving a merit-based salary increase, including an employee's current standing in the salary range, tenure in the position, and the work of the employee compared to other employees in the same position. Let's discuss these issues in more detail.

**Employee's position in the salary range**   Before providing a merit increase, consider the employee's current salary and where it fits into the range for the job title. For example, Tanya and Maurice are both customer service representatives. They perform the same job equally well. Tanya is at the high end of the salary range and Maurice is on the low end. In order to keep Tanya and Maurice within the same range, Maurice, with his salary on the low end, should receive a higher merit increase than Tanya. Typically, the midpoint of the salary range is the ideal place in the salary range for a fully trained, solid performing employee.

**Tenure in position (hire date/date of last promotion)**   It is important to consider how long an employee has held a job, the amount of time since the employee's last promotion, and the date of the last increase. For example, an employee who was recently promoted may still be learning a position and not performing all job requirements at a fully qualified level. The impact of this situation on the amount of increase would be to reduce the amount of the award so that the employee's salary is between the low and midpoints of the salary range. This would reflect the level of performance being delivered.

**Skill set and performance compared to peer group**   Human resource managers and supervisors should be aware of the marketable skills and current compensation of an employee relative to the employee's peers.

**Promotions**   Promotions may occur when employees are moved into new positions with different duties and greater responsibilities, or they may occur when employees develop a level of experience and skill enabling them to assume added responsibilities in their current positions. Typically, a promotion is accompanied by a change in title and salary level. In organizations with traditional pay structures, this also means an increase in salary grade.

Promotions can be very gratifying for employees and are often visible to the employee population. This visibility presents challenges for line managers who must balance internal equity and fairness within their workgroups.

## Seniority-Based Compensation

Companies that utilize a *seniority-based compensation* system base their pay decisions on length of time in the position and on years of related experience. A seniority-based compensation system is representative of an entitlement compensation philosophy, which I discussed earlier in the chapter.

A good example of seniority-based compensation is an organization with a union representing its workers. In a union context, long-term and short-term compensation decisions are the result of negotiations between the union and the employer. Because of this, they are not necessarily driven by an organization's compensation philosophy. In a union environment, annual increases are typically determined by seniority.

## Pay Differentials

Some organizations use pay differentials to encourage employees to perform work that is uncomfortable, out of the ordinary, inconvenient, or takes place under hazardous circumstances.

Pay differentials serve as incentives for employees to work on tough assignments or to be available to respond at inconvenient times. A *pay differential* provides additional pay for work that is considered beyond the minimum requirements of the job. For example, multinational employers who require employees to travel and work in potentially dangerous parts of the world may utilize hazard pay to make those jobs more attractive to employees.

Examples of pay differentials include overtime, shift pay, on-call pay, call-back pay, reporting pay, hazard pay, and geographic pay. Let's discuss these pay differentials in more detail.

## Overtime

While the FLSA only requires payment for overtime exceeding 40 hours in a week, some states have overtime laws that exceed federal requirements, and employees are paid at the more generous, state rate. Employers may require unlimited overtime as long as employees are paid at the required wage rate. It is not common practice to pay overtime to exempt employees, but doing so is not prohibited by the FLSA; however, doing so by definition requires employees to keep track of their time. As discussed previously, requiring exempt employees to keep track of their time is not prohibited by the FLSA as long as it does not result in a reduction of their pay based on the quality or quantity of work produced.

It is important for employers to take a leadership position in managing overtime costs. To prevent abuse, it is ideal for overtime work to be approved in advance. Employers may also want to develop a process or policy when scheduling overtime work for large groups of employees. Employees may be scheduled for overtime work based on skill set, seniority, or shift, depending on the needs of the employer. Overtime is an area that is commonly cut when employers face financial and/or economic challenges.

## Shift Pay

A *shift* is a scheduled block of time set by an organization for employees to perform job related duties. Shifts have a specific start and end time and are most applicable to nonexempt employees but can also affect exempt employees. There are three commonly recognized shifts: the day shift, with hours from 8 A.M. to 4 P.M.; the evening or *swing shift*, with hours from 4 P.M. to 12 A.M.; and the *graveyard shift*, with hours from 12 A.M. to 8 A.M. Shift work is necessary in industries with 24-hour operations, such as airlines, law enforcement, and some manufacturing operations.

Many employers pay more than state/federal requirements for shifts, agreeing to such things as pay for rest or meal periods. Compensating for time not covered under FLSA is typically reflective of the industry and market. Employers may decide to pay for these items to have a competitive compensation program to more effectively attract, motivate, and retain employees.

A *shift premium* is additional compensation provided for employees who work other than the day shift. Shift premiums may be paid as a percentage of base pay or may be factored into the hourly rate. For example, in high-tech manufacturing, it is common to pay a 10 percent shift premium for shifts that overlap 6:00 P.M. to midnight and 15 percent for shifts that overlap the midnight to 6:00 A.M. time period. The days and hours of a typical work week vary by industry. While it is most common for nonexempt employees to be paid shift premiums, they may also be paid to exempt employees.

Shift premium calculations can be a little bit tricky. Here's an example: Laura works as a nonexempt manufacturing technician at MonoCorp, working an 8-hour shift, 5 days a week, resulting in a 40-hour work week, making $10 an hour. Laura also works some hours on the second shift, from 4:00 P.M. to midnight, Monday through Friday. The second shift at MonoCorp pays a 10 percent shift premium. Table 6.2 illustrates the base pay and overtime costs for Laura's work.

**TABLE 6.2**   Laura's Schedule—Hours Worked

| Day | Shift/Scheduled Hours | Overtime |
|---|---|---|
| Monday | 8 | 0 |
| Tuesday | 8 | 2 |
| Wednesday | 8 | 0 |
| Thursday | 8 | 2 |
| Friday | 8 | 2 |
| Total Hours Worked | 40 | 6 |

As you can see, Laura worked a full 40-hour week and put in 6 hours of overtime. Table 6.3 illustrates Laura's pay based on her $10/hour salary and her 10 percent shift premium.

**TABLE 6.3**   Laura's Pay Schedule

| Category | Hours | Pay |
|---|---|---|
| Regular | 40 | $400 |
| Overtime | 6 | $90 ($1\frac{1}{2}$ time) |
| Sub Total | 46 | $490 |
| Shift Premium @ 10 percent | | $9 |
| Total | | $499 |

## On-Call Pay

While the FLSA establishes minimum requirements for on-call time, employers may decide to provide *on-call pay* that is more generous. Employees who are required to respond to work-related issues on short notice, typically emergencies, and who must be available via pager, telephone, or e-mail, may be paid an hourly or daily premium. In certain professions, being on-call is part of the job and on-call premiums are not paid.

### Call-Back Pay

Some companies may provide *call-back pay* to employees who are called to work before or after their scheduled work week. Nonexempt employees who are called into the facility or who work from home are paid their regular rate of pay and any other applicable premiums.

### Reporting Pay

When an employee is called into work and there is no work available, the employer may be required by state law or employment agreements to pay for a minimum number of hours of work. This is called a *reporting premium* and ensures the employee receives compensation for showing up for their regular shift or when called to the work site.

### Hazard Pay

*Hazard pay* is additional pay for dangerous and/or extremely uncomfortable working conditions. Hazard pay may be needed to attract candidates to jobs that require contact with hazardous elements such as radiation, chemicals, or extreme conditions. Firefighters commonly receive hazard pay, as they deal with extreme conditions and physically demanding duties. Examples of other professions that may receive hazard pay include medical positions that work with infectious diseases, police officers, and federal employees who are posted to assignments in countries that are considered dangerous due to wars and/or active hostilities. Although certain jobs may have risks, they may not provide a hazard pay premium and their compensation is instead reflective of the labor market. The Fair Labor Standards Act does not require hazard pay, but it does require employers who provide hazard pay to factor it into overtime calculations.

### Geographic Pay

Organizations utilize *geographic pay* to ensure that employees in different locations are paid at rates competitive in the labor market for specific jobs and locations. Geographic structures are put into place to make sure the employees are paid competitively and aligned with the organization's compensation philosophy. It is common to find nonexempt pay structures that vary by city and/or state due to the local cost of labor.

Exempt structures may adjust by region and have structure specific to the labor market. Having an exempt salary structure specific to the Northeast, Pacific Northwest, or Southeast may be appropriate for some labor markets. As an example, if a manufacturing organization is headquartered in the Silicon Valley in Northern California and has manufacturing plants in San Francisco, St. Louis, and Boston, it would be appropriate to have a salary structure specific to each location.

## Incentive Pay

*Incentive pay* programs reward employees for individual and organizational results. Individual and group incentive pay have become a common component of the total compensation package. According to several salary surveys, almost two-thirds of U.S. companies have some sort of *variable pay*. Incentive programs are also known as *pay for performance* because pay is based on individual and organizational results. When implemented correctly, incentive plans can motivate employees to achieve individual and/or organizational objectives.

Pay for performance through incentives can be based on individual or team performance or on the financial performance of the business unit or the corporation. When designing and implementing incentive plans, it is important to keep the employee's line of sight as a driving force of the program. Employees are motivated to achieve incentive plan objectives if they are able to impace or influence the incentive plan's performance objectives. Incentive plans should align with the organization's compensation philosophy. If developed and implemented appropriately, incentive plans will shape and change employee behavior.

Incentive pay has become a key component of a compensation package as the broad spreading of merit dollars may not always reinforce performance. Merit budgets have become smaller, on average, which can make it difficult to differentiate performance. In order to really reward employees through the merit process, given the average merit budget, requires many employees to be passed over for annual merit increases so the dollars can be spent on top performers.

The following section describes individual, group, and special incentives.

## Individual Incentives

Individual incentives are rewards for employees who achieve set goals and objectives. Individual incentives can be powerful tools for motivating individual performance. A characteristic of incentives is that they are prospective: they state the specific objectives that need to be achieved over a designated period of time. There is a pay-out target, a percentage base pay, or a flat dollar amount. There are three critical phases to successful incentive plan programs: plan design, review process, and communication and implementation.

### Plan Design

Incentive plan design should be kept simple. It should be easy and convenient for employees to understand and recall the performance goals (for instance, an employee or group needs to increase production by 10 percent or to decrease defective parts by 5 percent). Complicated incentive plans tend to create confusion and distrust and may not produce the desired results.

Research on incentive programs has found that a minimum bonus target of 10 percent is required to influence and change behavior. Bonus programs that are less than 10 percent may not give the employee the incentive to put forward the effort or spend the additional time to achieve incentive plan objectives. Bonus targets with a target of less than 10 percent of the employee's base pay may not produce the desired results.

### Review Process

Typically, bonus review and payment occurs on an annual basis corresponding to the end of the company's fiscal year. Some companies may choose to pay incentives more frequently than on an annual basis if the employees have a direct influence on revenue generation. As with most compensation programs, the *ability to pay* (the company affordability factor) is critical to any incentive program. Many bonus-based incentive programs define desired financial metrics that must be achieved before incentives are paid.

### Communication and Implementation

Individual incentive plan objectives are ideally communicated before or at the beginning of the review period. For example, annual, calendar-based plans are usually communicated in

January. Targets for incentive plans are commonly part of an offer package but can be modified as needed. When bonus targets are modified, whether they are increased or decreased, great care should be taken in communicating the rationale. When modifying bonus targets for employees based outside the United States, legal counsel and/or local HR representatives should be involved because changing variable compensation may require the need for new employment contracts. In addition, HR professionals may need to take steps to ensure that the changes follow local and state law.

Communication of an incentive plan program is key to ensuring employees understand the metrics of the plan. As part of a communication strategy, some organizations may choose to create and publish a plan document that describes the incentive program in detail.

## Organization or Group Incentives

*Organization incentives* or *group incentives* have many of the same characteristics as individual incentives. A sure step to a successful organization or group incentive plan is that the plan objectives align with the organization's compensation philosophy. Organization or group incentives are commonly put in place to increase productivity and foster teamwork while sharing the financial rewards with employees. Different types of group incentives include gainsharing, Improshare, the Scanlon Plan, profit sharing, and employee stock ownership plans (ESOPs). Benefits that are common to all group incentives include increased awareness and commitment to company goals. Group incentives do not take into account individual performance.

**Gainsharing**    *Gainsharing* programs involve employees and managers in improving the organization's productivity and sharing the benefits of success.

The key components of gainsharing include:

- Employees and management work together to review organizational performance.
- When measurable improvements are achieved, employees and managers share the success.
- The organization and the employees share the financial gains.

Some of the organizational benefits derived from gainsharing include:

- Teamwork, sharing knowledge and cooperation.
- Increased motivation.
- Employee focus and commitment to organizational goals.
- Greater employee acceptance of new methods, technology, and market changes.
- Perceived fairness of pay results in increased productivity at all levels.

**Improshare**    *Improshare* was developed in the 1970s by Mitchell Fein. It is differentiated from other group incentive plans because a key part of the program involves establishing the baseline of organization productivity and a baseline of productivity costs. The difference between the baseline productivity and the new output is used to calculate the group or organization's performance.

**Scanlon Plan**   The *Scanlon Plan* is one of the earliest pay for performance plans. In the 1930s, Joseph Scanlon created his plan to increase productivity and decrease costs through employee involvement. An organization's Scanlon Plan is administered by a committee that is representative of the employee population. The company's financial information and productivity metrics must be disclosed to the employee population. Through productivity gains and cost savings, the employees receive a portion of cost savings.

**Profit sharing**   Very similar to the Scanlon Plan, profit sharing is an incentive-based program that shares company profits. Profit sharing plans are typically qualified plans found across many industries and available at all employee levels, from individual contributors to senior management. Profit sharing plans distribute pretax dollars to eligible employees, typically based on a percentage of an employee's base salary. Distribution of profit sharing dollars typically occurs annually, after the close of the fiscal year. The set formula for a profit sharing plan defines individual contributions and distributions. It is typical for the plan to have a vesting schedule, and the plan document should detail when and how distributions occur at milestone events, such as employee termination, leave of absence, death, retirement, and so on. Profit sharing is discussed in more detail in the "Benefits" section of this chapter.

**Employee Stock Ownership Plans**   An Employee Stock Ownership Plan (ESOP) is a defined contribution plan that allows employees to own company stock. An employer sets up a tax-deductible trust that accepts tax-deductible contributions made by the company. Employee eligibility can be based on a formula that may include base salary, length of service, or other factors. At the time of termination, retirement, or death, employees are able to receive the vested portion of their ESOP. ESOPs become taxable at the time funds are distributed. An ESOP is considered an organization incentive, but it's also an organization benefit, and is discussed in more detail in the "Benefits" section.

## Special Pay Programs

Special pay programs benefit specific groups of employees such as executives, sales employees, and members of the board of directors. This section describes special pay in the form of bonuses, commissions, and stock options.

### Executive Pay

Executive compensation packages vary by industry and company culture, some having more pay at risk than others. The majority of executive compensation is in the form of short and long-term incentives. The size of the executive bonus pool is usually related to the profitability of the company. Key elements of executive compensation are the benefits and *perquisites*. Perquisites, often referred to as "perks," are additional benefits that provide comfort and luxury to the work and/or personal environment, usually intended for senior management and executives. Perquisites may include generous pension plans and access to a company jet, club memberships, limousine service, and so on. These perks are very attractive and effective in attracting, retaining, and motivating organization leaders. While these programs create loyalty, they do not pay for performance.

Recent legislation has impacted executive pay. In 1993, the Omnibus Budget Reconciliation Act (OBRA) modified certain aspects of executive compensation by limiting tax deductions for executives to $1,000,000 annually.

---

### Real World Scenario

#### Putting the Brakes on Excessive Executive Pay

In June 2003, New York Stock Exchange (NYSE) Chairman Richard Grasso was forced to resign from the NYSE amid outrage over his $140 million pay package (which included $48 million in special benefits). Grasso's situation at the NYSE is just one example of how executive-ranked businesspeople manage to be paid extraordinary amounts of money, even during poor economic times.

On their Executive Paywatch website, the American Federation of Labor-Congress of Industrial Organizations (AFL-CIO) (www.aflcio.org/corporateamerica/paywatch/) keeps track of U.S. trends on executive pay and benefits versus those of regular employees. The discrepancies are astounding. Citing the *New York Times*, the Paywatch site explains that median executive pay grew 6 percent in 2002, while stocks and corporate profits fell significantly.

According to the *New York Times*, the average CEO compensation package in 2002 was $10.83 million. Many CEOs received pay increases that year, while it proved to be a difficult one for many Americans, both in the job market and stock market. Furthermore, in 2002, the ratio of CEO pay to average employee pay was 500:1, according to professor Bruce Hutton at the University of Colorado, who has completed a research project on compensation.

With high profile executive greed associated with Enron and MCI WorldCom, executive pay has become more visible to the average employee and stockholder, and with the tough economy and bear market, the continuation of excessive pay packages for executives has been difficult for many to accept. The debate continues as stockholders scrutinize executive compensation packages and compensation committees of boards of directors take an active role in monitoring those packages.

---

### Bonus Plans

A bonus is additional compensation for performance above and beyond what was expected, and is paid in addition to an employee's base salary or hourly rate. Most bonuses are considered discretionary, meaning the bonus is optionally offered and is not based on an established objectives. An example of a *bonus plan* is a holiday bonus program that some organizations distribute at the end of the year. Individual bonus amounts and eligibility of employees is discretionary. Another example is a "spot bonus" plan which provides an immediate reward for outstanding performance. Bonus plans are different from incentive plans because incentives are communicated prior to the start of the project. Bonuses also take the form of performance and referral bonuses, patent awards, employee of the month rewards, and so on.

### Stock Options

A *stock option* is the right to purchase an employer's stock at a certain price (the strike price), at a future date, within a specified period of time. Options provide an employee with an opportunity to purchase shares, but do not require that the employee do so. The *grant price* or *strike price* of the stock is based on the market price at the time the options are issued. It is common to find stock options vesting to occur over a three- to five-year period as a retention tactic; they can be exercised for up to ten years. Stock options are only valuable if the stock price rises over time, so their value to employees depends upon the company's financial performance. While stock option plans vary between companies, all plans must be operated within parameters established by the SEC (Securities Exchange Commission) and IRS (Internal Revenue Service).

There are two types of stock options: *incentive stock options (ISO)* and *nonqualified stock options*. The difference between the option types is the tax treatment for the employer and employee.

**Incentive or qualified stock options**   ISOs are stock options that can be offered only to employees; consultants and external members of the board of directors are not eligible. The tax treatment for ISOs is often favorable for employees because they do not face taxes at the time the stock option is exercised—they do not have income to report until the stock is sold at a later date. When an ISO is sold, however, it is likely that capital gains taxes will be due and subject to the alternative minimum tax under certain conditions. Use of ISOs is not as favorable to employers because the company receives a tax deduction only if certain conditions are met.

**Nonqualified options**   Nonqualified stock options can be used for consultants and external members of the board of directors as well as for employees. The organization receives a tax deduction when the options are exercised, and employees pay tax on any gain they realize from the sale. Income from the stock is treated as compensation, and when the stock is sold there are further tax implications.

Two other types of stock options employers utilize are restricted stock and phantom stock.

**Restricted stock**   *Restricted stock* is common stock offered to employees, typically executives or employees who demonstrate outstanding performance. Restricted stocks are actual shares, not the option to buy shares, like stock options. Restricted stock usually follows a vesting schedule designed to reward retention. Employees may be motivated to stay with the organization to realize the full benefit of their restricted stock, which is why employees perceive these as "golden handcuffs" or a financial benefit that will be lost if they leave the organization. In a broad yet creative move to motivate its employees, Microsoft Corporation recently gave 600 employees restricted stock plans tied to their achievement of certain performance targets.

**Phantom stock**   *Phantom stock* is used in privately held companies to provide the benefits of employee ownership without granting stock. Organizations use phantom stock to motivate and retain employees without granting equity or sharing ownership in the company. Phantom stock can generate the kind of payoffs that stock options or restricted stock can yield. Executives and outside members of the board of directors are the most common recipients of phantom stock. There is usually a vesting schedule based on length of service and performance (individual or company). Like common stock, phantom stock follows the company's market price movements. There is a valuation formula that determines the value of the stock. When the phantom stock yields a pay-out, the employer is eligible to receive a tax deduction for the amount paid.

## Real World Scenario

### Stock Options and Compensation

Stock options have been a key part of employee compensation packages for decades, but they were never so popular as during the time of the dot-com boom. Employees at all levels, especially in the high-tech sector, were receiving stock options as part of their compensation packages. This was attractive for many reasons to both employers and employees. The alignment between employee, company, and market performance provided the upside opportunity for employees to profit if the company performed well in the stock market. During the dot-com boom, many average employees realized great wealth due to the performance of the stock market. Some employees believed so wholeheartedly in the value of their organizations that they declined salaries in exchange for more stock options. This outlook backfired on employees who lost their jobs and had nothing but worthless paper to show for their hard work.

Employers enjoyed this too, as there was the potential to create wealth without dipping into the company's cash flow. When the dot-com industry became unable to sustain itself in a declining economy, the opportunity for upside potential with stock options went away.

While stock options are no longer the highlight of a typical offer package, they are still a key component of total compensation. Due to financial abuses committed by companies such as Enron, there is pressure from regulators and legislators to change the way that options are expensed, requiring that the expense be recorded when they are issued instead of when they are exercised. While many companies object to this change due to concern that it will adversely affect their net profits, those companies that have voluntarily implemented this reporting change have found it has had little effect on their profits.

### Commissions and Bonuses

*Commissions* provide incentives to sales employees by paying them a percentage of the sale price for products and services sold to a customer. Commissions may serve as the entire cash compensation package, or they may used in combination with a base salary. When sales employees receive a base salary, it is usually a portion of their target cash compensation. The incentive or variable component is intended to drive sales objectives. Compensation for sales employees paid on a commission-only basis must meet at least the minimum wage.

An alternative to a commission plan is a sales bonus plan, in which a percentage of base pay compensates the employee for sales targets achieved. The difference between commission and bonus plans is the method of calculation, and this has has many implications for the design of sales compensation programs. For example, Joaquim sells new cars and has an annual quota of 100 cars. For every car Joaquim sells over 100, he receives a bonus of 1 percent of his base salary.

When performance targets are clearly communicated, commissions and bonuses are an excellent way to motivate sales employees to perform desired behaviors and achieve desired results.

### Board of Directors/Outside Directors

The board of directors is elected by shareholders to oversee the management of the corporation on behalf of its stockholders. Members of the board can be executives of the organization (known as inside directors) or those who are external to the organization (known as outside directors).

Inside directors receive the executive compensation packages, consisting of stock options, benefits, and base pay, to which they are entitled based on their roles as corporate executives. Outside directors commonly receive cash for meeting fees and retainers.

Now that you've learned about the different types of pay programs, let's take a look at how jobs are evaluated in organizations.

## Job Evaluation

The job evaluation process is a methodology for evaluating jobs that attempts to minimize reviewer opinions and preconceived ideas. Job evaluations are normally conducted when a job is developed, a job changes, or as part of a routine job evaluation process. HR professionals partner with line management when conducting job evaluations; using defined job evaluation methods allows for a repeatable process for this key component of the compensation system.

*Compensable factors* are characteristics that define and distinguish jobs from one another. Job evaluation methods identify and define the compensable factors of each job that are most relevant for the organization. For instance, a junior-level engineer's compensable factors might include:

- Bachelor's Degree in Electrical Engineering
- Two years of industry-related experience
- Two years experience testing products for quality and reliability

The two methods discussed in this chapter for job evaluation include the ranking method and classification method. Let's discuss each of these in greater detail.

### Ranking Method

The *ranking method* requires the evaluator to compare the value of jobs to one another. When evaluators use this subjective method, they are influenced by any preconceptions they may have about different positions or job duties and this impacts the way in which jobs are ranked. While ranking is a simple and cost-effective method for use in small organizations, it can become a very complicated process in a complex organization with many positions to be evaluated. In this method, it is also difficult to compare unrelated jobs.

Take this example of the ranking method in action: SkyLine Healthcare uses the ranking method to compare Judy, an administrative assistant, to Leonard, a file clerk. Both Judy and Leonard are administrative-level employees. Judy's job requires higher or more advanced qualifications and experience than Leonard's; therefore Judy's position is ranked higher than Leonard's.

### Classification Method

The *classification method* involves identifying key *benchmark positions*. Benchmark positions are jobs that are commonly found across organizations regardless of size or industry. Once a job is matched to a benchmark position, it may be classified according to value on a vertical scale. Benchmark positions are then associated with a grade on a hierarchical salary structure. Positions with similar characteristics are slotted into the same grade or level, which are identified by a similar level of knowledge, skills, and abilities.

In order to utilize the classification method, companies must determine *internal equity*, or the value of jobs to each other relative to their value to the organization. There are several ways to measure and assess internal equity, including broadbanding, the point factor method, and the HAY system.

**Broadbanding**    *Broadbanding* splits positions in the company into just a few specific levels, with each level shared by a variety of jobs. For example, a broadband classification structure may have four levels, such as individual contributor, manager, director, and VP. All jobs in the company fit into one of the four classifications. Broadbanding helps organizations remain flat and facilitates lateral career movement. In contrast, narrow banding or traditional pay classifications have many levels and are organized in a hierarchical and vertical fashion. These structures may not facilitate lateral movement and may create an employee focus on level.

**Point factor**    The *point factor* methodology provides companies with a system of points that are assigned to the position being evaluated. Based on the total number of points a position receives, a pay grade/range is assigned to the position. Each company that uses this complicated method for evaluating jobs may have abstract or very specific factors that broadly fall under five categories: education, skill, effort, responsibility, and working conditions.

**HAY system**    In 1943, Edward Hay, founder of The Hay Group, a professional services organization and consulting agency, developed the *HAY system*, a classification method that utilizes a complex point factor system. Jobs are evaluated using three factors: knowledge, problem solving, and accountability. Using the points from the evaluation, the job(s) are matched to a profile.

Now that you know the various methods for evaluating jobs (and thus determining their worth to the company), it's time to explore the various pay structures companies have to choose from.

# Compensation Administration

Compensation administration is a general term that describes how an organization develops pay structures and administers pay through daily activity. Compensation administration includes concepts and tools such as job pricing, pay ranges and grades, comparable worth, cost of living adjustments, and salary surveys that are used on a regular basis to manage compensation decisions. The application of these concepts and tools should be aligned with the organization's compensation philosophy, and a description of how the organization uses these concepts and tools may be kept in its policy manual.

Job pricing is a common practice when administering compensation. Many organizations, especially those going through high growth periods, use job pricing to ensure pay is competitive. Let's discuss job pricing in more detail.

## Job Pricing

*Job pricing* occurs when a job is new to the organization or when an existing job has undergone changes. Job pricing can be done in a four-step process designed to determine the appropriate pay level for a position. In order to price a job, an HR manager must:

1.   Review the job description and understand the level and scope of the job and its required responsibilities and skills.

2.   Select a salary survey (I will discuss salary surveys later in the chapter). When selecting a salary survey, consider the type and number of survey participants. For example, if doing a job pricing for a position in Austin, Texas, it may not be appropriate to use data from a salary survey if most of the participants are located in Silicon Valley. Most compensation managers like to see several competitors or other premier employers as part of the survey so the data is perceived as valid.

3.   Review compensation components, such as base pay, variable pay, equity pay, and so on. At this time it is also important to review a number of matches for a certain position. The more matches, the better, as the data will be more reliable and less likely to be skewed by outliers.

4.   Recommend a salary range. When developing a recommendation as a result of job pricing, keep in mind your organization's compensation philosophy of leading, matching, or lagging the market. In addition to a salary range, an HR professional may recommend incentive pay or special pay programs if applicable.

It is important for the HR manager to review the results of job pricing with management to validate that the survey positions and data match the job. Once a job is priced, it is appropriate to slot the job into the appropriate pay range and grade.

### Pay Ranges and Grades

*Pay ranges* include the minimum and maximum pay rate (hourly or annual) for all jobs in a particular pay or salary range. Depending on the compensation philosophy, some ranges are quite wide and cover many jobs, while others can be narrow and may only cover one job. A *pay grade* is the name or title given to the associated pay range. Some organizations denote a hierarchy of levels using a numerical or alphabetical system for pay grades.

Employees who are below the minimum of the salary range are commonly described as having a *green circle*. Employees may have a green circle because their experience and/or skills do not meet the requirements of the position or as a result of performance issues. Conversely, employees who have a *red circle* are above the maximum of the salary range. This may occur when an employee is demoted without a corresponding decrease to base pay, due to a transfer, or for some other unusual circumstance.

Pay ranges and grades provide the framework necessary for evaluating internal equity and comparing employees' base pay against the defined pay ranges. Pay ranges and grades provide structure when evaluating wage compression and when analyzing compa-ratios.

### Wage Compression

*Wage compression* occurs when new employees are hired at a rate of pay greater than that earned by incumbents for similar skills, education, and experience. These situations are usually the most challenging during high-growth economic times or when there is high demand for certain skill-sets. Compression may be reduced by providing salary adjustments for the incumbent population. Compression may also occur if the organization's pay practices, merit increases, and promotional budgets are not in line with the market.

### Compa-ratios

A *compa-ratio* is a simple calculation that compares an employee's base pay to the midpoint of the base salary range. This measure is commonly used for comparison against a group of employees, and is especially useful when providing recommendations for pay increases for promotions, merit increases, and so on.

Here's the formula for finding the compa-ratio:

Base Salary ÷ Midpoint of Salary Range × 100

An example of a compa-ratio in action is:

120,000 base salary ÷ 100,000 midpoint × 100 = 120 percent

A compa-ratio of 100 percent indicates that the base pay equals the midpoint of the salary range, for example, an HR manager, Elena, is evaluating the new base pay for Joseph, an executive who is about to be promoted to the next pay grade. Elena determines that incumbents in the new position have an average compa-ratio of about 110 percent. Because Joseph is entering this level for the first time, a compa-ratio of less than 100 percent may be most appropriate for him.

## Comparable Worth

*Comparable worth*, or *pay equity*, describes the concept of minimizing pay disparities between jobs traditionally held by women, such as teachers, with higher-paying jobs traditionally held by men, such as carpenters. This concept suggests that jobs with similar duties and responsibilities requiring similar levels of knowledge, skill, and ability should be paid similarly. Comparable worth does not reflect supply and demand in the labor market because it is about the inherent value of the job's content to society. The issue is complex because value is a subjective measure and how jobs are valued often depends on who is valuing them. Those opposed to this concept argue that the price of a particular job in the labor market is based on the supply and demand for its skills, and that social engineering is not an appropriate role for business.

## Cost of Living Adjustments (COLAs)

Cost of living adjustments are generally used during periods of high inflation to reduce the effects of wage compression. These adjustments are used more often in public sector jobs than in the private sector which relies on survey data to maintain compensation at a level that is competitive with the appropriate labor market, whether at the local or national level.

## Salary Surveys

*Salary surveys* allow organizations to gather compensation and benefits data that reflects current market trends. Surveys are provided by a professional services vendor. The vendor is responsible for confidentially collecting data, administering the survey and compiling this data into a usable format. Salary surveys identify changes in the cost of labor and are integral in ensuring that compensation and benefits programs continue to attract, retain, and motivate employees. There are different types of salary surveys for an organization to consider; these include government, industry, and company-sponsored surveys.

### Government Surveys

A great source for compensation data is the Bureau of Labor Statistics (BLS), an independent national statistical agency whose mission is to collect, analyze, and distribute statistical data. The BLS is a statistical resource to the Department of Labor and a great source for salary survey data.

### Industry Surveys

For certain jobs, it may be important to consider industry-specific salary surveys for greater validity. For example, the high-tech industry has specific surveys for companies in its sector. The hospitality industry also has industry specific surveys.

### Organization-Sponsored Surveys

A company may want to sponsor a salary survey to collect compensation and/or benefits data. This can be done formally or informally. An organization may want to work with a third party, such as a compensation consulting firm, to facilitate the data collection and analysis. This can be very costly and time consuming. As an informal process, an organization may want to simply make contact with other HR professionals to exchange information on pay practices. Another informal option is to work with a local/regional HR or compensation association and have the group facilitate the collection of pay practice data from participating members.

It is very important for HR professionals and employees to keep salary survey data confidential in order to comply with legislative mandates. Over the years, there have been a number of lawsuits against organizations and individuals who share salary data inappropriately.

## Payroll Systems and Administration

In many organizations, payroll is administered as a function of the finance department, but there are other organizations in which it is an HR responsibility. While an in-depth knowledge of payroll systems and administration is not required for the PHR/SPHR exams, candidates should have basic knowledge of payroll activities and how they interact with HR responsibilities.

### Payroll Systems

Whether an organization employs one person or hundreds of thousands, a payroll system must meet some basic requirements:

- It must accurately calculate payments due to employees.
- It must accurately calculate statutory and voluntary deductions.
- It must track payroll tax payments owed to federal and state agencies.
- It must provide accurate reports of payroll costs to management.
- It must provide security for payroll information.

In a small organization with a few employees, all of these requirements may be met with a manual system in which a qualified bookkeeper manually calculates the payments due to employees, uses federal and state tax publications to look up withholding information, and prepares checks. This process can be streamlined with the addition of an off-the-shelf accounting software program that makes the calculations, prints the checks, and tracks tax payments owed to federal and state agencies. As organizations grow, manual systems are no longer feasible and may be replaced by a service bureau, which performs the necessary calculations, prints the checks or deposits them electronically, and submits payroll tax payments on behalf of the organization. Very large organizations may develop proprietary software designed to handle their specific needs.

Because payroll systems collect some of the same information that is entered into HRIS systems, HR managers can benefit from systems that are able to interact and share information to reduce or eliminate the double entry of information into separate systems.

## Payroll Administration

Administering payroll is one of the most visible functions performed in any organization because it affects every employee from the CEO to the most junior assistant. Not only is it visible to everyone, payroll errors have the potential for profoundly affecting an employee's life, if only until the error can be corrected. Payroll administration is the function in the company that is responsible for calculating employee earnings and deductions and maintaining records of those payments.

### Employee Earnings

The payroll department is responsible for preparing employee paychecks and ensuring that earnings are calculated correctly. To calculate nonexempt earnings, the payroll department must know the employee's base pay rate, shift differentials, tips, bonuses, how many hours the employee worked during the pay period, and whether or not any paid leave was used. With this information, the *gross pay*, or earnings before taxes, can be calculated.

To calculate earnings for exempt employees, payroll will need to know the base salary, bonus amounts, and any paid leave that was used during the pay period.

### Statutory Deductions

As everyone knows, before you receive your paycheck, various deductions are made from your gross earnings. These deductions include:

- Social security
- Medicare
- Federal income tax
- State income tax
- Unemployment insurance (in some states)
- Disability insurance (in some states)
- Other state and local taxes

These amounts are withheld from employee earnings. As I will explain later in the "Social Security and Medicare" section, employers match the amount of social security and Medicare taxes that are withheld from employees. These amounts, along with the federal income tax withheld, are remitted to the IRS at regular intervals. Failure to remit taxes on time results in substantial penalties for employers. State and local taxes are remitted separately to the appropriate government agency according to payment schedules established by each agency.

At the end of each calendar quarter, reports of gross payroll and withheld taxes are filed with the federal, state, and local taxing authorities. These reports reconcile the amount of tax withheld to the amounts deposited during the quarter. At the end of the year, W-2 forms are prepared for each employee and submitted to federal and state tax agencies.

## Voluntary Deductions

There are a number of other deductions that may be made from an employee's paycheck. These include medical, dental, and other health benefit contributions; 401(k) contributions; union dues; and, in some cases, contributions to charities designated by employees.

## Involuntary Deductions

In some cases, employers may be required by court order or a tax levy to withhold additional funds from employee paychecks. These involuntary withholdings are known as *wage garnishments* and are issued to satisfy a debt owed by the employee. These garnishment orders may be issued by a court to force a parent to pay child support or by a federal, state, or local taxing agency to collect unpaid taxes. Garnishments may also be issued by a court to force payment of a debt to a third party. Wage garnishments are not voluntary, and employers have no discretion as to whether or not to honor them. Garnishments are subject to the requirements of the Consumer Credit Protection Act.

---

### Consumer Credit Protection Act of 1968

The Consumer Credit Protection Act, administered by the Wage and Hour Division of the DOL's Employment Standards Administration, limits the amount of an employee's earnings that may be garnished and prevents employees from being terminated for a single garnishment order, even if the order requires funds to be withheld from multiple paychecks.

---

## Record Keeping

The FLSA requires employers to keep accurate records that identify employees, such as their name, address, and Social Security number, along with their birth date if they are under 19 years of age, their sex, and their occupation. For nonexempt employees, the employer's records must include the work week (for example, 12:00 A.M. Sunday through 11:59 P.M. Saturday). Nonexempt records must also include the hours worked each day, total hours for the week and the basis for payment (the dollars per hour, per week, or per piece), as well as any differentials, bonuses, and other additions described previously. Finally, the records must include the pay period dates, how much straight-time and overtime pay was earned for the pay period, any deductions withheld, and the date of payment.

A more recent record keeping and reporting requirement was enacted by Congress to aid state and federal welfare agencies in collecting child support from parents who neglect to pay it, and is known as the Personal Responsibility and Work Opportunity Reconciliation Act of 1996.

---

**Personal Responsibility and Work Opportunity Reconciliation Act of 1996**

This legislation requires employers to report all new hires within 20 days of their hire date to the State Department of New Hires. The law requires only that employers forward the W-4 form to the state, but some states have developed their own forms for this purpose. As a side benefit for employers, the new hire reporting database has reduced and prevented fraudulent or erroneous unemployment payments that would otherwise be charged to the employer's unemployment insurance account. The database also cross-checks against workers' compensation claims which has reduced fraud and errors in those programs as well.

---

Payroll administration is often taken for granted until there are problems. The payroll process needs to be reliable to ensure employees are paid correctly and on time.

Now that we have discussed the basic components of compensation, it is time to consider how to evaluate the effectiveness of a compensation program.

# Evaluating Compensation Programs

Attraction, retention, and motivation are key to human resource objectives. By quantitatively and qualitatively reviewing their success in these three areas on a routine basis, the human resource group can ensure the organization is effectively achieving its goals and objectives in regard to its compensation philosophy. Quantitative data, such as turnover statistics and offer-to-accept ratios, can and should be measured. The HR department should also be concerned with qualitative information such as the performance management process and achievement of company objectives.

Ideally, the HR management team will collect this data and review the information with the organization's leadership on a regular basis. It is important for the success and appropriateness of the compensation programs to go through routine evaluation to ensure they remain competitive and that they continue to meet the organization's objectives.

In order to make sure your organization is attracting candidates and retaining and motivating employees, try these simple rules:

**Keep the compensation plan design simple.**    Compensation can become inherently complex. It can become quite easy to "not see the forest and get lost among the trees" and implement programs that are confusing to employees. Successful compensation programs must be simple and straightforward.

**Keep the compensation plan in line with the compensation philosophy.**    The compensation plan should be periodically reviewed to ensure that it continues to follow the organization's compensation philosophy. All compensation plans within the organization should keep its goal of leading, meeting, or lagging the market in sight when they are being developed, proposed, and implemented to ensure that the plan serves the organization's strategic goals.

**Do the research.**   Collecting market data and analyzing the results allows companies to assess whether or not their current pay structure and compensation program follows the organization's philosophy to lead, meet, or lag the market. Comparing incumbent data to market data is a proactive step to ensuring pay is in line with the company's pay philosophy. It also allows the human resource team to mitigate changes in the labor market, especially when compensation becomes more competitive for certain skill sets.

## Internal Evaluation

Evaluating internal pay practices and their effectiveness on a regular basis is a sound practice. This can be achieved through employee interviews, focus groups, and employee surveys, to name a few methods. Pay programs can become dysfunctional or outdated quickly. Reviewing compensation strategy and existing pay programs with executive management on a regular basis will help ensure that pay practices are aligned with the company's direction. Using the employee population to gather information from focus groups or employee opinion surveys provides valuable feedback on the success of compensation programs.

Regular review of pay is especially critical and time sensitive for sales employees and executive management. Because a greater proportion of their pay is part of special pay and/or incentive programs and they have such an immediate impact on the financial success of the organization, pay programs for sales employees and executives need to be reviewed on a regular basis.

## External Evaluation

In addition to collecting, analyzing, and comparing salary survey data against the organization's pay philosophy, pay programs, and incumbent population, it is helpful to use other external sources. Salary survey data is critical, but it may not keep up with the rapid changes that take place in the marketplace. Relationships with human resource counterparts at competitors can serve as a key resource. The local SHRM chapter and other HR associations can prove to be extremely helpful resources. Anecdotal compensation data from counterparts is helpful in supporting salary survey data and the organization's market position.

Once the compensation program's design is final, communication and implementation are critical to the success of the program.

## Communicating Compensation Programs

Taking the time to develop a compensation philosophy, participate in salary surveys, and develop new compensation programs does not help the organization unless results and objectives are clearly communicated to employees and managers.

For example, when rolling out the annual merit increase process, it is important to have timely communications geared toward both management and employee populations. Management typically receives different or additional information designed to facilitate their role as evaluator. Sharing salary survey results with management continues the dialogue about attracting, retaining, and motivating talent through existing or new programs.

Communicating compensation programs or philosophy involves a series of written communications. Updating the company intranet, the employee handbook, or plan documents are a few examples of written information that serve as a great resource for employees.

The compensation philosophy should be known by management and, in some organizations, all employees. Ultimately, communication of compensation programs should be simple, and the alignment to compensation philosophy should be visible.

# Benefits

When most employees think about their benefit packages, they think of medical and dental insurance, vacation and sick leave, and the retirement plan, but employers provide many other benefits that employees often overlook. These include such things as the location of their facilities and the length of the daily commute for employees, "dress down" days for employees, and salaries that are competitive with the industry and profession. These are all factors taken into consideration by candidates when considering whether or not to accept an offer. However, without specific effort on the part of employers, employees are often unaware of the value of the benefits provided for them because they rarely consider these costs when they think about their total income. Decisions about these facets of the employment relationship in each company can either help or hurt the efforts of the organization to attract and retain employees.

Employee benefit programs are an integral part of a company's total compensation plan and represent a significant cost to employers. The purpose of this section is to explore how HR professionals, working with senior management, can determine the mix of benefits that will attract and retain the type of employees needed by the company to achieve its goals.

While the level of cash compensation can be varied to attract candidates at different skill levels, the mix of employee benefits can be used to attract and retain different segments of the employee population. For example, an organization interested in attracting employees who are focused on maintaining a high level of knowledge in their chosen fields may offer a generous educational reimbursement benefit and provide training opportunities as a way of attracting and retaining those employees. There are a wide variety of benefits for companies to choose from at varying levels of cost. There are two main categories of benefits that may be offered, those that are legally mandated and those that are voluntary. Legally mandated benefits are easy. They include social security, Medicare, unemployment insurance, Family and Medical Leave, workers compensation, and COBRA benefit continuation.

The kinds of benefits that organizations may voluntarily provide are significantly more complicated. Table 6.4 provides some examples of the voluntary benefits.

**TABLE 6.4** Voluntary Employee Benefits

| Types of Benefits | Benefit Details |
| --- | --- |
| Deferred compensation | Qualified pension plans |
| | Nonqualified pension plans |
| Health and welfare benefits | Medical insurance |
| | Dental insurance |
| | Vision insurance |
| | Life insurance |
| | AD&D insurance |
| | Short-/long-term disability insurance |
| | Prescription coverage |
| Work-life balance | Vacation leave |
| | Sick leave |
| | Paid time off |
| | Paid holidays |
| | Child care |
| | Fitness |
| | Elder care |
| Other voluntary benefits | Employee assistance plans |
| | Relocation assistance |
| | Tuition reimbursement |
| | Flexible spending accounts |
| | Adoption assistance |
| | Section 529 plans |
| | Commute assistance |

Let's begin our discussion with a brief review of the benefits that are mandated by the federal government. Once again, keep in mind that legal requirements in your state may differ in some respects from the federal requirements. For purposes of the PHR/SPHR examinations, you must be familiar with the federal requirements.

# Legally Mandated Benefits

The first legally mandated employee benefits were introduced as part of President Franklin Delano Roosevelt's (FDR) New Deal programs during the mid-1930s to aid the millions of Americans who lost their jobs and were unable to find work during the Great Depression. Unemployment reached 25 percent at the low point of the Depression in 1933, leaving many families destitute, homeless, and living in shantytowns throughout the nation. In response to this economic crisis, when FDR was elected in 1932, he set about creating protections for American workers to provide a safety net during economic downturns.

## Social Security and Medicare

A key piece of the legislation introduced by FDR that has had an enduring impact on employers was the Social Security Act of 1935 (SSA). The SSA introduced *Old Age, Survivors, and Disability Insurance (OASDI)* that is to be paid to qualified workers upon retirement or disability or to their surviving dependents in the event of a worker's death. In addition to these social welfare benefits, the SSA established unemployment insurance (UI) for workers. The constitutionality of both the OASDI and UI was challenged in court, and in 1937, the U.S. Supreme Court ruled that both were valid and constitutional.

In the early 1960s, Presidents John F. Kennedy and Lyndon B. Johnson committed themselves to raising the standard of living among poor and elderly Americans, and in his State of the Union message in 1965, President Johnson presented a report to Congress recommending what became the Medicare program. This program was created by the Social Security Amendments of 1965 and provided medical and hospital insurance benefits for the elderly.

Taxes to support the OASDI and Medicare programs are paid equally by employers and employees. The original legal basis for the tax was contained in the SSA of 1935, but in 1939 Congress repealed the tax sections of the SSA and enacted the Federal Insurance Contributions Act (FICA) to replace them. The FICA transferred responsibility for collecting these taxes to the Internal Revenue Service, which remains the taxing authority for OASDI and the Medicare program. There have been many changes in both the tax rates and the wage base over the years based on changes in the economy. The tax rates for both programs are set by statute and reviewed as needed by Congress to ensure the fiscal viability of the programs. The wage base is currently revised each year according to a formula set by statute. Table 6.5 shows the changes in the taxable rate over several years.

**TABLE 6.5**  OASDI and Medicare Tax Rates for 1937–1958 and 1999–2003

| Year | OASDI Rate | Medicare Rate | Maximum Wage |
| --- | --- | --- | --- |
| 1937–49 | 1.000 | — | $3,000 |
| 1950 | 1.500 | — | 3,000 |
| 1951–53 | 1.500 | — | 3,600 |

**TABLE 6.5**   OASDI and Medicare Tax Rates for 1937–1958 and 1999–2003 *(continued)*

| Year | OASDI Rate | Medicare Rate | Maximum Wage |
| --- | --- | --- | --- |
| 1954 | 2.000 | — | 3,600 |
| 1955–56 | 2.000 | — | 4,200 |
| 1957–58 | 2.250 | — | 4,200 |
| | | | *data cut* |
| 1999 | 6.200 | 1.450 | 72,600 |
| 2000 | 6.200 | 1.450 | 76,200 |
| 2001 | 6.200 | 1.450 | 80,400 |
| 2002 | 6.200 | 1.450 | 84,900 |
| 2003 | 6.200 | 1.450 | 87,000 |

The complete table of OASDI and Medicare tax rates is available on the DOL website at www.ssa.gov/OACT/ProgData/taxRates.html.

As was discussed in the "Payroll Administration" section, employees must receive a statement of all taxes withheld from their paychecks each pay period. Depending upon the payroll system that is selected, the deduction for social security tax may be listed on paychecks as OASDI, FICA, or SSA. Deductions for the Medicare tax are listed separately and generally easier to identify as they are usually referred to as Medicare withholdings.

Another change in the OASDI program that affects employers is the change in the age at which workers may receive maximum benefits. This increase in the retirement age was necessary due to the improvements in health and resulting increased longevity of older Americans. This, combined with the impending retirement of employees born during the Baby Boom (people in the U.S. born between 1946 and 1964 are considered part of the Baby Boom) required Congress to take action to ensure the continued viability of the fund. In 1983, amendments to the SSA gradually increased the age at which workers are eligible to receive full retirement benefits based on a worker's year of birth. Table 6.6, based on data prepared by the Social Security Administration, shows the gradual increase for workers born in different years.

These increases in the retirement age mean that Americans will be part of the work force for a longer period of time. As discussed in Chapter 4, "Workforce Planning and Employment," this requires employers to consider these demographic changes when forecasting their needs for employees.

**TABLE 6.6**    Changes in Full Retirement Age

| Year of Birth | Full Retirement Age |
| --- | --- |
| 1937 or earlier | 65 |
| 1938 | 65 and 2 months |
| 1939 | 65 and 4 months |
| 1940 | 65 and 6 months |
| 1941 | 65 and 8 months |
| 1942 | 65 and 10 months |
| 1943–1954 | 66 |
| 1955 | 66 and 2 months |
| 1956 | 66 and 4 months |
| 1957 | 66 and 6 months |
| 1958 | 66 and 8 months |
| 1959 | 66 and 10 months |
| 1960 and later | 67 |

## Unemployment Insurance

Recall that the SSA of 1935 established the first federal unemployment insurance program. The SSA confers upon the states the responsibility for UI administration and distributes federal unemployment insurance funds to them for that purpose. Each state develops its own UI program, so eligibility requirements for *state unemployment insurance (SUI)* vary between states, as do the SUI tax rates. The state rates vary between employers as well, since states increase or decrease the amount of tax based on the number of employees terminated during the year.

When Congress moved taxing authority for OASDI to the IRS in 1939 by creating FICA, it also created the Federal Unemployment Tax Act (FUTA), moving unemployment taxing authority to the IRS as well. The FUTA tax rate is set by statute and is currently 6.2 percent of the first $7,000 earned by each worker during the year. All employers who make their SUI payments on time receive a credit of 5.4 percent toward their FUTA taxes, which means the effective FUTA tax rate is .8 percent for them.

Although unemployment is administered by the states, FUTA mandates minimum requirements for them to follow as described next.

### Employers Subject to FUTA

Amendments to FUTA have changed the definition of which employers are subject to FUTA since the law was first enacted. Currently, employers subject to FUTA include those who pay employees who are not farm workers or household workers. Those employers who paid wages of $1,500 or more in any calendar quarter in either 2002 or 2003 or employed one or more employees for a portion of a day in any 20 or more different weeks during the previous year or the current year to date are also subject to FUTA.

Employers of farm workers are subject to FUTA if they paid $20,000 or more to the workers during a calendar quarter in the previous year or the current year to date, or if 10 or more farm workers were employed during some part of a day (not necessarily at the same time) during any 20 or more different weeks during the previous year or the current year to date.

Employers of household workers are subject to FUTA tax if they pay $1,000 or more per calendar quarter to those who work in private homes, college clubs, or chapters of college sororities and fraternities.

### Employee Eligibility for Unemployment Benefits

As I mentioned before, each state determines SUI eligibility requirements within its jurisdiction. With few exceptions, unemployment compensation is paid for a maximum of 26 weeks, during which the recipient must be actively pursuing employment. From time to time when the unemployment rate is very high, Congress will submit a bill to the president extending this time period. If the president signs the bill, compensation will be paid, usually for an additional 13 weeks.

### Reducing Unemployment Tax Rates

As previously mentioned, employers are able to reduce the SUI tax rate by carefully managing their employment processes. There are a number of ways to do this, beginning with an effective hiring process that appropriately screens candidates to ensure that whoever is selected has all the qualifications for the position. Particularly in very large organizations, establishing a means of communicating between divisions and departments to avoid hiring new employees when employees in other areas of the organization with the necessary skills and experience are being laid off will make better use of the organization's investment in training and reduce the SUI tax rate. An effective performance management program in which employees are regularly coached and counseled about their performance so that they have an opportunity to improve will also reduce the need to terminate employees. When employees must be terminated for cause, maintaining accurate records of the reasons for termination will provide the basis for aggressively fighting claims that are not justified. Finally, the HR department must be diligent in following up with claims for unemployment to ensure that unjustified claims are challenged.

## Family Medical Leave Act

In 1993, President Bill Clinton signed the Family Medical Leave Act (FMLA), which was created to assist employees in balancing the needs of their families with the demands of their jobs. In creating the FMLA, Congress intended that employees not have to choose between keeping their jobs and attending to seriously ill family members. The FMLA provides three benefits for eligible employees of covered organizations:

1. 12 weeks of unpaid leave within a 12-month period
2. Continuation of health benefits
3. Reinstatement to the same position or an equivalent position at the end of the leave

FMLA applies to all public agencies and schools, regardless of their size and to private employers with 50 or more employees working within a 75-mile radius. The law provides detailed descriptions on how employers determine if these requirements apply to them:

**50 or more employees**    Employers must comply with the FMLA when they employ 50 or more employees for each working day during each of 20 or more calendar work weeks in the current or preceding year. The statute does not require the work weeks be consecutive. Guidelines in FMLA state that the number of employees at a worksite is determined by the number of employees on the payroll.

Employers remain subject to FMLA rules until the number of employees on the payroll is less than 50 for 20 nonconsecutive weeks in the current and preceding calendar year. This means that if employers with 50 employees on the payroll for the first 20 weeks in 2004 reduce the number of employees for the rest of 2004 and remain at the reduced level throughout 2005, they must continue to comply with FMLA through the end of 2005.

**Worksites within a 75-mile radius**    The number of employees at each worksite is based on the employees who report to work at that site, or in the case of outside sales representatives or employees who telecommute, the location from which their work is assigned.

This can either be a single place of business or a group of adjacent locations, such as a business park or campus.

A worksite may also consist of facilities that are not directly connected if they are in reasonable geographic proximity, used for the same purpose and share the same staff and equipment.

Employees, such as construction workers or truck drivers, who regularly work at sites away from the main business office, are counted as employees at the business site to which they report, the worksite that is their home base, or from where their work is assigned, not from a worksite where they may be temporarily deployed for the duration of a project.

## Employees Eligible for FMLA

FMLA also provides guidelines for determining which employees are eligible for leave. This includes employees who:

- Work for an employer who is subject to FMLA as described previously.
- Have been employed by the employer for at least 12 months, which need not be consecutive. Employees who received benefits or other compensation during any part of a week are counted as having been employed for that week.
- Have worked at least 1,250 hours during the 12 months immediately preceding the leave, based on the FLSA standards for determining compensable hours of work. If accurate time records are not maintained, it is up to the employer to prove that the employee did not meet

the requirement; if this is not possible, the law provides that the employee will be presumed to have met the requirement.

The determination of whether or not an employee meets the requirement for 1,250 hours of work within the past 12 months is counted from the date the leave begins. Within two days of notice by an employee of the intent to take an FMLA leave, the employer must confirm that the employee will meet the FMLA requirements as of the first day of the leave or advise the employee when they will become eligible for leave. Once the employer has confirmed an employee's eligibility, it may not be revoked at a later time. Similarly, if an employer neglects to inform an employee that they are ineligible for FMLA leave prior to the date the leave begins, the employee is considered eligible to take the leave and the employer may not deny it at that point.

## Key Employee Exception

FMLA leave is available to all employees of covered organizations who meet the FMLA eligibility requirements. FMLA includes a provision that key employees may be denied reinstatement to the position they held or an equivalent position if the employer demonstrates that the reinstatement would cause "substantial and grievous economic injury" to its operations. A key employee is defined by FMLA as a salaried employee among the highest-paid 10 percent of employees at the worksite as defined previously. The law requires that the determination of which employees are the highest paid is calculated by dividing the employee's year-to-date earnings (base salary, premium pay, incentive pay and bonuses) and dividing the total earnings by the number of weeks worked. Whether or not an employee meets the definition of a key employee is to be determined at the time leave is requested, and the employee must be advised of this status and its implications within a reasonable period of time.

## Reasons for FMLA Leave

FMLA presents covered employers with a list of circumstances under which FMLA leave must be provided if requested by an eligible employee:

- The birth of a child and caring for the infant. FMLA leave is available to both fathers and mothers; however, if both parents work for the same employer, the combined total of the leave may not exceed the 12-week total. In addition, the leave must be completed within 12 months of the child's birth.

- Placement of an adopted or foster child with the employee. The same conditions that apply to the birth of a child apply here as well; in this case, the leave must be completed within 12 months of the child's placement.

- To provide care for the employee's spouse, son, daughter, or parent with a serious health condition. For purposes of FMLA leave, a spouse must be recognized as such by the state in which the employee resides.

    A parent can be the biological parent of the employee or one who has legal standing *in loco parentis*, a Latin term that means "in place of the parent" and applies to those who care for a child on a daily basis. In loco parentis does not require either a biological or legal relationship.

    A son or daughter may be a biological child, adopted or foster child, stepchild, legal ward, or the child of someone acting in loco parentis. A child must also be under

18 years of age or, if over 18, unable to care for themselves due to a physical or mental disability.

Employers may require those employees requesting FMLA leave to provide reasonable documentation to support the family relationship with the person for whom they will be providing care.

- When an employee is unable to perform the functions of the job due to a serious health condition. According to FMLA, a serious health condition is an illness, injury, impairment, or physical or mental condition that requires:

  - Inpatient care or subsequent treatment related to inpatient care.

  - Continuing treatment by a health care provider due to a period of incapacity of more than three consecutive calendar days. Incapacity refers to an inability to work, attend school, or perform other daily activities as a result of the condition.

  - Incapacity due to pregnancy or prenatal care.

  - Treatment for a serious, chronic health condition.

### Types of FMLA Leave

FMLA provides for three types of leave: continuous, reduced leave, and intermittent. A *continuous FMLA leave* is one in which the employee is absent from work for an extended period of time. A *reduced FMLA leave schedule* is one in which the employee's regular work schedule is reduced for a period of time. This can mean a reduction in the hours worked each day or in the number of days worked during the week. An *intermittent FMLA leave* is one in which the employee is absent from work for multiple periods of time due to a single illness or injury. When utilizing intermittent leave, employees must make an effort to schedule the leave to avoid disruption of regular business operations. In addition, the employer may assign an employee requesting intermittent leave to a different position with equivalent pay and benefits in order to meet the employee's needs.

### Tracking Reduced and Intermittent FMLA Leave

While keeping track of the amount of FMLA used for a continuous leave is fairly straightforward, ensuring that accurate records of reduced and intermittent FMLA records are maintained can be a bit more difficult. In either case, only the amount of leave used may be deducted from the 12 weeks available to the employee. For example, an employee whose regular work schedule of 40 hours per week is reduced to 20 hours per week would be charged one-half week FMLA leave for each week that they work the reduced schedule.

For intermittent leave, employers may charge for leave in increments of not less than one hour. Employees should provide at least two days notice of the need to utilize the intermittent leave whenever possible.

### Ending FMLA Leave

FMLA leave ends when the employee has used the full 12 weeks of leave, the serious illness of the employee or family member ends, or, in some cases, when the family member or the employee dies. When one of these three circumstances occur, the employee may return to the same or equivalent position with no loss of benefits. If the employee wishes to continue the leave at that point, the company is under no obligation to grant it, unless there is a company policy in place to provide a longer leave.

### FMLA Implications for Employers

FMLA requirements are complex and confusing, particularly when used in conjunction with worker compensation or the ADA. There are some things employers can do to ensure that they comply with its requirements. HR professionals need to ensure that supervisors throughout their organizations are aware of the requirements for FMLA leaves and the consequences for noncompliance.

To start, review current leave practices to ensure that they comply with FMLA requirements and any state laws with more stringent requirements. FMLA leave policies should be included in the employee handbook; new hires should be advised of its availability. It is important for HR professionals to work with supervisors and managers throughout the organization to ensure that they understand the implications for situations that may be subject to FMLA regulations and encourage them to talk to HR about potential FMLA leave situations. HR needs to take an active role in educating the management team about the interaction of FMLA, ADA, and worker compensation requirements. Before an FMLA situation occurs, a documentation procedure and policy should be developed and HR should take an active role in ensuring that all leaves comply with established procedures to avoid possible claims of discriminatory practices. When workers compensation and FMLA leaves occur simultaneously, make sure to advise the employee that the leaves run concurrently.

The complete text of the FMLA can be found online at `www.dol.gov/dol/allcfr/ESA/Title_29/Part_825/toc.htm`.

## Workers Compensation

Workers compensation laws require employers to assume responsibility for all employee injuries, illnesses, and deaths that are related to employment. These laws are enacted and enforced by the individual states and provide benefits for employees that cover medical and rehabilitation expenses, provide income replacement during periods of disability when employees are unable to work, and pay benefits to their survivors in the event of an employee's death.

The amount of compensation paid is based on actuarial tables that take into account the seriousness of the injury, whether it is the disability is permanent or temporary, whether it is a full or partial disability (such as the loss of an eye or hand) and the amount of income lost due to the injury. In most cases, employers fund workers compensation obligations by purchasing coverage through private insurance companies or state-sponsored insurance funds. The premiums for workers compensation coverage are based on a percentage of the employer's payroll in various job categories. The percentages are different and depend on previous claim activity in each category. The rate charged for a roofer, for example, is much higher than that for an office worker due to the inherent danger of the job and the number and severity of claims that result.

In some states, companies may self-fund workers compensation programs, which means that they pay the total costs of any injuries or illnesses when they occur instead of paying insurance premiums. These are known as "nonsubscriber" plans and are rare; generally, self-funded insurance plans only make economic sense for very large organizations with the financial base to support the payment of large claims when they occur.

While increased emphasis on safety programs and training has led to a reduction in the number of nationwide workers compensation claims filed each year, the insurance rates are increasing due largely to increased medical costs. This is most evident in California, where employers saw costs double between 2000 and 2003, but it has also led to state reform of workers compensation programs in Florida, West Virginia, Washington state, and Texas.

Implementing programs aimed at reducing the cost of workers compensation coverage for their organizations is one way HR professionals can show a positive impact on the bottom line. Implementing safety training and injury prevention programs as discussed in Chapter 8, "Occupational Health, Safety, and Security," is one way to reduce job-related injury and illness and prevent claims. The costs of individual claims can be reduced by ensuring the availability of jobs that meet "light duty" medical requirements so that employees are able to return to work earlier, shortening the length of their leave.

## Health Benefit Continuation

Prior to 1986, employees who were laid off or resigned their jobs lost any health care benefits that were provided as part of those jobs. While no federal law requires employers to provide health benefits, organizations with 20 or more employees who provide health care benefits are required to continue the benefits for those who leave the company or for their dependents when certain qualifying events occur. The law requiring this, the Consolidated Omnibus Budget Reconciliation Act (COBRA) was signed by President Ronald Reagan in 1986. COBRA is an amendment to the Employee Retirement Income Security Act (ERISA). The requirements placed on employers by the law are discussed later in this chapter.

# Voluntary Benefits

Making decisions about the benefit package that is most appropriate for a particular organization's workforce requires consideration of many factors: demographics, industry standards, local area practices, the financial situation of the company, and the organizational culture. There are many possible benefits that employers can offer as part of the total compensation package, and finding the right mix can contribute to the ability of the organization to attract and retain employees with the desired qualifications. One way for HR professionals to demonstrate the strategic contributions that they can make to business operations is by developing alternative benefit packages and analyzing the impact of each on recruiting effectiveness, retention, and net profit as part of a cost benefit analysis. In doing so, it is important to consider all types of benefits that may appeal to the organization's employee base.

Determining which benefits will best suit a particular organization begins with a needs assessment, which is described in Chapter 2. Whatever benefits are offered, it is crucial that they meet the needs of the type of employees the organization is trying to attract and retain.

As previously described in Table 6.4, voluntary benefits fall into four main categories: deferred compensation, health and welfare benefits, work-life balance benefits, and other benefits. While there are no federal laws requiring employers to provide any of them, there are some federal laws that regulate pensions or benefits. Three of these laws have implications in both areas (pension and benefits) and are discussed here. Those laws that apply to only one area (pension or benefits) are discussed in subsequent sections.

**Employee Retirement Income Security Act (ERISA) of 1974**   ERISA was created by Congress to set standards for private pensions and some group welfare programs such as medical and life insurance. ERISA was amended in 1986 by the Consolidated Omnibus Budget Reconciliation Act (COBRA), which requires businesses with 20 or more employees to provide health plan continuation coverage under certain circumstances. The Health Insurance Portability and Accountability Act of 1996 (HIPAA) was another amendment to ERISA. HIPAA prohibits discrimination based on health status and limits restrictions that can be placed on individuals with pre-existing conditions. The requirements of these laws are discussed in detail in following sections.

**Older Worker Benefit Protection Act (OWBPA) of 1990**   In 1990, Congress passed the OWBPA in response to a Supreme Court decision that placed limitations on the Age Discrimination in Employment Act (ADEA) discussed in Chapter 4. The OWBPA amends the ADEA to include a prohibition on discrimination against older workers in all employee benefit plans unless any age-based reductions are justified by significant cost considerations. This amendment allows seniority systems as long as they do not require involuntary terminations of employees based on their age and extends ADEA protections to all employee benefits.

The OWBPA also defines the conditions under which employees may waive their rights to make claims under the act. To be acceptable, waivers must include the following components:

- Waiver agreements must be written in a way that can be understood by the average employee.
- Waivers must refer specifically to the rights or claims available under the ADEA.
- Employees may not waive rights or claims for actions that occur subsequent to signing the waiver.
- Employees must receive consideration in exchange for the waiver in addition to anything to which they are already entitled.
- The waiver must advise employees of their right to consult an attorney prior to signing the document.
- In individual cases, employees must be given 21 days to consider the agreement before they are required to sign; when a group of employees is involved, employees over 40 must be given 45 days to consider their decision.
- Once the waiver is signed, employees may revoke the agreement within seven days.
- In cases of group terminations, employees must be advised of the eligibility requirements for any exit incentive programs, any time limits for the programs, and a list of the job titles and ages of employees who have been selected or who are eligible for the program.

**Omnibus Budget Reconciliation Act (OBRA) of 1993**   The parts of the 1993 OBRA with relevance to HR have to do with changes that were made to employee benefit programs in addition to the cap on executive pay discussed in the relevant section earlier in this chapter. These changes require that health plans honor qualified medical child support orders for dependent children of employees when issued by a court. They also require that group health plans provide coverage for dependent adopted children when those children are placed for adoption in a covered employee's home.

## Deferred Compensation

Deferred compensation refers to tax-deferred retirement plans, such as IRAs, 401(k) programs, or traditional employer pension plans. There are some terms that will be used throughout this section with which candidates for the PHR/SPHR examinations should be familiar. The following list provides some definitions to aid in your understanding of the discussion of deferred compensation.

**Defined benefit**    *Defined benefit* plans are traditional pension plans in which the employer provides a specific benefit upon retirement. The funds are not accounted for individually.

**Defined contribution**    *Defined contribution* plans are individual plans in which the amount of funds contributed is known, but the amount of the benefit that is eventually paid out is not known because it depends on the investment returns that are earned. The funds are accounted for in individual accounts for each participant.

**Nonforfeitable**    A *nonforfeitable* claim is one that exists due to a participant's service. Nonforfeitable claims are unconditional and legally enforceable.

**Plan administrator**    The *plan administrator* is the person designated by the plan sponsor to manage the plan.

**Plan sponsor**    The *plan sponsor* is the entity that establishes the plan. This may be a single employer, a labor organization, or, in the case of a multi-employer plan, a group representing the parties that established the plan.

**Qualified plan**    A *qualified plan* meets ERISA requirements and provides tax advantages for both employees and employers. To be classified as a qualified plan, a pension plan cannot provide additional benefits for officers, shareholders, supervisors, or other highly compensated employees.

**Nonqualified Plan**    A *nonqualified retirement plan* is one in which the benefits exceed the limitations of qualified plans or do not meet other IRS requirements for favorable tax treatment.

Pension benefits for American workers were first provided in the late nineteenth century by business owners who used them to reward long-term employees. Early pension plans were defined benefit plans with all funds being provided by the employers. The payments to retirees were not set aside specifically for retirees but were made from business operating funds. As a result, a company that went out of business was no longer able to make the pension payments and employees did not receive the benefits that had been promised to them. To encourage businesses to provide pension benefits, in 1935 the SSA allowed employers who provided pension plans to deduct the full amount of the payments they made to employees, but there were no laws to govern how the plans operated or to require that the funds to pay pensions be set aside to ensure their availability for retirees. In 1958, Congress made its first attempt to exert some control over private pension plans when it passed the Welfare and Pension Disclosure Act (WPDA) requiring the administrators of health insurance, pension, and supplemental unemployment insurance plans to file descriptions of the plans and annual financial reports with the Department of Labor.

As the number of pension plans provided for employees by American businesses grew, some companies found ways to obtain tax benefits from pension plans while denying benefits to employees. There were no requirements for communicating information to plan participants, so many employees were unaware of eligibility requirements. There was also little oversight of the ways the plans were operated. Vesting schedules were inadequate and many long-term employees found themselves ineligible to receive pension benefits as a result. There were no established standards to ensure the viability of plans to pay promised benefits. The result of this was that many employees found themselves without pensions when they were ready to retire. Furthermore, some businesses set lengthy vesting schedules to obtain tax benefits but terminated long-term employees just before they became vested in the plan.

 **Real World Scenario**

**Life Before the Employee Retirement Income Security Act (ERISA)**

In 1963, almost 7,000 employees of the Studebaker Corporation lost all or most of their pension benefits due to a plant closure in Indiana. More than 4,000 of these employees had served an average of more than 22 years with the company and, at the time of the plant's closure, were an average of 52 years old. The pension fund failed largely because there was no legal precedent requiring organizations to set aside adequate funds with which to pay retirement benefits; plans at that time were still being funded from current operating funds within the Studebaker Corporation.

While the failure of the Studebaker Corporation fund was not unique, the large number of workers deprived of benefits focused national attention on the problem and led eventually to the passage of the Employee Retirement Income Security Act (ERISA). ERISA replaced the WPDA, increasing the reporting requirements, requiring that pension funds be separated from the operating funds of the business, establishing vesting schedules for plan participants, requiring employers to provide summary plan descriptions of the plans to employees, and setting minimum standards for fund management.

### ERISA Requirements

ERISA requires organizations to file three types of reports: a summary plan description, an annual report, and reports to participants of their benefit rights.

**Summary plan description (SPD)**   A *summary plan description (SPD)* provides plan participants with information about the provisions, policies, and rules established by the plan and advises them on actions they can take in utilizing the plan. ERISA requires that the SPD include the name and other identifying information about plan sponsors, administrators, and trustees, along with any information related to collective bargaining agreements for the plan participants. The SPD must describe what eligibility requirements must be met for participating in the plan and for receiving benefits, as well as the circumstances under which participants would be disqualified or ineligible for participation or be denied benefits.

The SPD must also describe the financing source for the plan and the name of the organization providing benefits. Information on the end of the plan year and whether records are maintained on a calendar, plan or fiscal year basis must be included in the description.

For health and welfare plans, the SPD must describe claim procedures, along with the name of the DOL office that will assist participants and beneficiaries with HIPAA claims. The SPD must also describe what remedies are available when claims are denied.

A new SPD reflecting all changes made must be prepared and distributed every five years unless no changes have occurred. Every ten years, a new SPD must be distributed to participants whether or not changes have occurred.

**Annual reports**    ERISA requires annual reports to be filed for all employee benefit plans. The reports must include financial statements, the number of employees in the plan, and the names and addresses of the plan fiduciaries. ERISA mandates that any persons compensated by the plan during the preceding year be disclosed, along with the amount of compensation paid to each, the nature of the services rendered, and any relationship that exists between these parties and any party in interest to the plan. Information that is provided with regard to plan assets must be certified by the organization that holds the assets, whether it is the plan sponsor, an insurance company, or bank.

The annual reports must be audited by a CPA or other qualified public accountant and any actuarial reports must be prepared by an *enrolled actuary*, who has been licensed jointly by the Department of the Treasury and the Department of Labor, to provide actuarial services for U.S. pension plans.

The DOL is given authority to simplify filing and reporting requirements for plans with less than 100 participants.

Once submitted, annual reports and other documents become public record and are made available in the DOL public document room. The DOL may also use this information to conduct research and analyze data.

**Participant benefit rights reports**    Participants may request a report of the total benefits accrued on their behalf along with the amount of the benefit that is nonforfeitable. If there are no nonforfeitable amounts accrued at the time the report is requested, the earliest date that benefits will become nonforfeitable must be provided. Participants are entitled to receive the report no more than once per year.

ERISA records must be maintained for six years from the date they were due to be filed with DOL. In addition to requiring the preparation of these reports, ERISA regulations stipulate that annual reports are to be filed with the DOL within 210 days of the end of the plan year. The DOL may reject reports that are incomplete or that contain qualified opinions from the CPA or actuary. Rejected plans must be resubmitted within 45 days or the DOL can retain a CPA to audit the report on behalf of the participants. ERISA authorizes the DOL to bring civil actions on behalf of plan participants if necessary to resolve any issues.

In addition to the reporting requirements it contains, ERISA sets minimum standards for employee participation, or eligibility requirements, as well as vesting requirements for qualified pension plans.

**Employee participation**    A *participant* is an employee who has met the eligibility requirements for the plan. The law sets minimum participation requirements as follows:

- When one year of service has been completed or the employee has reached the age of 21, whichever is later, unless the plan provides for 100 percent vesting after two years of service. In that case, the requirement changes to completion of two years of service or reaching age 21, whichever is later.

- Employees may not be excluded from the plan on the basis of age; that is, they may not be excluded because they have reached a specified age.

- When employees have met the minimum service and age requirements, they must become participants no later than the first day of the plan year after they meet the requirement, or six months after the requirements are met, whichever is earlier.

**Vesting**    Qualified plans must also meet minimum vesting standards. *Vesting* refers to the point at which employees own the contributions their employer has made to the pension plan whether or not they remain employed with the company. The vesting requirements established by ERISA refer only to funds that are contributed by the employer; any funds contributed by plan participants are owned by the employee. Employees are always 100 percent vested in their own money and earn the right to be vested in the employer's contribution.

Vesting may be immediate or delayed. *Immediate vesting* occurs when employees are 100 percent, or fully, vested as soon as they meet the eligibility requirements of the plan. *Delayed vesting* occurs when participants must wait for a defined period of time prior to becoming fully vested. There are two types of delayed vesting: cliff vesting and graded vesting.

- With *cliff vesting*, participants become 100 percent invested after a specified period of time. ERISA sets the maximum period at five years for qualified plans, which means that participants vest nothing until they have completed the five years of service, after which they are fully vested.

- *Graded vesting*, which is also referred to as *graduated or gradual vesting*, establishes a vesting schedule that provides for partial vesting each year for a specified number of years. A graded vesting schedule in a qualified plan must allow for at least 20 percent vesting after three years and 20 percent per year after that, with participants achieving full vesting after seven years of service. Table 6.7 illustrates a graded vesting schedule which complies with ERISA requirements.

**TABLE 6.7**    ERISA Graded Vesting Schedule

| Years of Service | Percent Vested |
| --- | --- |
| 3 | 20 percent |
| 4 | 40 percent |
| 5 | 60 percent |

**TABLE 6.7**   ERISA Graded Vesting Schedule *(continued)*

| Years of Service | Percent Vested |
| --- | --- |
| 6 | 80 percent |
| 7 | 100 percent |

**Benefit accrual requirements**   ERISA sets specific requirements for determining how much of an accrued benefit participants are entitled to receive if they leave the company prior to retirement. Plans must account for employee contributions to the plan separately from the funds contributed by the employer since the employees are entitled to all the funds contributed by them to the plan when they leave the company.

**Form and payment of benefits**   There are specific requirements for when payments are to be made when participants reach retirement age or when they leave the company. ERISA also provides guidance for employers to deal with *qualified domestic relations orders (QDRO)*, legal orders issued by state courts or other state agencies to require pension payments to alternate payees. An alternate payee must be a spouse or former spouse or child or other dependent of a plan participant.

ERISA also defines funding requirements for pension plans and sets standards for those who are responsible for safeguarding the funds until they are paid to employees. Finally, ERISA provides civil and criminal penalties for organizations that violate its provisions.

**Funding**   An enrolled actuary determines how much money is required to fund the accrued obligations of the plan, and ERISA requires that these funds be maintained in trust accounts separate from business operating funds. These amounts must be deposited on a quarterly basis; the final contribution must be made no later than eight and a half months after the end of the plan year.

**Fiduciary responsibility**   A *fiduciary* is a person, corporation, or other legal entity that holds property or assets on behalf of, or in trust for the pension fund. ERISA requires fiduciaries to operate pension funds in the best interest of the participants and their beneficiaries and at the lowest possible expense to them. All actions taken with regard to the plan assets must be in accord with the *prudent person standard of care*, a common law concept that requires all actions be undertaken with "the care, skill, prudence, and diligence . . . that a prudent man acting in like capacity" would use, as defined in ERISA itself.

Fiduciaries may be held personally liable for losses to the plan resulting from any breach of fiduciary responsibility that they commit and may be required to make restitution for the losses and be subject to legal action. They are not held liable for breaches of fiduciary responsibility that occur prior to the time they became fiduciaries.

ERISA prohibits transactions between pension plans and "parties in interest." A *party in interest* may be a fiduciary, a person or entity providing services to the plan, an employer or employee organization, a person who owns 50 percent or more of the business, relatives of any of the above, or corporations that are involved with the plan in any of these functions.

**Administration and enforcement**    Criminal penalties for willful violations of ERISA include fines of between $5,000 and $100,000 and imprisonment for up to one year. Civil actions may be brought by plan participants or their beneficiaries, fiduciaries, or by the DOL to recover benefits or damages or to force compliance with the law.

## Economic Growth and Tax Relief Reconciliation Act of 2001 (EGTRRA)

The EGTRRA made a number of changes to contribution limits, increasing many and allowing for catch-up contributions for employees over 50 years of age. The act provides a schedule of changes through the end of the year 2010, at which time they will revert to the levels in place prior to this act unless Congress extends them.

## Defined Benefit Plans

As mentioned previously in this chapter, a defined benefit plan is one in which the employer provides a pension for employees based on a formula. The formula looks at two factors: salary and length of service with the company. In most traditional defined benefit plans, the retirement benefit is based on the salary earned during the last five to ten years of earnings, but it may also be based on career average earnings, a flat dollar amount for each year of service, or a unit benefit plan in which the benefit payment is based on a percentage of earnings multiplied by the years of service.

In these plans, the company is committed to pay a specified benefit amount when an employee retires. How much the company must accrue each year may fluctuate based on the return earned on the invested funds. If the funds are invested in high growth investments, the company will need to transfer less cash from its operating funds to the pension trust, but if the return earned on the investment drops, the company may have to play "catch up" with larger than anticipated transfers of cash to maintain the viability of the plan. During the stock market boom of the late 1990s, many companies did not need to transfer large sums to fund their pension accounts, but when the stock market dropped, much of the value of the pension funds was lost. This required larger transfers to be made to maintain availability of the pension funds for employees.

## Cash Balance Plans

*Cash balance plans* (CBPs) have become increasingly popular since they were approved by the IRS in 1985—between 1996 and 2000, the percentage of cash balance plans nationwide grew from 4 to 23 percent. While some companies see them as a hybrid of the defined benefit and defined contribution plans, they are subject to the regulations placed on defined benefit plans. Cash balance plans are less costly for employers: in 1999, IBM revised its defined benefit plan to a CBP and projected savings of $500 billion over ten years as a result of the change.

In a CBP, benefits are determined by using a hypothetical personal pension account (PPA); each month this account is increased by a set rate, for example, 5 percent of the employee's salary. The account also accumulates interest, typically related to the interest rate on Treasury bills.

For employees, the benefit of the cash balance plan is that it is portable: when an employee resigns, the funds may be withdrawn in a lump sum payment, converted to an annuity, or remain in the employer's account and withdrawn at a later time. The downside to these plans is that they significantly reduce pension benefits for older workers when traditional defined benefit plans have been converted to CBPs. A number of lawsuits challenging these plans have been filed, alleging that the plans discriminate against older workers in violation of ERISA. Due to the controversy, the IRS suspended approval of conversions in 1999, pending resolution of the issue in the courts or by Congress. The federal district courts have been split in their rulings on this issue, but a case decided on July 31, 2003, *Cooper v IBM Personal Pension Plan and IBM Corporation*, in which the Court found that the plan did discriminate, may be the first to be reach a federal appeals court for clarification.

## Defined Contribution Plans

A defined contribution plan relies on contributions from employees and employers to fund individual retirement accounts. In these plans, the amount of the contribution is fixed, but the amount of the benefit available upon retirement can vary based on the type of investments that are made and the returns earned on them. There are several types of defined contribution plans:

**Profit sharing plans**  Also known as *discretionary contributions*, *profit-sharing plans* allow employers to contribute deferred compensation based on a percentage of company earnings each year. A maximum contribution of 25 percent or $40,000 may be made for an individual employee each year. The maximum amount was indexed to inflation in increments of $1,000 beginning in 2003. When calculating contributions, employers may only use the first $200,000 of an employee's compensation; as of 2003 this amount was indexed to inflation and adjusted annually in increments of $5,000. The percentage of the contribution may vary from year to year, and the company may elect to make no contributions in some years. The maximum tax deduction for contributions that can be taken by the employer is 25 percent of total employee compensation. Because the contributions may vary from year to year, profit sharing plans work well for companies with erratic profit levels.

**Money purchase plans**  A *money purchase plan* uses a fixed percentage of employee earnings to defer compensation. This type of plan works well for organizations with relatively stable earnings from year to year because the percentage is fixed and, once established, contributions must be made every year. The contribution limits are the same as the limits for profit sharing plans.

**Target benefit plans**  A *target benefit plan* is a hybrid plan, with similarities to a defined benefit plan and a money purchase plan. Instead of using a fixed percentage of employee salaries to determine annual contribution amounts, the contributions are calculated using actuarial formulas to calculate the amount needed to reach a predetermined benefit amount at retirement. Because this amount takes into consideration the current age of each employee, different amounts will be contributed for employees with equal compensation packages. As with other deferred contribution plans, the amounts are distributed to individual employee accounts, and the contribution limits are the same as the limits for profit sharing plans.

**Employee stock ownership plans (ESOPs)**  As previously discussed in the "Compensation" section of this chapter, ESOPs are a means by which employees can become owners of the company. For purposes of deferring compensation, ESOPs are often made part of an overall program that includes other plans. In the wake of the Enron collapse and scandal, ESOPs came under scrutiny by the federal government. As a result, limitations were placed on the amount of company stock that may be contained in a deferred compensation plan.

The website of the National Center for Employee Ownership has additional information at www.nceo.org.

**401(k) plans**  A common type of deferred compensation is the *401(k) plan*, established by the Revenue Act of 1978. A 401(k) plan allows for contributions from both employees and employers. Employees may defer a part of their pay before taxes up to limits established by the EGTRRA. Employers may make contributions as well; the limits for these are the same as those for profit sharing plans. Plans similar to the 401(k) are available for nonprofit workers (403(b) plans) and for public employees (457 plans). Any earnings or losses that accrue in the account impact on the funds available for retirement, and employees are ultimately responsible for ensuring that the funds are properly managed and available for use when they are ready to retire.

One requirement of 401(k) plans is that they may not provide greater benefits to *highly compensated employees (HCEs)* than other employees. An HCE is defined as a plan participant who, during the current or prior year, earned $90,000 or more, owns 5 percent or more of the company and, at the company's discretion, is one of the top paid 20 percent of employees. Each year, an *actual deferral percentage test (ADP)* must be conducted to ensure that the plan is within limits set by IRS regulations. When the ADP test indicates that HCE participants are realizing greater benefits from the plan than non-HCE participants, the company must take action to correct this or lose the tax benefits of the plan. To correct the problem, a company may refund the excess contributions to HCE participants, which will increase their taxable income for the prior year, or they may increase matching contributions to non-HCE employees in order to pass the test. Another option to correct imbalances is to aggregate the plan with other plans sponsored by the employer if available.

### Other Laws Impacting Deferred Compensation

Changes to different aspects of deferred compensation laws have been made at various times. They include the following:

**Retirement Equity Act (REA) of 1984**  The REA lowered age limits for participation and vesting in pension plans. It also required written approval from a spouse if the participant did not want to provide survivor benefits in the plan and placed restrictions on the conditions that could be placed on survivor benefits.

**Unemployment Compensation Amendments of 1992**  Among other provisions unrelated to pension administration, this act reduced rules for rolling over lump sum distributions of qualified retirement plans into other plans and subjected some distributions to 20 percent income tax withholding.

**Small Business Job Protection Act of 1996**  In order to relieve the costs of administering qualified plans for small businesses, this act simplified ADP tests for 401(k) plans and redefined highly compensated employees. In addition, it detailed minimum participation requirements and made changes to disclosure requirements for qualified plans.

## Nonqualified Deferred Compensation

Nonqualified deferred compensation plans are not protected by ERISA and are generally made available only to a limited number of employees at the executive level. Known as "top hat" plans, these benefits provide retirement funds that supplement qualified retirement benefits and are not subject to ERISA discrimination testing requirements. These plans allow highly compensated employees to defer income in excess of limits placed on qualified plans. Two types of nonqualified plans are grantor or rabbi trusts and excess deferral plans.

**Grantor or rabbi trusts**   Commonly known as a *rabbi trusts*, *grantor trusts* are nonqualified deferred compensation plans established to provide retirement income for officers, directors, and highly compensated employees (HCEs). The funds are unsecured and therefore subject to claims made by the organization's creditors. Benefits are taxable as ordinary income at the time they are paid to beneficiaries.

**Excess deferral plans**   An excess deferral plan allows the organization to make contributions to a nonqualified plan in order to reduce the impact of discrimination testing on highly compensated employees. This is done by making up the difference between what the executive could have contributed to the plan and what was actually allowed due to limits required by the qualified plan.

## Health and Welfare Benefits

Health and welfare benefits have come to be expected by most American workers. The benefits that fall into this category are listed in Table 6.4 at the beginning of this section and are described here in more detail.

**Medical insurance**   The cost of medical insurance is substantial for employers and employees. The costs can be controlled to a certain extent by the type of plan selected. Some plans to consider include:

**Health Maintenance Organizations (HMOs)**   HMOs are a type of managed care plan that focuses on preventive care and controlling health costs. HMOs generally utilize a *gate-keeper*, most often the patient's primary care physician, to determine whether or not patients need to be seen by a specialist.

**Preferred Provider Organizations (PPOs)**   PPOs utilize a network of health care providers for patient services and do not require patients to be referred by a gatekeeper. Employees who utilize health care services within the network make copayments and must also pay the difference between the fees negotiated by the plan and those charged by the physician.

**Point of service plans (POSs)**   POS plans include network physicians but allow for referrals outside of the network. When a network physician refers an employee to a care provider outside of the network, payment is covered by the plan, but when the employee sees a care provider outside the POS network, a coinsurance payment is required.

**Exclusive Provider Organizations (EPOs)**   An EPO also consists of a network and includes a hospital. Unlike physicians who participate in a PPO, EPO physicians may only see patients who are part of the EPO. Patients in an EPO may only see health care providers within the network; they receive no reimbursement for health care obtained outside of the network.

**Physician Hospital Organizations (PHOs)**   In a PHO, physicians join with a hospital and together rely on the PHO structure to develop and market their services and to negotiate and sign contracts. PHOs are unique in that they contract directly with employer organizations to provide services.

**Fee-for-service plans (FFSs)**    An FFS plan is typically the most expensive because it places no restrictions on the doctors or hospitals available to the patient. These plans require patients to pay for services out-of-pocket and submit claims for reimbursement of expenses.

**Dental insurance**    Employers may choose dental insurance plans to provide varying levels of coverage for preventive or restoration work, such as fillings; major restoration work, such as bridges; and orthodontia.

**Vision insurance**    One of the lowest-cost benefits available, vision insurance provides employees with reduced costs for eye examinations and contacts lenses or glasses.

**Prescription coverage**    Even though most medical plans include some form of coverage for prescription drugs, these plans are also offered separately. The cost of the plans is managed by controlling the amount of the required copayment and requiring the use of generic drugs instead of named brands.

Regardless of the health plans selected, it is crucial for HR professionals to manage the cost of the benefits by selecting the most cost-effective method for funding the benefits. There are several choices and determining the most appropriate choice for a particular organization depends upon factors such as the size of the organization and claim history.

One common funding method for smaller organizations is to purchase insurance coverage for the plan. The organization pays premiums for all participants in the plan and the insurance company manages payment to the service provider and claims issues. In this funding method, the insurer assumes the risk for any unusual claims that may result in claim costs exceeding premiums received. Insurers keep track of the claim history and will adjust the premiums in subsequent years to recover any losses.

In larger organizations, it may make sense to self-fund the insurance plan. A *self-funded plan* is one in which the employer creates a claim fund and pays all claims through it. Self-funded plans must conduct annual discrimination tests to ensure that HCEs are not utilizing the plan disproportionately to non-HCEs. In this case, the employer assumes the risk for unusual claims that may exceed the amount budgeted for the plan.

Another option is for organizations to implement a *partially self-funded plan*. These plans utilize *stop-loss insurance* to prevent a single catastrophic claim from devastating the claim fund. The employer agrees upon a preset maximum coverage amount that will be paid from the claim fund for each participant before the insurance company begins to pay the claim.

Self-funded organizations may decide to contract with an insurance company to manage and pay claims, which is known as an *administrative services only (ASO) plan*. A *third-party administrator (TPA)*, which provides claim management services only and is not part of an insurance company, may also be utilized for self-funded plans.

In order to take advantage of economies of scale, smaller employers may form *health purchasing alliances (HPA)* with other employers in the geographic area. The HPA will negotiate and contract for the plans on behalf of all members of the group.

**Life insurance**    Many insurance companies bundle basic life insurance with medical or dental insurance for a very low rate and offer supplemental insurance for employees who are willing to pay an additional premium for the coverage.

It is important to keep in mind that the IRS views group life insurance in excess of $50,000 as *imputed income* (any indirect compensation paid on behalf of employees) when the premiums are paid by employers. The calculation of imputed income for group life insurance is based on a table provided by the IRS. The table assigns a small amount per month for each $1,000 of coverage that exceeds $50,000 based on an employee's age. The amounts range from $.05 for employees who are 25 years old to $2.06 per month for employees age 70 and older.

A complete discussion of imputed income can be found at www.kennethjarvis.com /articles/imputedincomesec79.asp.

**Accidental Death and Dismemberment Insurance (AD&D) insurance**    AD&D insurance can provide insurance for employees and their dependents in the event of an accident that results in the death of the covered person or the loss of a bodily function. AD&D does not pay benefits in the event of death due to an illness.

**Short and long term disability insurance**    Disability insurance protects employees from income loss due to disability caused by illness or accident. Disability protection generally begins with sick leave provided by employers. When employees exhaust their sick leave, they may become eligible for short-term disability insurance, which can be in effect for anywhere between three and six months. Employees who are still disabled when short-term disability ends become eligible for long-term disability coverage, which can last for anywhere from two years until age 65.

Because these benefits are so common, businesses seeking to use them as recruiting and retention tools must find some way to differentiate their plans from those of their competitors. This need must be balanced with the skyrocketing cost of medical insurance and its impact on the bottom line. Companies looking for a way to increase the attractiveness of their benefit packages may want to reduce or eliminate the employee contribution toward premiums for themselves or for their families, or include coverage for domestic partners in the package.

## Flexible Spending Accounts

*Flexible spending accounts (FSAs)* were authorized by the Revenue Act of 1978. Also known as *Section 125 plans*, these plans allow employees to set aside pre-tax funds for medical expenses they plan to incur during the calendar year. Employees should be cautioned to be conservative when projecting the amounts they plan to spend during the year because any funds left in the FSA after all expenses for the year have been paid will be forfeited and may be used by the employer to pay the administrative costs of the plan. For employers, a downside to offering an FSA account is that employees may be reimbursed for expenses before the funds have been withheld from their paychecks. If they leave the company before the funds have been withheld, they are not required to reimburse the company for those expenses.

Expenses that may be included for reimbursement are the costs of any copayments and deductibles from the medical, dental, or vision care plans and other medical expenses approved by the IRS for reimbursement. Other allowable expenses include acupuncture treatments, orthodontia, psychiatric care, wheelchairs, physical therapy, Braille books and magazines, and a variety of other medical expenses. Some expenses that are not included are memberships to fitness clubs or gyms, elective cosmetic surgery, weight loss programs, and over the counter medications.

To receive reimbursement, employees must provide receipts for expenditures.

A similar *dependent care account* is authorized by Section 129. Employees may set aside a maximum of $5,000 to be used to care for dependent children or elders. To obtain reimbursement for dependent care expenses, employees must provide an itemized statement of charges from the caregiver. Unlike the flexible spending account for medical expenses, employees may not be reimbursed for expenses in excess of the amounts that have been withheld from their paychecks.

For employees to utilize either of these accounts, they must sign up at the beginning of the year, at the time they join the company, or during an open enrollment period. Once the contribution amount has been set for the year, it may only be changed if a qualifying event occurs, such as the birth, death, or adoption of a dependent or a change in employment status for the employee or the employee's spouse.

The IRS requires employers to conduct annual discrimination tests to ensure that FSA plans are being used consistently. Two types of tests are used to determine this: eligibility tests and utilization tests such as the key employee concentration test or dependent care test. A plan that does not pass the test may lose its favorable tax treatment.

As mentioned previously, there are no federal laws requiring employers to offer any of these benefits; when they are offered, amendments to ERISA, COBRA, HIPAA, and the Mental Health Parity Act of 1996 (MHPA) have implications for administering them.

## COBRA Requirements

As discussed previously in this chapter, COBRA requires employers with 20 or more employees during the previous year who provide group health coverage to continue this coverage for employees when specific qualifying events occur. Employers must notify employees of the availability of COBRA coverage when they enter the plan and again within 30 days of the occurrence of a qualifying event. Table 6.8 shows the qualifying events that will trigger COBRA, as well as the length of time coverage must be continued for each event.

**TABLE 6.8**   COBRA Qualifying Events and Coverage Requirements

| Qualifying Event | Length of Coverage |
| --- | --- |
| Employee death | 36 months |
| Divorce or legal separation | 36 months |
| Dependent child no longer covered | 36 months |
| Reduction in hours | 18 months |
| Reduction in hours when disabled* | 29 months |
| Employee termination | 18 months |

**TABLE 6.8**    COBRA Qualifying Events and Coverage Requirements *(continued)*

| Qualifying Event | Length of Coverage |
|---|---|
| Employee termination when disabled* | 29 months |
| Eligibility for SSA benefits | 18 months |
| Termination for gross misconduct | 0 months |

*An employee who is disabled within 60 days of a reduction in hours or a termination becomes eligible for an additional 11 months of COBRA coverage.

Employers may charge COBRA participants a maximum of 102 percent of the group premium for coverage and must include them in any open enrollment periods or other changes to the plans. Employers may discontinue COBRA coverage if payments are not received within 30 days of the time they are due.

Employees must notify the employer within 60 days of a divorce or separation or within 60 days of the time a dependent child is no longer dependent.

## HIPAA Requirements

HIPAA prohibits discrimination on the basis of health status as evidenced by an individual's medical condition or history, claims experience, utilization of health care services, disability, or evidence of insurability. It also places limits on health insurance restrictions for *preexisting conditions*, which is defined as a condition for which treatment was given within six months of enrollment in the plan. Insurers may exclude those conditions from coverage for 12 months, or in the case of a late enrollment, for 18 months.

Insurers may only discontinue an employer's group coverage if the employer neglects to pay the premiums, obtained the policy through fraudulent or intentional misrepresentation, or does not comply with material provisions of the plan. Group coverage may also be discontinued if the insurer is no longer offering coverage in the employer's geographic area, if none of the plan participants reside in the plan's network area, or if the employer fails to renew a collective bargaining agreement or fails to comply with its provisions.

In April 2001, the Department of Health and Human Services (HHS) issued privacy regulations that were required by the act. The regulations defined *protected health information (PHI)*, patient information that must be kept private, including physical or mental conditions, information about health care given, and payments that have been made. While these regulations were directed at *covered entities* that conduct business electronically, such as health plans, health care providers, and clearinghouses, they have had a significant impact on the way employers handle information related to employee health benefits. Many employers had to redesign forms for open enrollment periods and new hires and update plan documents and company benefit policies to reflect the changes. The regulations impact employers in other ways as well.

Although flexible spending accounts (FSAs) are exempt from other HIPAA requirements, they are considered group health plans for privacy reasons, so employers who sponsor FSAs must comply with the privacy requirements for them.

Employers who are self-insured or who have fully insured group health plans and receive protected health information are required to develop privacy policies that comply with the regulations, appoint a privacy official, and train employees to handle information appropriately.

While the HIPAA regulations do not prevent employees from seeking assistance from HR for claim problems or other issues with the group health plan, they do require employees to provide the insurance provider or TPA with an authorization to release information about the claim to the HR department.

The new regulations include stiff civil and criminal sanctions for violations; civil penalties of $100 per violation and up to $25,000 per person each year can be assessed. There are three levels of criminal penalties:

- A conviction for obtaining or disclosing PHI can result in a fine of up to $50,000 and one year in prison.

- Obtaining PHI under false pretenses can result in fines of up to $100,000 and five years in prison.

- Obtaining or disclosing PHI with the intent of selling, transferring, or using it to obtain commercial advantage or personal gain can be punished with a fine of up to $250,000 and ten years in prison.

### Mental Health Parity Act of 1986

The Mental Health Parity Act of 1986 requires insurers to provide the same limits for mental health benefits in their plans as they provide for other health benefits.

## Work-Life Balance Benefits

Many employers offer benefits that recognize employees have interests and obligations outside of work. These include benefits such as paid time off, parental leave, and adoption leave, as well as employee assistance programs and wellness initiatives.

### Paid Time Off

Paid time off, like health insurance coverage, is a benefit that employees have come to expect. Over time, businesses have developed different programs to accommodate various needs for time off.

**Vacation pay**    Vacation pay is generally earned as employees complete time in the job. Many companies require employees to work a specific period of time, usually three to six months before they are eligible to use any accumulated vacation pay. Some companies allow employees to accumulate vacation pay year-to-year, while others may have a "use it or lose it" policy, although some state laws prohibit companies from forcing employees to forfeit time off that has been earned. In those cases, companies may decide to pay employees for the leave that would otherwise be forfeited.

Most vacation pay policies require employees to schedule time off in advance and obtain approval from their supervisors before scheduling vacations.

**Sick pay**    Sick pay is provided for employees to use when they are ill or when they need to care for a sick child or other family member.

**Holiday pay**   Many companies provide paid holidays for between 6 and 12 holidays each year. These can include New Year's Day, President's Day, Martin Luther King's Birthday, Memorial Day, July 4th, Labor Day, Columbus Day, Veteran's Day, Thanksgiving, and Christmas.

**Paid time off (PTO)**   Many companies have combined all forms of time off into a single PTO bank that employees can use as they see fit to handle illnesses, personal needs, vacations, and other matters.

**Sabbaticals and leaves of absence**   In educational institutions, sabbaticals are a long-standing benefit provided for educators in which they receive a year off with pay to pursue further education, conduct research, or write books in their field of study. Some private companies have adopted this benefit for long-term employees to encourage professional development.

**Jury duty pay**   Employers are required to provide time off for employees who are called to jury duty, although most states do not require employees to be paid for this time. Many employers will pay the difference between the employee's regular earnings and the amount they are paid for performing jury duty.

**Bereavement leave**   Most companies allow employees time off with pay to attend funeral services for close relatives.

**Parental leave**   Some companies provide paid leave for parents of newborns or newly adopted children.

## Dependent Care Benefits

As more families find themselves caring for children as well as elder family members, some companies provide benefits that assist in providing necessary care. These include benefits such as flexible work schedules, job sharing programs, and telecommuting in addition to flexible benefit programs and reduced work schedules. Some companies are able to provide on-site child care facilities for young children, and others provide referrals and assistance in obtaining care for elder family members.

## Other Voluntary Benefits

As companies seek to differentiate themselves to attract and retain qualified employees, many different types of benefits have been tried. During the height of the Internet boom in Silicon Valley, California, along with more traditional benefit offerings, employers provided such benefits as bring your dog (or cat) to work day, free lunches on Friday, video game rooms, and breakfast and fresh fruit for employees each day. Some other voluntary benefits that employees find attractive are the following:

**Educational assistance**   Educational assistance or tuition reimbursement programs benefit both employees and employers. Employees are able to increase their knowledge and skills, and employers can make use of the new skills in meeting their goals. Reimbursement for job-related courses is nontaxable to employees, but those that are not job related are taxable. Employers may require proof of completion and a passing grade for the course prior to reimbursing the employee for expenses.

**Transportation benefits**   Employees who must travel on behalf of their employer or those who work in large urban areas with significant commute traffic appreciate benefits that help to offset these costs. For some employees, generally executives and sales personnel who travel regularly, a company car may be provided. Employees who use company cars for personal travel are taxed on a percentage of the cost of the car.

The National Energy Efficiency Act of 1992 set maximum tax exemption limits for mass transit passes, tokens, fare cards, vanpools, and similar assistance as well as for employee parking benefits. This amount is updated from time to time to reflect changes in the cost of living. During 2003, the tax exempt limit for mass transit was $100, while the maximum employee parking assistance was $190.

**Adoption assistance**   Some companies offer adoption assistance benefits to employees that offset the costs associated with adopting a child. During 2003, the IRS allowed a maximum of $10,160 to be excluded from an employee's gross income for this purpose. This amount is adjusted annually by the IRS for changes in the cost of living.

**Legal insurance**   Prepaid legal benefits are popular with some employees. These plans provide a variety of routine legal assistance, which can include writing letters to resolve issues for employees, preparing wills, and providing general legal counsel. Most of these plans prohibit their use in filing legal action against the employer and do not cover criminal cases.

# Global Compensation and Benefits

In addition to compensation and benefit legislation and practices within the United States, candidates for the PHR/SPHR examination should be aware of the impact of global operations on an organization's practices.

One important consideration is the question of internal equity. Employees at the same level in the organization, whether they remain in the home country or accept global assignments, must view organization compensation practices as fair and equitable. Compensation practices must allow for flexibility and movement between international assignments, and the policies must be designed to allow for consistency in the way employees are treated regardless of the countries in which they are working. The organization must view equity from the various perspectives discussed in Chapter 4: expatriates, inpatriates, third country nationals, and host country nationals. Expatriates, for example, must be compensated in a way that maintains equity with similar positions in the home country while at the same time is equitable with positions in the host country. Balancing these perspectives can present complex challenges for the organization.

When reviewing compensation outside the U.S., it is important to also implement pay practices that follow the country-specific cost of labor and pay practices. Comparing pay practices outside the U.S. against the U.S. market is an apples versus oranges comparison. Many countries have socialized welfare and economic and labor dynamics that make it inappropriate to compare compensation and benefits packages.

Benefits in different countries vary widely as well, and HR professionals with global responsibilities must be aware of local customs and legal requirements when developing benefit programs. For example, in many countries, Social Security programs are far more generous than those in the United States, while other countries may not have similar government programs in place. Some countries provide health care for citizens through the government while others may have rudimentary health care systems in place.

Holiday practices in each country are based on local customs as well. For example, many countries celebrate Independence Day, but the date varies depending on when each country became independent. Boxing Day is celebrated in Commonwealth Countries, as is the Queen's birthday. Mahatma Gandhi's birthday is celebrated in India. Japan celebrates Coming of Age Day and the Emperor's birthday.

In Western European countries, it is common for employees to be granted four to six weeks of paid vacation each year, while in other regions custom may provide for very little vacation.

Global compensation and benefit programs must take many factors into consideration if they are to attract and retain qualified employees.

# Summary

Compensation and benefits are two key factors in virtually every organization's pursuit of attracting and retaining employees who are best qualified to achieve its goals. The total compensation package is guided by the corporate mission and goals and reflects its organization culture. The culture in particular impacts the intrinsic and extrinsic rewards that employees derive from their work. Compensation philosophy drives the organization's ability to attract, retain, and motivate its employees to meet its strategic objectives.

Compensation philosophy is impacted by internal considerations such as an organization's willingness and ability to provide compensation and benefits that lead, meet, or lag the market. Whether an organization chooses a performance culture that rewards employee contributions or an entitlement culture which rewards employee service will have an impact on the motivation and loyalty of employees.

The first mandatory benefits, social security, Medicare, and unemployment insurance, were developed to provide a safety net for American workers. More recent benefits such as FMLA and COBRA require employers to more actively participate in and administer programs.

The mix of voluntary benefits chosen by an organization can help them to attract and retain employees with particular characteristics, for example, a generous educational reimbursement benefit will help the company attract employees who are committed to continuous learning and skill development.

# Exam Essentials

**Be aware of the federal laws that govern compensation and benefit programs.** The Fair Labor Standards Act in 1938 was the first to impact compensation in private businesses in America, and it continues to do so today. ERISA and its amendments, COBRA and HIPAA, required employers who offer benefits to meet minimum standards of fairness in benefit programs. IRS regulations often impact decisions on benefits that are offered.

**Understand the provisions of the FLSA.**   The FLSA (Fair Labor Standards Act) established a minimum wage, overtime requirements, laws protecting American children against labor exploitation, criteria for exempt and nonexempt employees, exemption tests to determine exemption status, and payroll record-keeping requirements.

**Be aware of the components of compensation.**   Base pay is the foundation of an employer's compensation program because it reflects the value placed on individual jobs by the organization. Differentials such as overtime and hazard pay motivate employees to spend longer hours at work or to accept assignments that may be unpleasant or hazardous. Incentive pay motivates and rewards employees when they achieve corporate goals.

**Understand the job evaluation process.**   Job evaluation is an objective mechanism used to determine the worth of different jobs to the company. Compensable factors distinguish jobs from each other and are used in determining their value to the organization.

**Understand the purpose of salary surveys and how they are conducted.**   Salary surveys are used to determine current market trends and competition for different skills and knowledge and assist the employer in setting pay levels that lead, meet, or lag the market. Surveys are conducted by gathering information about specific jobs in a large number of companies in an industry, profession, or geographic area and summarizing it by job.

**Understand how HR interacts with payroll systems.**   Whether HR interacts with or administers payroll, HR professionals are involved in ensuring that changes to employee pay and deductions are accurate.

**Be able to communicate the compensation and benefit program to employees.**   An effective communication program informs employees about the total compensation program so that they are able to take advantage of benefits that are offered and have an understanding of the full cost to the employer of providing the different programs.

**Be aware of the wide variety of benefits that are available.**   With an awareness of the various and sometimes unusual benefits that are available, employers are able to develop a benefit mix that meets the needs of employees at the lowest cost to net profits.

**Be aware of mandatory benefits.**   Mandatory employee benefits are determined by Congress and affect employers with varying minimum numbers of employees. Social security, Medicare, unemployment insurance, FMLA leave, and COBRA continuation benefits are required by statute.

**Understand how voluntary benefits influence employees.**   Voluntary benefits fall into four categories: deferred compensation, health and welfare, work-life balance, and other benefits. Some benefits such as medical insurance and paid time off have come to be expected by employees, while others will attract and retain different types of employees with different needs.

**Be aware of FMLA leave requirements.**   FMLA requires unpaid leave be provided by companies with 50 or more employees within 75 miles of the worksite. Employees who meet the eligibility requirements are entitled to leave for the birth or adoption of a child or a serious illness of an immediate family member or themselves.

# Key Terms

Before you take the exam, be certain you are familiar with the following terms:

401(k) plan

ability to pay

actual deferral percentage test (ADP)

administrative services only (ASO) plan

base pay

benchmark positions

bonus plan

broadbanding

call-back pay

cash balance plans

classification method

cliff vesting

commissions

comp time

comparable worth

compa-ratio

compensable factors

compensable time

compensation philosophy

compensatory time off

continuous FMLA leave

corporate culture

cost of labor

covered entities

defined benefit

defined contribution

delayed vesting

dependent care account

discretionary contributions

enrolled actuary

enterprise coverage

entitlement philosophy

exception reporting

exempt

extrinsic reward

fiduciary

Financial Accounting Standards Board (FASB)

flexible spending accounts (FSAs)

gainsharing

gatekeeper

geographic pay

graded vesting

graduated or gradual vesting

grant price

grantor trusts

graveyard shift

green circle

gross pay

group incentives

HAY system

hazard pay

health purchasing alliances (HPA)

highly compensated employees (HCEs)

immediate vesting

Improshare

imputed income

in loco parentis

incentive pay

incentive stock options (ISO)

individual coverage

intermittent FMLA leave

internal equity

intrinsic reward

job pricing

labor market

line of sight

merit pay

money purchase plan

nonexempt

nonforfeitable

nonqualified retirement plan

nonqualified stock options

Old Age, Survivors, and Disability Insurance (OASDI)

on-call pay

organization incentives

overtime

partially self-funded plan

participant

party in interest

pay differential

pay equity

pay for performance

pay grade

pay ranges

pay structure

performance-based pay

performance-based philosophy

perquisites

phantom stock

plan administrator

plan sponsor

point factor

positive time reporting

preexisting conditions

private letter ruling

profit-sharing plans

protected health information (PHI)

prudent person standard of care

qualified domestic relations orders (QDRO)

qualified plan

rabbi trusts

ranking method

red circle

reduced FMLA leave schedule

reporting premium

restricted stock

salary surveys

Scanlon Plan

Section 125 plans

self-funded plan

seniority-based compensation

shift

shift premium

state unemployment insurance (SUI)

stock option

stop-loss insurance

strike price

summary plan description (SPD)

swing shift

target benefit plan

third-party administrator (TPA)

time-and-a-half

total compensation

variable pay

vesting

wage compression

wage garnishments

# Review Questions

1. The Federal Insurance Contributions Act requires employers to
   A. Contribute to a defined benefit plan.
   B. Contribute to a deferred compensation plan.
   C. Withhold social security tax from pay.
   D. Provide health insurance for all employees.

2. Employers are required to provide a portable retirement plan to employees based on
   A. Employee Retirement Income Security Act
   B. Omnibus Budget Reconciliation Act
   C. Older Worker Benefit Protection Act
   D. Retirement benefits are not required by federal law

3. An example of an intrinsic reward is
   A. Recognition of accomplishments
   B. The satisfaction of a job well done
   C. A great supervisor
   D. An exciting assignment

4. Compensation philosophy can help achieve an organization's strategic goals by
   A. Attracting and retaining employees with the necessary KSAs
   B. Establishing a pecking order for jobs within the organization
   C. Positioning the company to lead the competition for employees
   D. Maintaining an entitlement culture

5. An entitlement culture is appropriate for a business that needs a work force that
   A. Continues to show productivity increases over time
   B. Has line of sight to retirement
   C. Is highly competitive in completing daily assignments
   D. Has a skill set in high demand

6. A company that wants to reduce the cost of its unemployment insurance should
   A. Aggressively fight unjustified claims for unemployment
   B. Establish an effective performance management program
   C. Retain employees who violate company policy
   D. All of the above

**7.** A reduced FMLA leave schedule is one in which

   **A.** The employee is absent from work multiple times for the same illness or injury

   **B.** The employee works fewer hours each day or week

   **C.** The employee's leave schedule is disruptive to the work schedule

   **D.** Accurate records of time off are maintained

**8.** The Older Worker Benefit Protection Act requires that an employee over 40 years of age who is asked to waive their rights under the act must be given

   **A.** 7 days to consider the agreement before signing it

   **B.** 21 days to consider the agreement before signing it

   **C.** 45 days to consider the agreement before signing it

   **D.** 60 days to consider the agreement before signing it

**9.** The Omnibus Budget Reconciliation Act of 1993 does not require that

   **A.** Group health coverage be offered for children placed for adoption before the adoption is final

   **B.** Group health plans honor qualified medical child support orders

   **C.** Tax deductions for executive pay be capped at $1,000,000 per year

   **D.** Income tax be withheld from some distributions to rollover accounts

**10.** A summary plan description is required all of the following except

   **A.** Defined contribution plans

   **B.** Defined benefit plans

   **C.** Flexible spending accounts

   **D.** AD&D insurance

# Answers to Review Questions

1. C. FICA requires employers to pay social security and Medicare for employees and to withhold an equal amount from employee paychecks.

2. D. No federal law requires employers to provide a retirement plan to employees.

3. B. Intrinsic rewards are those in which esteem is achieved from within oneself. A, C, and D are examples of extrinsic rewards which come from external sources.

4. A. Compensation philosophy helps determine what kind of employees will be attracted to the organization. Developing a philosophy to target employees with the KSAs needed by the organization can help to advance the organization's mission.

5. A. An entitlement culture rewards longevity in the job. If increased productivity is a function of time in the job, an entitlement culture will encourage employees to stay with the company.

6. D. A and B are both obviously correct. Many employers are hesitant to terminate employees for policy violations, but those terminated for cause are generally not eligible for unemployment insurance, so retaining an employee who is not contributing to the organization is a poor business decision. Maintaining adequate records that demonstrate the reasons for termination provides the tools to fight claims that are unjustified.

7. B. A reduced FMLA leave is one in which the employee's regular work schedule is reduced by some number of hours per day or days per week.

8. B. Workers over 40 who are asked to sign a waiver of their rights must be given 21 days to consider the agreement before signing it, unless they are part of a group termination or layoff. In that case, they must be given 45 days to sign the agreement. In both instances, they may revoke the agreement within 7 days.

9. D. OBRA capped executive pay, required that group health coverage be offered when children are placed for adoption before it is finalized and required health plans to honor qualified medical child support orders. The Unemployment Compensation Amendments of 1992 required 20 percent withholding from some distributions.

10. D. Summary plan descriptions are required only for group health plans.

# Chapter

# 7

# Employee and Labor Relations

---

## THE HRCI TEST SPECIFICATIONS FROM THE EMPLOYEE AND LABOR RELATIONS FUNCTIONAL AREA COVERED IN THIS CHAPTER INCLUDE:

✓ Ensure compliance with all applicable federal, state, and local laws and regulations.

✓ Develop and implement employee relations programs that will create a positive organizational culture.

✓ Promote, monitor, and measure the effectiveness of employee relations activities.

✓ Assist in establishing work rules and monitor their application and enforcement to ensure fairness and consistency (for union and nonunion environments).

✓ Communicate and ensure understanding by employees of laws, regulations, and organizational policies.

✓ Resolve employee complaints filed with federal, state, and local agencies involving employment practices.

✓ Develop grievance and disciplinary policies and procedures to ensure fairness and consistency.

✓ Implement and monitor grievance and disciplinary policies and procedures to ensure fairness and consistency.

✓ Respond to union organizing activity.

✓ Participate in collective bargaining activities, including contract negotiation and administration.

In this chapter, I will review the PHR and SPHR responsibility and knowledge requirements for Employee and Labor Relations (ELR). This area covers the functions necessary to sustain effective employment relationships in both union and nonunion environments. I will review the rights and responsibilities of both employers and employees in this relationship and HR's role in those processes.

In order to be fully prepared for the PHR/SPHR exam, candidates must be well versed in the basic knowledge for this functional area as well as some of the core knowledge requirements covered in Chapter 2, "Core Knowledge Requirements for HR Professionals," that pertain to ELR. The *PHR & SPHR Certification Handbook* described in the introduction to this book provides the detailed list of ELR knowledge requirements and should be reviewed prior to studying this area of the BOK. The HRCI core knowledge requirements that will be particularly helpful in understanding this functional area include motivation and leadership concepts, the ways in which interpersonal and organizational behavior affect employee relations programs, the impact of diversity on employee relations programs, the use of qualitative analysis tools in measuring employee satisfaction, and finally, the implications of employee relations programs across functional areas in the organization.

# Employee Relations

The employment relationship has broad implications for both employers and employees. An effective employee relations program can positively affect the bottom line through its impact on employee retention, employee morale, and the maintenance of union-free status. Employers rely on those they hire to produce the goods and services that bring money into the organization to operate the company, pay the employees, and produce a profit for the owners. Employees, particularly in the United States, spend the majority of their waking hours at work, which means that the effects of the employment relationship, good or bad, can spill over into other areas of the employee's life. Both employers and employees have rights that have either been granted through the legislative process or developed over time as the result of court decisions and common law practices. Along with these rights come associated responsibilities to act in a lawful and equitable manner within the relationship.

## Employer Rights and Responsibilities

Employee relations is covered by both common law legal concepts and statutory requirements that protect employers and employees and require certain actions and behaviors. Employers (be they individuals or stockholders represented by a board of directors) have the right to structure organizations in the most cost-effective way in order to fulfill the vision, strategy, mission, and goals they have developed in order to earn a profit. Employers have the right to determine how to run their organizations to achieve that outcome and to develop the policies, procedures, and work rules necessary to make that happen. With those rights comes the responsibility to provide safe working conditions, pay wages for all work done by employees, and reimburse employees for expenses incurred on behalf of the employer.

Employment relationships are generally covered either by the common law doctrine of employment at-will or by employment contracts. Employment disagreements may result in legal action on the basis of a breach of the terms of a contract, or on a tort action. A *tort* is a civil action based on a duty or obligation that has been breached by one party, causing an injury of some kind to the other.

In the absence of an employment contract, there are common law doctrines that apply to employment relationships.

## Common Law Doctrines

*Common law doctrine* has been developed over centuries as a result of legal decisions made by judges in individual cases. There are a number of doctrines with implications for employment relationships, the most common of which is the concept of employment at-will. Other common law issues that employers must take into consideration when making employment decisions are constructive discharge and defamation.

### Employment At-Will

In *Payne v The Western & Atlantic Railroad Company* in 1884, Justice Ingersoll of the Tennessee Supreme Court defined employment at-will in this way: ". . . either party may terminate the service, for any cause, good or bad, or without cause, and the other cannot complain in law." This definition allowed employers to change employment conditions, whether it be to hire, transfer, promote, or terminate an employee, at their sole discretion. It also allowed employees to leave a job at any time, with or without notice. In the absence of an employment contract that could be legally enforced, this definition was unaltered for over 70 years.

While there have always been exceptions to at-will employment based on employment contracts, beginning in 1959, the doctrine began to be eroded by both court decisions and statutes. This erosion resulted in several exceptions to the at-will concept, including public policy exceptions, the application of the doctrine of good faith and fair dealing to employment relationships, and the concepts of promissory estoppel and fraudulent misrepresentation.

**Contract exceptions**    Employment at-will intentions may be abrogated by contracts, either express or implied. An *express contract* can be a verbal or written agreement in which the parties state exactly what they agree to do. Employers have been known to express their gratitude for a job well done with promises of continued employment, such as, "Keep doing that kind of work and you have a job for life." or "You'll have a job as long as we're in business." Statements such as these can invalidate the at-will doctrine.

An *implied contract* can be created by an employer's conduct and need not be specifically stated. For example, an employer's consistent application of a progressive discipline policy can create an implied contract that an employee will not be terminated without first going through the steps set forth by the policy. A disclaimer can offset the effects of an implied contract; however, there is little agreement in the courts as to what and how the disclaimer must be presented in order to maintain at-will status.

**Statutory exceptions**   The at-will doctrine has been further eroded by legislation. At-will may not be used as a pretext for terminating employees for discriminatory reasons as set forth in equal opportunity legislation or other legislation designed to protect employee rights.

**Public policy exceptions**   Erosion of the doctrine of at-will employment began in 1959 when the California Court of Appeals heard *Petermann v International Brotherhood of Teamsters* in which Mr. Petermann, a business agent for the union, alleged that he was terminated for refusing to commit perjury on behalf of the union at a legislative hearing. The court held that it is ". . . obnoxious to the interest of state and contrary to public policy and sound morality to allow an employer to discharge any employee, whether the employment be for a designated or unspecified duration, on the ground that the employee declined to commit perjury, an act specifically enjoined by statute."

The public policy exception to employment at-will was initially applied conservatively by the courts, but over time, its application has been expanded. There are generally four areas in which the public policy exception has been applied. The first is exemplified by the *Petermann* case—an employee who refuses to break the law on behalf of the employer can claim a public policy exception. The second application covers employees who report illegal acts of their employers; the third covers employees who participate in activities supported by public policy, such as cooperating in a government investigation of wrong-doing by the employer. Finally, the public policy exception covers employees who are acting in accordance with legal statute, such as attending jury duty or filing a worker's compensation claim.

While the public policy exception to at-will employment originated in California, it has been adopted by many, although not all, states.

**Duty of good faith and fair dealing**   This tenet of common law provides that parties to a contract have an obligation to act in a fair and honest manner with each other to ensure that benefits of the contract may be realized. The application of this doctrine to at-will employment issues varies widely from state to state. The Texas Supreme Court, for example, has determined that there is no duty for good faith and fair dealing in employment contracts. On the other hand, the Alaska Supreme Court has determined that it is implied in at-will employment situations.

**Promissory estoppel**   Promissory estoppel occurs when an employer entices an employee (or prospective employee) to take an action by promising a reward. The employee takes the action, but the employer does not follow through on the reward. For example, an employer promises a job to a candidate who resigns another position to accept the new one and then finds the offered position has been withdrawn. If a promise is clear, specific, and reasonable, and an employee acts on the promise, the employer may be required to follow through on the promised reward or pay equivalent damages.

**Fraudulent misrepresentation**   Similar to promissory estoppel, fraudulent misrepresentation relates to promises or claims made by employers to entice candidates to join the company. An example of this might be a company that decides to close one of its locations in six months, but in the meantime, needs to hire a general manager to run the operation. If, when asked about the future of the company during the recruiting process, the company tells candidates that the plant will be expanded in the future and withholds its intention to close the plant, they would be fraudulently misrepresenting the facts about the position.

In addition to employment at-will, the common law doctrines of constructive discharge and defamation can have serious and costly implications for employers.

### Constructive Discharge

*Constructive discharge* occurs when an employer makes the workplace so hostile and inhospitable that an employee resigns. In many states, this gives the employee a cause of action against the employer. The legal standard that must be met varies widely between the states, with some requiring the employee to show that the employer intended to force the resignation, while others require the employee only to show the conditions were intolerable.

### Defamation

Accusations of defamation in employment relationships most often occur during or after termination. *Defamation* is a communication that damages an individual's reputation in the community, preventing them from obtaining employment or other benefits. Concerns about defamation have caused many employers to stop giving meaningful references for former employees. Employers are generally protected by the concept of "qualified privilege" if the information provided is job-related, truthful, clear, and unequivocal. Obtaining written authorization prior to providing references and limiting responses to the information being requested without volunteering additional information can reduce the risks of being accused of defamation.

## Legal Statutes

Legal statutes are laws that have been enacted by the legislature, as with the Civil Rights Act of 1964, or pronounced by the president in the form of executive orders. In Chapter 4, "Workforce Planning and Employment," I discussed extensively the requirements of equal employment opportunity legislation as it relates to hiring and terminations. Those legal statutes govern the employment relationship as well; in this section, I will cover those aspects that apply more specifically to existing employment relationships.

### Sexual Harassment

Title VII of the Civil Rights Act of 1964 (covered in depth in Chapter 4), and its subsequent amendments require that employers furnish a workplace that is free from sexual harassment. There are two forms of sexual harassment: quid pro quo and hostile work environment.

*Quid pro quo* is a legal term which means, in Latin, "this for that." Quid pro quo harassment, therefore, occurs when a supervisor or manager asks for sexual favors in return for a favorable employment action. "Sexual favors" is a broad term that covers actions ranging from unwanted touching to more explicit requests.

A *hostile work environment* has been defined by the EEOC as one in which an individual or individuals are subjected to unwelcome verbal or physical conduct "when submission to or rejection of this conduct explicitly or implicitly affects an individual's employment, unreasonably interferes with an individual's work performance, or creates an intimidating, hostile, or offensive work environment." *Unlike the quid pro quo form of harassment, a hostile work environment can be created by coworkers, suppliers, customers, or other visitors to the work place.* When investigating these charges, the EEOC looks at many factors. In most cases, a single incidence of inappropriate and unwelcome behavior does not rise to the level of a hostile work environment, but in some cases when the actions or behavior are particularly offensive or intimidating, the EEOC may find that harassment has occurred. A hostile work envirnoment can also be found to exist for victims who have been affected by unwelcome offensive conduct toward someone other than themselves.

Courts have held employers responsible for the harassing actions of their employees, whether or not the employer was aware of the harassment. Beginning in 1986, the Supreme Court issued a number of rulings to clarify employer responsibilities in the prevention of sexual harassment. The most commonly cited of these for HR purposes are *Meritor Savings Bank v Vinson* (1986), *Harris v Forklift Systems* (1993), and two cases decided at the same time in 1998, *Burlington Industries v Ellerth* and *Faragher v City of Boca Raton.*

**Meritor Savings Bank v Vinson (1986)**   Mechelle Vinson applied for a job at a branch of Meritor Savings Bank in 1974 when Sidney Taylor was a vice president and manager of the branch. Taylor hired Vinson, who worked at the branch for four years, starting as a teller trainee and working her way up to assistant branch manager based on her performance in the jobs she held. Once she passed her probationary period as a trainee, Vinson claims that Taylor began to harass her, requesting that they go to a motel to have sexual relations. Although Vinson refused Taylor's advances initially, she gave in eventually because she believed she would lose her job if she did not. Vinson claims that Taylor's harassment escalated to the point that she was fondled in front of other employees and expected to engage in sexual relations at the branch both during and after work. In September 1978, Vinson took an indefinite medical leave and the bank terminated her in November 1978.

The Supreme Court issued its opinion in June 1986, finding that a claim of "hostile environment" sex discrimination is actionable under Title VII. The Court rejected the idea that the "mere existence of a grievance procedure and a policy against discrimination" is enough to protect an employer from the acts of its supervisors. The opinion indicated that a policy designed to encourage victims of harassment to come forward would provide greater protection.

**Harris v Forklift Systems (1983)**   In April 1985, Teresa Harris was employed by Forklift Systems, Inc., as a manager, reporting to the company president, Charles Hardy. Hardy insulted Harris frequently in front of customers and other employees and made sexually suggestive remarks. When Harris complained in August 1987, Hardy apologized and said he would stop the conduct. But in September of that year, Hardy once again began the verbal harassment, and Harris quit on October 1.

Harris then filed a lawsuit against Forklift, claiming that Hardy had created a hostile work environment on the basis of her gender. The District Court found that although Hardy's conduct was offensive, it did not meet the required standard of severity to seriously affect her psychological well-being.

The Supreme Court agreed to hear the case in order to resolve conflicts in the lower courts on what conduct was actionable for a hostile work environment. The Court found that the appropriate standard is one that falls between that which is merely offensive and that which results in tangible psychological injury. While this is not a precise guideline, it does allow courts to take into consideration a number of factors about the work environment, the frequency and severity of the conduct, the level of threat or humiliation that the victim is subjected to, and whether the conduct interferes unreasonably with performance of the employee's job.

**Faragher v City of Boca Raton (1998)** Beth Faragher and Nancy Ewanchew were two of about six females out of 40 to 50 lifeguards for the City of Boca Raton in Florida from 1985 to 1990. During their tenure, they were verbally and physically harassed by two supervisors, Bill Terry and David Silverman. They both complained to a third supervisor, Robert Gordon, about the harassment, but did not file a formal complaint, and no corrective action was taken. Ewanchew resigned in 1989 and wrote to the city manager in 1990 to complain about the harassment. The city investigated and, when it found that both Terry and Silverman had acted inappropriately, reprimanded and disciplined them both.

The Supreme Court found that employers are responsible for actions of those they employ and have a responsibility to control them. Going further, the Court determined that a supervisor need not make an explicit threat of an adverse *tangible employment action (TEA)*, which the Court defined as "a significant change in employment status, such as hiring, firing, failing to promote, reassignment with significantly different responsibilities, or a decision causing a significant change in benefits" in order for harassment to be actionable. The Court determined that subordinates know that the possibility of adverse supervisory actions exists whenever requests are made, even if the adverse actions are not stated.

**Burlington Industries v Ellerth (1998)** Kimberly Ellerth worked for Burlington Industries in Chicago as a salesperson from March 1993 to May 1994. During that time, Ellerth claims that she was subjected to ongoing sexual harassment by Ted Slowick, who was not her direct supervisor but did have the power to approve or deny a TEA with regard to her employment. While Ellerth was aware of Burlington's policy prohibiting sexual harassment during her employment, she did not complain about the harassment until after she resigned. After resigning, she filed a complaint with the EEOC and, when she received a right-to-sue letter in October 1994, filed suit against Burlington.

A key issue in this case was that of *vicarious liability*, a legal concept which, in this context, means that an employer may be held accountable for the harmful actions of its employees, whether or not the employer is aware of those actions. The Supreme Court decided in part that, "An employer is subject to vicarious liability to a victimized employee for an actionable hostile environment created by a supervisor with immediate (or successively higher) authority over the employee."

The costs to employers for sexual harassment can be substantial, as a partial list of recent cases illustrates:

**$34,000,000** In June 1998, Mitsubishi agreed to a consent decree and the largest sexual harassment settlement in the history of the EEOC to date, in a case brought on behalf of women on the assembly line in the Illinois factory who were subjected to a hostile work environment by coworkers and supervisors.

**$9,850,000**   In February 1998, Astra USA agreed to a settlement and consent decree with the EEOC on behalf of female employees who were subjected to both quid pro quo and hostile work environment harassment. Astra fired the president, who had been aware of the activities, and took action against other employees and customers who had taken part in the harassment.

**$7,750,000**   In 1999, Ford Motor Company agreed to settle a case regarding harassment of women in two plants in the Chicago area. The women were subjected to crude remarks, groping, and sexually explicit graffiti. As part of the settlement, Ford also agreed to conduct sensitivity training in its plants nationwide, promote more women into management positions, and hold supervisors accountable for inaction against harassment they observe but allow to continue by making them ineligible for promotion and bonuses.

---

### 🌐 Real World Scenario

#### Oncale v Sundowner Offshore Services, Inc.

In late October 1991, Joseph Oncale was a roustabout employed by Sundowner Offshore Services on an oil rig in the Gulf of Mexico. During the time he worked on the rig, three of his coworkers, including two who had supervisory authority over him, humiliated him in front of other employees on the rig using sexually explicit words and actions. At one point, Oncale was physcially assaulted and threatened with rape. When Oncale complained to other supervisors about the harassment, no corrective action was taken, and one of them, the company's safety compliance clerk, told him that he too was subjected to similar treatment by the three. When Mr. Oncale quit his job, he gave his reason for leaving as being "due to sexual harassment and verbal abuse."

Mr. Oncale filed a complaint against Sundowner, alleging discrimination on the basis of his sex. The district court denied the complaint, and on appeal, the Fifth Circuit Court of Appeals upheld the district court. Oncale then appealed to the U.S. Supreme Court. The Court heard oral arguments in the case in December 1997, and comments of the justices during the arguments gave a rare early indication of the way they were leaning: Chief Justice Rehnquist commented, "I don't see how we can possibly sustain the holding."

In March 1998, Justice Scalia wrote the majority opinion, referencing in part the Court's opinion in an earlier sexual harassment case that, "When the workplace is permeated with discriminatory intimidation, ridicule, and insult that is sufficiently severe or pervasive to alter the conditions of the victim's employment and create an abusive working environment, Title VII is violated." (*Harris v Forklift Systems, Inc.*)

Scalia went on to say that even though the intent of Title VII was to protect harassment of women in the workplace, "sexual harassment of any kind that meets the statutory requirements" must be covered as well.

The courts have been divided on the question of same-sex harassment. Since sexual orientation does not constitute a protected class under federal law, some courts have been reluctant to classify cases of same-sex harassment as unlawful. In 1997, the first case of same-sex harassment reached the U.S. Supreme Court. In the majority opinion issued for *Oncale v Sundowner Offshore Services, Inc.* (see sidebar), Justice Antonin Scalia observed that ". . . male on male sexual harassment was assuredly not the principal evil congress was concerned with when it enacted Title VII. But statutory prohibitions often go beyond the principal evil to cover reasonably comparable evils . . ." A number of cases following Oncale resulted in substantial awards or settlements in cases of same-sex harassment:

**$1,900,000**   In 1999, the EEOC reached a settlement with the Long Prairie Packing Company in Minnesota in the amount of $1.9 million dollars, along with a consent decree that required the company to establish a zero-tolerance policy for sexual or disability harassment and to conduct mandatory sexual harassment training for all employees in the company.

**$1,050,000**   In 2000, $1.7 million dollars was awarded to the plaintiff in *Jones v Yellow Freight Systems, Inc.* in a civil law suit.

**$500,000**   The EEOC obtained a $500,000 settlement in August 2000 on behalf of a complainant who was harassed at a Chevrolet dealership in Denver, Colorado. As part of the settlement agreement, the dealer also agreed to provide mandatory sexual harassment training to its employees.

## EEOC Guidelines for the Prevention of Sexual Harassment

The EEOC has developed guidelines to assist employers in developing policies that clearly express the employer's prohibition against harassment. These guidelines are fully described at www.eeoc .gov/docs/harassment.html#VC1. To summarize, employers are encouraged to develop anti-harassment policies, along with complaint procedures for those who feel they have been harassed. The policy should clearly explain unacceptable conduct and reassure employees who complain that they will be protected against retaliation. The complaint process should describe multiple avenues for reporting harassment and provide assurances of confidentiality to the extent it is possible. Investigations of allegations should be prompt and impartial and, should the investigation find that harassment did indeed occur, the policy should provide for immediate corrective action.

## Glass Ceiling Act

In 1991, Senator Robert Dole included the Glass Ceiling Act as part of Title II of the Civil Rights Act of 1991. An article in the *Wall Street Journal* in 1986 had coined the term *glass ceiling* to describe the limitations faced by women and minorities when it came to advancing into the senior ranks of corporate management. The act established a commission whose purpose was to determine whether or not a glass ceiling existed and, if it did, to identify the barriers to placing more women and minorities in senior management positions. The commission found that although CEOs understood the need to include women and minorities in the ranks of senior management, this belief was not shared at all levels in the organization. The study went on to identify three barriers that prevented women and minorities from advancing to senior levels:

**Societal barriers**   Result from limited access to educational opportunities and biases related to gender, race, and ethnicity.

**Internal structural barriers**   Encompass a wide range of corporate practices and shortcomings over which management has some control, including outreach and recruiting programs that do not try to find qualified women and minorities, and organizational cultures that exclude women and minorities from participation in activities that will lead to advancement, such as mentoring, management training, or career development assignments.

**Governmental barriers**   Are related to inconsistent enforcement of equal opportunity legislation and poor collection and dissemination of statistics that illustrate the problem.

The commission also studied organizations that have successfully integrated glass ceiling initiatives into their operations and found some common traits that can be adopted by other organizations. These successful initiatives begin with full support of the CEO, who ensures that the initiative becomes part of strategic planning in the organization and holds management accountable for achieving goals by tracking and reporting on progress. These comprehensive programs do not exclude white men, but do include a diverse workforce population. Organizations implementing programs to increase diversity benefit with improved productivity and bottom-line results for shareholders.

As a result of the study, the EEOC conducts glass ceiling audits to monitor the progress of including women and minorities at all levels in corporate organizations.

## Uniformed Services Employment and Reemployment Rights Act of 1994 (USERRA)

Congress enacted the Uniformed Services Employment and Reemployment Rights Act (USERRA) in 1994 to protect the rights of reservists called to active duty in the armed forces. The act provides reemployment and benefit rights and is administered through the Veterans Employment and Training Service (VETS) of the Department of Labor, and applies to all public and private employers in the United States, including the federal government. Some of the stipulations of USERRA include:

- In most circumstances, the employee must give verbal or written notice to the employer that they have been called to active service.

- The employer must grant a leave of absence for up to five years, although there are several exceptions that extend coverage beyond five years.

- The employer must reinstate the employee to a position that the employee would have earned had they remained on the job, referred to as an "escalator position."

- The employee continues to accrue seniority and other benefits as though they are continuously employed.

- The employer must make reasonable accommodation to provide training or retraining to reemploy a returning service member disabled as a result of service; if reasonable accommodation creates an undue hardship, reemployment can be made to a position "nearest approximate" in terms of status and pay and with full seniority to which the person is entitled.

- The employer is required to grant pension plan benefits that accrued during military service.

- For leave greater than 30 days duration, the employer must offer COBRA-like health coverage upon request of the employee; for service less than 30 days, and at the employee's request, the employer must continue health coverage at the regular employee cost.
- Reemployment rights are forfeited if the employee has been discharged dishonorably or other than honorably from the service, has been expelled as a result of a court martial, or been AWOL (absent without leave) for 90 days.

To be eligible for reemployment rights, the service member must report back to work within time frames that vary according to the length of service. Table 7.1 shows the reporting time requirements established by USERRA.

**TABLE 7.1** USERRA Reemployment Reporting Times

| Length of Service | Reporting Time |
| --- | --- |
| 1 to 30 days *or* absence for "fitness for service" exam | The first regularly scheduled work day that falls 8 hours after the end of the calendar day. |
| 31 to 180 days | Submit application for reemployment no later than 14 days after the end of service, or on the next business day after that. |
| 181 or more days | Submit application for reemployment no later than 90 days after the end of service, or on the next business day after that. |
| Disability incurred or aggravated | Reporting or application deadline is extended for up to two years. |

Visit www.dol.gov/vets/whatsnew/uguide.pdf to view the full text of USERRA.

## Employee Rights and Responsibilities

As discussed in the previous section, employment rights developed over time from common law doctrines as well as from statutes. In essence, statutory law provides employees with the right to expect equal opportunity in a workplace free from harassment. The common law doctrine of employment at-will provides employees with the right to leave a job at any time, with or without notice.

Due process, while not a legal requirement for private employers, is a practice that is in the best interest of the employer. *Due process* in the employment context means that employment actions are taken in accordance with established procedures, including notifying employees of pending actions and providing the opportunity to respond to any allegations prior to making a final adverse employment decision.

Employees have responsibilities in the employment relationship as well. The *duty of diligence* requires an employee to act "with reasonable care and skill" in the course of performing work for the employer. The *duty of obedience* requires employees to act within the authority granted by the employer and to follow the employer's reasonable and legal policies, procedures, and rules. The *duty of loyalty* requires that employees act in the best interest of the employer and not solicit work away from the employer to benefit themselves.

## Policies, Procedures, and Work Rules

Employers need a consistent and understandable means to communicate important information about how the company operates and what is expected of employees. This is best done through *policies*, which are broad guidelines developed by the employer to guide organizational decisions. *Procedures* provide further explanation and more details on how the policy is to be applied, and work rules state what employees may or may not do to be in compliance with the policy. For example:

**Policy**   Employees will conduct business in a manner consistent with the highest standards of business ethics.

**Procedure**   Employees should avoid situations in which the best interest of the company conflicts with the employee's self-interest.

**Work Rule**   Employees may not own, in whole or in part, any venture that seeks to do business with, or is a competitor of, this organization.

Some employment policies are required by law, such as the sexual harassment policy previously discussed. Other policies help to ensure that consistent employment practices are applied throughout the organization, and still others serve to motivate employees, such as education reimbursement, recognition, or telecommuting policies. The number and type of policies in each organization should be reflective of the mission, values, and culture of the organization and seek to further successful employment relationships. Regardless of how policies are utilized in any organization, it is important that they be reviewed and updated periodically to ensure that they are still relevant for the organization.

HR policies, procedures, and work rules are developed in conjunction with line management. The role of HR in this process is to advise management on current best practices and legal requirements and work with management to develop policies that are consistent with organization goals, easily communicated, and viewed by employees as equitable. Once developed, HR is responsible to advise management on appropriate ways to administer the policies, procedures, and work rules and provide training as needed.

Employee handbooks can be useful as a way of communicating policies, procedures, and work rules to employees in an organized fashion and providing a reference. Poorly worded handbooks have, in some cases, been found by the courts to create an implied contract, requiring employers to abide by its contents. If the organization wishes to maintain status as an at-will employer, it is important to clearly state this in the handbook, and more importantly, to have the handbook reviewed by legal counsel to ensure that it will accomplish the purpose intended without a negative impact.

Handbooks generally begin with a welcoming statement from senior management and a statement of the organization's employee relations philosophy. Some handbooks provide a history of the organization to give new employees a feel for the type of organization they have joined. Handbooks also contain legally required policies, such as statements of the organization's compliance with equal employment opportunities, prohibitions against unlawful harassment, and information about federally mandated leaves such as the FMLA (Family and Medical Leave Act). The employer then has the opportunity to describe the terms and conditions of employment in the organization, including such things as work hours, safety, ethics, employment status, eligibility for benefits, and benefit programs. The handbook is a good place to inform employees of workplace privacy considerations; if the organization has a policy of monitoring the workplace or places restrictions on Internet usage, clear descriptions of those policies can prevent future problems.

It is advisable to include a tear-out acknowledgment form for employees to sign, or, if the employer utilizes an online handbook, an electronic acknowledgment. The acknowledgment should include statements that employment is at-will, that the employer has the right to unilaterally change the terms and conditions described in the handbook, and that the employee has received, read, and understands the contents of the handbook. While some of this language may be viewed negatively by employees, it provides documentation for the employer in any future disciplinary or legal actions that may occur.

# Effective Employee Relations

Employee relations (ER) is, by definition, concerned with relationships in the workplace: how employees interact with each other and with management, how they feel about the work they do, and whether they feel that they are treated fairly. While employee relations as a concept is difficult to quantify, the impact it has on the organization can be considerable. During times of organizational downsizing, if employees are unsure of the future of the organization and of their continued employment, they spend work time worrying about the future instead of doing their jobs, which reduces productivity. When employees feel supported and fairly treated, they are able to concentrate fully on their work, and productivity increases.

While some aspects of employee relations are governed by the law, as previously discussed, the fact is that employers who wish to have a profitable organization will increase the chances of doing so by treating their employees with dignity and respect. Senior and executive management may not always recognize the connection between fair treatment and profitability, and it is up to the HR professional to build the business case for implementing effective ER programs by showing the connection.

## Elements of Employee Relations Programs

An effective employee relations program is based on mutual respect, open and honest communications, fair and equitable treatment, and mutual trust. These characteristics begin at the top. If the executive team behaves autocratically, expecting adherence to strict and restrictive policies, procedures, and work rules, this demonstrates a lack of trust in the ability of employees to do competent work. When the executive team supports employees in making decisions and taking risks, it demonstrates trust in the competence of its employees. Employees who are empowered to take ownership of the work they do, accepting the rewards of good work and consequences of errors, are more productive.

An organization characterized by mutual respect is one in which management listens to employee ideas and concerns and acts on them, and in which employees feel that they are partners with management in the workplace. Management can demonstrate respect for the workforce by actions such as promoting from within, providing training for employees to prepare them for increased responsibility, and giving employees opportunities to demonstrate their capabilities. Employees demonstrate respect for management and each other by listening to differing points of view and supporting decisions that are made.

The role of open and honest communications in the organization cannot be underestimated. Communication must be both top-down and bottom-up; management must be willing to hear and act on information that may be contrary to its decisions. To be effective, management needs to solicit information from those employees closest to the issue being discussed in order to make fully informed decisions. Employees must feel comfortable in approaching management with relevant information when they are aware it has not been included in the decision-making process.

The concept of fair and equitable treatment goes beyond that which is required by legal statute and common law doctrine. An effective ER program is one in which favoritism does not exist and where employees can see that employment decisions, even the ones they may not agree with, are based on objective criteria and equitable treatment. When disputes occur, an effective ER program has a nondiscriminatory process for adjudicating them, and it provides a means for employees to appeal unfavorable decisions to an impartial party.

Finally, none of the preceding concepts work effectively in the absence of an atmosphere of mutual trust within the organization. Trust is built over time, when management continuously demonstrates that its actions are based on fairness and equity and gives employees input into decisions that affect them. A key element of building trust occurs when management communicates not only the "rosy scenario" but an honest evaluation of problems and challenges being faced by the organization. This accomplishes two goals: it encourages employees to come up with creative solutions to the problem or challenge, and it demonstrates that management both respects and values employees and trusts them to handle the information appropriately. The role of the HR professional in employee relations is to provide expertise in developing programs containing these elements and develop methods for measuring the impact of ER programs on the bottom line.

## Communicating with Employees

Because communications is a large element of an ER program, it's important to know the most effective ways of providing information to employees. Depending on the size of the organization, communication may be as simple as an "all-hands meeting" in which the owner talks to the whole company about issues, or it may be as complex as a web broadcast for a multinational corporation. The most effective communication methods are those that occur between the employee and their direct supervisor because these provide the best opportunities for a meaningful exchange of information.

**Open-door policy**   Open-door policies are an effective means for managers to both keep their fingers on the pulse of operations and stay in touch with employee concerns. Giving employees access to the decision makers who can provide support, answer questions, or address concerns also shows a commitment from management to the needs of employees.

**Management By Walking Around**   Publicized in the 1980s by Tom Peters in his book *In Search of Excellence*, Management By Walking Around (MBWA) is a practice first used at Hewlett-Packard in which management provided employees with goals and then spent time with them observing their progress and listening to their concerns or ideas.

**Department staff meetings**   Regularly scheduled meetings in which direct supervisors meet with their staff for updates and coordination of activities, as well as to disseminate information about organization policies and changes, provide a vehicle for employees to voice their questions and concerns and have input into their schedules.

**All-hands staff meetings/town hall meetings**   From time to time, employees like to hear from senior management to find out what's really going on with the company. The all-hands meeting is a means by which executives can update employees on the "state of the company" and answer questions about its future direction, new products, or stock prices. Depending on the size of the company, these meetings can occur in person, via video teleconferencing, or as a web broadcast.

**Brown-bag lunches**   A brown-bag lunch program provides an informal setting for a small group of employees to meet with a senior manager to learn more about the company or a specific goal and ask questions. These informal meetings get their name from the fact that they occur over a lunch period on company premises, with employees bringing their own lunches.

**Newsletters**   Newsletters can provide employees with regular updates on company projects, profits, and goals. They are an effective means for introducing employees to other areas of the organization, reporting on financial issues, and soliciting input for changes in the employment relationship.

**Intranet**   An employee intranet can be an effective, easily updated source for information to employees. In many organizations, the employee handbook is available on the intranet, as are the company newsletter and updates on company goals.

**Word of mouth**   In many organizations, word of mouth is the main means by which employees obtain information. This, of course, has drawbacks. While word-of-mouth communications based on accurate information from management can be an effective way to "get the message out," the information tends to be distorted by the employee grapevine.

**E-mail**   E-mail provides a virtually instantaneous means of communicating information to large groups of employees at the same time. However, e-mail, by its very nature, can be the source of problems, for example, when an executive sends a confidential communication about pending layoffs to all staff instead of to the executive team. Particularly with regard to human resource issues, e-mail should be used cautiously to avoid embarrassment and legal complications because it is discoverable in the event of legal action.

## Employee Involvement Strategies

A significant factor in effective employee relations is the extent to which employees are involved in making decisions that affect them on a day-to-day basis. This requires a commitment from senior management to both ask for and listen to what employees have to say and, whenever possible, implement changes suggested by employees. It's also important that management communicate to employees that the changes were implemented. Employee involvement can be very simple, such as a suggestion box, or more complex, such as a self-directed work team. The previous section discussed a number of communication strategies that are a key aspect of effective employee involvement programs. Other strategies for involving employees include the following:

**Suggestion boxes**   As mentioned in Chapter 2, a suggestion box provides an anonymous means by which employees can provide management with ideas for improvements. As with any method of soliciting information from employees, it is important that suggestions be acted upon in a timely manner, or the concept of the suggestion system loses its credibility.

**Delegating authority**   As discussed earlier in this chapter, management demonstrates respect for its employees by trusting them to make the decisions necessary to do their jobs. To do this effectively, management needs to delegate a sufficient level of authority to employees for making decisions or incurring expenses so that they are free to act without waiting for approval to take necessary action.

**Task force**   A task force is brought together to research and recommend solutions for a significant undertaking or problem; once the solution has been determined, the task force disbands. A task force might be created to analyze technological improvements in a manufacturing plant and recommend improvements that will meet the long term strategic objectives of the organization.

**Committees**   Committees are often formed to address ongoing issues in the organization and may be permanent, such as a safety committee, or ad hoc, such as a group appointed to plan a company function.

**Work team**   A work team is made up of employees who work together each day to accomplish their assignments. The team can be composed of members within a single functional area, or it can have members from several functions that are needed to accomplish the goal. A functional work team might be made up of employees in the marketing department who develop collateral pieces for company products. A cross-functional work team might be made up of employees from the research and development, manufacturing, marketing, operations, and accounting departments who are responsible for developing, launching, and marketing a specific product.

**Virtual work team**   A virtual work team operates in much the same way as a work team, with one major exception: team members are not located in the same building, but may work anywhere in the world and connect through the Internet to accomplish team assignments.

**Self-directed work team**   A self-directed work team is a group of employees who are jointly responsible for accomplishing ongoing assignments. Team members set the work schedules, determine who will do which jobs, and hold each other accountable for accomplishing goals.

## Retention Strategies

One goal of effective employee relations programs is to retain employees. An effective employee relations program with the components I have discussed in this chapter contains the building blocks for retention. In addition, development of "employee-friendly" policies and programs that provide flexibility and recognize that employees have obligations outside the workplace can enhance the employer's ability to retain employees. Advances in technology have made non-traditional work arrangements feasible that were not possible in the past:

**Telecommuting** Employees who telecommute connect to the company network via the Internet and communicate with coworkers and managers via e-mail, fax, and telephone, all from their homes. The telecommuting solution for organizations who are willing to embrace it has many benefits for the company, the employee, and the community. The company is able to hold on to employees who might otherwise choose to leave, maintaining the KSAs and training that have been invested in the individual. The employee is able to continue working and yet be able to handle personal needs, such as caring for an ill child or parent. The community benefits from reduced rush-hour traffic congestion.

**Flextime** Flextime allows employees to work the hours that enable them to take care of personal business, such as taking children to school, attending classes, or avoiding heavy commute traffic. Many organizations set "core hours" during which all employees are required to be at work, but other than that allows employees to determine what hours meet their needs.

**Compressed work weeks** Some organizations allow employees to work four 10-hour days or a 9/80 schedule in which the employee works nine 9-hour days in each two-week period and has a day off every other week. There are a number of variations to these schedules; employers must be aware of FLSA overtime requirements for nonexempt employees and ensure that the compressed work week does not violate those requirements.

**Part-time work** Occasionally, an employee may wish to reduce their hours for a variety of reasons such as attending school or caring for parents or young children. Employers who agree to a regular part-time schedule will retain qualified employees who would otherwise need to leave the organization.

**Job sharing** Job sharing is a situation where two part-time employees share one job. The employer can benefit from this practice in several ways. First, it allows accommodation of an employee's request for a part-time schedule yet maintains full-time coverage for the job. Second, it can allow the employer to hire two people with complementary skills that enhance results.

# Organizational Feedback

A key component of effective employee relations programs is staying in touch with how well the programs are meeting the needs of employees. Some of the communication techniques just described gather this information in an informal way; there are also several more structured methods to do this:

**Employee surveys** As you recall from Chapter 3, "Strategic Management," employee surveys can be used to gather information on any number of issues and are often the most effective means for obtaining information from large numbers of employees. Surveys can be outsourced to companies who develop and conduct them regularly or can be developed in-house. Outsourcing a survey can result in more honest feedback because the identity of participants can be protected.

**Employee focus groups**   When it is impractical to solicit input from all employees, a focus group consisting of a cross-section of employees from various departments and levels in the organization can be used to involve employees in decisions.

**Skip-level interviews**   A *skip-level interview* process in which employees are interviewed by their manager's manager provides insight into employee goals and job satisfaction, as well as an opportunity for career counseling.

## Analyzing and Reporting Feedback Results

> You can prove anything with statistics.
> —Carl Jung

When an organization undertakes a feedback initiative, it is critical that the results be reported back to both management and employees. The HR professional should carefully review the data to ensure that it is accurate. If the results are quantified, they should be viewed critically to make sure they make sense and accurately reflect what is truly happening in the organization. Any quantitative analyses should be carefully reviewed for data entry errors or inadvertent misrepresentations of the information. For example, if only a representative sample of the employee population was surveyed, are the results skewed because the members of the group were not truly representative of the entire population? If the entire workforce was surveyed, did the phrasing of the questions influence the results? There are many ways in which statistical data can be misinterpreted, intentionally or unintentionally. Before reporting any survey results, it is important to ensure that they are accurate.

## Measuring Employee Relations Effectiveness

While employee relations as a concept is difficult to measure, there are two indicators of employee satisfaction that can be measured—absenteeism and turnover. Excessive unplanned absences can be an indication of employee stress, dissatisfaction with job requirements, supervisory conflicts, and feeling undervalued by the employer. Measuring absence rates over time can provide feedback on the success of ER programs, as well as provide indicators of supervisory issues that may be resolved through coaching or training. As discussed in Chapter 4, the turnover rate is the ultimate indicator of dissatisfaction with the supervisor, company, and/or employee relations programs.

# Disciplinary Procedures

As in any relationship, there are times when disagreements occur; in the employment relationship, these disagreements are usually related to some form of performance issue and result in a disciplinary action. Much has been written about this topic, as it can become a source of legal action if the employer does not act appropriately. HR's role in the disciplinary process is to provide the expertise needed to set up a fair and equitable process that is applied consistently throughout the organization.

Organizations with effective employee relations programs work to prevent the need for disciplinary action. Many of the elements of an effective ER program contribute to preventing disciplinary actions: the establishment and publication of clear policies, procedures and work rules, and clearly communicated expectations for individual employees are the cornerstones of prevention. In addition, employees who receive feedback, both positive and negative, on a regular basis are able to correct problems when they are still minor. When this happens, employees are not surprised by negative feedback and are able to improve performance issues when they are easily remedied. When a performance problem cannot be resolved at this level, the supervisor moves into a formal progressive disciplinary process. You can find a full discussion of the five steps in a disciplinary process in Chapter 2.

---

**Weingarten Rights**

In 1975, the Supreme Court upheld a decision by the National Labor Relations Board (NLRB) that unionized employees have the right to request a union representative be present at any investigatory interview which the employee believes could result in disciplinary action. Known as "Weingarten rights," the NLRB extended similar rights to nonunion employees in July 2000. Employers are not required to inform employees of this right, but if an employee requests that a coworker be present, the employer can discontinue the interview until the coworker arrives, decide not to conduct the interview at all and make any disciplinary decision based on other facts, or give the employee the choice of voluntarily waiving the Weingarten rights and continuing the interview or having the employer make disciplinary decisions without an interview.

Employees invoking Weingarten rights are entitled only to the presence of another coworker (in nonunion settings) or a union representative, but they are not entitled to have a family member or attorney present.

---

## Disciplinary Terminations

If, after having been informally coached and receiving three formal warnings (one verbal and two written), the employee has still shown no improvement, it is time to move to the termination stage. When this becomes necessary, the manager should work with HR to ensure that, to the extent possible, all necessary steps to prevent legal action as a result of the termination have been taken. As discussed earlier in this chapter, due process is not required in employment actions taken by private employers, but ensuring that employees are informed of the issues and given the opportunity to tell their side of the story demonstrates that the employer treats them in a fair and equitable manner.

In cases where employee actions create a dangerous situation for the employer, as in theft of company property or violence in the workplace, the employer should move immediately to the termination phase of the disciplinary process. When this occurs, the best course of action is to suspend the employee pending an investigation, conduct the investigation in a fair and expeditious manner, and, should the results of the investigation support termination, terminate the employee. Terminations are always difficult situations, and HR professionals need to be able to provide support for managers who must take this action. There are two areas in which HR's expertise is critical: the termination meeting and providing information so that managers avoid wrongful termination claims.

### The Termination Meeting

Termination meetings are among the most difficult duties any supervisor has to perform. When termination becomes necessary, HR should meet with the supervisor to ensure that the documentation supports the action to be taken and to coach the supervisor on how to appropriately conduct the meeting. By this stage in the process, the employee should not be surprised by the termination, since it should have been referred to as a consequence if improvement did not occur. The meeting should be long enough to clearly articulate the reasons for the termination and provide any final papers or documentation that are necessary. Managers should be counseled to be professional, avoid debating the action with the employee, and conclude the meeting as quickly as possible. The timing of termination meetings is a subject of disagreement as to the "best" day and time. Taking steps to ensure that the termination occurs with as little embarrassment for the employee as possible should be the guiding factor in making this decision. Once completed, and, of course, depending on corporate policy and the circumstances surrounding the termination, the employee should be escorted from the building. Company policies differ on this part of the process: some companies have a security officer escort the employee from the building; others allow the employee to pack up their personal items from the desk with a supervisor or security officer present. While the supervisor is conducting the termination meeting, facilities and IT personnel are often advised of the termination in order to take steps to prevent the employee from accessing the company network or facilities once the termination has been completed.

In any situation with the possibility of the employee becoming violent, HR should arrange for security personnel to be nearby, or, in extreme cases, ensure that the local police department is advised of the situation.

### Wrongful Termination

Wrongful terminations occur when an employer terminates someone for a reason that is prohibited by statute or breaches a contract. For example, an employee may not be terminated because they are a member of a protected class. If an employer gives a different reason for the termination, but the employee can prove that the real reason was based on a discriminatory act, the termination would be wrongful. Similarly, an employee may not be terminated as retaliation for whistle-blowing activity or for filing a worker's compensation claim.

## Dispute Resolution

Most employment disputes are resolved within the organization, but on some occasions that is not possible. In the worst case, employment disputes are resolved in court—a very long and expensive process for all parties. *Alternative dispute resolution (ADR)* covers a range of methods used to solve disagreements without litigation. These alternatives are often able to resolve problems with less animosity than occurs when a lawsuit is filed, and at far less cost to the parties.

Initially, the parties involved in the dispute may attempt a cooperative problem solving meeting, where they work together to find a solution to the problem. Another internal ADR technique is known as a *peer review panel*, which consists of management and nonmanagement employees who are trained in company policies, procedures, and work rules. The panel hears disputes and makes decisions which, depending upon the individual program, can be final and binding on both parties to the dispute. Some companies have established an *ombudsman* or ombuds, an impartial person not involved in the dispute, who can speak with both parties and suggest alternative solutions. An ombudsman can be someone within the company or an outsider.

## Arbitration

Arbitration is a means of resolving conflicts without the expense of a lawsuit. *Voluntary arbitration* occurs when both parties to a disagreement agree to submit the conflict to an arbitrator for resolution. *Compulsory arbitration* can be a contract requirement or may be mandated by a court system as a means of reducing the backlog of civil lawsuits or by legal statute as with public employee unions which are prohibited from striking.

Arbitration decisions may either be binding or nonbinding. In *binding arbitration*, the parties agree to accept the arbitrator's decision as final. In *nonbinding arbitration*, either party may reject the decision and continue the dispute by filing a lawsuit.

There are a number of organizations offering arbitration services throughout the country; most of them have a roster of individuals with expertise in a variety of business and legal disciplines so that the arbitrator assigned to a particular case will be knowledgeable in its requirements and common practices. These organizations develop standards for those selected as arbitrators to ensure that they have the qualifications necessary to make fair and impartial decisions in the matters they hear. For example, the oldest of these organizations, the American Arbitration Association (AAA), requires that its arbitrators have a minimum of 10 years senior-level experience and educational degrees and/or professional licenses in their area of expertise as well as training in arbitration or dispute resolution. In addition the AAA wants their arbitrators to demonstrate professional recognition for excellence in their field and memberships in professional associations.

Arbitration proceedings begin with the selection of the arbitrator. The arbitration service provides a list of individuals with relevant expertise, and each party to the arbitration has an opportunity to eliminate those who may have a conflict of interest in the proceedings.

There are three types of arbitrators: ad hoc, permanent, and a tripartite panel. An *ad hoc arbitrator* is one who is selected to hear only a single case. A *permanent arbitrator* is one who both parties agree is fair and impartial to resolve any disputes arising between them. A *tripartite arbitration panel* consists of three arbitrators who hear the issues and reach a joint decision in the matter.

In an arbitration proceeding, each party makes an opening statement describing their case for the arbitrator. The parties then present evidence, in the form of documents or witnesses, to support their case. The arbitrator asks questions of both sides to obtain additional information, and then each side makes a closing statement to sum up the evidence that was presented. The arbitrator then weighs the evidence and renders a decision, notifying the parties by mail.

## Mediation

Mediating a grievance involves having the parties work together with the aid of a mediator to devise a solution for a problem. The decisions of a mediator are not binding on the parties, and if the process fails, the parties may continue to the arbitration process. Mediation is an informal undertaking without evidentiary rules, and no formal record of the proceedings is retained. Mediators assist the parties by using a variety of problem-solving skills to move the disagreement to a resolution.

There are several steps in the mediation process, described in the following list:

**Structure**   Before the parties meet, the mediator develops a structure for the mediation, deciding on the time, place, and attendees for the session.

**Introductions**   The mediator makes introductions, explains the mediation process, and sets expectations and goals for the mediation.

**Fact-finding**   During the mediation, each party presents its side of the issue in a joint session and, generally, the mediator meets with each party individually as well, to ask questions and ensure that everyone has the same facts and that the issues are clearly identified.

**Options**   As the parties present their facts and listen to those of the other side, alternative solutions may become clear; the mediator may guide the parties to this as well.

**Negotiating**   Once the possible alternatives are on the table, the mediator facilitates negotiations during which the parties come to an agreement.

**Writing the agreement**   The mediator or the parties will write the agreement that has been reached and the parties will sign it.

Mediation is a cost-effective solution that successfully resolves many employment disagreements. In mediation, the parties are in control of the decision-making process and resolving the conflict; the mediator facilitates the process that allows this to occur.

In either mediation or arbitration (unless it is a binding arbitration), if either party is dissatisfied with the decision, they may choose to continue the dispute by taking the matter to court. In most cases, the use of either of these methods results in an agreement that is acceptable to both sides.

The implications of arbitration and mediation in a union environment are discussed in the section entitled "Contract Enforcement."

## Maintaining a Union-Free Environment

Most employers prefer to operate in a union-free environment. An effective employee relations program and organization culture that treats employees with dignity and respect is more likely to remain union-free because employee needs are being met without a union. When employees are treated poorly, overworked, and stressed about their jobs and don't have management support, union promises of better pay and working conditions are attractive and they often turn to unions with the hope that the union will be able to improve their work situation. Unions also offer leadership opportunities for members who become shop stewards and union officers.

# Labor Relations

The history of American labor relations begins in 1869, with the formation of the Knights of Labor. This organization was an advocate of the 8-hour work day when 12 or 14 hours per day was the norm. Over the next century, labor unions grew in importance, but in recent years they have lost some of their appeal to working people. As unions became more powerful and threatened business profitability at the end of the 19th century, federal laws were used to hinder union growth. In reaction, Congress enacted labor legislation that supported union growth. The pendulum swung back and forth several times over the course of the next century, and next I will discuss the various labor laws that were enacted and their impact on unionism in the United States.

## Labor Laws and Organizations

The first piece of legislation that impacted the labor movement was the Sherman Anti-Trust Act, passed in 1890. This legislation was originally intended to control business monopolies that conspired to restrain trade in the United States. The act allowed *injunctions*, court orders that either require or forbid an action by one party against another, to be issued against any person or group that conspired to restrain trade. It was first used against a labor union to obtain an injunction against the American Railway Union in 1894 to end its strike against the Pullman Palace Car Company.

The Clayton Act, passed in 1914, limited the use of injunctions to break strikes and exempted unions from the Sherman Act.

In 1926, Congress enacted the Railway Labor Act, the intention of which was to avoid interruptions due to strikes, protect the rights of employees to join a union, and allow for a cooling off period of up to 90 days if the president deems a strike to be a national emergency. Originally intended to cover the railroad companies, today this act applies to airlines as well.

The Norris-La Guardia Act was passed in 1932 and protected the rights of workers to organize and strike without the interference of federal injunctions. It also outlawed *yellow dog contracts*, which employers had used to prevent employees from joining unions by requiring them to sign an agreement that the employee was not a member of union, would not become one in the future, and that joining a union would be sufficient grounds for dismissal in the future.

In 1935, the National Labor Relations Act (NLRA), or Wagner Act, was passed as part of President Franklin Roosevelt's New Deal. At the time, it was referred to as "labor's bill of rights" and represented a marked change in government attitudes toward unions. The NLRA allowed employees to organize, bargain collectively, and engage in "concerted activities for the purpose of collective bargaining or other mutual aid or protection." The right to engage in concerted activities applies not only to union employees, but to nonunion employees as well. The NLRA went on to identify five employer unfair labor practices and created the *National Labor Relations Board (NLRB)*. The NLRB was established by the NLRA to enforce provisions of the act. It is charged with conducting elections and preventing and remedying unfair labor practices. The NLRB does not instigate actions on its own; it only responds to charges of unfair labor practices or petitions for representation elections filed in one of its offices.

In 1947, when a Republican majority was elected to Congress, the Taft-Hartley Act, or Labor-Management Relations Act (LMRA) was passed in response to employer complaints about union abuse. Not surprisingly, union leaders decried the act as a "slave labor" law. The LMRA prohibits closed shops and allows union shops only with the consent of a majority of employees. It also provides that states have the right to outlaw closed and union shops by passing "right to work" laws. Jurisdictional strikes and secondary boycotts were also prohibited.

When employers bring replacement workers in during an economic strike, they may permanently replace union workers; however, if the strike is in response to unfair labor practices committed by the employer, the union members will be reinstated when the strike ends. The LMRA established the Federal Mediation and Conciliation Service to "prevent or minimize interruptions of the free flow of commerce growing out of labor disputes" by providing mediation and conciliation services.

An important feature of Taft-Hartley is the power granted to the president to obtain an injunction ending a strike or lockout for an 80-day "cooling off" period if, in the president's estimation, the continuation of the strike could "imperil the national health or safety." This power is rarely invoked since its record of leading to successful long-term agreements is mixed.

The Labor-Management Reporting and Disclosure Act (LMRDA) of 1959, also known as the Landrum-Griffith Act, placed controls on internal union operations. Congress felt this was necessary due to "a number of instances of breach of trust, corruption, disregard of the rights of individual employees, and other failures to observe high standards of responsibility and ethical conduct" on the part of union leadership. The act provided a bill of rights for union members which required equal rights for all members to participate in the union, granted freedom of speech and assembly for union members to gather and discuss union issues, and restricted increases in dues and assessments to those that were approved by majority vote of the union. Landrum-Griffith gave employees the right to sue the union and provided safeguards against retaliatory disciplinary actions by the union. The act also prohibited "extortionate picketing" by unions and required that union leadership elections be conducted no less often than every three years for local unions and every five years for national or international officers.

## Employee Rights

The NLRA grants employees the right to organize, join unions, bargain collectively, and engage in other "concerted activities" for mutual aid or protection, as well as the right to refrain from doing so.

The NLRA also protects the right of employees to strike, and identifies lawful versus unlawful strikes:

**Lawful strikes**   One reason that lawful strikes occur is for economic reasons: to obtain better pay, hours, or working conditions from the employer. In an economic strike, employers may hire permanent replacements for striking employees, and are not required to rehire the strikers if doing so means the replacement would be fired. If employees make an unconditional request to return to work, they may be recalled at a later time when openings occur.

The other lawful strike is one that occurs when the employer has committed an unfair labor practice and employees strike in protest. These strikers may not be discharged or permanently replaced.

**Unlawful strikes**   Unlawful strikes are those whose purpose is unlawful, such as a strike that occurs in support of an unfair labor practice committed by a union. Strikes that occur in violation of a no-strike clause in the contract are unlawful. Strikes can become unlawful if the strikers engage in serious misconduct as well.

# Unfair Labor Practices

An *unfair labor practice (ULP)* is an action by an employer or a union that restrains or coerces employees from exercising their rights to organize and bargain collectively or to refrain from doing so. As discussed previously in this chapter, Congress has identified ULPs for both employers and unions.

## Employer Unfair Labor Practices

Employers who attempt to restrain or otherwise interfere with the right of employees to organize and bargain collectively can, in a worst-case scenario, be ordered by the NLRB to bargain with a union even if an election did not take place or if the union loses an election. For that reason, it is extremely important for employers to be certain that all supervisory personnel are aware of what constitutes an unfair labor practice. An acronym that is helpful in avoiding prohibited activity is *TIPS*: employers may not threaten, interrogate, promise, or spy on employees. The ULPs defined by the NLRA are as follows:

**Interfere with, restrain, or coerce unionization efforts**   Employers may not interfere in any way with attempts to unionize the workplace, including organizing activity, collective bargaining, or "concerted activity" engaged in by employees for mutual aid or protection. Interfering also includes inhibiting free speech of employees who advocate unionization.

**Dominate or assist a labor organization**   Employers are precluded from forming company unions that are controlled by management and, therefore, do not allow employees an independent representative. Employers are also prohibited from showing favoritism to one union over another.

**Discriminate against employees**   Employers may not discriminate against union members in any of the terms and conditions of employment. This includes taking disciplinary action against employees for participating in union activities.

**Discriminate against NLRB activity**   Employers may not retaliate against employees who have filed charges or participated in an investigation conducted by the NLRB.

**Refuse to bargain in good faith**   Employers must bargain with a union once it has been designated by a majority of the employees and the union has made a demand to bargain.

**Enter into a hot cargo agreement**   It is unlawful for employers and unions to enter into an agreement in which, at the union's request, employers stop doing business with another employer.

## Union Unfair Labor Practices

The LMRA identified the following union actions that were considered ULPs:

**Restrain and coerce employees**   Union conduct that interferes with an employee's right to choose a representative or to refrain from participating in organizing or collective bargaining activity is a ULP. The act identifies some of the coercive behavior that is unlawful, including assaults, threats of violence, and threats to interfere with continued employment. Unions are also held responsible for coercive acts committed by union members in the presence of union representatives if the representatives do not renounce the actions.

**Restrain or coerce employers**   Unions may not refuse to bargain with representatives chosen by the employer to negotiate with the union or fine or expel from the union a supervisor based on the way the supervisor applies the contract during the course of business. Unions may not insist that employers accept contract terms the union has negotiated with other bargaining units.

**Require employers to discriminate**   Unions may not require the employer to terminate an employee for working to decertify the union or require employers to hire only union members or others of whom the union approves.

**Refuse to bargain in good faith**   Unions must meet and confer with employer representatives at reasonable times to negotiate the terms and conditions of the contract.

**Engage in prohibited strikes and boycotts**   Unions may not engage in hot cargo actions or secondary boycotts (these will be covered in detail later in this chapter).

**Charge excessive or discriminatory membership fees**   Membership fees must be reasonable and in line with the members' wages and industry standards.

**Featherbedding**   Unions may not require employers to pay for services that are not rendered. For example, unions may not require employers to continue to pay employees to do jobs that have been rendered obsolete by changes in technology. An example of this is the fireman on a train who fed coal into the fire on a steam engine to keep the water hot enough to run the train. When diesel trains came along, the fireman was no longer needed to run the train. If a union insisted on keeping the firemen on the trains even though they were not necessary, this was known as "featherbedding."

**Organizational and recognitional picketing**   Picketing is discussed later in this chapter in the "Union Organizing Tactics" section.

### Consequences of Unfair Labor Practices

If, as the result of an investigation, an employer or a union has been found to have committed a ULP, the NLRB can order remedial actions to be taken. The NLRB goal is to eliminate the ULP and to undo the effects of the illegal action to the extent possible. One of the requirements is that the offending party post notices in the workplace advising employees that the ULP will be discontinued and describing the actions to be taken to correct the offense.

**Employer remedies**   The NLRB may require that the employer disband an employer-dominated union, reinstate employees to positions they held prior to the ULP, or engage in the collective bargaining process and sign a written agreement with the union.

**Union remedies**   Unions may be required to agree to reinstatement of employees it caused to be terminated or rejected for employment, refund excessive dues with interest to members, or engage in the collective bargaining process and sign a written agreement with the employer.

## Filing an Unfair Labor Practice Charge

ULP charges can be filed by an employee, an employer, or a union representative (the charging party) on a form available from the NLRB. Charges may be filed in person, by fax, or by mail at the regional office of the NLRB where the alleged violation occurred. The statute of limitations for ULPs requires that they be filed within six months of the incident.

Once the case has been received by the NLRB, the charged party is notified, invited to submit a written statement of the facts and circumstances about the case, and advised that they have the right to counsel. The case is then assigned to a board agent for investigation.

The board agent conducts interviews with all parties to the action, as well as with any witnesses, and makes a recommendation to the regional director for disposition of the case. At this stage, the charges may be dismissed if unwarranted or result in a complaint if valid. Depending on the nature and severity of the offense, the complaint may result in an informal or formal settlement agreement. An informal settlement agreement requires that the charged party will take specified actions to remedy the ULP and does not involve a board order or court decree. A formal settlement involves a complaint issued by the NLRB against the charged party and results in a board order or court hearing.

Charges that are not settled are heard by an administrative law judge (ALJ), who conducts a hearing on the evidence, reviews the record, and issues a "decision and order." If a party is not satisfied with the order of the ALJ, they have 28 days to file an exception with the NLRB office in Washington, D.C., which will issue a final order concurring with or amending the finding of the ALJ.

If the charged party is not satisfied with the NLRB findings, an appeal can be filed with the U.S. Court of Appeals in the appropriate jurisdiction.

# Union Organization

By the time management notices signs of union activity, the organizing process may already be well underway. Early indications that an organizing campaign has begun are changes in employee behavior more than anything else. Employees may begin to challenge management decisions and use union terminology related to benefits or employee rights.

## What Can an Employer Do?

Just as union organizers work to convince employees to join the union, management may communicate the reasons for its opposition to a union. During any organizing campaign, management should procure the services of an experienced labor attorney to review communications about the union before they are disseminated. Once that has been done, first line supervisors should be made aware of information necessary to effectively represent the management view to employees. First line supervisors have more influence with their direct reports than any other member of management, and employers should make use of this relationship.

In response to union claims, employers can make truthful statements about the consequences of unionization as long as the TIPS guideline is followed.

Finally, unions understand that the enthusiasm and support for the union peaks at a certain point and then support begins to dwindle. For that reason, unions like to schedule elections to coincide with the peak of interest, and they gear their organizing activities to that goal. If management can delay the election, it increases the chances of prevailing in the election.

# Union Organizing Tactics

At their peak in 1953, unions represented 35.7 percent of the private sector workforce. Numbers released by the Bureau of Labor Statistics in February 2003 revealed that unions represented only 8.5 percent of the private sector workforce in 2002. However, unions are far more prevalent in today's public sector: 37.5 percent of public sector employers are unionized. As unions struggle to maintain membership levels, they have had to re-examine their strategies for attracting new members.

As the economy in the United States moved from a manufacturing to an informational base, the workforce changed from predominantly blue-collar workers, traditional union members, to white-collar workers who have not traditionally been attracted by union membership. While the strategies vary with each union, the general trend is to find ways of attracting white-collar workers to union membership. Once potential members indicate interest in unionizing their place of work, there are a number of methods used to organize the employees:

**Internet**   Many unions have sophisticated websites that provide information for employees who are interested in forming a union. The sites contain information on labor laws, unfair labor practices, advice on beginning a campaign, and opportunities for interested workers to contact union personnel.

**Home visits**   This tactic is most often used when the union is trying to gain initial supporters in the company. It provides an opportunity for organizers to have private conversations with potential inside organizers. Because home visits are expensive for the union and can be viewed as an unwanted invasion of privacy, they are not widely used.

**Inside organizing**   The most effective organizing process occurs when one or more employees work from within the organization to build support for the union. Insiders can use their influence on coworkers, identify those most likely to respond to the effort, and encourage participation.

**Salting**   Salting occurs when a union hires a person to apply for a job at an organization they have targeted. Once hired, the employee acts in much the same way as an inside organizer who was already employed by the company.

**Meetings**   Union organizing meetings bring together experienced organizers, inside organizers from the company, and employees who are undecided about supporting the organizing process. Meetings provide opportunities for communicating the benefits of membership and exerting peer pressure on potential members.

**Leafleting**   The goal of union leaflets is to point out the advantages the union will bring to the workforce and to counter information that management provides to employees about the benefits of remaining union-free. Leaflets are generally utilized when the organizing campaign is well under way.

**Media**   Unions have developed expertise in getting their message out. When management commits an unfair labor practice or takes any action the union perceives as unfavorable, the union will issue a press release that interprets the action in the most favorable way for the union. For example, in 1999, the Union of Needletrades, Industrial, and Textile Employees (UNITE) was conducting an organizing campaign at Loehmann's Department Store in New York City. Just over a month before the scheduled NLRB election, the store fired one of the leaders of the organizing campaign. UNITE issued a press release that concentrated on the fact that the employee had an exemplary work record at the store and was a single mother. The union went on to allege that the store had spied on the employee during her lunch break in order to find a reason to fire her. The union used this as the basis for encouraging the public to boycott the store.

**Picketing**    *Picketing* occurs when a group of employees patrols the entrance to a business in order to inform customers and the public about disputes, or to prevent deliveries to a business that the union is trying to influence in some way. It can also occur to advise the public about unfair labor practices the union believes the employer has committed. The NLRB recognizes three types of picketing:

**Organizational picketing**    *Organizational picketing* occurs when the union wants to attract employees to become members and authorize the union to represent them with the employer.

**Recognitional picketing**    *Recognitional picketing* occurs when the union wants the employer to recognize the union as the employee's representative for collective bargaining purposes. The NLRA places a limit of 30 days on recognitional picketing, after which a petition for an election must be filed.

**Informational or publicity picketing**    *Informational or publicity picketing* is done to truthfully advise the public that an employer is a union-free workplace.

There are three instances when picketing is prohibited. First, when another union has been lawfully recognized as the bargaining representative for the organization; second, when a representation election has been held within the previous 12 months; and third, when a representation petition is not filed with 30 days of the start of the picketing.

## The Recognition Process

There are seven basic elements in the recognition process, but not all of them occur in every situation. The process consists of authorization cards, a demand for recognition, a petition to the NLRB, an NLRB conference, a pre-election hearing, a campaign, and finally, the election.

The goal of the union during the organizing process is to obtain signed authorization cards from employees. An *authorization card* is the means by which the NLRB determines that there is sufficient support for a union to hold an election. The NLRB will hold an election if 30 percent of the eligible employees in the anticipated bargaining unit sign the authorization cards. In practice, the union would like to have far more signed cards before submitting a petition for an election—generally they would like to have signed cards from at least 50 percent of the eligible employees.

When the union has a sufficient number of authorization cards, they are ready to petition the NLRB for an election. The petition can be filed by an individual or group of employees, by the union, or by the employer. However, before the union can file a petition, they must have first approached the employer with a demand for recognition.

### Voluntary Recognition

An employer may choose to recognize a union voluntarily under some circumstances; this should only be done after conferring with legal counsel. An employer may choose to do this if the union provides evidence that a majority of employees support the union, or if the union convinces the employer to do so. One way unions may seek voluntary recognition is to approach management with signed authorization cards to have management witness its majority status by accepting the cards. There are a number of NLRB cases involving union claims that management has witnessed majority status by counting the authorization cards, so supervisors and management should be made aware of the consequences of handling the cards.

## Petitioning the NLRB

If management refuses to grant voluntary recognition, the union files a petition for an election with the NLRB, along with evidence of employee interest in union representation. The NLRB reviews the petition to determine that it represents an appropriate level of interest in union representation and whether or not signatures on the petition or authorization cards are valid.

When the NLRB is satisfied with the legitimacy of the petition, it schedules a conference with the employer and employee representatives. If either party disputes issues related to the bargaining unit, legitimacy of the authorization cards, or timing of the election, a formal hearing is held by the NLRB to resolve those issues.

### Bargaining Units

The makeup of the bargaining unit is a critical factor to both union and employer points of view. The union wants the unit to be as large as possible and include a majority of employees who are in favor of the union. Management, of course, wants to limit the size of the unit and include a majority of employees who choose to remain union-free.

The NLRA grants broad discretion for bargaining unit determinations to the NLRB. Guidance in the act is that ". . . the unit appropriate for the purposes of collective bargaining shall be the employer unit, craft unit, plant unit, or subdivision thereof." Aside from that, the only specifics provided are that a bargaining unit may not consist of both professional and nonprofessional employees unless the professional employees vote to be included in the unit, and that individuals hired as guards to protect the employer's premises or property may not be included in a unit with other employees. The NLRB looks at several objective criteria to devise a bargaining unit that is appropriate for the individual situation, beginning with determining if there is a "community of interest" within the unit; that is, that the interests of members of the unit are sufficiently similar to preclude disagreements during the bargaining process. The NLRB looks as well at factors such as how the employer administers its business (whether it's with standard policies across the entire company or diverse policies in different locations), geography (how far apart the locations are in the proposed unit), whether the unit is comprised of employees involved in a major process of the company, whether employees are cross-trained or frequently transfer between locations, what unit the employees want to be part of, and any relevant collective bargaining history. Finally, the NLRB considers the extent to which employees are already organized, although the act makes it clear that this may not be the determining factor.

Bargaining units may be comprised of two or more employees in one employer location, or employees in two or more locations of a single employer. If there is an employer industry association, the bargaining unit may include employees of two or more employers in several locations.

Some employees are not eligible for inclusion in a bargaining unit. These include confidential employees, supervisors, and management personnel. The act also excludes independent contractors and some agricultural laborers from bargaining units.

### Temporary Workers

In August 2000, the NLRB made a significant change to its previous rulings on the inclusion of temporary workers in an employer's bargaining unit in a case involving M. B. Sturgis, Inc. Sturgis is a gas hose manufacturer in Missouri that was the target of an organizing campaign. When the union petitioned for an election, Sturgis wanted to include the temp workers on its site in the bargaining unit, but the union did not want them included. The NLRB reversed two long standing positions in this case by deciding that the determining factor in this decision is whether or not a community of interest in wages, scheduling, and working conditions exists between the regular employees and the temp workers, and that a unit including temp workers is not considered a multi-employer unit needing consent of both employers.

## Conducting the Election

During the conference, the NLRB representative reviews any jurisdictional issues, the makeup of the bargaining unit, eligibility of voters in the proposed unit, and the time and place of the election. If all these issues are resolved, a *consent election* is scheduled within 30 days of the conference to determine whether or not a majority of employees in the unit desire to be represented by the union. A *directed election* occurs when a pre-election hearing is required to resolve those issues prior to scheduling the election. An *Excelsior list* containing the names and addresses of all employees in the bargaining unit must be provided by the employer to the union within 7 days of the consent to or direction of the election.

During the time between the NLRB decision and election day, both management and union present the case for their point of view to employees in the bargaining unit. The employer is required to post notice of the election in prominent locations frequented by employees in the bargaining unit. In the 24 hours immediately preceding the campaign, the NLRB prohibits the employer from holding company meetings for the purpose of influencing the vote.

On the day of the election, neither the employer nor the union may conduct campaign activities in or around the polling area.

To be eligible to vote in the election, an employee must have worked during the pay period prior to the election and must be employed by the business on the day of the election. Employees who are sick, on vacation, on military leave, or have been temporarily laid off may vote subject to rules established by the NLRA. Economic strikers who have been replaced by bona fide permanent employees may vote in any election that takes place within 12 months of the beginning of the strike.

During the election, representatives of the employer and the union may challenge the eligibility of any vote before it is placed in the ballot box. These votes are set aside and, if it is possible that the challenged votes would change the result of the election, the NLRB will determine whether or not they are valid after the election ends.

The NLRB representative counts the votes at the end of the voting period and provides the vote count to the parties at that time. If the union receives 50 percent plus one vote, the union is certified as the bargaining representative for the unit. In the event of a tie vote, the union is not certified.

After a vote, the party that lost the election may file charges that the prevailing party interfered with the election results by committing ULPs. The NLRB will investigate the charges in accordance with its administrative procedures and, should they be justified, will take remedial action against the offending party.

For those unfamiliar with the organizing process, the 1979 movie *Norma Rae* provides dramatic insight into the unionization of a garment factory in the South. Based on a true story, the movie follows the efforts of a union organizer from New York to build support for a union in a textile factory in a small southern town. The organizer begins by visiting the homes of some of the workers, distributing leaflets at the front gate of the factory, and enlisting the support of one of the workers who becomes the "inside" organizer. This insider lends credibility to the union representative by introducing him to co-workers, sponsoring organizing meetings, and obtaining signed union authorization cards. In the course of the campaign, management commits several unfair labor practices. One of the final scenes dramatizes the vote count: as the NLRB official observes, representatives for management and the union count each vote.

## Bars to Elections

The NLRA will not allow elections in some circumstances; these are known as election bars:

*Contract bar*   Except in very limited circumstances, the NLRB will not direct an election while a bargaining unit is covered by a valid collective bargaining agreement.

*Statutory bar*   The NLRA prohibits an election in a bargaining unit which had a valid election during the preceding 12-month period.

*Certification-year bar*   When the NLRB has certified a bargaining representative, an election will not be ordered for at least one year.

*Blocking-charge bar*   An election petition will be barred when there is a pending unfair labor practice charge.

*Voluntary-recognition bar*   If an employer has voluntarily recognized a union as the representative for a bargaining unit, an election will be barred for a reasonable period of time to allow the parties to negotiate a contract.

*Prior-petition bar*   When a union petitioning for an election withdraws the petition prior to the election, then no elections will be approved for six months.

## Union Decertification

Employees may petition the NLRB for *decertification* if they are dissatisfied with the union's performance. A decertification petition requires signatures of at least 30 percent of the employees before the NLRB will act upon it. Employees may want to decertify the union for a variety of reasons, including poor performance by the union in its representation of the employees or the desire of the employees to be represented by a different union. Decertification may also occur because the employee relationship with management is a good one, and employees no longer feel the need for union representation. It is critical for HR professionals and management to understand that the employer may not encourage or support employees in the decertification process.

Doing so constitutes an unfair labor practice and may well result in employees being compelled to continue to be represented by the union.

## Union Deauthorization

Employees may wish to maintain the union but remove a union security clause, such as union-shop, dues check-off, or maintenance of membership clause. The NLRB will approve *deauthorization* based on a petition by 30 percent or more of the members of the bargaining unit. As with decertification, employers must not participate in the effort to deauthorize the union as doing so is considered to be an unfair labor practice.

# Collective Bargaining

The NLRA imposes a duty to bargain on employers and unions. Mandatory subjects for the bargaining process include wages, hours, terms and conditions of employment, the agreement itself, and any questions that arise from the agreement. Bad faith in the bargaining process can be evidenced by a lack of concessions on issues, refusing to advance proposals or to bargain, stalling tactics, or withholding information that is important to the process. Evidence of bad faith by management in the bargaining process can also be evidenced by attempts to circumvent the union representative by going directly to employees with proposals before they have been presented to the union. Another indicator of bad faith bargaining by management occurs when unilateral changes are made to working conditions. An indication of bad faith by the union would be failing to notify management of the intent to renegotiate the contract within 60–90 days before it expires.

## Collective Bargaining Positions

Before I can really discuss the components of collective bargaining, it is important to understand the different bargaining positions that can be taken and how each position impacts the bargaining process. There are two basic approaches to the negotiating process: positional bargaining and principled bargaining.

**Positional bargaining**    *Positional bargaining* is a strategy represented by demands made by each side. During positional negotiations, each side views the object of the negotiation as something finite that must be shared, stakes out the position they believe is in their own interest, and concentrates on "winning" that position for their side. This makes the process an adversarial, competitive one. Also known as *hard bargaining* or *distributive bargaining*, positional bargaining is a zero-sum game: in order for one side to gain something, the other side must lose something.

**Principled bargaining**    *Principled bargaining* as a negotiating strategy is characterized by parties who are more interested in solving a problem than they are in winning a position. In doing so, the parties remain open to looking at the problem in new ways, brainstorming for ideas, and often coming up with an agreement that solves the original problem in a way that was not originally contemplated by either side. The most common forms of principled bargaining are integrative bargaining and interest-based bargaining.

**Integrative bargaining**   *Integrative bargaining* is a form of principled bargaining in which the parties look at all the issues on the table and are able to make mutually agreeable trade-offs between those issues.

**Interest-Based Bargaining (IBB)**   *Interest-based bargaining (IBB)*, another form of principled bargaining, is based on the concept that both sides in the negotiation have harmonious interests. In labor-management negotiations, for example, both labor and management have an equal interest in the continuing viability of the business—for management, to earn profits and for labor, to have continued employment.

## Collective Bargaining Strategies

In addition to collective bargaining positions, HR professionals should be aware of the three basic negotiating strategies used in union environments:

**Parallel bargaining**   In *parallel bargaining*, also known as *pattern bargaining*, *whipsawing*, or *leapfrogging*, the union negotiates with one employer at a time. Once a contract has been reached with this employer, the union uses the gains made during the negotiation as a base for negotiating with the next employer.

**Multi-employer bargaining**   In *multi-employer bargaining*, the union negotiates with more than one employer in an industry or region at a time. This situation can occur when temporary workers are part of a client employer's bargaining unit and the union negotiates with both the temp agency and the client employer on employment issues.

**Multi-unit bargaining**   *Multi-unit bargaining*, or *coordinated bargaining*, occurs when several unions represent different bargaining units in the company. An example of this occurs in the airline industry, when the employer negotiates with the unions representing pilots, flight attendants, and mechanics or other employee classes. This allows the employer to coordinate negotiations on mandatory and permissive bargaining subjects while allowing the unions to cooperate on issues that have similar meaning to their various members.

## Collective Bargaining Subjects

The subjects open for negotiation during the collective bargaining process fall into four areas.

**Mandatory subjects**   The NLRA defines the subjects that are mandatory in the collective bargaining process. These are wages, hours, other terms and conditions of employment, and the negotiation of the agreement and bargaining related to questions that arise from the agreement. Both parties must bargain on mandatory subjects, and unresolved issues on them are the only ones that may be the subject of a strike or lockout.

**Illegal subjects**   The NLRA also identifies topics that are unlawful for inclusion in a collective bargaining agreement, including topics such as hot cargo clauses or closed shop security agreements.

**Voluntary subjects**   Voluntary or permissible subjects for negotiation would be any lawful topic other than those identified as mandatory by the NLRA. These generally include management rights, such as production scheduling, and operations or selecting supervisors.

**Reserved rights doctrine**   Management generally includes a clause in the contract that states that any rights not covered specifically in the agreement are the sole responsibility of management.

## Collective Bargaining Agreement (CBA)

The *collective bargaining agreement* is a contract governing the employment relationship for a specified period of time. The clauses contained in the CBA will, of course, be reflective of the bargaining topics in individual companies; some of the clauses found in many contracts include the following:

**Wages, hours, terms and conditions of employment**    The clauses that describe the wages, medical and other benefits, overtime, hours, and other conditions of employment are the backbone of the collective bargaining agreement.

**Union security clauses**    The union security clause requires members of the union to provide financial support to the union. A security clause helps to ensure that the union will be financially able to carry out its bargaining obligations.

A *union shop* clause requires that all employees join the union within a grace period specified by the contract, but no fewer than 30 days, or, in the construction industry, 7 days.

An *agency shop* clause specifies that all employees must either join the union or pay union dues if they choose not to join the union.

A *closed shop* clause requires that all new hires be members of the union before they are hired. The closed shop is illegal except in the construction industry.

A *maintenance of membership* clause allows employees to choose whether or not to join the union, but once they join, they must remain members until the expiration of the contract. The employee must notify the union to discontinue membership within 30 days of the contract expiration.

**No strike/no lockout clause**    These clauses are considered very important to both unions and management because they provide economic protection from work stoppages on both sides. Strikes and lockouts are discussed more fully in the "Lockouts and Strikes and Boycotts...Oh My!" section of this chapter.

**Contract administration**    This clause covers the nuts and bolts of how the contract will be administered over its duration. Procedures for disciplinary actions, grievance resolution, and arbitration, as well as agreements on how clauses may be modified during the contract term, can be included in this clause.

**Dues check-off**    Most unions prefer to have employees agree to automatic deduction of their union dues. To be enforceable, employees must give written authorization for the deductions.

**Zipper clause**    A *zipper clause* or *totality of agreement* clause is an agreement between the parties that the CBA is the entire agreement between them and that anything not in the agreement is not part of the agreement. The purpose of this clause is to prevent reopening of negotiations during the term of the contract.

## Contract Enforcement

Disagreements that arise during the course of the contract may take many forms; some are easily resolved through the grievance process established in the CBA, others may go to arbitration before they are resolved.

### Grievance Procedure

When disagreements occur in a union environment, the grievance process described in the CBA provides the framework for resolving them. The framework describes the steps to be taken and the time frames within which actions must be implemented to either resolve or reply to the grievance. Many grievances can be resolved at the first step in the process with the immediate supervisor, grievant, and union steward working together to solve the problem. If resolution is not possible at that level, a union official takes the dispute to the next level of company management, where the grievant generally does not attend but is represented by the union representative. If the dispute is not resolved at the second level, a member of the union grievance committee meets with the next level of management in the company. Grievances that are serious enough to be unsolved at the highest management level in the process then go to a third party for resolution. Depending on the terms of the CBA, this may involve binding arbitration, as is the case in the majority of contracts, or it may utilize mediation or another form of alternative dispute resolution.

### Binding Arbitration

As discussed previously in the section entitled, "Dispute Resolution," arbitration is one method of resolving disputes without litigation. In the union environment, binding arbitration is used to resolve conflicts without resorting to work stoppages. Compulsory arbitration is mandated by legal statute to resolve disputes in the public sector where labor strikes are prohibited.

### Mediation

The process used to mediate disputes in a union environment is the same as it is in a non-union environment. With the aid of the mediator, the parties to the disagreement are able to develop a solution that is acceptable to both of them.

### Court Injunctions

As explained earlier in this chapter, injunctions are sought when immediate action is needed to temporarily prevent something from occurring. One example of the use of injunctions in the collective bargaining process is the national emergency strike. The Taft-Hartley act empowers the president to seek an injunction to stop a strike or lockout for an 80-day "cooling off" period.

## Duty of Successor Employers

In the event that a company with collective bargaining agreements is acquired by a new company, the new management may be required to maintain the union contract. Whether or not the NLRB will consider an acquiring owner to be a successor employer is based on the following factors:

- There is substantial continuity in operations.
- The number of employees assimilated into the new company.
- Similarity of operations and products.
- The agreement with the previous employer.

While the terms and conditions may be changed by the new employer, the changes are required to be made through the collective bargaining process, and may not be made unilaterally by the employer.

## Lockouts and Boycotts and Strikes . . . Oh My!

For a variety of reasons, such as when communication between union and management breaks down and tempers flare, when workplace conditions become so hazardous that employees are afraid they will be maimed or seriously injured on the job, one party or the other may determine that the only course of action left to them is a work stoppage.

### Lockouts

A *lockout* occurs when management shuts down operations to keep the union from working. This can happen for several different reasons. For example, union members may be engaging in a work slowdown, and it may be costing management more to have the employees working slowly and producing a limited number of goods or services than it would cost to shut down the operation.

### Boycotts

Boycotts occur when the union and the employees in the bargaining unit work together against an employer to make their dissatisfaction with the employer's actions known or to try to force the employer into recognizing the union or conceding to the demands of the union. Boycotts occur in several ways:

**Ally doctrine**     The *ally doctrine* states that when an employer whose workers are on strike contacts a neutral employer and asks the neutral employer to produce the work that would normally be performed by the striking workers, the neutral employer becomes an ally of the struck employer and is therefore a legitimate target of a picket line.

**Alter ego doctrine**     The *alter ego doctrine* developed originally as a means to protect creditors from frauds perpetrated by shareholders. Its application has been extended to labor relations to preclude employers from dodging their collective bargaining responsibilities. An alter ego employer consists of two or more businesses with substantially identical management, business purposes, operations, equipment, customers, supervision, and ownership. In 1965, the Supreme Court heard a case, *Radio Union v Broadcast Services, Inc.*, in which it identified four criteria that determine whether or not a single employer exists: interrelation of operations, central control of labor relations, common management, and common ownership. When these four criteria are present, the NLRB may determine that employees of the alter ego employer are part of the bargaining unit.

**Double breasting**     Double breasting refers to a common owner of two businesses, one of which is a union shop and the other a nonunion shop. Unions would like to include both businesses in a bargaining unit due to their common ownership. Historically, as long as each business had different management, equipment, and customers and a legitimate business purpose separate and apart from the other company, the union was prohibited from striking the second business because that was considered a secondary boycott by the NLRB. More recently, the NLRB has determined that unionization of both businesses may be a legitimate topic for contract negotiation, and if the owner refuses to bargain, the union may strike.

**Straight line operations**   A straight line operation is one in which two businesses perform operations that complement each other's operations. If one business is struck, the other may be as well because they are engaged in a single economic enterprise.

## Strikes

A *strike* occurs when the union decides to stop working. Earlier in the chapter, I discussed the difference between unlawful and lawful strikes. Whether or not a strike is lawful depends on the purpose of the strike, and the NLRA identifies several specific strikes:

- A strike in support of a ULP committed by the union is an unfair labor practice and therefore an unlawful strike.

- A strike that occurs in violation of a no-strike clause in a CBA is not a protected activity, and employees engaging in this type of activity may be terminated or disciplined.

- Strikers who engage in serious misconduct during a strike, including violence, threats of violence, physically blocking someone from entering or leaving the place of business, or attacking management personnel will cause a strike to be deemed unlawful.

- Work slowdowns are considered unlawful strikes and may result in disciplinary action, including termination.

- A *wildcat strike* is one that occurs in violation of a contract clause prohibiting strikes during the term of the contract.

- A *sit-down strike*, in which employees stop working and stay in the building, is considered an unlawful strike.

- Strikes in support of a hot cargo clause are prohibited.

## Picketing

As discussed in the section, "Union Organizing Tactics," picketing can be a lawful activity and a way for unions to advertise their message. Although picketing often occurs in connection with a strike or work stoppage, it is not the same thing as a strike. The difference is that picketing occurs to simply inform other parties about issues under dispute, while a strike occurs when the employees stop working. Even in the public sector where strikes are prohibited by law, picketing can be used to inform the public about the issues. The three different kinds of picketing that PHR/SPHR candidates should be familiar with are the following:

**Common Situs picketing**   *Common Situs picketing* happens when an employer shares a building with other employers. Because picketing a common business location can interfere with the ability of secondary businesses to operate, the union must ensure that picket signs clearly state the name of the business they are striking, and where possible, restrict picketing to an entrance that is used only by the primary employer.

**Consumer picketing**   *Consumer picketing* is done to advise consumers that goods have been produced by a business whose workers are on strike.

**Hot cargo pickets**   Hot cargo was described earlier in the chapter. Because it is an unlawful activity, picketing against hot cargo issues is prohibited.

# Summary

Effective management of Employee and Labor Relations is a critical element of a successful business. Employees who are treated with dignity and respect and given the tools they need to succeed reward the employer with increased production, fewer sick days, and a loyal and committed workforce. Organization culture begins with management attitudes toward employees and ranges from those that are based on an autocratic philosophy characterized by "top-down" communications and interactions to those of employee empowerment where individuals and work teams make the decisions necessary to get their job done.

Effective dispute resolution programs that solve employment disagreements without the need for legal action are both cost-effective and more successful than lawsuits. Establishing programs in the workplace that provide opportunities for employees who feel they have been mistreated is one way for HR professionals to add value to their organizations.

Management of the employment relationship is subject to the laws prohibiting discrimination in all terms and conditions of employment, as well as to common law doctrines. HR professionals must be aware of the requirements of these statutes and doctrines in order to provide sound advice to management in making employment decisions, and to ensure that the programs and policies developed by HR are in compliance with them.

Labor Relations is governed by a number of laws designed to protect the rights of employees. The unionization process is strictly regulated by the NLRB, which conducts union recognition elections and adjudicates charges of unfair labor practices by both unions and employers. Unions, whose membership has steadily declined over the past 20 years, are now seeking to expand their organizing efforts by targeting nontraditional union members and developing sophisticated methods for attracting new members. The most effective way for management to avoid unionization of the workplace is to treat employees fairly and give them a voice in decisions that affect their day-to-day work.

# Exam Essentials

**Be aware of the requirements of equal employment opportunity legislation on the employment relationship.**   EEO legislation requires employers to provide equal opportunities and a safe workplace that is free from harassment. Federal EEO legislation established protected classes for race, color, religion, sex, national origin, age, and disability. Employers must ensure that all employees are aware that the business does not tolerate harassment on the basis of any protected category, and they must create written policies that clearly state the employer's position and consequences that will occur if employees violate the policy.

**Be aware of the impact of an effective employee relations program on the bottom line.** Providing a workplace environment in which employees are treated with dignity and respect, are involved in making decisions that affect them each day, and have work that is satisfying and challenging benefits employers. Employees who feel respected and valued are more productive and loyal to the company and, in the long run, have a positive impact on the bottom line.

**Be aware of employer unfair labor practices.**   Employers may not interfere with attempts of employees to organize unions or assist a union in organizing, nor can they discriminate against employees who advocate for the union or who engage in protected NLRB activities.

**Be able to establish fair and effective disciplinary processes.**   The most effective disciplinary process is one that prevents performance problems by providing clear performance expectations and regular feedback, both positive and negative, on how the employee is meeting those expectations. A fair and effective process tells employees clearly what the problem is, allows the employee to respond, and involves the employee in developing a solution to the problem.

**Be able to identify various methods for alternative dispute resolution.**   Lawsuits are costly and time consuming for employers and generally disruptive to operations. Establishing alternative methods of resolving employment disputes demonstrates that the employer has provided due process to employees. An effective ADR program involves successively higher levels of management in resolving disputes.

**Know how to identify and respond to union organizing activity.**   Union organizing activity is most effective when conducted by employees within the organization. Some signs that an organizing effort is underway include employees who begin challenging management in staff meetings, talking with employees that they haven't had contact with before, and a newly hired employee who is very vocal about perceived management abuses toward employees.

**Understand the collective bargaining process.**   The collective bargaining process is required by the National Labor Relations Act and provides that employers must bargain in good faith with the union representative chosen by the employees. Employers have a duty to bargain in good faith on mandatory subjects, which include wages, hours, and other terms and conditions of employment.

# Key Terms

Before you take the exam, be certain you are familiar with the following terms:

| | |
|---|---|
| ad hoc arbitrator | authorization card |
| agency shop | binding arbitration |
| ally doctrine | blocking-change bar |
| alter ego doctrine | certification-year bar |
| alternative dispute resolution (ADR) | closed shop |

collective bargaining agreement

common law doctrine

Common Situs picketing

compulsory arbitration

consent election

constructive discharge

consumer picketing

contract bar

coordinated bargaining

deauthorization

decertification

defamation

directed election

distributive bargaining

due process

duty of diligence

duty of loyalty

duty of obedience

Excelsior list

express contract

glass ceiling

hard bargaining

hostile work environment

implied contract

informational picketing

injunctions

integrative bargaining

interest-based bargaining (IBB)

leapfrogging

lockout

maintenance of membership

multi-employer bargaining

multi-unit bargaining

National Labor Relations Board (NLRB)

nonbinding arbitration

ombudsman

organizational picketing

parallel bargaining

pattern bargaining

peer review panel

permanent arbitrator

picketing

policies

positional bargaining

principled bargaining

prior-petition bar

procedures

publicity picketing

quid pro quo

recognitional picketing

sit-down strike

skip-level interview

statutory bar

strike

tangible employment action (TEA)

TIPS

tort

totality of agreement

tripartite arbitration panel

unfair labor practice (ULP)

union shop

vicarious liability

voluntary arbitration

voluntary-recognition bar

whipsawing

wildcat strike

yellow dog contracts

zipper clause

# Review Questions

1.  A supervisor has called an employee in for a interview about an inventory shortage. When the supervisor begins asking questions, the employee invokes his Weingarten rights. The supervisor has the option to

    A.  Stop the discussion while the employee calls an attorney.

    B.  Stop the discussion until a coworker is available upon return from vacation in 4 days.

    C.  Discontinue the interview and make the determination based on other evidence and documentation.

    D.  Continue the interview while waiting for the coworker to return from lunch.

2.  An employee has resigned and during the exit interview tells HR that the reason for the resignation is that for the last three months the supervisor has been hostile, refused to provide instructions on work assignments, given the employee all of the most unpleasant tasks in the department, and verbally reprimanded the employee in front of coworkers and customers. The employee may have a cause of legal action based on

    A.  The employer's duty of good faith and fair dealing

    B.  Constructive discharge

    C.  Promissory estoppel

    D.  Fraudulent misrepresentation

3.  All of the following statements about employment at-will are true except:

    A.  The employer may terminate the employee at any time for any reason.

    B.  The employee may resign at any time, with or without notice.

    C.  The employer may terminate the employee for cooperating with an SEC investigation.

    D.  The employer may withdraw an offer of employment after the employee has accepted the position and resigned another job.

4.  During a unionizing campaign, management may do the following in response to union allegations:

    A.  Point out the consequences of unionization based on past facts.

    B.  Encourage nonunion employees to talk about the reasons they don't want the union.

    C.  Tell employees the company will have to move the jobs to another country if the union is elected.

    D.  Ask employees what the union is saying about the company.

5.  As a result of the Sturgis case,

    A.  Temporary employees may only form a union and bargain with the temp agency.

    B.  The temporary agency must agree to bargain with a client company's union.

    C.  Temporary employees who work side-by-side with regular employees may be part of the bargaining unit.

    D.  Temporary employees may not be unionized.

6. If employees no longer want the union to represent them, they may petition the NLRB for
   A. Decertification
   B. Deauthorization
   C. Contract bar
   D. Statutory bar

7. A union security clause that requires all employees to join the union after they are hired is
   A. An agency shop clause
   B. A union shop clause
   C. A closed shop clause
   D. A maintenance of membership clause

8. Double breasting occurs when
   A. An employer has two companies that are substantially identical.
   B. A neutral employer performs work that is normally done by striking employees.
   C. An employer has two businesses, one union and one nonunion, that do substantially the same work but have different management, equipment, and customers.
   D. Two businesses perform operations that are part of the same product.

9. During a representation election, votes may be challenged
   A. By management or the union at any time
   B. By management or the union before the votes are counted
   C. By management only
   D. By the union only

10. Salting is a practice in which
    A. The union hires an individual to publicize its reasons for targeting an employer for unionization.
    B. The union hires an individual to distribute leaflets to employees as they are leaving work at the end of the day.
    C. The union hires an individual to picket the employer's business.
    D. The union hires an individual to apply for a job with an employer and begin to organize the company.

# Answers to Review Questions

1. **C.** Weingarten rights give all employees the right to have a coworker present during an interview if the employee believes the interview could lead to disciplinary action. The interview must be discontinued until the coworker is available or the employer may decide to use other facts available without interviewing the employee if there will be a lengthy delay while waiting for the coworker.

2. **B.** Constructive discharge occurs when the employer forces an employee to resign by creating a work environment that is so unpleasant a reasonable person would resign.

3. **C.** The public policy exception to the at-will doctrine prevents an employer from terminating an employee who is cooperating in a government investigation of wrong-doing.

4. **A.** The company may make truthful statements about a unionized environment during an organizing campaign, such as pointing out that employees will have to pay dues to the union.

5. **C.** Temporary employees who have a community of interest with regular employees of the client company may become part of the bargaining unit whether or not the temp agency agrees to bargain with the union.

6. **A.** The NLRB will conduct a decertification election if the employees present a petition signed by 30 percent of the employees in the bargaining unit. Management may not participate in or encourage employees to circulate the petition or provide any support in the process. Doing so is considered an unfair labor practice.

7. **B.** A union shop requires all new employees to join the union within a grace period specified by the contract, no less than 30 days, except in the construction industry where the grace period must be 7 days.

8. **C.** Double breasting occurs when an employer has two companies that are separate and distinct from each other but do the same type of work, and one company is union while the other is nonunion. This occurs most often in the construction industry when contractors have two different crews for bidding on union and nonunion jobs.

9. **B.** Votes may be challenged by the union representative or by management only before the vote goes into the ballot box.

10. **D.** Salting occurs when a union hires an individual experienced at organizing tactics to apply for a job with a company that has been targeted for an organizing campaign.

# Chapter

# 8

# Occupational Health, Safety, and Security

**THE HRCI TEST SPECIFICATIONS FROM THE OCCUPATIONAL HEALTH, SAFETY, AND SECURITY FUNCTIONAL AREA COVERED IN THIS CHAPTER INCLUDE:**

✓ Ensure compliance with all applicable federal, state, and local workplace health and safety laws and regulations.

✓ Determine safety programs needed for the organization.

✓ Develop and/or select injury/occupational illness prevention programs.

✓ Implement injury/occupational illness prevention programs.

✓ Develop and/or select safety training and incentive programs.

✓ Implement safety training and incentive programs.

✓ Evaluate the effectiveness of safety prevention, training, and incentive programs.

✓ Implement workplace injury/occupational illness procedures (for example, worker's compensation, OSHA)

✓ Determine health and wellness programs needed for the organization.

✓ Develop/select, implement, and evaluate (or make available) health and wellness programs.

✓ Develop/select, implement, and evaluate security plans to protect the company from liability.

✓ Develop/select, implement, and evaluate security plans to protect employees (for example, injuries resulting from workplace violence).

✓ Develop/select, implement, and evaluate incident and emergency response plans (for example, natural disasters, workplace safety threats, evacuation).

The connection between work and health was first studied in sixteenth-century Europe when two traveling physicians, Philippus Aureolus (writing under the name Paracelsus) and Georgius Agricola wrote about mine conditions and advocated changes to protect workers. One treatise by Paracelsus entitled, "On the Miner's Sickness and Other Mine Diseases," investigated the relationship between the occupation and an illness and identified the "Miner's Sickness," which today we know as silicosis, a disabling and often fatal disease that still takes the lives of more than 250 American workers each year.

Prior to the Industrial Revolution, however, work done for hire was largely agrarian, and the potential for large-scale injury or illness did not exist in the way it does today. When steam-powered machinery and equipment took the place of animals and hand tools in the workplace and workers moved from agricultural to industrial jobs, lung diseases were the first to be noticed and addressed by government regulation. Early safety legislation in the United States was enacted by state governments and focused on conditions in factories and mines, often spurred as a result of a tragic accident. In 1869, the federal government established the Bureau of Labor to study and report on job-related accidents, but it had no ability to require changes in safety practices.

There was a long period of time in America when it was cheaper for employers to fight lawsuits filed on behalf of workers killed or injured on the job than it was to implement safety programs. Because the courts rarely held employers accountable for worker injuries, most employers chose this approach. Employer attitudes in this regard did not change until the shortage of skilled workers during World War II gave employees plentiful options for places to work—and they opted to work for employers who provided safe environments over those who did not.

For over a hundred years beginning in 1867, sporadic legislation was enacted by different states and the federal government to address specific safety concerns, usually in regard to mine safety or factory conditions, but there was no comprehensive legislation requiring employers to protect workers from injury or illness. That changed with the Occupational Safety and Health Act of 1970 (the OSH Act), a comprehensive piece of federal legislation that continues to impact employers in virtually every company in America. In order to be fully prepared for the PHR/SPHR exam, candidates must have the basic knowledge needed to fully understand, develop, implement, and evaluate programs related to the activities detailed in the test specifications for Occupational Health, Safety, and Security. Knowledge of the OSH Act and other federal laws in this area is key to understanding these requirements. Candidates should understand safety and security risks for the company and its employees, be aware of potentially violent behaviors and conditions in the workplace, and understand processes for preventing or reducing the impact of violence in the workplace. The exams require a thorough knowledge of health and safety practices and the ability to develop and implement response plans. Questions on the exams will require knowledge of internal investigation and surveillance techniques, as well as employee assistance and wellness programs. PHR/SPHR candidates will need to be able to recognize the signs of substance abuse and dependency and be aware of the legally appropriate ways to respond to situations involving illegal drug use.

The HRCI core knowledge requirements that will be particularly helpful in understanding this functional area include needs assessment and analysis, communication strategies, documentation requirements, adult learning concepts, motivation, liability, and risk management.

# Employment Legislation

In the years prior to the OSH Act, there was a growing recognition that employers were largely unwilling to take preventative steps to reduce the occurrence of injuries, illnesses, and fatalities in the workplace. On December 6, 1907, 362 miners died in an explosion at the Monongah coal mine in West Virginia—the single worst mining disaster in American history. In that year alone, a total of 3,242 coal miners lost their lives. As a result, in 1910 Congress established the Bureau of Mines to investigate mining accidents.

Annual fatalities in the railroad industry also peaked in 1907 when there were 4,218 work-related deaths. Railroad safety technology began developing at the end of the nineteenth century, but most railroad owners did not implement these preventative measures until much later, partially as a result of federal legislation requiring safety improvements.

The tragic nature of large accidents in the railroad and mining industries captured public attention and created pressure on the federal government to take action. This led Congress to enact legislation requiring safety improvements in the coal mining and railroad industries, but these measures were specifically targeted to those industries. Little attention was paid to equally dangerous workplace safety and illness issues that did not produce the spectacular accidents prevalent in mines or on railroads. By the late 1960s, 14,000 American workers lost their lives each year due to injuries or illnesses suffered while on the job. The federal government had been working on solutions, but was mired in bureaucratic turf battles over which agency should have control of the process. The Department of Health, Education, and Welfare wanted legislation that applied only to federal contractors, and the Department of Labor, spurred by Secretary Willard Wirtz's personal interest in the subject, wanted to protect *all* American workers. After several years of this infighting, the proposal by the Department of Labor was sent to the Congress and enacted as the Occupational Safety and Health Act of 1970. A key component of this legislation was the creation of the *Occupational Safety and Health Administration (OSHA)*, which now sets safety standards for all industries and enforces those standards with the use of fines, and in case of criminal actions, can call on the Department of Justice to file charges against offenders.

In this section, we will discuss the OSH Act and other legislation that protects workers, as well as worker compensation requirements that are, with some exceptions, covered by state laws.

## Occupational Safety and Health Act of 1970

The major piece of federal legislation applicable to the functional area of Health, Safety, and Security is the Occupational Safety and Health Act of 1970, as amended. The intent of Congress, as stated in the preamble to the OSH Act, is to assure safe and healthful working conditions for American workers. To accomplish this purpose, the act sets forth three simple duties:

1. Employers must provide every employee a place to work that is "free from recognized hazards that are causing or are likely to cause death or serious physical harm."

2. Employers must comply with all safety and health standards disseminated in accordance with the act.

3. Employees are required to comply with occupational safety and health standards, rules, and regulations that impact their individual actions and behavior.

As mentioned previously, the OSH Act created the Occupational Safety and Health Administration (OSHA) and gave it the authority to develop and enforce mandatory standards applicable to all businesses engaged in interstate commerce. The definition of interstate commerce is sufficiently broad to cover most businesses, except those sole proprietors without employees, family farms employing only family members, and mining operations, which are covered by the Mine Safety and Health Act (to be discussed later in this section). The act encouraged OSHA to work with industry associations and safety committees to build on standards already developed by specific industries, and it authorized enforcement action to ensure that employers comply with the standards. OSHA was charged with developing reporting procedures to track trends in workplace safety and health so that the development of preventative measures would be an ongoing process that changed with the development of new processes and technologies.

The OSH Act also created the *National Institute of Occupational Safety and Health (NIOSH)* as part of the Department of Health and Human Services. NIOSH is charged with researching and evaluating workplace hazards and recommending ways to reduce the effect of those hazards on workers. NIOSH also supports education and training in the field of occupational safety and health by developing and providing educational materials and training aids and sponsoring conferences on workplace safety and health issues.

The NIOSH website (`www.cdc.gov/niosh/homepage.html`) provides a wealth of information that may be of assistance to PHR and SPHR candidates looking for additional study resources.

Finally, the OSH Act encourages the states to take the lead in developing and enforcing safety and health programs for businesses within their jurisdictions by providing grants to help states identify safety and health issues in their specific jurisdictions and to develop programs for enforcement and prevention.

## Mine Safety and Health Act of 1977 (MSH Act)

The MSH Act established the *Mine Safety and Health Administration (MSHA)* to ensure the safety of workers in coal and other mines. The act established mandatory safety and health standards for mine operators and monitors operations throughout the United States. MSHA has developed a comprehensive website (`www.msha.gov/`) that is a resource for miners and mine operators, providing access to information on preventing accidents, year-to-date fatalities, and guidance on specific mine hazards. The site also contains a link to the complete text of the act.

# Drug-Free Workplace Act of 1988

The Drug-Free Workplace Act applies to businesses with federal contracts of $100,000 or more each year. Contractors subject to the act must take the following steps to be in compliance:

**Develop and publish a written policy**     Contractors must develop a written policy that clearly states that they provide a drug-free workplace and that illegal substance abuse is not an acceptable practice in the workplace. The policy must clearly state what substances are covered and clearly indicate the consequences for violation of the policy.

**Establish an awareness program**     The employer must develop a program to educate employees about the policy and communicate the dangers of drug abuse in the workplace, discuss the employer's policy, inform employees of the availability of counseling or other programs to reduce drug use, and notify employees of the penalties for violating the policy. The program can be delivered through a variety of media—seminars, brochures, videos, web-based training—whatever methods will most effectively communicate the information in the specific environment.

**Notify employees about contract conditions**     Employees must be made aware that a condition of their employment on a federal contract project is that they abide by the policy and inform the employer within 5 days if they are convicted of a criminal drug offense in the workplace.

**Notify the contracting agency of violations**     In the event that an employee is convicted of a criminal drug offense in the workplace, the employer must notify the contracting agency within 10 days of being informed of the conviction by the employee.

**Establish penalties for illegal drug convictions**     The employer must have an established penalty for any employees convicted of relevant drug offenses. Within 30 days of notice by an employee of a conviction, the employer must take appropriate disciplinary action against the employee, or require participation in an appropriate drug rehabilitation program. Any penalties must be in accordance with requirements of the Rehabilitation Act of 1973.

**Maintain a drug-free workplace**     Contractors must make a good faith effort to maintain a drug-free workplace in accordance with the act, or they are subject to penalties, including suspension of payments under the contract, suspension or termination of the contract, or exclusion from consideration from future contracts for a period of up to 5 years.

# Other Legislation Impacting Occupational Health, Safety, and Security (OHSS)

While the OSH Act of 1970 is the major piece of federal legislation that impacts employers, other legislation has less well-known requirements related to occupational health and safety. This additional legislation includes the following:

**Fair Labor Standards Act**     Components of the Fair Labor Standards Act (FLSA), more fully discussed in Chapter 6, "Compensation and Benefits," apply to children in the workforce. Minors between the ages of 16 and 18 may not be employed in jobs considered particularly hazardous to them, including those that expose them to explosives, logging operations, power-driven tools, radiation, mining operations, and other jobs that require the use of equipment that poses a significant danger to the child.

**Small Business Regulatory Enforcement Fairness Act of 1996 (SBREFA)**    SBREFA was enacted to give a voice to small businesses without the resources to hire lobbyists to affect the decision-making process in federal agencies. The act provides that the Chief Counsel for Advocacy of the Small Business Administration (SBA) work with small business advocacy groups to advise agencies of appropriate businesses to consult with during decision-making processes.

**Needlestick Safety and Prevention Act of 2000**    This law was enacted in response to the ongoing public health issue of exposure to blood-borne pathogens by health care workers subjected to accidental needlestick or sharps injuries. The act mandates that all needlestick and sharps injuries be recorded, requires involvement of front-line employees in finding safer devices to replace needles and sharps, and protects employees who have endured needlestick injuries.

## Worker Compensation

As long as there have been workers and employers, there has been a debate about financial responsibility for injuries suffered on the job. The first written record of this is in the Hammurabic Code, written some 4,000 years ago. Of course, at that time, the workers were slaves, and compensation for injuries was paid to their masters, but, nonetheless, there was a recognition of financial liability when injuries occurred.

Over time, three common law doctrines developed that were applied to workers who were injured on the job: the fellow servant rule, the doctrine of contributory negligence, and voluntary assumption of risk.

1.  The *fellow servant rule* absolved employers of responsibility if a coworker's actions caused the injury.

2.  The *doctrine of contributory negligence* was used to mitigate the employer's responsibility if the worker's actions contributed in any way to the injury.

3.  *Voluntary assumption of risk* said that workers who knew the dangers of the job when they took it assumed the associated risks, and the level of pay accepted reflected the amount of danger involved so the employer had no responsibility when death or injury occurred.

For workers, these doctrines presented many problems. First, they assumed that the employer and the worker were equals in the labor market so the law treated employment relationships the same as it did contracts between business owners. It assumed that if the terms and conditions of employment were not agreeable to the worker, the worker could simply seek other employment.

Second, these doctrines required workers injured on the job to seek recompense through the court system. Employers for the most part could afford the best attorneys to represent them while few employees could afford a lengthy legal battle.

These common law doctrines became known as the "unholy trinity" because the results were almost always in favor of the employer: only 50 percent of cases brought on behalf of workers killed or injured on the job resulted in any kind of compensation; of those that did receive compensation, it was rarely more than a few month's pay. As governments recognized the blatant unfairness of the lopsided way these doctrines were applied, states began enacting worker compensation laws to level the playing field for workers. Wisconsin was the first state to pass a Worker Compensation Act in 1911, and New Jersey followed in the same year.

Worker compensation laws for private employers are in most cases the purview of state government; however, there are a few industries with federal legislation to protect injured workers. These include the federal government, the longshore industry, coal mines, and the Department of Energy. Legislation pertaining to these industries is covered by the following laws:

**Federal Employees Compensation Act of 1916 (FECA)**    FECA is administered by the DOL and is the federal employee's equivalent of worker compensation, providing similar benefits for workers injured during the course of performing their jobs.

**The Longshore and Harbor Workers' Compensation Act of 1927 (LHWCA)**    LHWCA provides worker compensation benefits for maritime workers whose injuries occur on the navigable waters of the U.S. or on piers, docks, or terminals.

**Black Lung Benefits Act of 1969 (BLBA), amended in 1977**    The BLBA provides benefits to coal miners who have been disabled by pneumoconiosis as a result of their work in the mines. Benefits are also paid to surviving dependents if the miner dies from the disease.

**Energy Employees Occupational Illness Compensation Program Act of 2000 (EEOICPA)**
This act was created to provide compensation for employees and contractors of the Department of Energy who were subjected to excessive radiation while producing and testing nuclear weapons.

# Occupational Safety and Health Administration (OSHA)

Any discussion of the topic of occupational safety and health must begin with OSHA, because it exerts overwhelming influence on workplace safety and health issues. OSHA statistics, developed through the record-keeping requirements of the OSH Act, show significant improvements in workplace safety and health since 1971: fatalities have been reduced by 62 percent, and injury and illness rates have been reduced by 42 percent, even though the workforce has more than doubled in the same time period. In May 2003, OSHA unveiled its new five-year strategic management plan to further reduce workplace fatalities by an additional 15 percent and workplace injuries and illnesses by 20 percent by the year 2008.

These improvements in working conditions are a result of many factors—the change from a manufacturing to a service economy and improvements in technology among them—but underlying them all has been OSHA, with its unwavering focus on establishing health and safety standards to improve the safety of the American workplace.

## OSHA Standards

Although the OSH Act did not clearly define workplace hazards, it did empower OSHA to define *occupational safety and health standards* that would result in improved workplace safety and health as quickly as possible. Wherever possible the act encouraged OSHA to use previously existing federal standards or industry standards that already had substantial agreement within the industry. The resulting standards range from those that are job and industry specific, such as standards for handling toxic chemicals used in manufacturing processes, to those that apply to many businesses.

Let's review some of the more generally applicable standards now. Each standard is identified here with the OSHA title and the number assigned to it in the Code of Federal Regulations (CFR).

**The General Duty Standard, Section 5**    The *general duty standard* requires employers to provide jobs and a workplace environment that are free from recognized safety and health hazards that could potentially cause death or serious physical harm. This standard also requires employers to comply with all OSHA rules, regulations, and standards.

Employees are required to comply with OSHA standards and rules that apply to their own conduct in the course of performing their duties.

**Emergency Action Plans, 1910.38**    Employers are required to have *emergency action plans* in place to inform employees of appropriate procedures to follow during a fire or evacuation. The plan must designate employees who will remain behind during an evacuation to maintain or shut down critical operations. Employers must also develop a process to account for all employees after an evacuation and identify those employees who are responsible to carry out rescue and medical duties in the event of an emergency. Employers must provide training for employees when the plan is first developed, when new employees are hired, and when an employee is assigned new responsibilities for execution of the plan.

The plan must also identify the person responsible for maintaining it who can be contacted by employees who have questions about the plan.

**Fire Prevention Plans, 1910.39**    An OSHA-required fire prevention plan must describe the major fire hazards and appropriate procedures for handling and storing hazardous materials to prevent fires. The employer must develop and implement procedures to control the accumulation of flammable or combustible refuse and ensure that devices on heat-producing machinery that prevent ignition of fires are adequately maintained.

The fire prevention plan must also inform employees about any fire hazards they will face when first assigned to a new job and what actions they should take to protect themselves in the event of a fire.

**Occupational Noise Exposure, 1910.95**    This standard establishes permissible noise levels for the workplace, establishes measurement procedures, requires implementation of hearing conservation programs when average noise levels reach 85 decibels or greater, and requires audiometric testing for employees who work in environments with noise at those levels. Audiometric test results indicating a hearing loss of 10 decibels must be reported on OSHA form 300.

**Personal Protective Equipment, 1910.132**    OSHA has established standards for personal protective equipment (PPE) to be used in jobs in which employees come in contact with hazardous materials, compressed gases, explosives and blasting agents, liquid petroleum, and ammonia. The standard requires PPE to protect the eyes and face, respiration, head, feet, and hands. It also requires that gear be provided to protect employees from electrical shocks or other injuries. The standard requires that PPE be provided, used, and maintained in working condition.

Employers are required to train employees in the appropriate use of PPE and are responsible for ensuring that employee-owned equipment is adequately maintained for use in hazardous situations.

**Sanitation, 1910.141**    This standard requires that the workplace be clean to the extent the type of work allows and sets forth specific guidelines for maintaining sanitary conditions.

**Specifications for Accident Prevention Signs and Tags, 1910.145**    OSHA has developed specifications for hazard signs and tags and requires that all workplace signs conform to the OSHA specifications. These specifications describe the colors to be used for different levels of warning, and in some cases, such as biohazard and slow-moving vehicle signs (among others) provide specifications for size, color, and design of the sign.

In general, OSHA defines red as the background color for danger, yellow for caution, orange for warning, and fluorescent orange or orange-red for biological hazards. Lettering or symbols on the signs is specified as being of a contrasting color for the background.

**Permit-Required Confined Spaces, 1910.146**    OSHA requires permits for employees to enter spaces that may become filled with a hazardous atmosphere that is immediately dangerous to life or health. The atmosphere in confined spaces must be tested prior to an employee's entrance into them and other personnel are required to be in close proximity to the entrance to render assistance if needed. Employees who will be entering the space have the opportunity to observe the testing process if they desire to do so.

**The Control of Hazardous Energy (Lockout/Tagout), 1910.147**    The lockout/tagout standard applies to machinery that may start unexpectedly when a guard or other safety device must be removed to perform a service or maintenance process and any part of an employee's body may be subjected to injury in the course of the process.

**Medical Services and First Aid, 1910.151**    OHSA requires that employers provide adequate first aid supplies and either have medical personnel available, or ensure that one or more workers are trained in first aid to assist injured employees in an emergency.

**General Requirements for All Machines (Machine Guarding), 1910.212**    OSHA requires that woodworking machines; cooperage machinery; abrasive wheel machinery; mills; power presses; forging machines; portable power tools; welding, cutting, and brazing tools; and tools for specific industries such as paper, textile, bakery, and sawmill, among others, use guards to protect employees from injury. These guards can be barrier-type guards, two-hand tripping devices, electronic safety devices, or other guards or devices that effectively prevent injuries.

**Selection and Use of Electrical Work Practices, 1910.333**    Employers must ensure that employees who work on or around electrical equipment or circuits are protected from injury that could result from direct or indirect contact with electrical currents.

**Blood-Borne Pathogens, 1910.1030**    Blood-borne pathogens are pathogenic microorganisms in human blood that can cause disease in humans. The Hepatitis B Virus (HBV) and Human Immunodeficiency Virus (HIV) are examples of blood-borne pathogens, but are not by any means the only ones. Workers in the health care industry are those most at risk for exposure to blood-borne pathogens, and OSHA regulations require employers to take steps to prevent exposure, including a written exposure control plan that informs employees of preventive steps, post-exposure evaluation and follow-up, record keeping, and incident evaluation procedures.

**Hazard Communication Standard (HCS), 1910.1200** The HCS requires employers to provide employees with information about physical and health hazards related to the use of any chemicals in the workplace. Employers must develop and maintain an ongoing written HCS plan that is to be updated as changes occur in the materials that are used in the workplace. The *material safety data sheets (MSDS)* provided by chemical manufacturers provide sufficient information for communication and training of employees.

 The comprehensive list of OSHA standards can be accessed at www.osha.gov/pls/oshaweb/owastand.display_standard_group?p_toc_level=1&p_part_number=1910&p_text_version=FALSE.

## Enforcement of OSHA Standards

OSHA's success is the result of strong enforcement of the standards it has developed. As business owners demonstrated in the nineteenth and twentieth centuries, without the threat of financial penalty, some companies would choose to ignore injury and illness prevention requirements. That being the case, OSHA established fines and penalties that can be assessed against businesses that violate required standards. Table 8.1 describes the violation levels and associated penalties for noncompliance.

**TABLE 8.1** Categories of OSHA Violations

| Violation | Description | Fine |
|---|---|---|
| Willful | Assessed when there is evidence of an intentional violation of the OSH Act or "plain indifference" to its requirements. | $5,000 to $70,000 per violation |
| Serious | Assessed when there is substantial probability of death or serious physical harm as a result of the hazard. | Up to $7,000 |
| Other-than-Serious | The hazard could have a direct and immediate effect on the safety and health of employees. | Up to $7,000 |
| Repeat | OSHA has previously issued citations for substantially similar conditions. | Up to $70,000 per violation |
| Failure to Abate | The employer failed to abate a prior violation. | Up to $7,000 per day past the abatement date |
| *De-minimus* | Assessed for violations with no direct or immediate relationship to safety or health. | $0 |

During fiscal year 2002, OSHA conducted 37, 493 inspections. Tables 8.2 and 8.3 provide a breakdown of the numbers and reasons for inspections, as well as the costs of violations identified during the inspections.

**TABLE 8.2**    OSHA Inspections During Fiscal Year 2002

| Number | Percent | Reason for Inspection |
|---|---|---|
| 9,007 | 24% | Complaint/accident related |
| 20,511 | 55% | High hazard targeted |
| 7,975 | 21% | Referrals, follow-ups, etc. |
| **Number** | **Percent** | **Industry Sector** |
| 21,347 | 57% | Construction |
| 8,270 | 22% | Manufacturing |
| 7,876 | 21% | Other industries |

Source: OSHA Facts, www.osha.gov/as/opa/oshafacts.html

**TABLE 8.3**    Violations and Penalties from 2002 Inspections

| Violations | Percent | Type | Current Penalties |
|---|---|---|---|
| 416 | 0.5% | Willful | $11,799,539 |
| 54,842 | 70% | Serious | $48,312,043 |
| 1,969 | 2.5% | Repeat | $7,710,736 |
| 231 | 0.3% | Failure to Abate | $597,301 |
| 20,749 | 26% | Other | $2,145,151 |
| 226 | 0.3% | Unclassified | $2,268,508 |
| 78,433 | TOTAL | | $72,827,278 |

Source: OSHA Facts, www.osha.gov/as/opa/oshafacts.html

## Employer Responsibilities

As discussed earlier in this chapter, the OSH Act has three requirements, two of which pertain to employers. Not only must employers provide a workplace that is safe and healthful for employees, they must also comply with established standards. OSHA has established other requirements for employers as required by the law:

- Employers are expected to take steps to minimize or reduce hazards and ensure that employees have and use safe tools, equipment, and PPE and ensure that they are properly maintained.

- Employers are responsible to inform all employees about OSHA, posting the OSHA poster in a prominent location, and making them aware of the standards that apply in the worksite. If an employee requests a copy of a standard, the employer must provide it to them.

- Appropriate warning signs that conform to the OSHA standards for color coding, posting, or labels must be posted where needed to make employees aware of potential hazards.

- Compliance with OSHA standards also means that employers must educate employees about safe operating procedures and train them to follow the procedures.

- Businesses with 11 or more employees must maintain records of all workplace injuries and illnesses and post them from February 1 through April 30 each year.

- Within 8 hours of a fatal accident, or one resulting in hospitalization for three or more employees, a report must be filed with the nearest OSHA office.

- The accident report log must be made available to employees, former employees, or employee representatives when reasonably requested.

- When employees report unsafe conditions to OSHA, the employer may not retaliate or discriminate against them.

## Employer Rights

Employers have some rights as well, including the right to seek advice and consultation from OSHA and to be active in industry activities involved in health and safety issues. Employers may also participate in the OSHA Standard Advisory Committee process in writing or by giving testimony at hearings. Finally, employers may contact the National Institute for Occupational Safety and Health (NIOSH) for information about substances used in work processes to determine whether or not they are toxic.

At times, employers may be unable to comply with OSHA standards due to the nature of specific operations. When this happens, employers may apply to OSHA for temporary or permanent waivers to the standards along with proof that the protections developed by the organization meet or exceed those of the OSHA standard.

## Employee Rights and Responsibilities

When the OSH Act was passed in 1970, employees were granted the basic right to a workplace with safe and healthful working conditions. The act intended to encourage employers and employees to collaborate in reducing workplace hazards. Employees have the responsibility to comply with all OSHA standards and with the safety and health procedures implemented by their employers. The act gave employees the following specific rights to:

- Seek safety and health on the job without fear of punishment.

- Know what hazards exist on the job by reviewing the OSHA standards, rules, and regulations that the employer has available at the workplace.

- Be provided with the hazard communication plan containing information about hazards in the workplace and preventive measures employees should take to avoid illness or injury, and to be trained in those measures.

- Access the exposure and medical records employers are required to keep relative to safety and health issues.

- Request an OSHA inspection, speak privately with the inspector, and accompany the inspector during the inspection. Employees may also respond to questions asked by the inspector during the inspection.

- Observe steps taken by the employer to monitor and measure hazardous materials in the workplace, and access records resulting from those steps.

- Request information from NIOSH regarding the potential toxic effects of substances used in the workplace.

- File a complaint about workplace safety or health hazards with OSHA and remain anonymous to the employer.

## OSHA Record-Keeping Requirements

The fact that companies must keep specific records of injuries and illnesses allows OSHA and NIOSH to identify new hazards to be researched and addressed by standards that reduce the possibility of injury or illness. Employers must also keep records of their compliance with OSHA regulations. These records include up-to-date files for exposures to hazardous substances and related medical records, records of safety training meetings, and OSHA logs that record work-related injuries and illnesses.

As of January 1, 2002, OSHA revised the requirements for maintaining records of workplace injuries and illnesses in order to collect better information for use in prevention activities, simplify the information collection process, and make use of advances in technology. Three new forms were developed:

1. OSHA Form 300, Log of Work-Related Injuries and Illnesses
2. OSHA Form 300A, Summary of Work-Related Injuries and Illnesses
3. OSHA Form 301, Injury and Illness Incident Report

Completion of the forms does not constitute proof of fault on the part of either the employer or the employee and does not indicate that any OSHA violations have occurred. Recording an injury or illness on the OSHA forms does not mean that an employee is eligible for worker compensation benefits. Detailed guidance about completing the forms is available at www.osha.gov/recordkeeping/detailedfaq.html#1904.0.

The following list covers the basic requirements for OSHA record-keeping, including who should file OSHA reports, which employers are exempt from filing, and what injuries are considered work related:

**Who must complete and file OSHA forms?**   All employers with 11 or more employees are required to complete and file the OSHA forms just discussed.

**Exempted employers**   Employers with 10 or fewer employees are not required to file the forms. In addition, OSHA has identified industries with low injury and illness rates and exempted them from filing reports. These include the retail, service, finance, insurance, and real estate industries. Unless OSHA has notified a business in writing that reports must be filed, they are exempt from the requirement.

**What must be recorded?**   There are three considerations taken into account in determining whether an injury or illness should be recorded. First, is the employee covered by OSHA? Second, is the employee covered by OSHA regulations? And finally, is it a new case?

Injury or illness to any employee on the employer's payroll must be recorded, regardless of how the employee is classified, full or part time, regular or temporary, hourly or salary. Injuries to employees of temp agencies, if under the employer's direct supervision on a daily basis, must also be recorded. The owners and partners in sole proprietorships and partnerships are not considered employees for OSHA reporting purposes.

*Privacy concern cases* are new protections developed by OSHA to protect employee privacy by substituting a case number for the employee name on the OSHA 300 log. Cases where this is appropriate include injury or illness that involved an intimate body part or resulted from a sexual assault; HIV infection, hepatitis or tuberculosis; needlestick injuries involving contaminated needles; or other illnesses when employees request that their names not be included on the log.

An injury or illness is generally considered to be work related if it occurred in the workplace. Table 8.4 is provided in the regulations to provide guidance in determining when an injury or illness is not considered to be work related.

**TABLE 8.4**   Injuries and Illnesses Not Considered Work Related

| 1904.5(b)(2) | **You are not required to record injuries and illnesses if ....** |
| --- | --- |
| (i) | At the time of the injury or illness, the employee was present in the work environment as a member of the general public rather than as an employee. |
| (ii) | The injury or illness involves signs or symptoms that surface at work but result solely from a non-work-related event or exposure that occurs outside the work environment. |
| (iii) | The injury or illness results solely from voluntary participation in a wellness program or in a medical, fitness, or recreational activity such as blood donation, physical examination, flu shot, exercise class, racquetball, or baseball. |

**TABLE 8.4**   Injuries and Illnesses Not Considered Work Related *(continued)*

| 1904.5(b)(2) | You are not required to record injuries and illnesses if .... |
| --- | --- |
| (iv) | The injury or illness is solely the result of an employee eating, drinking, or preparing food or drink for personal consumption (whether bought on the employer's premises or brought in). For example, if the employee is injured by choking on a sandwich while in the employer's establishment, the case would not be considered work related. **Note:** If the employee is made ill by ingesting food contaminated by workplace contaminants (such as lead), or gets food poisoning from food supplied by the employer, the case would be considered work related. |
| (v) | The injury or illness is solely the result of an employee doing personal tasks (unrelated to their employment) at the establishment outside of the employee's assigned working hours. |
| (vi) | The injury or illness is solely the result of personal grooming, self medication for a non-work-related condition, or is intentionally self inflicted. |
| (vii) | The injury or illness is caused by a motor vehicle accident and occurs on a company parking lot or company access road while the employee is commuting to or from work. |
| (viii) | The illness is the common cold or flu. **Note:** Contagious diseases such as tuberculosis, brucellosis, hepatitis A, or plague are considered work-related if the employee is infected at work. |
| (ix) | The illness is a mental illness. Mental illness will not be considered work related unless the employee voluntarily provides the employer with an opinion from a physician or other licensed health care professional with appropriate training and experience (psychiatrist, psychologist, psychiatric nurse practitioner, etc.) stating that the employee has a mental illness that is work related. |

Source: OSHA Regulations Section 1904.5

Once the employer has determined whether or not the injury or illness is work related, the employer must determine whether it is a new case or a continuation of a previously recorded case. To a certain extent, this is left to the employer's common sense and best judgment. OSHA considers a new case to have occurred when an employee has not had a previous injury or illness that is the same as the current occurrence, or when the employee had recovered completely from a previous injury or illness of the same type.

**Annual summary**   At the end of each year, employers must review the OSHA 300 log and summarize the entries on the form 300A, which must then be certified by a company executive as correct and complete, and then posted as previously mentioned in February of the following year.

**Retention**   The OSHA 300 log and annual summary, privacy case list, and 301 Incident Report forms must be retained for 5 years following the end of the calendar year that they cover.

**Employee involvement** Employers are required to provide employees and employee representatives, former employees, or a personal representative of an employee with information on how to properly report an injury or illness, and they are also required to allow limited access to employees or their representatives to the records of injury and illness.

The OSHA 300 log must be provided to these requestors by the end of the following business day.

The OSHA 301 Incident Report must be provided by the end of the next business day when the employee who is the subject of the report requests a copy. When an employee representative requests copies, they must be provided within 7 calendar days, and all information except that contained in the "Tell Us About the Case" section must be removed.

## OSHA Inspections

OSHA is empowered by the OSH Act to inspect workplaces. Most inspections are conducted without notice by a Compliance Safety and Health Officer (CSHO) who has been trained on OSHA standards and how to recognize safety and health hazards in the workplace. OSHA has established a hierarchy of situations to give priority to inspection of the most dangerous workplace environments. Table 8.5 describes the priorities OSHA uses in allocating time for inspections.

**TABLE 8.5** OSHA Inspection Priorities

| Priority | Hazard | Description |
| --- | --- | --- |
| First | Imminent Danger | A reasonable certainty that immediate death or serious injury from existing workplace hazards will occur before normal enforcement procedures can take place. |
| Second | Catastrophes and Fatal Accidents | Employers must report fatal accidents or serious injuries resulting in the hospitalization of 3 or more employees within 8 hours. OSHA will inspect to determine if any safety violations contributed to the accident. |
| Third | Employee Complaints | Employees may request inspections when they feel violations exist that threaten physical harm. |
| Fourth | Programmed High-Hazard Inspections | Based on statistical analysis, OSHA conducts planned inspections of industries or jobs that have high incident rates for death, injury, and illness. |
| Fifth | Follow-up Inspections | CSHOs follow up on previously issued citations to ensure that the employer has taken action to correct the violation. |

During an inspection, OSHA follows a distinct procedure. In advance of the inspection, the CSHO prepares by reviewing records related to any previous incidents or inspections or employee complaints. The inspector also determines what, if any, special testing equipment will be necessary for the inspection. Upon arrival at the worksite, the inspection commences with an opening conference, proceeds to a workplace tour and ends with a closing conference.

1. First, the CSHO arrives at the worksite and presents his credentials; if the CSHO doesn't, the employer should insist upon seeing them before the inspection begins. It is critical that any employee who may be the initial contact at the worksite be instructed as to who should be contacted when this occurs. Any observation of trade secrets during the inspection remains confidential; CSHOs who breach this confidentiality are subject to fines and imprisonment. Employers have the right to require the inspector to have a security clearance before entering any secure areas.

2. Next, the inspector holds an *opening conference*, during which the inspector will explain why the site was selected, the purpose of the visit, the scope of the inspection, and discuss the standards that apply to the worksite. The CSHO will request an employee representative to accompany the CSHO on the inspection along with the management representative. If no employee accompanies the inspector on the tour, the CSHO will talk to as many employees as necessary to understand the safety and health issues in the workplace.

3. The next step is a tour of the facilities. During the tour, the inspector will determine what route to take, where to look, and to which employees the CSHO will talk. During this part of the inspection, the CSHO may talk privately to employees, taking care to minimize disruptions to work processes. Activities that can occur during an inspection include the following:

   - Review of the safety and health program
   - Examination of records, including OSHA logs, records of employee exposure to toxic substances, and medical records
   - Ensuring that the OSHA workplace poster is prominently displayed
   - Evaluation of compliance with OSHA standards specific to the worksite
   - Pointing out unsafe working conditions to the employer and suggesting possible remedial actions

4. Finally, the inspector holds a *closing conference*, where the inspector, the employer, and, if requested, the employee representative discuss the observations made and corrective actions that must be taken. At this time the employer may produce records to assist in resolving any corrective actions to be taken. The CSHO will discuss any possible citations or penalties that may be issued, and the OSHA Area Director makes the final determination based on the inspector's report.

Should the OSHA Area Director determine that citations are necessary to ensure employer compliance with OSHA, the director will issue citations and determine the penalties that will be assessed according to established guidelines that consider various factors, including the size of the company. The OSHA Area Director also determines the seriousness of the danger, how many employees would be impacted, and good faith efforts on the part of the employer to comply with the standards, among others. OSHA regulations allow for adjustments to penalties based on the size of the employer, the gravity of the offense, and the employer's good-faith efforts to cooperate with the inspector.

During the course of an OSHA inspection, an employer may raise an affirmative defense to any violations observed by the inspector. Possible affirmative defenses include:

- An isolated case caused by unpreventable employee misconduct. This defense may apply when the employer has established, communicated, and enforced adequate work rules that were ignored by the employee.

- Compliance is impossible based on the nature of the employer's work, and there are no viable alternative means of protection.

- Compliance with the standard would cause a greater hazard to employees, and there are no alternative means of protection.

The employer has the burden to prove an affirmative defense exists. If successfully proven, the OSHA Area Director may decide that a citation and penalty are not warranted. The employer has specific responsibilities and rights during and after the inspection:

- Employers are required to cooperate with the CSHO by providing records and documents requested during the inspection and by allowing employees or employee representatives to accompany the inspector on the worksite tour.

- Should a citation be issued during the inspection, the employer must post it at or near the worksite involved, where it must remain for 3 working days or until the violation has been abated, whichever is longer. It goes without saying, of course, that the employer is required to abate the violation within the time frame indicated by the citation.

- Employers may file a Notice of Contest within 15 days of a citation and proposed penalty. If there will be an unavoidable delay in abating a violation because the materials, equipment, or personnel will not be available, the employer may request a temporary variance until the violation can be corrected.

Employees have the right to object in writing to the abatement period set by OSHA for correcting violations within 15 days of receipt of the citation by the employer. Employees who have requested an inspection have the right to be advised by OSHA of the results of the inspection.

# OSHA Assistance

OSHA provides many sources for employers and employees to obtain information about workplace health and safety issues. Chief among these is an extensive website (www.osha.gov), which provides access to the laws, regulations, and standards enforced by OSHA as well as general information on prevention. In addition to the website, OSHA publishes a number of pamphlets, brochures, and training materials that are available for use in businesses.

## OSHA Consultants

Educating employers and employees about workplace health and safety issues is key to preventing injuries and illnesses in the workplace. OSHA provides training programs for consultants who work with business owners in establishing effective health and safety programs. These free consultation services give employers an opportunity to learn which of the standards apply in their worksite, involve employees in the safety process, and correct possible violations without a citation and penalty. Once the consultant becomes involved, the employer must abate any violations or the consultant will refer the violation to an OSHA inspector.

The *Safety and Health Achievement Recognition Program (SHARP)* recognizes small, high-hazard employers who have requested a comprehensive OSHA consultation, corrected any violations, and developed an ongoing safety management program. To participate in the program, the business must agree to ask for additional consultations if work processes change.

## Partnerships and Voluntary Programs

The *Strategic Partnership Program* is a means for businesses and employees to participate in solving health and safety problems with OSHA. Partnerships currently exist for metal recycling, grain handling, and janitorial contractors working to develop solutions specific to their businesses.

The *OSHA Alliance Program* provides a vehicle for collaboration with employer organizations interested in promoting workplace health and safety issues. The program is open to trade and professional organizations, businesses, labor organizations, educational institutions, and government agencies, among others.

The *Voluntary Protection Program (VPP)* involves employers with tough, established safety programs. VPP participants must meet OSHA criteria for the program and, having done so, are removed from routine scheduled inspection lists. The program serves to motivate employees to work more safely, reduce workers compensation costs, and encourage further improvements to safety programs.

# Health

As mentioned earlier in this chapter, the connection between occupations and illnesses was first established almost 500 years ago by physicians caring for miners in Germany. In 1700, Bernardino Ramazzini published his "Discourse on Diseases of Workers," which sought to connect additional illnesses with environmental conditions in the workplace. One of the connections he made was to identify "irregular" or "unnatural" body movements that affect the safety and health of workers—we know this concept today as the science of ergonomics.

OSHA estimates the cost to business of occupational illness and injury to be $170 billion a year. The focus of occupational health is to prevent those illnesses from occurring in the first place, to protect workers and, in the long run, to reduce the costs incurred by businesses by reducing turnover and worker compensation costs, increasing productivity, and eliminating OSHA fines and penalties assessed for violations of health standards. In this section, we are going to discuss health hazards that occur in the workplace and the ways employers can eliminate or reduce those hazards. We'll talk about developing an illness prevention plan and how an effective plan both protects employers and saves money for employers.

## Environmental Health Hazards

*Environmental health hazards* in the modern workplace come in many forms, from physical hazards such as noise and extreme temperatures to chemicals used for everything from making copies to manufacturing products to biological hazards from viruses and bacteria. The effects of these various hazards differ between individual employees—some are more affected than others—and employers must take steps to prevent serious health consequences in the workplace. Table 8.6 provides a list of some of the more common environmental health hazards.

**TABLE 8.6**   Examples of Environmental Health Hazards

| Chemical | Physical | Biological |
| --- | --- | --- |
| Asbestos | Electrical currents | Bacteria |
| Battery acid | Ergonomic design | Contaminated water |
| Corrosives | Extreme temperatures | Dusts |
| Gas fumes | Light | Fungi |
| Pesticides | Noise | Molds |
| Polyurethane foam | Radiation | Plants |
| Solvents | Vibrations | Viruses |

## Chemical Health Hazards

Many of the OSHA standards deal with specific *chemical health hazards* in the workplace. Every chemical present in the workplace should have an MSDS provided by the chemical manufacturer to provide information on how to both prevent and treat an injury. The MSDS identifies the ingredients in the substance, how the substance reacts to changes in the atmosphere such as at what temperature it will boil or become a vapor, and information about its explosive and flammable qualities. The MSDS tells employees whether it is stable or unstable, what materials it must not be in contact with, and what additional hazards are present when the substance decomposes or degrades.

Most importantly for physical safety, the MSDS provides information about how the chemical may be absorbed by the body; whether it can be inhaled, ingested, or enter through the skin; whether it is carcinogenic; and what protective equipment is required to handle the substance to prevent illness.

There are some chemicals, known as *teratogens*, that have no effect on a pregnant woman but do affect an unborn child. Some employers, concerned about the health of the employee and her child as well as about potential liability, have developed policies to protect the fetus. These policies, while well-intentioned, violate the Pregnancy Discrimination Act, which prohibits sex-specific fetal protection policies.

### 🌐 Real World Scenario

#### *Automobile Workers v Johnson Controls, Inc.*

Johnson Controls, Inc. manufactures batteries, a process in which lead is a primary ingredient. Occupational exposure to lead can have serious health consequences, including posing a risk to the health of an unborn child. Prior to 1964, Johnson Controls did not employ women in any of the battery manufacturing jobs in its plant. After passage of the Civil Rights Act in 1964, women were given the opportunity to work in those jobs.

In June 1977, Johnson developed its first fetal protection policy, which stated, "(P)rotection of the health of the unborn child is the immediate and direct responsibility of the prospective parents. While the medical profession and the company can support them in the exercise of this responsibility, it cannot assume it for them without simultaneously infringing their rights as persons." Although this policy did not exclude women from the manufacturing jobs, the company discouraged women who wished to have children from taking these jobs and required them to sign a statement that they had been advised of the risks of lead exposure to a fetus.

In 1982, after eight women became pregnant while maintaining high levels of lead in their blood, the policy changed: ". . .women who are pregnant or who are capable of bearing children will not be placed into jobs involving lead exposure or which could expose them to lead through the exercise of job bidding, bumping, transfer, or promotion rights." The policy went on to define lead levels that would make a job inaccessible to women and required that women who wished to work in those positions supply medical proof of their inability to bear children.

In 1984, a class action petition challenging the fetal-protection policy was filed. Among the individuals in the class were Mary Craig, who had chosen to be sterilized so that she could keep her job; Elsie Nason, a 50-year-old divorcee who had been transferred out of a job where she was exposed to lead to a job that paid less; and Donald Penney, who had requested and been denied a leave of absence so that the lead level in his blood could be lowered in order for him to become a father.

Johnson Controls argued that its policy was a business necessity.

Both the District Court and the Federal Court of Appeals found for Johnson Controls. The case was then appealed to the U. S. Supreme Court in 1990, where the lower court decisions were reversed. The Supreme Court found that there was clear bias because the policy required only female employees to prove that they were not capable of conceiving children, and it was therefore in violation of the PDA.

The Supreme Court ruled that "Decisions about the welfare of the next generation must be left to the parents who conceive, bear, support, and raise them, rather than to the employers who hire those parents."

## Physical Health Hazards

There are many *physical health hazards* that are easy to identify and remedy. One such condition would be an open hole without any warning signs or barriers to prevent someone from accidentally falling. Another would be an electrical or telephone cord crossing a walkway that is not covered or secured to prevent someone from tripping. Another physical hazard would be a walk-in freezer storage unit that could not be opened from inside the unit. Other physical hazards occurring in the workplace are less obvious, such as ergonomics.

*Ergonomics* is a science that addresses the way a physical environment is designed and how efficient and safe that design is for the people in the environment.

Poor ergonomic designs can cause *musculoskeletal disorders* or MSDs. An MSD is the result of repeated stress to various parts of the body, including the back, arms, shoulders, and other areas, that is caused by the way tasks are performed. MSDs are referred to by several other names as well, including *repetitive stress injuries (RSI)* and *cumulative trauma injuries (CTI)*. MSD injuries that can result from poor ergonomics in the workplace include tendinitis, bursitis, and carpal tunnel syndrome. According to BLS statistics, these and other MSD injuries account for one-third of workplace injuries and illnesses each year, which makes them the largest job-related health and safety problem in the United States. Factors that contribute to MSDs include awkward postures; forceful lifting, pushing, or pulling; prolonged repetitive motions; contact stress; and vibration, such as that which occurs while using power tools for an extended period of time.

Development of an ergonomics program provides a means by which employers can determine whether or not MSDs are a problem in their workplaces. An effective ergonomics program requires management support and involves employees in the process. After a review of OSHA logs and worker compensation claims for injury patterns, an analysis of job tasks, beginning with an observation of the work area while work is being done, is needed to determine if the risk factors for potential injury exist. Jobs with poor ergonomics may be redesigned to make them less hazardous and reduce injuries.

OSHA has developed tools to assist employers in reducing potential ergonomic hazards. The tools are provided in a checklist format for various activities that are statistically prone to ergonomic injury, including handling baggage, sewing, and working at a computer workstation. The checklists provide guidance in the form of basic principles that can be used to reduce ergonomic injuries. For example, the computer workstation checklist provides guidelines for placement of the monitor, keyboard, mouse, desk, chair, and telephone along with a discussion of some common problems that can occur. The checklists may be viewed online at http://www.osha.gov/dts/osta/oshasoft/index.html#eTools. In addition to those currently available, OSHA is in the process of developing similar checklists for specific industries and jobs.

As with any HR program, it is important to provide a quantitative measurement of the results. With an ergonomics program, this can be accomplished by using OSHA's recordable case rate formula to calculate the incidence rate of ergonomic injuries before the program is implemented and taking periodic measures as the program progresses to determine the reduction in injuries. The recordable case rate formula uses a base of 100 full time employees working 40 hours per week, 50 weeks per year, or 200,000 hours. Figure 8.1 illustrates the formula for calculating the ergonomic injury rate before implementation of the program, when 53 injuries occurred, and after implementation, when the injuries were reduced to 35. The example assumes that an individual employee works 2000 hours per year (40 hours per week time 50 weeks per year).

**FIGURE 8.1**    Quantitative analysis of ergonomic injury program

$$\text{Ergonomic Injury Rate} = \frac{\text{Number of Ergonomic Injuries} \times 200{,}000}{\text{Total hours worked by all employees during the period}}$$

Total number of employees: 350 FTE
Number of Ergonomic injuries = 53

$$\text{EIR} = \frac{53 \times 200{,}000}{350 \times 2{,}000} = \frac{10{,}600{,}000}{700{,}000} = 15.15\%$$

Total number of employees: 350 FTE
Number of Ergonomic injuries = 35

$$\text{EIR} = \frac{35 \times 200{,}000}{350 \times 2{,}000} = \frac{7{,}000{,}000}{700{,}000} = 10\%$$

# Biological Health Hazards

*Biological health hazards* come in many forms, from unsanitary conditions in a food preparation area to serious diseases contracted through needlestick injuries. Infectious diseases are spread by different means to employees, but the resulting impact on the health of the workforce or the community can be substantial. Although the health care and food preparation industries are at greater risk than other industries, HR professionals should understand the implications of infectious disease in all workplaces.

**HIV/AIDS**    Human Immunodeficiency Virus (HIV) and Acquired Immune Deficiency Syndrome (AIDS) are blood-borne pathogens transmitted through blood or other bodily fluids. For this reason, transmission to coworkers in workplaces other than in the health care industry is relatively unlikely. Persons with HIV/AIDS are protected by the ADA; as long as they are able to perform their essential job functions, they are entitled to remain employed.

**HBV**    The Hepatitis B Virus (HBV) is another blood-borne pathogen posing risks to health care workers. Because transmission chiefly occurs as the result of an accidental needlestick, health care workers are at the greatest risk of infection in the workplace. The CDC recommends that health care workers at high risk of infection be vaccinated to prevent them from contracting the disease.

**Tuberculosis**    Tuberculosis is a lung disease that is spread through the air. Exposure occurs when someone with TB coughs or sneezes, expelling pathogens. Those at higher risk for contracting TB in the workplace are people who share the same breathing space, such as coworkers or health care workers, particularly in nursing homes.

**Severe Acute Respiratory Syndrome (SARS)**    SARS is the latest communicable disease to be of concern to employers. While it has not yet become a major health problem in the United States, it has affected business travel and had a negative effect on some industries, particularly the travel industry. The disease appears to be transmitted by close person-to-person contact when an infected person coughs or sneezes. Preventing the spread of SARS in the workplace requires frequent hand washing and the use of common household cleaners to frequently clean surfaces.

Employees with infectious diseases who do not pose a threat to coworker health and safety are protected by ADA requirements for reasonable accommodation and may not be subjected to adverse employment actions because of their disease.

## Employee Assistance Programs

An *employee assistance program (EAP)* is sponsored by the employer as a benefit. EAPs are often as advantageous for employers as they are for employees because they are generally a low-cost benefit that provides a resource for employees with problems that are not work related and cannot be solved within the work context. In some cases, this assistance allows people who might not otherwise be able to remain employed to stay on the job.

EAPs offer a variety of counseling services, for problems ranging from alcohol and drug abuse to legal assistance or financial counseling. Many EAPs are a source for outplacement counseling during a layoff, and some programs offer on-site smoking cessation. During times of crisis, for example, the death of an employee or an incident of workplace violence, the EAP can be a resource for employees to come to grips with their feelings so that they are able to continue with their jobs.

EAP services are most often provided through a third party to ensure the confidentiality of employee information, but some employers have in-house programs with counselors on staff. Smaller businesses may join together in a consortium and jointly contract with an EAP to lower costs.

## Health and Wellness Programs

Employers have developed *health and wellness programs* to prevent employee illnesses and to lower health care costs. As with any program proposal, it is essential that HR professionals show management how the company will benefit from the program, how much it will cost, and what return the company can expect on its investment. Being able to provide specific costs and savings that will be realized demonstrates HR's ability to develop programs that serve the long-term strategic goals of the business. Table 8.7 illustrates some of the benefits and costs to be considered in analyzing the advantages of a wellness program to the company.

**TABLE 8.7**    Costs and Benefits of Wellness Programs

| Benefits | Costs |
| --- | --- |
| Increased productivity | Program implementation |
| Reduced turnover | Ongoing vendor costs |
| Reduced medical costs | Administrative costs |

**TABLE 8.7**    Costs and Benefits of Wellness Programs *(continued)*

| Benefits | Costs |
|---|---|
| Reduced absenteeism | Liability issues |
| Enhanced ability to attract top-quality employees | |
| Reduced worker compensation premiums | |

A typical wellness program must be voluntary for employees and will include a physical screening to assess each employee's current fitness level and needs, nutrition counseling, education programs for weight control, smoking and stress reduction, and a program of physical exercise. Other programs could include education about substance abuse, back care, and prenatal care, depending on the needs of the particular employee population. Health and wellness programs can take many forms, depending on the budget of the employer, the needs of the employees, and the availability of services in the local area.

Employees like wellness programs because they provide convenient opportunities to make healthful lifestyle choices that result in more energy and less stress, both on and off the job.

The size of the budget available for a wellness program will obviously dictate how the program is offered. Some large companies provide fitness centers on site, along with employee cafeterias that serve healthful meals. Smaller organizations may engage a wellness vendor to provide the educational piece of the program and offer employees subsidies for gym memberships or develop walking or sports programs for employee participation.

An important consideration for programs that include on-site fitness centers will be to analyze the total costs, including not only the space and equipment, but fitness personnel and liability for injuries suffered while an employee is working out. Recommendations for on-site programs should therefore include an assessment of the possible risks involved as part of the cost analysis.

## Substance Abuse

Government statistics indicate that more than 70 percent of substance abusers have jobs. They are all working in someone's business—some of them might work in your business. Substance abusers cost employers with tardiness and absenteeism, increased errors, accidents, and increases in health care costs and worker compensation claims. When a substance abuser's job is to drive a semi-trailer or operate heavy equipment, an employer faces increased costs for injuries or damages that occur as a result of an accident. If the employer is a federal contractor subject to the Drug-Free Workplace Act, continued substance abuse at the workplace could result in the loss of the contract.

There are six components for an effective substance abuse program in the workplace:

- Support for the substance abuse policy from top management. (As with any policy, this is the most important component.)

- A written policy clearly stating that substance abuse will not be tolerated in the workplace.

- Training for managers and supervisors to ensure that they understand and can explain the policy, are able to recognize the signs of substance abuse, understand the importance of documenting poor performance, and know what steps to take when they become aware of a substance abuser.

- Education programs for new hires and employees to inform them of the policy and explain the consequences for violations. The drug testing program should be explained. Employees should be made aware of resources in the community or through the EAP, as well as the effects of substance abuse on themselves, their families, and the costs to the employer.

- An EAP provides confidential counseling for substance abusers as needed.

- An ongoing drug testing program is fair and consistent and complies with federal, state, and local laws and union contracts. The program should identify who will be tested, when tests will occur, which drugs will be tested for, and what happens if the test is positive.

## Drug Testing Programs

There are several decisions to make when a company decides to implement a drug testing program. First, the program must be implemented in a fair and consistent manner to avoid charges of discrimination. Next, the company must decide what type of testing will be done:

*Pre-employment testing*    Lawful only after an offer of employment has been made. Before beginning a testing program, the employer must decide which applicants will be tested. This decision may be based on the type of work done in different jobs; for example, a company may decide to test all employees who operate machinery. The test must be conducted fairly and consistently on all applicants for the designated jobs.

*Random drug testing*    Done on an arbitrary, unscheduled basis. To make the testing truly random and reduce the risk of legal challenges, employers may want to make use of a computer program that randomly selects employees.

*Scheduled drug testing*    Can be useful when monitoring rehabilitation progress of employees but has limited value because employees who may be currently using drugs are generally able to stop long enough before the test to clear their systems of the drugs.

*Reasonable suspicion drug testing*    Can be used any time there has been an accident in the workplace or when a supervisor suspects, based on behavior, that an employee is under the influence of drugs.

Regardless of the substance abuse testing schedule that is used, it is important to keep in mind that implementation must be fair and equitable to avoid charges of discrimination. If employers choose to test specific job categories, then all employees in those categories must be subjected to the testing process. If random testing is used, all employees in the selected category must be included in the selection group.

HR professionals must also keep in mind that , under the ADA, abusers of alcohol and drugs are considered disabled as long as they are in recovery. Employees who are current abusers do not have protection under the ADA.

## Job-Related Stress

In 1999, NIOSH published the results of a study entitled *Stress at Work*, which defined job *stress* as "harmful physical and emotional responses that occur when the requirements of the job do not match the capabilities, resources or needs of the worker." As companies continue to downsize operations, even employees who are able to keep their jobs feel the stress of having to pick up the work that was done by others who are no longer in the workplace. High levels of stress can reduce an employee's productivity and increase errors, and this is expensive for employers in lost productivity and turnover costs. There are some things employers can do to alleviate situations that are known stressors.

First, encouraging employees to balance their work with personal pursuits provides relief from stress, as does physical exercise. Clearly communicating expectations to employees and providing them with avenues for feedback is one action management can take to relieve stress, as are providing employees with the resources required to successfully perform their work and giving them some control over their jobs. Ensuring that managers and supervisors are well trained in management techniques and receive coaching when needed to improve management skills can relieve stress for employees who report to them. Table 8.8 describes some of the symptoms of stress.

**TABLE  8.8**   Symptoms of Stress

| Physical | Emotional | Mental |
|---|---|---|
| Headaches | Mood swings | Forgetfulness |
| Indigestion | Irritability | Inability to concentrate |
| Fatigue | Depression | Disorganization |
| Intestinal problems | Hostility | Poor judgment |

Managers who notice these symptoms in an employee should refer them to the EAP for counseling. The NIOSH study mentioned earlier provides additional information on the causes of job-related stress along with steps managers can take to reduce job stress. The study is available free of charge at www.cdc.gov/niosh/stresswk.html.

# Safety

Much of the first part of this chapter was spent in describing the various laws, regulations, and standards that govern workplace safety. So what exactly is workplace safety? In a word (or two): accident prevention. *Safety* is about identifying possible hazards in the workplace and reducing the likelihood that an accident will happen by correcting the hazard. Management and employees are partners in this process. Because employees are close to the possible hazards, they should feel empowered to take the steps necessary to reduce hazards that are within their control, whether that means correcting the hazard themselves or reporting the hazard to management with suggestions on how to correct it.

Workplace accidents impact the bottom line in many ways. They reduce productivity because an injured employee must be given time to recover from an injury. A high accident/injury rate increases insurance costs and, when employees sense that management is unconcerned about their safety, lowers morale and increases turnover. Employees who are not satisfied with their work care less about what kind of job they do, which has a negative impact on quality. Poor quality products tarnish the company's reputation, which makes it more difficult for the company to compete against other products. All of these consequences of poor safety policies reduce the company's ability to earn a profit, which reduces the value of the company to its owners. All of this happens when employers don't think safety matters!

Accident prevention begins with a commitment from the top that safety does matter and that the health and well-being of employees is important to the company. Employers need to provide safe operating procedures, train workers to use those procedures, and then enforce the procedures by rewarding positive safety actions and disciplining employees who fail to comply with procedures.

Because the employees doing the job know best what is safe and what is unsafe, they must be involved in developing safe operating procedures. Working in partnership, management and employees can identify the hazards present in the workplace and develop strategies to reduce or eliminate them. An added benefit of including employees in this process is that they will have a greater stake in maintaining safe operations that they were a part of creating. As safe operating procedures are identified, they become part of a safety and health management plan.

Employers who have developed effective safety management programs have safer work environments for their employees. Over the last 30 years, through workplace investigation and analysis of injury and illness statistics, OSHA has determined that effective Safety and Health Management Plans have four common characteristics:

1. Senior management is committed to a safe work environment, and employees are involved in the decisions and activities to make it happen.

2. The company is engaged in an ongoing worksite analysis to identify potential safety and health hazards.

3. The company has active hazard prevention and control programs in place to correct hazards before injury or illness occurs.

4. Safety and health training is an ongoing process in the company.

An effective plan will identify the person who is responsible for its overall implementation and create a safety committee with representatives from both management and labor to address safety concerns and develop workable solutions to safety problems. An effective plan will identify hazards that exist in the work environment, whether they are physical, chemical, or biological, and provide guidance, in the form of OSHA safety standards, on the appropriate way to work with each hazard. The plan will provide a mechanism for employee complaints so that they reach the appropriate management level for speedy resolution to prevent injuries. If the work environment requires the use of machinery, equipment, tools, or PPE, the plan will spell out the appropriate methods for using and maintaining them and include consequences for failing to comply with the standards.

The plan describes how to report accidents, who must be notified, and the time frames in which the notifications must occur and provides an accident investigation procedure, identifying who will conduct the investigation, what records must be kept, and how and where they are filed. As a result of the investigation, the plan should include a process that ensures all employees are advised of the accident circumstances and what steps should be taken to avoid similar accidents in the future.

Part of an effective plan is ongoing training for employees that addresses accidents that have occurred and ways to prevent similar occurrences in the future.

# Security

*Security* in the workplace covers a broad spectrum of topics related to protecting the company from threats of one kind or another, including fires, earthquakes, hurricanes, tornadoes, and other natural disasters and manmade threats such as terrorist attacks, computer hackers, workplace violence and theft, or unintentional release of trade secrets or confidential information. Many of these topics are not ultimately the responsibility of HR professionals, but a working knowledge of the impact they have on the workforce is essential to understanding the ways HR interacts with other functional areas in the company. HR professionals must be able to provide the expertise required to appropriately handle the suspected inappropriate conduct by employees in order to protect the company from liability.

Workplace security measures are those taken by employers to ensure the safety of the people and assets of the business and begin with assessing the possible risks. When the potential risks have been identified, plans for protection of the people and the assets of the organization can be made and implemented. In this section, we will briefly review security issues with which HR professionals may become involved.

**Risk assessment**    Before an employer can put plans in place to reduce the risks faced by the organization, the threats (external forces) and vulnerabilities (internal weaknesses) must be identified. *Risk assessment* is the process by which the employer determines how likely it is that an emergency will occur, the cost of an emergency to the business should it occur, and the impact it would have on the ability of the business to continue operations. With this knowledge, it is possible to identify what controls must be in place to protect the company and which emergencies are most likely to occur so that preventive measures can be taken to protect it.

A risk assessment is most often a collaborative effort between internal managers and outside consultants with expertise in security issues. Depending on the nature of the business, consultants with different types of expertise would be required; for example, a software company developing a new product will have significantly different needs than a manufacturing plant whose employees may go on strike. Risk assessments are most frequently accomplished using a qualitative analysis, where all the possible emergencies are listed along with the potential financial costs and impact on operations. The emergencies can then be ranked so that those with the greatest possible impact on the business can be addressed.

Identifying and ranking the risks provides business owners with the opportunity to be proactive and implement controls to prevent damage to the assets of the business. There are four basic types of company assets: financial assets, such as cash, securities and accounts receivable; physical assets, such as buildings, machinery and equipment; human assets; and information assets.

**Protecting physical assets**   When we think of security, often what comes most readily to mind are building security measures such as guards, security cameras, keys or card-key lock systems, and entry barriers such as fences or security gates. The size, nature, and budget of each business will determine which systems are most appropriate.

**Protecting human assets**   Providing protection for employees takes many forms. Many of the security measures that protect physical assets also protect employees; in addition an ongoing safety training program can include information on ways in which employees can protect themselves in different situations.

Protecting employees working outside of the United States presents different issues for employers. Issues of political stability and animosity toward American companies and people require programs and vendors that specialize in protecting them abroad.

Another security issue for large corporations involves the special needs for preventing executives from kidnapping. Corporations whose executives may be at risk have several protective options, including body guards and vendors who specialize in corporate protection.

**Protecting financial assets**   Financial assets, including cash, inventory, accounts receivable, and securities, are vulnerable to theft and embezzlement. Implementing policies and procedures to protect financial assets is generally the responsibility of a company's chief financial officer (CFO). CFOs are responsible for implementing *internal controls* to ensure that cash and negotiable securities are not mishandled, along with inventory controls to reduce employee pilferage or customer theft. In most organizations, CFOs implement processes to ensure that purchase commitments at certain dollar levels are reviewed and approved by higher level management to prevent mismanagement.

**Protecting confidential information**   The most effective way to protect confidential information is to ensure that employees know what the company considers confidential before they are hired with an *Intellectual Property Agreement (IPA)* and/or *Non-Disclosure Agreement (NDA)*. Because the types of confidential information vary widely between different companies, it's important that an attorney develop an agreement that meets the needs of the individual company. An IPA should identify what the company considers to be confidential information (such as customer lists, financial information, or trade secrets) and how its use is limited by the agreement, as well as how long the information must remain confidential after the agreement expires. The agreement may contain a "non-solicitation" clause limiting the ability of employees who leave the organization to hire coworkers. IPAs should contain clauses that require employees to describe any discoveries or inventions they may have made prior to entering into the agreement and require that they don't share confidential information from other companies with the new employer or disclose who owns the inventions or discoveries made during the course of employment. Finally, the agreement should state that materials containing confidential information are the property of the company and may not be removed from a given location.

These agreements help to prevent employees from sharing confidential proprietary information with other companies or individuals. For these documents to be effective, the company must advise employees on a regular basis that even inadvertently sharing this information can damage the company.

While this discussion has been limited to the use of IPAs and NDAs in employment relationships, these documents are equally important when sharing proprietary information with business partners or others with whom the company shares the information in the course of doing business.

**Workplace violence**   *Workplace violence* occurs when an employee with poor behavior control becomes highly stressed. The stress may or may not be work related, but it is often set off by an incident in the workplace. Under OSHA's General Duty Clause, employers are required to be aware of employees exhibiting the signs of possible violent behavior and take steps to prevent its occurrence. Employees who commit acts of violence in the workplace frequently show recognizable signs of stress before they commit the acts. It is up to employers to train managers and supervisors to identify these signs so that employees who are having difficulty can be referred to an EAP for counseling or directed to social services if needed.

Some of the more common signs of stress include a change in work habits, a decline in productivity, conflicts with coworkers, depression, and refusing to take responsibility for individual actions.

Even though not everyone who exhibits signs of stress is likely to become violent, any employee who exhibits these signs should be counseled and referred to appropriate professional assistance. As part of the Emergency Action Plan described in the previous section, a plan for responding to an incident of workplace violence should be developed and communicated to employees. This plan, in addition to other requirements, should include code words to be used when employees feel threatened so they can alert coworkers to call for help, along with a resource book for managers and supervisors that contains referral agencies for different types of issues to assist employees who are troubled.

OSHA has identified workplace emergencies as natural or manmade occurrences that threaten businesses, employees, customers, and the community. These emergencies can include earthquakes, floods, hurricanes, tornadoes, fires, toxic gas releases, chemical spills, and explosions, to name but a few. To ensure the safety of employees and business assets, an emergency action plan, combined with ongoing employee training, is essential. By developing a plan and having regular drills to reinforce the steps to be taken in an emergency, employers can improve the chances that all employees will be safe in an emergency.

The OSHA emergency action plan standard requires, at a minimum, that the employer define the preferred method for reporting fires and other emergencies, an evacuation policy and procedure, and floor plans or maps that define escape procedures and assign evacuation routes. The plan must have contact information for individuals who can provide additional information during an emergency and provide procedures for employees who will remain behind to perform essential services during the emergency. Employees who will perform rescue and medical duties are to be included in the plan as well. The plan requires alarm systems to notify all employees, including those who are disabled, of the need to evacuate.

 **Real World Scenario**

**Sample Emergency Action Plan**

**Section 1: Responsibilities**   In this section is a description of everyone who has a role to play during an emergency. Who will make the decision to evacuate the building? If critical machinery must be shut down, who will do that? Who is responsible to "take roll" and ensure that all employees have been safely evacuated from the building? Which employees are certified to perform first aid until medical personnel arrive on the scene? How will the emergency be reported to authorities, and who is responsible for doing that? Finally, this section should include the names of those who have been designated to answer questions and explain duties required by the plan.

**Section 2: Emergency Escape Procedures**   This section of the plan identifies the emergency escape procedures that employees are to follow and provides a diagram of the building showing escape routes from each floor and each area. In this section, special procedures for evacuating persons with disabilities, visitors to the building, and others with special needs should be spelled out. A safe meeting area should be designated so that all employees know where they should go in the event of an evacuation.

**Section 3: Critical Plant Operations**   Particularly in manufacturing operations, there are processes that must be shut down according to specific protocols. In this section, these processes should be identified, along with instructions for employees on recognizing when they must evacuate themselves, even if the operation is not yet complete.

**Section 4: Accounting for Employees**   In the event of an evacuation, it is critical that rescue personnel know whether or not people are trapped in the building. Equally important is that rescue personnel not endanger themselves if everyone has been successfully evacuated. In this section of the plan, the procedures to be followed should be described, including where employees will meet, and who will account for employees and visitors to the area.

**Section 5: Reporting Emergencies**   This section describes how emergencies are to be reported to the appropriate authorities.

**Section 6: Identify Emergency Contacts**   In this section, the plan should identify who should be contacted for specific information. This may be a single person, or it may be several individuals who are responsible for different sections of the plan.

**Section 7: Alarm System**   This section of the plan should describe how employees will be notified of an emergency, where alarms are located, if there are different alarms for different emergencies, what they sound like, and whether or not the alarm system automatically notifies emergency personnel.

**Section 8: Types of Evacuations**   If the building is located in an area in which the potential for different types of emergencies exist, such as fires, tornadoes, and floods, this section of the plan describes the evacuation plan for each type of emergency.

**Section 9: Training Requirements**   In this section, the plan should describe how employees will be trained in emergency procedures and how often. The person responsible for training employees should be identified, along with a schedule for emergency drills.

**Section 10: Record-keeping**   In this section, the plan should include documents that might be required in an emergency. This could include information on MSDSs for chemicals in the worksite, maintenance records for safety equipment, equipment inspection records, building plans and OSHA forms.

Although not required by the standard, good business practice would indicate appropriate off-site storage for copies of records and legal documents needed to maintain operations in an emergency. Identifying and making arrangements for alternative means of communicating during an emergency is suggested as well. Assigning a gathering place for employees to meet during an evacuation so that rescue personnel can be advised of missing employees can save lives in an emergency.

# OHSS Plans and Programs

Throughout this chapter we have discussed requirements for various occupational health, safety, and security plans. In this section, we will recap the requirements for these plans. Some elements are present in all of the plans, and others are related only to individual plans. OSHA requires the following plans:

- Safety and Health Management Plan (also known as an Injury and Illness Prevention Plan)
- Emergency Action Plan (also referred to as an Emergency Response Plan)
- Fire Prevention Plan

Generally, employers with 10 or fewer employees are not required to provide written plans unless they have been notified by OSHA to do so.

# Elements Common to All Plans

Some elements are important enough for inclusion in each of the plans. They include:

- A clear statement of the company policy regarding the program
- The commitment and full support of senior management
- A process for including employees in the process, whether through the establishment of a safety committee or some other means
- Identification of those with responsibilities under the plan, including employees, vendors, and public health and safety officials, and contact information for those individuals
- A clear, unambiguous process for reporting hazards or concerns to the responsible parties
- A description of the process to be used in training employees
- Procedures for maintaining records required by OSHA

## Safety and Health Management Plan

In addition to the "Elements Common to All Plans," a Safety and Health Management Plan will also include:

- A process to ensure two-way communications between management and labor
- An assessment of known hazards
- Procedures to correct known hazards
- A procedure to ensure that the company engages in an ongoing analysis of workplace hazards and conducts updated training on changes
- Maintenance procedures for any equipment, machinery, tools, or personal protective equipment used in the workplace
- An accident investigation procedure
- An accident reporting procedure

## Emergency Action Plan

The Emergency Action Plan begins with the common elements described previously and also includes:

- Emergency escape procedures, including a floor plan or diagram for employees to follow

- Procedures for shutting down critical plant operations
- Process to account for employees after an evacuation
- A description of the alarm system that will notify employees of an emergency, including how persons with disabilities, visitors, and temporary employees will be notified
- Procedures to follow for different types of emergencies, such as fires, tornadoes, earthquakes or terrorist attacks

### Fire Prevention Plan

The Fire Prevention Plan may be included as part of the Emergency Action Plan. Whether the plan is included with it or separate, it must provide information about the following:

- All major fire hazards, how they should be handled and stored, a description of possible causes of igniting them and how to prevent that from happening, and a description of the appropriate equipment to suppress each hazard
- The location of fire extinguishing systems or portable fire extinguishers
- The procedure describing how waste materials that are flammable or combustible will be stored before disposal

## OHSS Training Programs

OSHA has developed guidelines to assist employers in developing effective training programs that reduce work-related injury and illness. These guidelines can be modified to fit the specific industry and work site requirements for individual businesses.

1. Determine if training is needed. In other words, is the safety problem something that can be corrected with training, or is another correction necessary?
2. Identify the training needs. What should employees be doing that they are not doing? The program should inform them of appropriate methods for doing the job.
3. As with any other training program, objectives for the training must be developed.
4. When the learning needs and objectives have been identified, methods for delivering the training can be developed. Will classroom training be best? One-on-one training with an experienced employee? Demonstration and practice? This will depend on the specific training needs for the organization.
5. Conduct the training.
6. Evaluate how well the training worked using the methods discussed in Chapter 5, "Human Resource Development."
7. Based on the evaluation, adjust the training to improve its effectiveness.

## Evaluating OHSS Effectiveness

Evaluating health, safety, and security programs is a simple matter: compile statistics on a regular basis and compare them over time. If the trend is downward, great! Your programs are working to prevent injury and illness to employees. If the trend is up, well, it's time to identify what injuries or illnesses caused the increase, review the plan to determine what changes are necessary to correct the problems, and implement the changes.

# Summary

Occupational Health, Safety, and Security has been a source of concern to workers and physicians for centuries, but until relatively recently, employers were not required to protect employees from dangerous work environments and were rarely held accountable when death, injury, or illness occurred as a result of hazards in the businesses they managed. The OSH Act of 1970 was the first comprehensive, effective legislation that required employers to provide safe and healthful workplaces for their employees and provided an enforcement process that penalized employers who did not comply with safety standards. OSHA has been successful where other attempts to do the same thing have failed because Congress provided strong enforcement powers to the agency.

In the past, employers were also not willing to compensate workers who were injured during the course of their jobs and made full use of the "unholy trinity" of common law doctrines to avoid financial responsibility for injured workers. In 1911, Wisconsin was the first state to provide workers with a more equitable process for determining compensation due to them for injuries suffered during the course of their work by passing the first worker compensation law. This enabled workers to receive compensation for injuries and illnesses without having to utilize the court system which was, at that time, heavily weighted in favor of employers.

OSHA has been a key proponent and motivator in identifying workplace health, safety, and security hazards and in developing processes designed to protect workers in a variety of situations. Once employers realized the financial benefits of creating safer working environments, they developed employee benefits to enhance health and safety programs, such as employee assistance and wellness programs that serve employee needs as well as add value to the business bottom line.

# Exam Essentials

**Be familiar with federal legislation and regulations for workplace health and safety.**   The major federal legislation for this functional area is the Occupational Safety and Health Act of 1970. This law created OSHA, which develops and enforces workplace health and safety standards.

**Understand the safety needs of organizations and be able to design, implement, and evaluate a safety program, train employees, and evaluate program effectiveness.**   Employers are responsible for ensuring that those who work for them have a workplace that is free from danger. To provide this, employers must be committed to a safe workplace, involve employees in meeting safety standards by giving them the information they need to be safe in the workplace, and provide training for the equipment and materials employees will use to perform their jobs.

**Understand health and wellness programs and be able to develop, implement, and evaluate one for an organization.**   Health and wellness programs are a means by which employers can impact the health of their employees through programs designed to enhance their physical well being. These programs benefit employers through reduced health insurance costs.

**Understand the purpose of an emergency response plan and be able to design and implement one and evaluate its effectiveness.**   The emergency response plan is created in advance of an emergency. It describes what roles are to be played in the emergency and who will play them, communicates to all employees a place to meet in the event of an evacuation, and assigns some responsibilities for implementing the plan in the event of an emergency.

**Understand the security need of organizations and employees and be able to develop, implement, and evaluate workplace security plans.**   Organizations and employees must both feel secure in the work environment. Employees must be safe in order to work productively; employers must feel secure that the assets of the business will continue to be available for use in the business.

# Key Terms

Before you take the exam, be certain you are familiar with the following terms:

| | |
|---|---|
| biological health hazards | internal controls |
| chemical health hazards | Material Safety Data Sheets (MSDS) |
| closing conference | Mine Safety and Health Administration (MSHA) |
| cumulative trauma injuries (CTI) | musculoskeletal disorders |
| de-minimus | National Institute of Occupational Safety and Health (NIOSH) |
| doctrine of contributory negligence | Non-Disclosure Agreement (NDA) |
| emergency action plans | Occupational Safety and Health Administration (OSHA) |
| employee assistance program (EAP) | occupational safety and health standards |
| environmental health hazards | opening conference |
| ergonomics | OSHA Alliance Program |
| fellow servant rule | physical health hazards |
| general duty standard | pre-employment testing |
| health and wellness programs | privacy concern cases |
| Intellectual Property Agreement (IPA) | random drug testing |

reasonable suspicion drug testing

repetitive stress injuries (RSI)

risk assessment

safety

Safety and Health Achievement Recognition Program (SHARP)

scheduled drug testing

security

Strategic Partnership Program

stress

teratogens

voluntary assumption of risk

Voluntary Protection Program (VPP)

workplace violence

# Review Questions

1.  An OSHA violation with substantial probability of death or serious physical harm as the result of a workplace hazard is

    **A.** Willful

    **B.** Serious

    **C.** Repeat

    **D.** De-minimus

2.  Under OSHA regulations, employers do *not* have the right to

    **A.** Refuse to allow an OSHA inspector on the premises.

    **B.** Request a variance to an OSHA standard while waiting for repairs.

    **C.** Consult with OSHA to correct hazards without fear of a citation and penalty.

    **D.** File a Notice of Contest within 30 days of the citation.

3.  What is the *best* way to ensure that employees comply with the Drug-Free Workplace Act?

    **A.** Develop and publish a written policy.

    **B.** Notify employees about contract conditions.

    **C.** Establish penalties for drug arrests.

    **D.** Establish an awareness program.

4.  The 16-year-old son of one of your friends is looking for a summer job and has been offered a job at a coal mine. Which law makes this illegal?

    **A.** Mine Safety and Health Act

    **B.** Occupational Safety and Health Act

    **C.** Fair Labor Standards Acts

    **D.** Hazard Communication

5.  The company receptionist has always been cheerful and warm when greeting customers and has taken the initiative to do what needed to be done without waiting to be told. She's always kept the front desk tidy and presentable for visitors. Over the last few weeks, the receptionist has become moody and called in sick several times complaining of headaches, and the reception area looks disorganized all the time. This receptionist is showing classic signs of

    **A.** Stress

    **B.** Job dissatisfaction

    **C.** Substance abuse

    **D.** SARS

6. The union rep has requested copies of all of the incident reports filed during the last year. You are required to

   A. Furnish the copies by the end of the day.

   B. Furnish copies within 15 calendar days, but only of the "Tell Us About the Case" section.

   C. Furnish the copies by the end of the next business day.

   D. Furnish copies within 7 calendar days, but only of the "Tell Us About the Case" section.

7. An employee assistance plan will *not* assist employees with

   A. Outplacement counseling

   B. Substance abuse

   C. Gambling problems

   D. Legal assistance

8. Which of the following injuries or illnesses is considered work-related?

   A. An employee has twisted an ankle at an aerobics class the company sponsored.

   B. An employee fell while taking a shower at work.

   C. An employee is hit by a car in the parking lot while walking into the building.

   D. An employee disregards the safety procedures and is cut by a table saw.

9. An effective Safety and Health Management Plan does *not* include:

   A. Senior management support

   B. Ongoing worksite analysis

   C. Regular OSHA inspections

   D. Active hazard prevention program

10. How can an employer determine if a job creates an ergonomic hazard for an employee?

    A. Review and analyze the OSHA logs.

    B. Review and analyze the worker compensation records.

    C. Review the MSDS.

    D. Observe the incumbent performing the job duties.

# Answers to Review Questions

1.  **B.**  A serious violation is the second level of violation. Willful violations are, in addition to having the potential for serious harm or injury, done intentionally or with "plain indifference" to the requirements.

2.  **D.**  A Notice of Contest must be filed within 15 days of the citation.

3.  **A.**  While all of these are steps in the process, the *best* way to ensure that employees will comply with the Drug-Free Workplace Act is to develop and publish a written policy.

4.  **C.**  The FLSA defines a list of jobs not suitable for children between the ages of 16 and 18.

5.  **A.**  The receptionist is exhibiting symptoms of all three types of stress: physical, emotional, and mental.

6.  **D.**  The employee representative is entitled to receive copies of incident reports with the identifying information covered up. Employers have 7 calendar days to provide the information to an employee representative.

7.  **C.**  EAPs provide counseling for a variety of employee needs, including financial and legal counseling, substance abuse, and help to quit smoking. The plans do not cover gambling.

8.  **D.**  Injuries that occur while performing the job are reportable, whether or not the employee was at fault.

9.  **C.**  OSHA inspections are only conducted at the request of an employee based on a safety violation, as a preprogrammed high-hazard inspection, or an a random basis.

10.  **D.**  While a review and analysis of OSHA logs can be used to determine any injury patterns occurring in the workplace, observation of the incumbent performing the work is necessary to determine whether or not there is an ergonomic hazard in the job.

# Appendix A

# Federal Employment Legislation and Case Law

This appendix provides a brief overview of federal employment legislation and case law that is required knowledge for HR professionals. All of the legislation has been covered in detail in the appropriate chapters, as have most of the cases. I have included some additional cases in this table that exam candidates may find useful during their review. This information is not presented as or intended to replace legal advice. Please consult your employment attorney for advice on specific employment situations.

The abbreviation "USSC" refers to decisions made by the United States Supreme Court.

| Year | Name | Key Requirements | Chapter |
|------|------|------------------|---------|
| 1884 | Payne v The Western & Atlantic Railroad Company | Defined employment at-will. | 7 |
| 1869 | Bureau of Labor Statistics | Established to study industrial accidents and maintain accident records. | 8 |
| 1890 | Sherman Anti-Trust Act | Controlled business monopolies; allowed court injunctions to prevent restraint of trade. | 7 |
| 1914 | Clayton Act | Limited use of injunctions to break strikes; exempted unions from the Sherman Act. | 7 |
| 1916 | Federal Employees Compensation Act | Provided benefits similar to worker compensation for federal employees injured on the job. | 8 |
| 1927 | Longshore and Harbor Workers' Compensation Act | Provided workers' compensation benefits for maritime workers injured on navigable waters of the U.S. or on piers, docks, and terminals. | 8 |
| 1926 | Railway Labor Act | Protected unionization rights; allowed for 90-day cooling off period to prevent strikes in national emergencies. Covers railroads and unions. | 7 |

| Year | Name | Key Requirements | Chapter |
|------|------|------------------|---------|
| 1932 | Norris-La Guardia Act | Protected right to organize; outlawed yellow dog contracts. | 7 |
| 1935 | National Labor Relations Act (Wagner Act) | Protected the right of workers to organize and bargain collectively; identified unfair labor practices; established the NLRB. | 7 |
| 1935 | Federal Insurance Contributions Act/Social Security Act | Required employers and employees to pay social security taxes. | 6 |
| 1936 | Federal Unemployment Tax Act | Required employers to contribute a percentage of payroll to an unemployment insurance fund. | 6 |
| 1936 | Public Contracts Act (Walsh-Healey Act) | Required contractors to pay prevailing wage rates. | 6 |
| 1938 | Fair Labor Standards Act | Defined exempt and nonexempt employees; required and set the minimum wage to be paid to nonexempt workers; required time-and-a-half to be paid for nonexempt overtime hours; limited hours and type of work for children; established recordkeeping requirements. | 6 |
| 1947 | Labor-Management Relations Act (Taft-Hartley) | Prohibited closed shops; restricted union shops; allowed states to pass "right to work" laws; prohibited jurisdictional strikes and secondary boycotts; allowed employers to permanently replace economic strikers; established the Federal Mediation and Conciliation Service; allowed 80-day cooling off period for national emergency strikes. | 7 |
| 1947 | Portal-to-Portal Act | Clarified definition of "hours worked" for the FLSA. | 6 |
| 1952 | Patent Act | Established U.S. Patent and Trademark Office. | 5 |

| Year | Name | Key Requirements | Chapter |
|---|---|---|---|
| 1959 | Labor-Management Reporting and Disclosure Act (Landrum-Griffin) | Controlled internal union operations; provided bill of rights for union members; required majority vote of members to increase dues; allowed members to sue the union; set term limits for union leaders. | 7 |
| 1963 | Equal Pay Act | Required that employees performing substantially similar or identical work be paid the same wage or salary rate. | 6 |
| 1964 | Title VII of the Civil Rights Act of 1964 | Established EEOC; prohibited employment discrimination on the basis of race, color, religion, national origin, or sex. | 4 |
| 1965 | EO (Executive Order) 11246 | Prohibited employment discrimination on the basis of race, creed, color, or national origin; required affirmative steps for all terms and conditions of employment; required a written AAP for contractors with 50 employees. | 4 |
| 1965 | Immigration and Nationality Act | Eliminated national origin, race, and ancestry as bars to immigration; set immigration goals for reunifying families and preference for specialized skills. | 4 |
| 1965 | Service Contract Act | Required government contractors to pay prevailing wages and benefits. | 6 |
| 1967 | Age Discrimination in Employment Act | Prohibited discrimination against persons 40 years of age or older; established conditions for BFOQ (Bona Fide Occupational Qualification) exceptions. | 4 |
| 1967 | EO 11375 | Added sex to protected classes in EO 11246. | 4 |
| 1968 | Consumer Credit Protection Act | Limited garnishment amounts on employee wages; prohibited discharge of employees for a single garnishment order. | 6 |

| Year | Name | Key Requirements | Chapter |
|------|------|------------------|---------|
| 1969 | EO 11478 | Included disabled individuals and those over 40 years of age in protected classes established by EO 11246. | 4 |
| 1969 | Black Lung Benefits Act | Provided benefits for coal miners suffering from pneumoconiosis due to mine work. | 8 |
| 1970 | Occupational Safety and Health Act | Required employers to provide a safe workplace and comply with safety and health standards; established OSHA to enforce safety regulations; established NIOSH to research, evaluate, and recommend hazard reduction measures. | 8 |
| 1970 | Fair Credit Reporting Act | Required employers to notify candidates that credit reports may be obtained; required written authorization by the candidate and that the employer provide a copy of the report to the candidate before taking an adverse action. | 4 |
| 1971 | Griggs v Duke Power | Required employers to show that job requirements are related to the job; established that lack of intention to discriminate is not a defense against claims of discrimination. | 4 |
| 1972 | Equal Employment Opportunity Act | Established that complainants have burden of proof for disparate impact; provided litigation authority for EEOC; extended time to file complaints. | 4 |
| 1973 | Rehabilitation Act | Expanded opportunities for individuals with physical or mental disabilities and provided remedies for victims of discrimination. | 4 |
| 1974 | Privacy Act | Prohibited federal agencies from sharing information collected about individuals. | 4 |

| Year | Name | Key Requirements | Chapter |
|------|------|------------------|---------|
| 1974 | Vietnam Era Veterans Readjustment Assistance Act | Provided equal opportunity and affirmative action for Vietnam veterans. | 4 |
| 1974 | Employee Retirement Income Security Act | Established requirements for pension, retirement, and welfare benefit plans including medical, hospital, AD&D, and unemployment benefits. | 6 |
| 1975 | Albemarle Paper v Moody | Required that employment tests be validated; subjective supervisor rankings are not sufficient validation; criteria must be tied to job requirements. | 4 |
| 1975 | NLRB v J. Weingarten, Inc. | Established that union employees have the right to request union representation during any investigatory interview that could result in disciplinary action. | 5 |
| 1976 | Washington v Davis | Established that employment selection tools that adversely impact protected classes are lawful if they have been validated to show future success on the job. | 4 |
| 1976 | Copyright Act | Defined "fair use" of copyrighted work; set term of copyright effectiveness. | 5 |
| 1977 | Mine Safety and Health Act | Established mandatory mine safety and health standards and created MSHA. | 8 |
| 1977 | Automobile Workers v Johnson Controls, Inc. | USSC: "Decisions about the welfare of the next generation must be left to the parents who conceive, bear, support and raise them, rather than to the employers who hire those parents." | 8 |
| 1978 | Uniform Guidelines on Employee Selection Procedures | Established guidelines to ensure that selection procedures be both job related and valid predictors of job success. | 4 |

| Year | Name | Key Requirements | Chapter |
|------|------|------------------|---------|
| 1978 | Pregnancy Discrimination Act | Required that pregnancy be treated the same as any other short-term disability. | 4 |
| 1978 | Civil Service Reform Act | Created Senior Executive Service, Merit Systems Protection Board, Office of Personnel Management, and the Federal Labor Relations Authority. | 6 |
| 1978 | Revenue Act | Established Section 125 and 401(k) plans for employees. | 6 |
| 1979 | EO 12138 | Created National Women's Business Enterprise Policy; required affirmative steps to promote and support women's business enterprises. | 4 |
| 1980 | Guidelines on Sexual Harassment | Assisted employers to develop antiharassment policies, establish complaint procedures, and investigate complaints promptly and impartially. | 4 |
| 1984 | Retirement Equity Act | Lowered age limits on participation and vesting in pension benefits; required written spousal consent to not provide survivor benefits; restricted conditions placed on survivor benefits. | 6 |
| 1986 | Consolidated Omnibus Budget Reconciliation Act | Provided continuation of group health coverage upon a qualifying event. | 6 |
| 1986 | Tax Reform Act | Reduced income tax rates and brackets. | 6 |
| 1986 | Immigration Reform and Control Act | Prohibited employment of individuals who are not legally authorized to work in the U.S.; required I-9s for all employees. | 4 |
| 1988 | Drug-Free Workplace Act | Required federal contractors to develop and implement drug-free workplace policies. | 4 |
| 1988 | Employee Polygraph Protection Act | Prohibited use of lie detector tests except under limited circumstances. | 4 |

| Year | Name | Key Requirements | Chapter |
|------|------|------------------|---------|
| 1988 | Worker Adjustment and Retraining Notification Act | Required 60 days' notice for mass layoffs or plant closings; defined mass layoffs and plant closings; identified exceptions to the requirements. | 4 |
| 1990 | Americans with Disabilities Act | Required reasonable accommodation for qualified individuals with disabilities. | 4 |
| 1990 | Older Worker Benefit Protection Act | Amended ADEA to prevent discrimination in benefits for workers over 40; added requirements for waivers. | 6 |
| 1990 | Immigration Act | Required prevailing wage for holders of H1(b) visas; set H1(b) quotas. | 4 |
| 1991 | Civil Rights Act | Allowed compensatory and punitive damages; provided for jury trials; established defenses to disparate impact claims. | 4 |
| 1991 | Glass Ceiling Act | Established commission to determine whether or not a glass ceiling exists and identify barriers for women and minorities. As a result, the EEOC conducts audits of the representation of women and minorities at all corporate levels. | 4 |
| 1992 | Unemployment Compensation Amendments | Reduced rollover rules for lump-sum distributions of qualified retirement plans; required 20 percent withholding for some distributions. | 6 |
| 1992 | National Energy Efficiency Act of 1992 | Set maximum transit subsidy at $60 per month for employees; limited tax-free parking benefits to $155 per month. | 6 |
| 1993 | Family and Medical Leave Act | Required qualifying employers to provide 12 weeks of unpaid leave to eligible employees for the birth or adoption of a child or to provide care for defined relatives with serious health conditions; or to employees unable to perform job duties due to a serious health condition. | 6 |

| Year | Name | Key Requirements | Chapter |
|------|------|------------------|---------|
| 1993 | Taxman v Board of Education of Piscataway | Found that in the absence of past discrimination or under-representation of protected classes, preference may not be given to protected classes in making layoff decisions. | 4 |
| 1993 | Harris v Forklift Systems | Defined actionable hostile work environment as that which falls between merely offensive and that which results in tangible psychological injury. | 7 |
| 1993 | Omnibus Budget Reconciliation Act | Revised rules for employee benefits, set maximum deduction for executive pay at $1,000,000; mandated some benefits for medical plans. | 6 |
| 1994 | Uniformed Services Employment and Reemployment Rights Act | Protected the re-employment and benefit rights of reservists called to active duty. | 7 |
| 1995 | Congressional Accountability Act | Required all federal employment legislation passed by Congress to apply to congressional employees. | 4 |
| 1996 | Illegal Immigration Reform and Immigrant Responsibility Act | Reduced number and types of documents to prove identity. | 4 |
| 1996 | Mental Health Parity Act | Required insurers to provide the same limits for mental health benefits that are provided for other types of health benefits. | 6 |
| 1996 | Health Insurance Portability and Accountability Act | Prohibited discrimination based on health status; limited health insurance restrictions for pre-existing conditions; required a Certificate of Group Health Plan Coverage upon plan termination. | 6 |
| 1996 | Personal Responsibility and Work Opportunity Reconciliation Act of 1996 | Required employers to provide information about all new or rehired employees to state agencies to enforce child support orders. | 6 |

| Year | Name | Key Requirements | Chapter |
|------|------|-----------------|---------|
| 1996 | Small Business Job Protection Act | Redefined highly compensated individuals; detailed minimum participation requirements; simplified 401(k) tests; corrected qualified plan and disclosure requirements. | 6 |
| 1996 | Small Business Regulatory Enforcement Fairness Act | Provided that an SBA ombudsman act as an advocate for small business owners in the regulatory process. | 8 |
| 1998 | EO 13087 | Expanded coverage of protected classes in EO 11246 to include sexual orientation. | 4 |
| 1998 | Burlington Industries v Ellerth | Established that employers have vicarious liability for employees victimized by supervisor with immediate or higher authority over them who create an actionable hostile work environment. | 7 |
| 1998 | Faragher v City of Boca Raton | Established that employers are responsible for employee actions and have a responsibility to control them. | 7 |
| 1998 | Oncale v Sundowner Offshore Services, Inc. | Extended the definition of sexual harassment to include same-sex harassment. | 7 |
| 2000 | Epilepsy Foundation of Northeast Ohio | NLRB extended Weingarten rights to nonunion employees by allowing employees to request a coworker to be present during an investigatory interview that could result in disciplinary action. | 7 |
| 2000 | M. B. Sturgis, Inc. | Established that temporary employees may be included in the client company's bargaining unit and that consent of the employer and temp agency are not required to bargain jointly. | 7 |
| 2000 | Needlestick Safety and Prevention Act | Mandated recordkeeping for all needlestick and sharps injuries; required employee involvement in developing safer devices. | 8 |

| Year | Name | Key Requirements | Chapter |
|------|------|------------------|---------|
| 2000 | Energy Employees Occupational Illness Compensation Program Act | Provided compensation for employees and contractors subjected to excessive radiation during production and testing of nuclear weapons. | 8 |
| 2000 | EO 13152 | Added "status as a parent" to protected classes in EO 11246. | 4 |

# Additional Cases

There is a great deal of case law that impacts human resource management. I have included many of those significant cases in the chapters where they have the most impact, but there are many more that impact HR practice on a daily basis. You should be prepared to see some of these included in questions on the exam.

## 1968: *Rosenfeld v Southern Pacific*

Leah Rosenfeld began working for Southern Pacific (SP) in 1944 and was a member of the Transportation Communication Employees Union, which represented employees at that location. As part of its Collective Bargaining Agreement (CBA) with SP, the union had negotiated a clause that stated, "Employees shall be regarded as in line for promotion, advancement depending upon faithful discharge of duties and capacity for increased responsibility. Where ability is sufficient, seniority shall govern."

In 1966, Ms. Rosenfeld applied for the position of agent-telegrapher at the SP office in Thermal, CA, and was the most senior employee bidding for the opening. She was fully qualified for the position based on all the standards established by the CBA and was fully qualified to perform the services of the position, including required overtime and the physical duties required by the position. The company did not perform any tests or evaluation of her abilities for requirements of the job.

A male employee with less seniority was selected for the position.

SP gave two reasons for refusing the job to her:

1. The California Labor Code limited the number of hours of work per day that could be performed by women and placed a limit of 25 pounds on the weight that could be lifted by a woman.

2. Hiring Ms. Rosenfeld was contrary to SP's discretion as an employer.

Rosenfeld filed suit, claiming that the labor code sections were discriminatory on the basis of sex based on Title VII and that the requirements were not BFOQ (Bona Fide Occupational Qualification).

The Ninth Circuit Court of Appeal determined that the labor code did not create a BFOQ and was, in fact, discriminatory, that SP did violate Title VII, and that the refusal of SP to assign her to the position was not a lawful exercise of SP's discretion as an employer. SP was ordered to consider her for future openings.

## 1969: *Weeks v Southern Bell Telephone Co.*

In 1947, Lorena Weeks began working for Southern Bell (Bell) in Georgia and was a member of the union that represented the workers. The union had a CBA with the company including a clause that seniority would be the deciding factor in determining which job bidders were placed in positions if they otherwise met all the requirements for an opening.

In 1966, Ms. Weeks and one other employee applied for an opening as a switchman. Bell refused her application, telling her they had decided not to place women in this position. The other applicant, a man, had less seniority than Ms. Weeks.

Ms. Weeks filed a complaint with the EEOC, claiming that the company had discriminated against her on the basis of her sex and later filed suit against the company on the same basis. Bell admitted a prima facie violation of Title VII but claimed that sex was a BFOQ for the position, basing this claim on the Georgia Commissioner of Labor's Rule 59, which prohibited women and minors from lifting over 30 pounds. Ms. Weeks argued that the limit was unreasonably low, arbitrary, and that it both violated the Equal Protection Clause of the Fourteenth Amendment and was contrary to Title VII.

In 1969, the Fifth Circuit Court of Appeal ruled that Bell had not proven that sex was a BFOQ for this position. The fact that by then Georgia had repealed Rule 59, replacing the specific weight limit with a requirement that the weight of loads be limited to avoid strains or undue fatigue, was noted by the court in its decision.

## 1973: *McDonnell Douglas Corp. v Green*

Mr. Green was an African-American man working as a mechanic for McDonnell Douglas Corp. in St. Louis, MO from 1956 until he was laid off at the end of August 1964 as part of a general reduction in the company's work force. Mr. Green claimed that his termination and the company's hiring practices in general were racially motivated. To protest this alleged discrimination, Mr. Green, a member of the Congress for Racial Equality (CRE), participated in a "stall-in" with other members of the group that was designed to block access to the company's plant during the morning rush hour. Mr. Green was arrested for his part in the action and pled guilty to obstructing traffic. Some time later, the CRE conducted a "lock-in" at the plant that prevented some McDonnell Douglas employees from leaving the building.

When McDonnell Douglas advertised for mechanics a few weeks after the lock-in, Mr. Green applied and was turned down based on his participation in the stall-in and lock-in. He filed a complaint with the EEOC, claiming that he was turned down because of his race and his participation in the civil rights movement. Mr. Green sued McDonnell Douglas in 1968 for violations of Title VII, and the case was heard by the U.S. Supreme Court in 1973.

In issuing its findings in 1973, the Supreme Court defined the requirements for a finding of a prima facie case of discrimination as follows: "The complainant in a Title VII trial must carry the initial burden under the statute of establishing a prima facie case of racial discrimination. This may be done by showing (i) that he belongs to a racial minority; (ii) that he applied and was qualified for a job for which the employer was seeking applicants; (iii) that, despite his qualifications, he was rejected; and (iv) that, after his rejection, the position remained open and the employer continued to seek applicants from persons of complainant's qualifications."

## 1978: *Regents of California v Bakke*

While the Bakke case was based on a college admissions program, its results impacted the use of affirmative action programs in general.

The Medical School at the University of California Davis utilized two admissions programs to qualify students for the medical program. Both the regular and the special admissions programs evaluated applicants based on a number of criteria and ranked them with a "benchmark score" based on the results. Applicants for both programs were rated on similar criteria, but those in the special admissions program were not rated against those in the regular admission program when decisions were made as to which applicants would be offered admission. In addition, there were a specific number of spots allotted to applicants from the special admissions program.

In 1973 and 1974, Mr. Bakke's applications for admission to the medical program through the regular admission process were rejected, while applicants from the special admissions program, who ranked lower than he did on the admission criteria, were accepted. Mr. Bakke filed suit, claiming that the special admissions program was in violation of the Equal Protection Clause of the Fourteenth Amendment to the Constitution, as well as Title VI of the Civil Rights Act of 1964 and a provision of the California constitution. The Supreme Court handed down its decision in 1978, finding that Mr. Bakke's rights had indeed been violated by the special admissions program, which operated as a quota for admitting minorities to the medical program.

The Court's decision acknowledged the need to consider race in admission decisions when it was necessary to correct prior discriminatory practices but ruled that quotas were not an acceptable method to accomplish this.

## 1979: *United Steelworkers v Weber*

This case began with an Affirmative Action Plan (AAP) that had been negotiated by the United Steelworkers of America (USWA) and Kaiser Aluminum & Chemical Corp. (Kaiser) as part of a collective bargaining agreement. The AAP had been negotiated to "eliminate conspicuous racial imbalances" in skilled craft positions at 15 Kaiser plants by reserving 50 percent of openings in the in-plant training programs for black employees until the percentage of black craftworkers in each plant corresponded with the percentage of blacks in the local labor force. Employees were selected for the program based on their seniority, as long as 50 percent of the trainees were black.

Mr. Weber filed suit against Kaiser and the USWA when he was rejected for a spot in the training program in favor of black employees who had less seniority than he did. Mr. Weber claimed that this was a violation of Title VII of the Civil Rights Act of 1964. The Supreme Court found that the AAP was permissible because it allowed that half of the participants would be white, that it had been designed to remedy prior discrimination and that it was a temporary measure designed to eliminate a racial imbalance.

## 1981: *Texas Department of Community Affairs v Burdine*

In 1972, Ms. Burdine was hired by the Texas Department of Community Affairs (TDCA) as an accounting clerk in the Public Service Careers Division (PSC) whose mission was to train unskilled workers for public sector jobs. Six months later, Ms. Burdine, who had previous training experience, was promoted to the position of field service coordinator. The project director (her supervisor) resigned a few months later and Ms. Burdine applied for the position, but it was not filled and remained open for another six months. At that point, the U.S. Department of Labor, which funded the PSC and was concerned about the quality of its operations, decided to cease funding in 30 days. Based on the efforts of the TDCA, with input from Ms. Burdine, the DOL was convinced to continue funding for the PSC if it was reorganized and a permanent director was hired.

The TDCA reassigned a male from another division to the project director position. He terminated three employees, including Ms. Burdine, retaining one male employee. Shortly after the termination, Ms. Burdine was rehired by the TDCA in another division at the same salary as was paid to the project director of the PSC.

Ms. Burdine filed this suit, claiming gender discrimination had motivated both the refusal of TDCA to promote her and her subsequent termination from PSC. The District Court determined that gender had not been a factor in either decision. The Fifth Circuit Court of Appeals found that the male hired for the project director position may have been better qualified than Ms. Burdine for the position, but that the TDCA had not proved that there were legitimate, nondiscriminatory reasons for Ms. Burdine's termination.

The Supreme Court held that employers are not required to prove the nondiscriminatory reasons for an employment action but are required only to explain the nondiscriminatory reasons for the action.

## 1987: *Johnson v Santa Clara County Transportation Agency*

Paul Johnson, a male employee of the Santa Clara County Transportation Agency (SCCTA) was passed over for a promotion in favor of a female employee, Diane Joyce. Both candidates were deemed to be well qualified for the position of road dispatcher, a job classified as a Skilled Craft Worker by the EEOC. The director of the agency made the final decision based on a number of factors, including the qualifications of both candidates, the selection committee recommendation, and affirmative action issues, among others.

The affirmative action issues included the fact that the agency had established a voluntary affirmative action plan in 1978 that had as one of its goals to increase the participation of women in the Skilled Craft Worker category. At the time Ms. Joyce applied for this position, none of the 238 SCCTA positions classified as such was held by a woman.

Mr. Johnson filed a complaint with the EEOC, received a right-to-sue letter in 1981, and filed suit against the agency for violating Title VII. The Supreme Court handed down its decision in 1987.

The Supreme Court held that the SCCTA acted appropriately in promoting Ms. Joyce into the position. The Court stated that the plaintiff has the burden to prove a prima facie case of discrimination. Once that occurs, the employer has the burden to prove that there is a non-discriminatory rationale for the decision (that is, the AAP). At that point, the burden is once again on the plaintiff to show that the AAP is invalid.

The agency's AAP was determined to be "a moderate, flexible, case-by-case approach" consistent with Title VII requirements. Key elements in this finding were that the AAP was flexible and temporary, designed only to correct an existing workforce imbalance. That being the case, it is acceptable for an employer to place a less qualified member of a protected class in a job.

# 1987: *School Board of Nassau v Arline*

Gene Arline contracted tuberculosis in 1957 and was hospitalized until the disease went into remission. In 1966, Ms. Arline became an elementary school teacher in Nassau County, FL, where she taught for 13 years. In 1977, the TB became active again off and on through the 1978–79 school year. The school board suspended her with pay twice to accommodate her recovery, but in 1979 decided to terminate her employment due to the contagious nature of her ongoing illness.

Ms. Arline sued the district, alleging that her dismissal was a violation of Section 504 of the Rehabilitation Act of 1973 because its terms qualified her as a handicapped person based on her illness.

Section 504 is based on Title VI of the Civil Rights Act of 1964 and defines a handicapped individual as "any person who (i) has a physical or mental impairment which substantially limits one or more of such person's major life activities, (ii) has a record of such an impairment, or (iii) is regarded as having such an impairment." Regulations formulated by the Department of Health and Human Services define "major life activities" as "functions such as caring for one's self, performing manual tasks, walking, seeing, hearing, speaking, breathing, learning, and working."

The case centered around whether or not a person with a contagious disease could be considered a handicapped individual under Section 504 of the Rehabilitation Act.

In 1987, the Supreme Court handed down its decision that a person afflicted with tuberculosis can be a handicapped person as defined by Section 504.

Justice Brennan, writing for the majority, stated, "The fact that some persons who have contagious diseases may pose a serious health threat to others under certain circumstances does not justify excluding from the coverage of the act all persons with actual or perceived contagious diseases." The decision also stated that the determination of whether or not someone with a contagious disease poses a serious health threat to others should be left to the medical judgments of public health officials.

## 1989: *Martin v Wilks*

The basic issue in this case was whether an employee can sue for reverse discrimination when hiring and promotion decisions are made pursuant to a consent decree.

The city of Birmingham, AL and the Jefferson County Personnel Board were sued by Martin and six other black individuals in 1974, alleging that the city and the board had unlawfully discriminated against blacks when making hiring and promoting decisions for public service jobs. The case was resolved when the parties entered into consent decrees that established AAPs intended to increase the hiring and promotion of black firefighters.

At a public fairness hearing and in other subsequent actions, objections and a request for injunctive relief to prevent enforcement of the decrees by the Birmingham Firefighters Association (BFA) and white firefighters were denied by the District Court.

A third group of firefighters (including Wilks) then filed suit against the city and the board, alleging that they were being denied promotions in favor of less-qualified blacks, and that this was a violation of Title VII. Martin and the other black individuals sought to have the Wilks suit dismissed, claiming that the consent decree precluded any claims of reverse discrimination.

The Supreme Court held that, because the white firefighters were not involved in the original litigation that resulted in the consent decrees, they could not be held to employment decisions based on them and were entitled to challenge the validity of the consent decrees.

## 1992: *Electromation, Inc. v NLRB*

This case resulted from an unfair labor practice charge filed against Electromation by the Teamsters union.

Electromation is a small company with 200 employees that was having financial problems in late 1988. As a result, management decided to eliminate the employee attendance bonus policy and the wage increase for 1989. Instead, they made lump-sum payments to employees based on an individual's length of service. Shortly after this decision was made, the president received a petition signed by 68 employees objecting to the change in policy. The president first met with supervisory personnel to discuss the complaints; then decided to meet directly with a group of employees to discuss their concerns. After meeting with the employees, the president realized that the employee issues were unlikely to be resolved without employee participation. The company decided to create five action committees, one for each area of concern:

1. Absenteeism/infractions
2. No smoking policy
3. Communication network
4. Pay progression for premium positions
5. Attendance bonus program

The committees met weekly, beginning in late January 1989, and included management personnel as well as employees as members. While employees were allowed to sign up for the committees, management determined how many were allowed and limited employees to serving on one committee. Management communicated to the committee members that they were expected to talk with their coworkers for ideas that could be incorporated into the work of the committees. Management also expected committee members to inform coworkers about "what was going on."

On February 13, 1989, the Teamsters union made a demand for recognition to Electromation; at that point management advised the committees that management was no longer able to participate but that the committees could continue their work if they wished to do so.

The NLRB Administrative Law Judge determined that the action committees were unlawful, employer-dominated labor organizations because:

1. They included employees, supervisors, and management as members, and management personnel had the ability to reject recommendations.

2. Management expected committee members to represent coworkers by soliciting ideas from them to be presented to the committee.

3. They included discussions about conditions of employment. Formation of the committees was a direct result of the company's unilateral change to the attendance bonus policy.

4. Management organized them by establishing their goals, determining what each committee would work on, deciding how many employees would be allowed on each committee and how they would operate, and determining their functions.

5. The company provided support in the form of a place to meet, supplies, materials, and payment for time spent on committee work.

In its decision, the NLRB indicated that not all employee-participation committees are employer-dominated organizations and that they can serve a useful purpose if they are not. It also determined that paying employees who participate in committees at work does not in and of itself violate the NLRA.

## 1993: *E. I. DuPont & Co. v NLRB*

This case was initiated by the Chemical Workers Union which represents clerical workers, production personnel, and maintenance employees at DuPont's plant located in Deepwater, NJ. The union claimed that six safety committees and a fitness committee established by DuPont were company-dominated labor organizations and that the company was bypassing the union by dealing with the committees on bargainable issues. DuPont claimed that the committees were "a management vehicle to enhance the safety of employees through labor-management communication or to carry out similar management functions."

The NLRA sets three conditions that must be met in order for a labor organization to exist:

1. Employees participate in the organization.

2. A function of the organization is dealing with the employer.

3. The function of the organization is concerned with some form of "conditions of work," including grievances, labor disputes, wages, rates of pay, or hours of employment.

The purpose of this case was to determine whether or not DuPont was using these committees to bypass the union in dealing with the employees, since clearly employees were participating in them and they dealt with safety issues, which are a mandatory subject for collective bargaining.

Some of the reasons the NLRB found these to be employer-dominated labor organizations include the following:

- Each committee included at least one member of management who set the weekly agenda and had veto power over any decisions or recommendations made by committee members.

- DuPont controlled the number of members on each committee.

- DuPont determined how many and which employees served on each committee.

- DuPont could unilaterally restructure the committees.

The board also found that DuPont was using the committees to circumvent the union. For example, the union had repeatedly requested that changes be made to the ventilation system in the welding shop. Until one of the committees made the suggestion, DuPont took no action, but once the committee suggestion was acted upon, DuPont constructed a new shop. In another instance, DuPont had consistently refused the union's request for employee fitness facilities, but when the committee made the suggestions, management acted upon them.

DuPont was required to disband the action committees and to post a notice at the plant that read, in part:

"We will not deal with these committees or their successors. We will not bypass the Chemical Workers Association as your bargaining agent. We will not unilaterally implement these committees' proposals concerning safety awards and fitness facilities without affording the union an opportunity to bargain."

## 1993: *St. Mary's Honor Center v Hicks*

St. Mary's Honor Center is a halfway-house run by the Missouri Department of Corrections and Human Resources (MDCHR), which hired Melvin Hicks as a correctional officer in 1978 and, in 1980, promoted him to one of the six shift commander positions at St. Mary's. Mr. Hicks' work performance during this time was deemed to be satisfactory by his supervisors. As the result of an investigation by MDCHR, the supervisory structure of St. Mary's was reorganized in January 1984, at which time Mr. Hicks' immediate supervisor was replaced, as was the superintendent of the facility. Shortly after this change, his new supervisors singled out Mr. Hicks for disciplinary actions that his peers were not subjected to. In fact, they were more lenient with his peers even with regard to more serious violations, in some cases disregarding them entirely. At one point Mr. Hicks was suspended, and he was later demoted from his supervisory position. In June he was terminated for threatening his supervisor during a heated argument.

At this point, Mr. Hicks filed suit, alleging discrimination on the basis of his race in violation of Title VII of the Civil Rights Act of 1964. Mr. Hicks was able to convince the District Court that a prima facie case of discrimination existed. St. Mary's then provided evidence of legitimate, nondiscriminatory reasons for its actions (the rules infractions for which Hicks had been disciplined). Once that occurred, the burden fell once again to Mr. Hicks to show that those reasons were actually a pretext, designed to hide the racial motivation of St. Mary's. The District Court found that, although the court did not believe the reasons given by St. Mary's, Mr. Hicks had not proved that his termination was racially motivated. Based on the evidence offered, there was no way to determine whether the termination had been racially motivated (unlawful) or based on personal dislike for Mr. Hicks (lawful).

The Eighth Circuit Court of Appeals determined that since the Mr. Hicks had proved the reasons were a pretext, he was entitled to a judgment in his favor.

When the case reached the Supreme Court, it relied on two prior cases in making its decision: *McDonnell Douglas Corp. v Green*, and *Texas Dept. of Community Affairs v Burdine*. Based on *Green*, Mr. Hicks was required to establish that a prima facie case of discrimination existed. (He did.) Once that happened, according to *Burdine*, St. Mary's needed to provide a lawful explanation for the adverse employment actions taken against Mr. Hicks. (They did). Once St. Mary's provided a nondiscriminatory reason for the employment actions, it was once again up to Mr. Hicks to prove that those reasons were racially motivated and not based on some other, lawful motivation.

## 1995: *McKennon v Nashville Banner Publishing Co.*

Christine McKennon was employed by Nashville Banner Publishing Company (Banner) for 30 years. At age 62, Ms. McKennon's employment was terminated as part of a workforce reduction that was needed to reduce costs. Ms. McKennon believed that the termination was in fact unlawfully based upon her age and filed suit claiming that this violated the Age Discrimination in Employment Act of 1967 (ADEA). During a deposition, she admitted copying confidential documents that she had access to in the course of her employment. Within a few days of the deposition, Banner notified her that removal of the documents was in violation of her job responsibilities and once again terminated her employment. Banner claimed in the letter that, had Banner known of this wrongdoing, her employment would have been terminated immediately based on this fact alone. The District Court then granted summary judgment for Banner, finding that her misconduct was grounds for her termination and that she was not entitled to any remedy in light of her actions.

The Supreme Court agreed to hear the case in order to resolve the question of whether or not all relief must be denied when an employer has violated the ADEA in its discharge of an employee but later discovers employee conduct that would have justified a lawful termination. The Court ruled that after-acquired evidence of employee misconduct that would have resulted in a termination does not relieve the employer for liability in discharging the employee for an unlawful, discriminatory reason.

## 2001: *Circuit City Stores v Adams*

In 1995, Saint Clair Adams applied for and was hired as a sales counselor at a Circuit City store in Santa Rosa, CA after signing an employment application that contained a condition requiring that all employment disputes to settled through binding arbitration based on the

Federal Arbitration Act of 1925 (FAA). In 1997, Mr. Adams filed a discrimination claim against Circuit City in state court and the store responded with a federal suit seeking to stop the state action and force Mr. Adams to arbitration per the agreement he had signed. The District Court agreed with Circuit City, and Mr. Adams appealed the decision to the Ninth Circuit Court of Appeals, which ruled that the FAA does not apply to employment contracts. Because this ruling conflicted with all other circuits of the Federal Court of Appeals, the Supreme Court granted certiorari in 2000.

The Supreme Court reversed the Ninth Circuit, finding that mandatory arbitration agreements in employment contracts are enforceable under the FAA except for transportation workers, which are specifically exempted from the FAA.

# Appendix

# B

# Resources

There are literally thousands of references available for every aspect of human resources, so it's just not possible to include every great resource here. The resources we have included are those that add dimension or different perspectives to the information presented in this book. While the best preparation for both the PHR and SPHR examinations is diverse generalist experience, these resources will provide a more in-depth "refresher" than is possible in this guide.

**A word about the Internet**   There is a wealth of information available on the Internet that is current and easily accessible. The best way to access this information is through a search engine such as Google (www.google.com) or Ask Jeeves (www.ask.com). If you haven't used a search engine before, you can get instructions on how to search by clicking the Help button on each search page. When you type in the phrase you want to research, you will get a list of websites to check out.

**Information about the test**   For information about eligibility requirements and test dates, the best source is the Human Resource Certification Institute (HRCI). There are three sources for information from HRCI. The first is the *PHR & SPHR Certification Handbook*, described in the Introduction, which is free of charge and published annually. The handbook provides all the information necessary to apply for the exams and includes pricing, deadlines, and general information. The second source is the HRCI website (www.hrci.org). The website contains a great deal of information about the exams and also allows you to view the handbook online, download a copy, or request that a hard copy be mailed to you. The third HRCI information source is the *HRCI Certification Guide*. This inexpensive guide explains the testing process, discusses various study methods, and contains sample questions and answers; it can be purchased from several national online booksellers.

**Professional associations**   Professional associations are often a great source of information about current trends in a particular practice area. Some of these are member-only sites, but even those very often have useful information available to nonmembers.

As mentioned earlier, there are many HR sources available. The inclusion of these materials is not an endorsement of the information contained in them. They are provided only as suggestions for further reading should you feel the need for more detail in one of these areas. For ease of use, the list is organized according to functional area.

At the time of publication, the URLs included below were operational; given the changing nature of the World Wide Web, some of them may have been changed or no longer exist.

# Strategic Management

Resources included with Strategic Management cover general human resource books and resources for other business disciplines with which HR professionals interact on a daily basis.

**Books**  Chase, Richard B., F. Robert Jacobs, and Nicholas J. Aquilano. *Operations Management for Competitive Advantage*, 9th ed., New York City, NY: McGraw-Hill/Irwin, 2001.

Fitz-Enz, Jac. *How to Measure Human Resources Management*, 3rd ed., New York City, NY: McGraw-Hill Trade.

Gardner, Christopher. *The Valuation of Information Technology: A Guide for Development, Valuation, and Financial Planning*, New York City, NY: John Wiley & Sons, Inc., 2000.

Hiam, Alexander. *Marketing for Dummies*, New York City, NY: John Wiley & Sons, Inc., 1997.

Kaplan, Robert S., and David P. Norton. *The Balanced Scorecard: Translating Strategy into Action*, Boston, MA: Harvard Business School Press, 1996.

Mathis, Robert L., and John H. Jackson. *Human Resource Management*, 10th ed., Cincinnati, OH: South-Western College Publishing, 2000.

Tracy, John A. *How to Read a Financial Report*, 5th ed., New York City, NY: John Wiley & Sons, Inc., 1999.

**Professional Associations**  American Institute of Certified Public Accountants, `www.aicpa.org`

American Management Association, `www.amanet.org`

American Marketing Association, `www.marketingpower.com`

The Human Resource Planning Society, `www.hrps.org`

The Institute for Management of Information Systems, `www.weball.org`

The Institute of Operations Management, `www.iomnet.org`

The International Association for Human Resource Information Management, `www.ihrim.org`

Society for Human Resource Management, `www.shrm.org`

Strategic Management Association, `www.smsweb.org`

# Workforce Planning and Employment

These resources are some of the many related to planning for workforce recruiting and employment. In Chapter 4, "Workforce Planning and Employment," we provided links to government agencies enforcing employment laws should you wish to read more about them.

**Books**   Ahlrichs, Nancy S. *Competing for Talent: Key Recruitment and Retention Strategies for Becoming an Employer of Choice*, Palo Alto, CA: Davies-Black Books, 2000.

Bechet, Thomas P. *Strategic Staffing*, New York City, NY: AMACOM, 2002.

McCarter, John, and Ray Schreyer. *Recruit and Retain the Best: Key Solutions for HR Professionals*, Manassas Park, VA: Impact Publications, 2000.

Smalley, Larry R. *On-The-Job Orientation and Training*, San Francisco, CA: Jossey-Bass, 1999.

Steingold, Fred S. *The Employer's Legal Handbook*, 5th ed., Berkeley, CA: Nolo Press, 2003.

Truesdell, William H. *Secrets of Affirmative Action Compliance*, 5th ed., Walnut Creek, CA: The Management Advantage, Inc. 2001.

**Professional Associations**   American Staffing Association, www.staffingtoday.net (look for the issue papers)

Employee Relocation Council, www.erc.org

International Labour Organization, www.ilo.org

International Public Management Association for Human Resources, www.ipma-hr.org

# Human Resource Development

These resources provide additional information about developing talent within organizations.

**Books**   Anderson, Dean, and Linda Ackerman Anderson. *Beyond Change Management: Advanced Strategies for Today's Transformational Leaders*, San Francisco, CA: Jossey-Bass/Pfeiffer, 2001.

Becker, Brian E., Mark A. Huselie, and Dave Ulrich. *The HR Scorecard: Linking People, Strategy, and Performance*, 1st ed., Boston, MA: Harvard Business School Press, 2001.

Fitz-Enz, Jac. *The ROI of Human Capital: Measuring the Economic Value of Employee Performance*, New York City, NY: AMACOM, 2000.

Grote, Dick. *Discipline without Punishment: The Proven Strategy That Turns Problem Employees into Superior Performers*, New York City, NY: AMACOM, 1995.

Knowles, Malcolm S., Elwood F. Holton, and Richard A. Swanson. *The Adult Learner: The Definitive Classic in Adult Education and Human Resource Development*, 5th ed., Houston, TX: Gulf Publishing Company, 1998.

Philips, Jack, and Ron D. Stone. *How to Measure Training Results: A Practical Guide to Tracking the Six Key Indicators*, 1st ed., New York City, NY: McGraw-Hill Trade, 2002.

Senge, Peter M. *The Fifth Discipline*, 1st ed., New York City, NY: Currency/Doubleday, 1994.

Kline, Peter, and Bernard Saunders. *Ten Steps to a Learning Organization*, 2nd ed., Arlington, VA: Great Ocean Publishing, 1998.

**Professional Associations**   American Society for Training and Development, www.astd.org

# Compensation and Benefits

Additional information about compensation and benefit issues and processes is available in the following resources.

**Books**   Beam, Burton T. Jr., and John J. McFadden. *Employee Benefits*, 6th ed., Chicago, IL: Dearborn Trade Publishing.

Berger, Lance A. (Editor), and Dorothy R. Berger (Editor). *The Compensation Handbook*, 4th ed., New York City. NY: McGraw-Hill Trade, 1999.

Plachy, Roger J., and Sandra J. Plachy. *Building a Fair Pay Program: A Step-by-Step Guide*, 2nd ed., New York City, NY: AMACOM, 1998.

**Professional Associations**   American Payroll Association, www.americanpayroll.org

Employee Benefit Research Institute, www.ebri.org

International Foundation of Employee Benefit Plans, www.ifebp.org

International Society of Certified Employee Benefits Specialists, www.iscebs.org

World at Work (formerly American Compensation Association), www.worldatwork.org

# Employee and Labor Relations

These resources provide additional information on labor and employee relations.

**Books**   Brounstein, Marty. *Coaching and Mentoring for Dummies*, 1st ed., New York City, NY: John Wiley & Sons Publishing, Inc., 2000

Costantino, Cathy A., and Christina Sickles Merchant. *Designing Conflict Management Systems: A Guide to Creating Productive and Healthy Organizations*, San Francisco, CA: Jossey-Bass, 1996.

Holley, William H., Kenneth M. Jennings, and Roger S. Wolters. *The Labor Relations Process*, 7th ed., Cincinnati, OH: South-Western College Publishing, 2000.

Grazier, Peter B., *Before It's Too Late: Employee Involvement... An Idea Whose Time Has Come*, Chadds Ford, PA: Teambuilding, Inc., 1989.

Kaye, Beverly, and Sharon Jordan-Evans. *Love 'Em or Lose 'Em: Getting Good People to Stay*, San Francisco, CA: Berrett-Koehler Publishers, Inc., 1999.

Larkin, T.J., and Sandar Larkin (Contributor). *Communicating Change: Winning Employee Support for New Business Goals*, 2nd ed., New York City, NY: McGraw-Hill Trade, 1994.

Loughran, Charles S. *Negotiating a Labor Contract: A Management Handbook*, Washington, D.C.: BNA Books, 1992.

Delpo, Amy, Lisa Guerin, and Janet Portman. *Dealing with Problem Employees: A Legal Guide*, 2nd ed., Berkeley, CA: Nolo Press, 2001.

National Labor Relations Board, Office of the General Counsel, *A Guide to Basic Law and Procedures under the National Labor Relations Act*, Washington, D.C.: U.S. Government Printing Office, 1997 (can be downloaded from www.nlrb.gov/publications/basicguide.pdf).

Spitzer, Dean R., *Supermotivation: A Blueprint for Energizing Your Organization from Top to Bottom*, New York City, NY: AMACOM, 1995.

**Professional Associations**   Employment Management Association, www.shrm.org/ema

National Public Employer Labor Relations Association, www.npelra.org

# Occupational Health, Safety, and Security

These are some of the many resources available for workplace health, safety, and security issues.

**Books**   Bible, Jon D., and Darien A. McWhirter. *Privacy in the Workplace*, Westport, CT: Greenwood Publishing Group, 1990.

Blanco, James A. (Editor), et al. *Business Fraud: Know It and Prevent It,* Huntington, WV: Humanomics Publishing, 2000.

Fay, John J. *Contemporary Security Management*, 1st ed., St. Louis, MO: Butterworth-Heinemann, 2001.

Geller, E. Scott. *The Psychology of Safety: How to Improve Behaviors and Attitudes on the Job*, Boca Raton, FL: CRC Press, 1996.

Levy, Barry S. (Editor), and David H. Wegman (Editor). *Occupational Health: Recognizing and Preventing Work-Related Disease and Injury*, 4th ed., Philadelphia, PA: Lippincott Williams & Wilkins, 2000.

Mitroff, Ian I., et al. *The Essential Guide to Managing Corporate Crises: A Step-by-Step Handbook for Surviving Major Catastrophes*, New York City, NY: Oxford University Press, 1996.

**Professional Associations**   National Association of Safety Professionals, www.naspweb.com

National Safety Council, www.nsc.org

The American Society of Safety Engineers, www.asse.org

# Employment Documents and Retention

HR professionals should be well aware of the many different requirements for maintenance and retention of employment documents. In enacting employment legislation, Congress has mandated retention requirements for various documents which, unfortunately, are not consistent. In addition, many state and local governments have retention requirements that differ from federal requirements. Table C.1 lists federal document retention requirements for the PHR/SPHR exams; these may be different from the state and local requirements where you practice, so keep that in mind while you are studying. As with any other conflicting requirements, documents should be retained in accordance with the most strict requirement.

**TABLE C.1**   Federal Employment Document Retention Requirements

| Federal Law or Regulation | Document(s) Covered | Retention Period | Covered Employers |
|---|---|---|---|
| Title VII of the Civil Rights Act of 1964 (Title VII) | Current EEO-1 Report | 1 year | 15+ employees |
| | Records of all employment actions: employment applications, resumes, hire, rehire, layoffs, recalls, terminations, promotions, demotions, transfers, compensation | | |
| | Apprentice selection records | | |
| | Name, address, social security number, gender, date of birth, occupation, job classification | | |
| | Compensation records (direct and indirect), tax forms, records of hours worked, benefit payments, tax deductions | | |
| Title VII of the Civil Rights Act of 1964 (Title VII)<br><br>Americans with Disabilities Act (ADA)<br><br>Age Discrimination in Employment Act (ADEA)<br><br>Rehabilitation Act of 1973 (RA) | Personnel records related to discrimination charges | Required: Until resolution<br><br>Best practice: 7 years after employee leaves (for use in future litigation) | 15+ employees (ADA/Title VII)<br><br>20+ employees (ADEA)<br><br>Federal contractors and subcontractors with contracts of $10,000+ |

**TABLE C.1** Federal Employment Document Retention Requirements *(continued)*

| Federal Law or Regulation | Document(s) Covered | Retention Period | Covered Employers |
|---|---|---|---|
| Americans with Disabilities Act (ADA) | Job announcements, advertisements, and job orders sent to agencies or unions | 1 year | 15+ employees |
| | Records of all employment actions: applications, resumes, promotions, transfers, demotions, layoffs, terminations | | |
| | Reasonable accommodation requests | | |
| | Name, address, social security number, gender, date of birth, occupation, job classification | | |
| | Compensation records (direct and indirect), tax forms, records of hours worked, benefit payments, tax deductions | | |
| Age Discrimination in Employment Act (ADEA) | Compensation records (direct and indirect), tax forms, records of hours worked, benefit payments, tax deductions | 3 years | 20+ employees |
| | Name, address, social security number, gender, date of birth, occupation, job classification | | |
| | Employee benefit plans | 1 year after plan ends | 20+ employees |
| | Written merit plans | | |
| | Temporary employee records | 90 days | 20+ employees |
| | Job announcements, advertisements, and job orders sent to agencies or unions | 1 year | 20+ employees |
| | Records of all employment actions: applications, resumes, promotions, transfers, demotions, layoffs, terminations | | |
| | Pre-employment records for temp positions | | |
| | Employment test results | | |
| | Physical examination results | | |
| | Training records | | |

**TABLE C.1** Federal Employment Document Retention Requirements *(continued)*

| Federal Law or Regulation | Document(s) Covered | Retention Period | Covered Employers |
|---|---|---|---|
| Consolidated Omnibus Budget Reconciliation Act (COBRA) | Written COBRA procedures<br><br>Payment records and correspondence<br><br>Documentation that COBRA notices are sent within specified time period | 6 years (required by ERISA) | 20+ employees |
| Davis Bacon Act | Name, address, social security number, gender, date of birth, occupation, job classification<br><br>Compensation records (direct and indirect), tax forms, records of hours worked, benefit payments, tax deductions | 3 years from end of contract | Federal construction contractors and subcontractors (contracts over $2,000) |
| Employee Polygraph Protection Act (EPPA) | Reason for test administration<br><br>Test results | 3 years | All employers |
| Employee Retirement Income Security Act of 1974 | Dated and signed documentation of employee receipt of plan reports and disclosures<br><br>Beneficiary designation and distribution elections—beneficiary distribution<br><br>Documentation for eligibility determinations (age, length of service record, marital status) | Indefinitely | All employers except churches and governments |
| | Copies of summary plan descriptions and annual reports, COBRA notices, and other plan reports<br><br>Wage and hour records used to determine retirement benefits | 6 years after filing date | All employers except churches and governments |
| | Beneficiary designation and distribution elections—participant distribution | 3 years | All employers except churches and governments |

**TABLE  C.1**    Federal Employment Document Retention Requirements *(continued)*

| Federal Law or Regulation | Document(s) Covered | Retention Period | Covered Employers |
|---|---|---|---|
| Equal Pay Act (EPA) | Date of birth for employees under 19<br>Gender<br>Occupation<br>Payroll records (time cards, wage/salary rate, deductions, explanation for difference between rates for men and women) | 3 years | All employers |
| Executive Order 11246 | Affirmative Action Plan and supporting documents | Update annually | Federal contractors and subcontractors with 50+ employees and contracts over $50,000 |
| Fair Labor Standards Act (FLSA) | Collective bargaining agreements<br>Individual employment contracts<br>Sale and purchase records<br>Date of birth for employees under 19<br>Payroll records, including record of name, birth date, gender, occupation<br>Basis for salary calculations for exempt employees<br>Written training agreements, job and selection criteria, records of minority and female applicants | 3 years | All employers |
|  | Regular pay rate<br>Beginning of work week, start time<br>Straight time and overtime earnings calculations (day/week)<br>Total wages for pay period<br>Pay deductions<br>Pay period and date of payment<br>Basis for payment of wages<br>Work schedules | 2 years | All employers |

**TABLE C.1**    Federal Employment Document Retention Requirements *(continued)*

| Federal Law or Regulation | Document(s) Covered | Retention Period | Covered Employers |
|---|---|---|---|
| Fair Labor Standards Act (FLSA) | Job announcements, advertisements, and job orders sent to agencies or unions | 1 year | All employers |
| | Certificate of Age | Until termination | All employers |
| Family and Medical Leave Act (FMLA) | Basic employee information (name, address, title, compensation, employment terms, hours worked, wage deductions) | 3 years | 50+ employees within a 75 mile radius |
| | Employee notices and description of policy | | |
| | Records of leave dates and hours of intermittent leave | | |
| | Benefit premium payments | | |
| | Documentation of disputes about FMLA leave | | |
| Federal Insurance Contributions Act (FICA) | Income tax withholding information | 4 years | All employers |
| Federal Unemployment Tax Act (FUTA) | Income tax withholding information | 4 years | All employers |
| Immigration Reform and Control Act (IRCA) | I-9 signed by employee and employer | 3 years from hire date *or* 1 year after termination, whichever is longer | 4+ employees |
| National Labor Relations Act (NLRA) | Collective bargaining agreements | 3 years | All employers |
| | Individual employment contracts | | |
| | Sale and purchase records | | |
| | Written training agreements, job and selection criteria, records of minority and female applicants | | |

**TABLE  C.1**    Federal Employment Document Retention Requirements *(continued)*

| Federal Law or Regulation | Document(s) Covered | Retention Period | Covered Employers |
|---|---|---|---|
| National Labor Relations Act (NLRA) | Straight time and overtime earnings calculations (day/week) | 2 years | All employers |
| | Basis for payment of wages | | |
| | Total wages for pay period | | |
| | Pay deductions | | |
| | Pay period and date of payment | | |
| | Work schedules | | |
| | Certificate of Age | Until termination | All employers |
| Occupational Health and Safety Act (OSHA) | Safety and health training records | 3 years | 11+ employees |
| | Illness and injury logs | 5 years | 11+ employees |
| | Supplementary injury and illness records | | |
| | Employer records of adverse reaction to chemical substances | | |
| | Medical exam records for exposures to toxic substances | 30 years | 11+ employees |
| | Medical exam records for exposures to blood-borne pathogens | | |
| | Hazardous material exposure records | | |
| Rehabilitation Act of 1973 (RA) | Job announcements, advertisements, and job orders sent to agencies or unions | Retain for 2 years (1 year if less than 150 employees) | Federal contractors and subcontractors with contracts of $10,000+ |
| | Records of all employment actions: applications, resumes, promotions, transfers, demotions, layoffs, terminations | | |
| | Employment test results | | |
| | Physical examination results | | |
| | Training records | | |
| | Name, address, social security number, gender, date of birth, occupation, job classification | | |
| | Compensation records (direct and indirect), tax forms, records of hours worked, benefit payments, tax deductions | | |

**TABLE C.1** Federal Employment Document Retention Requirements *(continued)*

| Federal Law or Regulation | Document(s) Covered | Retention Period | Covered Employers |
|---|---|---|---|
| Service Contract Act (SCA) | Name, address, social security number, gender, date of birth, occupation, job classification<br><br>Compensation records (direct and indirect), tax forms, records of hours worked, benefit payments, tax deductions<br><br>Wages and tax deductions | 3 years from end of contract | Federal service contractors and subcontractors with contracts of $2,500+ |
| Social Security Act | Employee name and ID number<br><br>Social security number<br><br>Employee home address with zip code | 4 years from tax due date | All employers |
| Toxic Substance Control Act (TSCA) | Documentation of hazardous material exposures<br><br>Documentation of significant adverse reactions to work environment<br><br>Claims of occupational disease or health problems | 30 years from report date | Manufacturers, importers, processors or distributors of toxic chemicals |
| Uniform Guidelines on Employee Selection Procedures (Guidelines) | Applicant race and sex<br><br>Employee race and sex<br><br>Veteran status<br><br>Disability status | 2 years for 150 employees; 1 year if less | Employers subject to Title VII, EO 11246, and other EEO laws (ADEA and RA are exempt) |

**TABLE C.1**    Federal Employment Document Retention Requirements *(continued)*

| Federal Law or Regulation | Document(s) Covered | Retention Period | Covered Employers |
|---|---|---|---|
| Vietnam Era Veterans' Readjustment Act (VEVRA) | Affirmative Action Plan for current and prior year<br><br>Documentation of good faith effort to comply with AAP<br><br>Job announcements, advertisements, and job orders sent to agencies or unions<br><br>Records of all employment actions: applications, resumes, promotions, transfers, demotions, layoffs, terminations<br><br>Employment test results<br><br>Physical examination results<br><br>Training records<br><br>Name, address, social security number, gender, date of birth, occupation, job classification<br><br>Compensation records (direct and indirect), tax forms, records of hours worked, benefit payments, tax deductions | 2 years | Federal contractors and subcontractors with contracts of $25,000+ |
| Walsh-Healey Public Contracts Act (PCA) | Name, address, social security number, gender, date of birth, occupation, job classification<br><br>Compensation records (direct and indirect), tax forms, records of hours worked, benefit payments, tax deductions | 3 years from end of contract | Federal contractors and subcontractors with contracts of $10,000+ |

# Glossary

# Numbers

**401(k) plan**   A common type of deferred compensation that allows for contributions from both employees and employers. Employees may defer a part of their pay before taxes up to limits established by the EGTRRA.

# A

**ability to pay**   An organization's financial resources determine the level of compensation it is able to pay its employees.

**accounting**   The organizational function concerned with recording financial transactions, paying bills, collecting revenue from customers and producing financial statements.

**acquired needs theory**   David McClelland's theory states that people are motivated by experiences acquired throughout their lives. Overall, humans are motivated to excel in either achievement, affiliation, or power.

**active training methods**   Methods in which the learning experience is focused on the learner.

**actual deferral percentage (ADP) test**   An annual test required by ERISA to ensure that highly compensated employees (HCEs) do not receive greater benefits from a 401(k) plan than those received by other employees. (For more on ERISA, see Appendix A.)

**ad hoc arbitrator**   A person who is selected to hear only a single case.

**ADDIE model**   ADDIE is an acronym that describes the five elements of the instructional design process: analysis, design, development, implementation, and evaluation.

**adverse impact**   Any negative result of an employment action.

**administrative services only (ASO) plan**   A benefit plan utilized by some self-funded organizations. These organizations contract with an insurance company to manage and pay claims.

**Affirmative Action Plan (AAP)**   An AAP analyzes a workforce to determine whether or not protected classes are underutilized in different job groups and describes how an organization will address any underutilization that exists.

**agency shop clause**   A clause in a labor contract that specifies that all employees must either join the union or pay union dues if they choose not to join the union.

**ally doctrine**   If an employer whose workers are on strike asks a neutral employer to produce the work that would normally be performed by the striking workers, the ally doctrine states that the neutral employer becomes an ally of the struck employer and is therefore a legitimate target of a picket line.

**alter ego doctrine**   When two businesses have interrelated operations, central control of labor relations, common management, and common ownership, they are considered alter ego employers, and the NLRB may determine that employees of the alter ego employer are part of the bargaining unit.

**alternative dispute resolution (ADR)**    ADR covers a range of methods used to solve disagreements without litigation. These alternatives are often able to resolve problems with less animosity than occurs when a lawsuit is filed, and at far less cost to the parties.

**andragogy**    The study of how adults learn; education in which the learner participates in decisions about what will be taught and how it will be delivered.

**auditory learners**    One of the three learning styles. Auditory learners retain information best when they hear it.

**authorization card**    The means by which the NLRB determines that there is sufficient support for a union to hold an election. The NLRB will hold an election if 30 percent of the eligible employees in the anticipated bargaining unit sign the authorization cards.

**average bias**    A bias characterized by a group of candidates (in a selection process) or employees (in a performance management process) who are all rated about the same because the interviewer or reviewer has difficulty deciding which one is best.

# B

**balance sheet**    A report providing a picture of the financial condition of the organization on a specific day, usually the last day of the accounting period. Information on the balance sheet includes the company's assets, liabilities, and equity. Called a balance sheet because the total of the liabilities and the equity must equal the total of the assets as represented by the balance sheet formula: Assets = Liabilities + Owner Equity.

**balanced scorecard**    Utilized by managers to track information in four key areas: financial results, customer results, key internal processes, and how people are hired and trained to achieve organization goals.

**base pay**    A preset salary or hourly rate paid to an employee for performance of job responsibilities.

**behavior evaluation method**    The third level of a training evaluation model developed by Donald Kirkpatrick; uses a test to measure how well participants learned the information that was presented in the training.

**behavioral reinforcement**    B.F. Skinner's study of behavioral reinforcement or behavior modification revealed that behavior can be changed through the use of four intervention strategies: positive reinforcement, negative reinforcement, punishment, and extinction.

**benchmark positions**    Jobs that are commonly found across organizations regardless of size or industry.

**binding arbitration**    A way of resolving conflicts without resorting to work stoppages. The parties to a dispute agree to accept the arbitrator's decision as final.

**biological health hazard**   This type of environmental health hazard spreads infectious diseases to people and is caused by many factors, including unsanitary conditions in a food preparation area or serious diseases contracted through needlestick injuries.

**bona fide occupational qualification (BFOQ)**   A requirement that is reasonably necessary to business operations for an employee be a particular religion, sex, or national origin. For instance, it is assumed that an opening for a Baptist minister at a local Baptist church would be filled by a minister who is actually a person who celebrates the Baptist religion, and not say, the Episcopalian religion.

**bonus plan**   A strategy for paying additional compensation, above and beyond an employee's base salary or hourly rate, used as an incentive for desired behaviors or results achieved. Examples of bonuses include discretionary performance bonuses, referral bonuses, patent awards, and employee-of-the-month rewards.

**broadbanding**   A classification method that consolidates multiple pay grades into a few broad "bands" with a wide range between the minimum and maximum of the band.

# C

**call-back pay**   Compensation paid to employees when they are called to work before or after their scheduled work time.

**case study**   A report that reproduces a realistic situation providing learners with the opportunity to analyze the circumstances just as though it was one encountered in the course of business. Case studies provide learners with the opportunity to investigate, study, and analyze a situation.

**cause and effect diagram**   A quality management tool developed by Dr. Kaoru Ishikawa for use in brainstorming sessions to organize information.

**centralized organization**   An organization in which the decision-making authority is held at senior levels or is concentrated at corporate headquarters.

**certiorari**   A Latin term used when the Supreme Court agrees to review a case so that all lower courts are "certain" how to interpret the law.

**change agent**   Someone who listens to various stakeholders' concerns during the change process and moves them toward acceptance of and commitment to the change.

**change management**   A broad term used to describe the strategies used by organizations to facilitate the acceptance of change by employees.

**change process theory**   Kurt Lewin's theory describes three stages for change: unfreeze, move, refreeze.

**check sheet**   The simplest quality management tool, often used to gather data and count items. A check sheet consist of a list of items; each time an item occurs, a check mark is placed next to it.

**chemical health hazard**   A type of environmental health hazard that can cause illness or injury. All chemical substances in the workplace should have a material safety data sheet provided by the manufacturer that describes the hazards associated with the chemical, how they should be handled, and how employees may protect themselves from injury or illness.

**classification method**   A job evaluation system that identifies benchmark positions and places them in salary grades, then matches positions with similar KSAs and slots them into the same grade.

**cliff vesting**   A form of delayed benefit vesting in which participants become 100 percent invested after a specified period of time. ERISA sets the maximum vesting period at five years for qualified plans.

**closed shop clause**   A clause in a collective bargaining agreement requiring all new hires to be members of the union before they are hired. The closed shop is illegal except in the construction industry.

**closing conference**   A conference held at the end of an OSHA inspection during which the inspector, employer and employee representatives discuss the observations made and corrective actions that must be taken.

**collective bargaining agreement**   A contract governing the employment relationship for a specified period of time.

**commissions**   A method of employee compensation that allots a percentage-of-sales price for products and services sold to a customer. Commissions may serve as the entire cash compensation package or work in combination with a base salary.

**common law doctrine**   A doctrine developed over centuries as a result of legal decisions made by judges in individual cases.

**common situs picketing**   Common situs picketing occurs when an employer shares a building with other employers. Because picketing a common business location can interfere with the ability of secondary businesses to operate, the union must ensure that picket signs clearly state the name of the business they are striking, and where possible, restrict picketing to an entrance that is used only by the primary employer.

**communication strategy**   A communication strategy establishes the plan and the means to disseminate business information out to the organization and builds employee trust in the organization in the process.

**comparable worth**   A concept that suggests that jobs requiring similar levels of knowledge, skill, and ability should be paid similarly.

**compa-ratio**   A calculation tool that compares an employee's base pay to the midpoint of the base salary range; it is commonly used when comparing salaries within a group of employees, especially when providing recommendations for pay increases related to promotions or merit reviews.

**compensable factors**   Characteristics that define and distinguish different jobs from one another. These factors are used when determining their value when using the various job evaluation methods.

**Compensation and Benefits**   The functional area of the HR body of knowledge that is concerned with development, implementation, and maintenance of total compensation programs to support an organization's compensation philosophy.

**compensation philosophy**   A mission statement that guides the development and implementation of compensation programs. Factors that go into developing a compensation philosophy include internal and external market conditions, the organization's financial and market performance, and the corporate culture.

**compensatory time (comp time)**   Paid time off from work in lieu of overtime pay when extra hours are worked. Only available for public employees.

**compulsory arbitration**   Arbitration mandated by legal statute to resolve disputes in the public sector where labor strikes are prohibited.

**computer-based training (CBT)**   An interactive training method that combines elements of the lecture, demonstration, one-on-one, and simulation methods allowing the learner to have a real-world learning experience.

**concurrent validity**   A type of criterion validity that correlates a test measurement to behavior. In concurrent validity, a test is given and the behavior is measured at the same time.

**conference**   A combination of a lecture or presentation with question-and-answer sessions involving the participants.

**conflict resolution**   A process of developing strategies for resolving issues and maintaining or rebuilding effective working relationships.

**consent election**   A union election that is held after an NLRB conference if the employer and the union agree to jurisdictional issues, the makeup of the bargaining unit, eligibility of voters in the proposed unit, and the time and place of the election.

**continuous feedback program**   A performance management process in which feedback occurs regularly during the year.

**constructive discharge**   Constructive discharge occurs when the employer forces an employee to resign by creating a work environment that is so unpleasant a reasonable person would resign.

**consumer picketing**   An action performed to advise consumers that goods have been produced by a business whose workers are on strike.

**construct validity**   Construct validity measures the connection between candidate characteristics and job performance. It is not widely used due to its complexity.

**continuous FMLA leave**    A continuous FMLA leave occurs when an employee is absent from work for a single block of extended time.

**contract**    A legally enforceable agreement between two or more parties in which all parties benefit in some way.

**contract workers**    Workers who are employed by brokers or agencies who negotiate contracts for the workers and act as the employer of record, as well as providing payroll, marketing, and other services for them.

**contributory negligence**    A legal doctrine used to mitigate an employer's responsibility if a worker's actions contributed in any way to an injury.

**contrast bias**    A form of bias that occurs when the interviewer or reviewer compares candidates to each other or compares all candidates to one candidate who may be either very weak or very strong.

**coordinated bargaining**    Also known as multiunit bargaining, coordinated bargaining occurs when several unions represent different bargaining units in the company.

**core competencies**    Characteristics valued by an organization as unique to its vision, mission, and method of operation.

**corporate culture**    See *organization culture*.

**correlation**    In regard to quantitative analysis, a correlation measures two variables to determine if there is a relationship between them. For example, if the HR department posts a quarterly reminder for employees about the referral bonus that is paid for new hires, a correlation analysis could be used to determine if there is an increase in referrals in the weeks after the reminder.

**correlation coefficient**    Describes the relationship between two variables and is stated as a number between −1.0 and +1.0.

**cost-benefit analysis**    A cost-benefit analysis compares the costs of various possible decisions to each other, forecasts the net impact of each on the bottom line, and recommends the best alternative.

**cost of labor**    The cost to employers of hiring and retaining employees.

**covered entities**    Health plans, health care providers and clearinghouses identified by HIPAA privacy rules as bearing responsibility for maintaining the confidentiality of patient information. Employers who process or have access to employee health benefit information may also be considered covered entities for purposes of HIPAA privacy requirements.

**cultural noise**    A form of bias that occurs when candidates answer questions based on what they think the interviewer wants to hear instead of what they believe or know about themselves.

**cumulative trauma injuries (CTI)**    See *musculoskeletal disorder*.

**cycles**    A trend characterized by a pattern of repeated performance for a period of more than one year.

# D

**de-minimus**   A de-minimus violation is the lowest level of OSHA violation and does not pose a direct or immediate threat to safety or health.

**decentralized organization**   An organization in which decision-making authority is held by the managers who are closest to operating activities.

**decertification**   Employees may petition the NLRB to decertify a union if they are dissatisfied with the union's performance. A decertification petition requires signatures of at least 30 percent of the employees before the NLRB will act upon it.

**defamation**   A communication that damages an individual's reputation in the community, preventing them from obtaining employment or other benefits.

**defined benefit**   A deferred compensation plan in which the employer provides a specific benefit upon retirement. The funds are not accounted for individually.

**defined contribution**   An individual deferred compensation plan in which the amount of funds contributed are known, but the amount of the benefit that is eventually paid out is not known because it depends on the investment returns that are earned. The funds are accounted for in individual accounts for each participant.

**Delphi technique**   A qualitative method of analysis in which input is obtained from a group of individuals, summarized, and resubmitted to the group for additional input until consensus is reached. The Delphi technique is unique because the group members do not meet in person but conduct the analysis in writing.

**delayed vesting**   A vesting plan in which participants must wait for a defined period of time prior to becoming fully vested. There are two types of delayed vesting: cliff vesting and graded vesting.

**demonstration**   A method of training that can be used as part of an on-the-job training program or combined with a lecture program. Demonstrations involve the trainer first explaining the process or operation, demonstrating it on the equipment, and then having the learner perform it under the guidance of the trainer.

**Department of Labor (DOL)**   The federal agency charged with enforcement of various federal laws, including the Fair Labor Standards Act, the executive orders related to workplace discrimination, the Occupational Safety and Health Act, the Employment Retirement Income Security Act, and others.

**dependent care account**   A flexible spending account authorized by Section 129 of the Internal Revenue Code in which employees may set aside a maximum of $5,000 to be used to care for dependent children or elders. To obtain reimbursement for dependent care expenses, employees must provide an itemized statement of charges from the caregiver.

**design patents**   A patent that protects new, original, and ornamental designs of manufactured items. Design patents are limited to 14 years.

**directed election**    A union representation election that occurs after an NLRB pre-election hearing has resolved issues about jurisdiction, the bargaining unit, voter eligibility, and the time and place of the election.

**discretionary contributions**    Also known as profit-sharing programs, discretionary contributions allow employers to contribute deferred compensation based on a percentage of company earnings each year.

**disparate impact**    This occurs when an employment practice that appears to be fair unintentionally discriminates against members of a protected class.

**distance learning**    Similar to lectures, this training method allows simultaneous training to occur in geographically dispersed multiple locations. Distance learning provides participants with the ability to communicate with presenters and participants in other locations utilizing web technology or video conferencing.

**distributive bargaining**    See *positional bargaining*.

**diversity initiative**    An initiative that seeks to increase the personality, racial, ethnic, religious, educational, and economic diversity of an organization's workforce or to increase the effectiveness of an already diverse workforce.

**diversity training**    This type of training educates all groups about the cultures, needs, and attitudes of other groups in the workforce to ensure the inclusion of all groups in workplace activities.

**doctrine of contributory negligence**    This common law doctrine lessens an employer's liability if a worker's actions contribute in any way to an injury.

**downsizing**    Actions taken by organizations to reduce the size of their workforces as a result of a change in strategic direction or in reaction to different economic conditions.

**due process**    In the employment context, employment actions that are taken in accordance with established procedures. This includes notifying employees of pending actions and providing them with the opportunity to respond to any allegations prior to making a final employment decision.

**duty of diligence**    A common law doctrine requiring an employee to act "with reasonable care and skill" in the course of performing work for the employer.

**duty of loyalty**    A common law doctrine requiring employees to act in the best interest of the employer and not solicit work away from the employer to benefit themselves.

**duty of obedience**    A common law doctrine requiring employees to act within the authority granted by the employer and to follow the employer's reasonable and legal policies, procedures, and rules.

# E

**emergency action plans**    A plan that informs employees of appropriate procedures to follow during a fire or evacuation.

**emotional intelligence (EI or EQ)**   A measurement of how people deal with their feelings and how they perceive and interact with others.

**Employee Assistance Program (EAP)**   A program that offers employees a variety of benefits that provide a resource for problems that cannot be solved within the work context. Some typical services available through an EAP include legal assistance, financial counseling, and alcohol and drug abuse counseling.

**Employee and Labor Relations**   The functional area of the HR body of knowledge that addresses employment relationships in both union and nonunion environments.

**Employee Stock Ownership Plan (ESOP)**   A defined compensation plan in which employees are able to purchase stock in the organization at a reduced price.

**employment practices liability insurance (EPLI)**   Insurance coverage that protects employers against lawsuits brought by current or former employees.

**enrolled actuary**   An actuary in charge of analyzing insurance and annuity premiums who has been licensed jointly by the Department of the Treasury and the Department of Labor to provide these services for U.S. pension plans.

**enterprise coverage**   The Fair Labor Standards Act (FLSA) coverage category requiring businesses employing at least two employees with at least $500,000 in annual sales or employers who are hospitals, schools, or government agencies to comply with its requirements.

**entitlement philosophy**   An approach to compensation based on rewarding employee longevity. This philosophy can foster a culture in which employees expect certain benefits and treatment.

**environmental health hazards**   These hazards come in many forms, including physical hazards such as noise and extreme temperatures, exposure to chemicals used for everything from making copies to manufacturing products, and biological hazards from viruses and bacteria.

**environmental scan**   A method for collecting information about the organization, industry, marketplace, and technology relevant to the planning process. There are two elements to the scanning process: internal assessment and external assessment.

**Equal Employment Opportunity Commission (EEOC)**   The federal agency responsible for enforcement of Title VII of the Civil Rights Act of 1964.

**equity theory**   J. Stacy Adams's equity theory states that people are constantly measuring what they put into work against what they get from work. If an employee's perception is that it is a fair trade, they are motivated to continue contributing at the same level. When an employee perceives that there is an imbalance and they are putting more into their work than they are receiving, they become demotivated and lose interest in their work, decreasing productivity and quality.

**ergonomics**   A science that addresses the way a physical environment is designed and how efficient and safe that design is for the people in the environment.

**ERG theory**   Clayton Alderfer's ERG theory of motivation identifies three levels of needs: existence, relatedness, and growth.

**essential job functions**   Those functions of a job that are the reasons for its existence.

**ethnocentric**   A global staffing strategy in which all key management positions are filled by expatriates.

**Excelsior list**   A list containing the names and addresses of all employees in the bargaining unit designated by the NLRB that must be provided by the employer to the union within seven days of the consent to or direction of an election.

**executive orders**   An order from the president of the United States; a presidential proclamation which, when published in the Federal Register, becomes law after 30 days.

**exempt**   Positions determined to be exempt from requirements of the Fair Labor Standards Act (FLSA). Exempt positions must be paid on a salary, not an hourly basis, and must meet the requirements established by DOL exemption tests for administrative, professional, outside sales, executive, or other jobs exempted by DOL regulations.

**exit interview**   An interview conducted with employees when they leave the organization to determine why they are leaving, what improvements could be made to the organization and to learn if there are any specific issues that need to be addressed.

**expatriates**   Employees who originate from the corporate home country and work in another country.

**expectancy theory**   Victor Vroom's expectancy theory of motivation maintains that people are motivated by the expectation of the reward they will receive when they succeed, and that each individual calculates the level of effort required to receive a particular reward to determine if the reward is worth the effort that is required to attain it.

**experiential training methods**   Training methods that provide experience in real time situations through demonstrations, one-on-one training, or performance-based training.

**express contract**   A verbal or written agreement in which the parties state exactly what they agree to do.

**extrinsic reward**   A form of nonmonetary compensation in which esteem is achieved from others, such as fulfillment from working with a talented team of peers.

# F

**fast track program**   A program that provides specific training opportunities, beyond those offered to most employees, to individuals who have been identified as having high potential for leadership.

**fellow servant rule**   A rule that absolves employers of responsibility for worker injuries if a coworker's actions caused the injury.

**fiduciary responsibility**   The obligation put upon executives to make decisions that will benefit the organization or a pension trust fund instead of making decisions that benefit them personally.

**final written warning**   When documenting performance issues, this warning advises the employee that continued inability or refusal to make necessary performance changes will result in further action, up to and including termination of employment.

**finance**   The business function in an organization that is responsible for obtaining credit to meet the organization's needs, granting credit to customers, investing and managing cash for maximum return on investment, and establishing banking relationships for the organization.

**Financial Accounting Standards Board (FASB)**   A board that establishes standards of financial accounting and reporting intended to regulate and guide financial accounting practices. Such standards are essential to the efficient functioning of the economy because investors, creditors, auditors, and others rely on credible, transparent, and comparable financial information.

**first written warning**   When documenting performance issues, the first written warning is a formal memo to the poorly performing employee describing disciplinary steps that have already been taken. This message spells out the performance problems and the steps that need to be taken to avoid future warnings as well as any agreements that have been made about performance changes.

**fiscal year**   An annual reporting period that is different from a calendar year, such as July 1 of one calendar year to June 30 of the next calendar year.

**flexible spending accounts (FSAs)**   Plans authorized by the Sections 125 and 129 of the Revenue Act of 1978 that allow employees to set aside pretax funds for medical or dependent expenses they expect to incur during the calendar year.

# G

**gainsharing**   An organization or group incentive plan in which employees and managers come together for the common purpose of improving the organization's productivity and sharing the benefits of success.

**gap analysis**   In a needs assessment, a gap analysis compares the objective to the current situation and results in a list of people, actions, or items that will be needed to attain the objective of the assessment. The goal of the gap analysis is to close the gaps.

**gatekeeper**   One who controls the input or output of a situation or activity. For example, in a health and welfare benefits setting, a patient's primary care physician is a gatekeeper in charge of determining whether or not patients need to be seen by a specialist.

**general duty standard**   OSHA's general duty standard requires employers to provide jobs and a workplace environment that are free from recognized safety and health hazards that could potentially cause death or serious physical harm. This standard also requires employers to comply with all OSHA rules, regulations, and standards.

**geocentric**    A global staffing approach that places the best-qualified person into a position regardless of the country of origin.

**glass ceiling**    A term first used by the *Wall Street Journal* to describe the limitations faced by women and minorities when it comes to advancing into the senior ranks of corporate management.

**goal**    A desired outcome that guides the direction to be taken and what will be achieved.

**graded vesting**    Also referred to as graduated or gradual vesting, graded vesting is a delayed vesting schedule that provides for partial vesting each year for a specified number of years. A graded vesting schedule in a qualified plan must allow for at least 20 percent vesting after three years and 20 percent per year after that, with participants achieving full vesting after seven years of service.

**graduated (or gradual) vesting**    See also *graded vesting*.

**grant price**    See *strike price*.

**graveyard shift**    The night to morning shift, such as midnight to 8 A.M. The graveyard shift is generally thought of as an undesirable time to work.

**green circle**    Refers to salaries that are below the minimum of the salary range.

**group incentives**    Benefits or bonuses in which all employees within the organization or within a department share a stake. Also known as organizational incentives, group incentives are commonly put in place to increase productivity and foster teamwork while sharing the financial rewards with employees. Types of group incentives include gainsharing, Improshare, the Scanlon Plan, profit sharing, and employee stock ownership plans (ESOPs).

**gut feeling bias**    This bias occurs when the interviewer relies on intuition to determine whether or not a candidate will be a good or bad fit for the position.

# H

**halo effect bias**    This bias occurs when an interviewer bases a positive assessment on a single characteristic and allows it to overshadow other, negative characteristics.

**hard bargaining**    See *positional bargaining*.

**harshness bias**    The harshness bias occurs when an interviewer rates a candidate negatively based on a single characteristic, allowing it to overshadow other, positive characteristics. See also *horn effect*.

**HAY system**    Developed by Edward Hay of The Hay Group, the HAY system is a classification method that utilizes a complex point factor method. Jobs are evaluated using three factors: knowledge, problem solving, and accountability. Using the points from the evaluation, the job(s) are matched to a profile.

**hazard pay**   Additional pay provided for dangerous and/or extremely uncomfortable working conditions.

**health and wellness programs**   Voluntary programs that seek to prevent employee illnesses and lower health care costs.

**health purchasing alliances (HPA)**   An allegiance that small employers make with other employers in a geographic area to take advantage of economies of scale. The HPA will negotiate and contract for benefit plans on behalf of all members of the group.

**high involvement organizations**   An organization in which employees are involved in designing their own work processes, empowered to take the actions necessary to complete their work, and accountable for the results. Jobs in these organizations are broadly defined within self-directed work teams. These organizations are characterized by flat hierarchies in which continuous feedback is provided and information flows between and among work teams.

**hierarchy of needs**   Abraham Maslow, a behavioral scientist, developed his hierarchy of needs to explain how people meet their personal needs through work. His theory describes needs that begin with the most basic requirements for life (food, shelter, and basic physical comforts) and progress through stages of growth as people strive to fill higher-level needs.

**highly compensated employees (HCEs)**   The Economic Growth and Tax Relief Reconciliation Act of 2001 defines a highly compensated employee as a 401(k) plan participant who, during the current or prior year, earned $90,000 or more, owns 5 percent or more of the company and, at the company's discretion, is one of the top-paid 20 percent of employees.

**histograms**   A quality management tool, often used in conjunction with a check sheet, that provides a graphical representation of the effects of changes on a process and can be used to set standards.

**horn effect**   Also called the harshness bias, the horn effect occurs when an interviewer rates a candidate negatively based on a single characteristic, allowing it to overshadow other, positive characteristics.

**host-country nationals (HCNs)**   A citizen of the country in which they work for a business that is domiciled in another country.

**hostile work environment**   As defined by the EEOC, an environment in which an individual or individuals are subjected to unwelcome verbal or physical conduct "when submission to or rejection of this conduct explicitly or implicitly affects an individual's employment, unreasonably interferes with an individual's work performance, or creates an intimidating, hostile, or offensive work environment."

**Human Resource Certification Institute (HRCI)**   The credentialing body for the human resource profession.

**Human Resource Development**   The functional area of the HR body of knowledge concerned with training, development, change, and performance management programs to ensure that individuals with the required knowledge, skills, and abilities are available when needed to accomplish organization goals.

**human resource information system (HRIS)**   A database that serves as a repository of information and as an aid to effective decision making, thus reducing the amount of paper that the human resource department uses and consolidating the various data needed to keep HR information stored easily.

**HR body of knowledge**   The information necessary to be an effective practitioner of the human resource profession.

# I

**immediate vesting**   Vesting that occurs 100 percent, or fully, as soon as employees meet the eligibility requirements of the vesting plan.

**implied contract**   A contract that can be created by an employer's conduct and need not be specifically stated or written.

**Improshare®©**   Developed in the 1970s by Mitchell Fein, Improshare plans are group incentive plans that establish a baseline of productivity and reward employees with 50 percent of any gains made over the base.

**in loco parentis**   Latin term meaning "in place of the parent." Applies to those who care for a child on a daily basis. In loco parentis does not necessarily refer to a biological or legal relationship.

**incentive pay**   A compensation program that rewards employees for individual and organizational results. Individual and group incentive pay have become a common component of the total compensation package. Also known as variable pay.

**Incentive Stock Options (ISO)**   Stock options that can be offered only to employees; consultants and outside members of the board of directors are not eligible.

**income statement**   Also knows as the profit and loss (P&L) statement, an income statement provides information about financial results of operations during the reporting period. The report includes such information as revenue that was produced from various sources, costs to produce the goods or services, overhead expenses, and profit or loss for the period.

**independent contractors**   Self-employed individuals who work for multiple customers and clients on a project or fee basis.

**individual coverage**   The Fair Labor Standards Act (FLSA) coverage category requiring companies whose employees' daily work involves interstate commerce to comply with its requirements.

**individual level training**   Training that seeks to address the performance needs of individual employees. It can be indicated by poor performance reviews or requests for assistance by the employee.

**information technology (IT)**   The functional area of the business responsible for managing systems such as voice mail, computer networks, software, websites and the Internet, and the data collected by these systems.

**informational picketing**   Also known as publicity picketing, informational picketing is done to truthfully advise the public that an employer is a union-free workplace.

**injunction**   A court order that either requires or forbids an action by one party against another. The Sherman Anti-Trust Act of 1890 allows injunctions to be issued against any person or group that conspires to restrain trade.

**inpatriates**   Employees brought to the home office for training to become accustomed to the corporate culture and practices before returning to their countries of origin to work as host-country nationals.

**integrative bargaining**   A form of principled bargaining in which the parties look at all the issues on the table and make mutually agreeable trade-offs among those issues.

**Intellectual Property Agreement (IPA)**   An agreement that identifies what a company considers to be confidential information (such as customer lists, financial information, or trade secrets) and how its use is limited by the agreement. In addition, the agreement may contain a nonsolicitation clause limiting the ability of former employees to hire coworkers if they leave the organization, as well as how long the agreement must remain confidential after it expires.

**interest-based bargaining (IBB)**   A form of principled bargaining based on the concept that both sides in the negotiation have harmonious interests.

**intermittent FMLA leave**   Intermittent FMLA leave occurs when an employee is absent from work for multiple periods of time due to a single illness or injury.

**internal controls**   Policies and procedures designed to protect financial assets from being mishandled.

**internal equity**   The value of jobs relative to their value within the organization. Also means the equitable ranking of one job to another within any organization.

**internship programs**   Programs that give students the opportunity to gain work experience in their chosen profession prior to graduation. They are often unpaid, but the student may be given academic credit for the work done.

**intrinsic reward**   A noncompensatory reward that encourages individual employee self esteem, such as satisfaction from challenging work.

# J

**job analysis**   The process used to identify the tasks, processes, or functions that make up the responsibilities of a job.

**job bidding**   A process that allows employees to express interest in positions before they become available.

**job competencies**   Broad statements of the factors needed to be successful in the organization.

**job description**   A document describing the tasks, processes, or functions that are part of an employee's responsibilities.

**job enrichment**   According to Fredrick Herzberg's research, this is the result of increasing the significance of the tasks in a job to provide challenging work and growth opportunities.

**job posting**   An internal job announcement providing basic information about the position to current employees who may be interested in and qualified for the position.

**job pricing**   A process used to determine the appropriate pay for a new position or one that has changed significantly. The process involves reviewing the job description, matching the job to a salary survey, reviewing the various compensation components in the survey, and recommending an appropriate salary or wage.

**job sharing**   A setup that allows two part-time employees to share the duties and responsibilities of a full-time position.

**job specifications**   Descriptions of the KSAs necessary for successful performance of the essential functions of a position.

**just-in-time (JIT) inventory**   An inventory system characterized by the purchase of small amounts of supplies frequently to reduce inventories and ensure a steady supply of products for distribution.

# K

**kinesthetic learners**   Learners who retain information best when they are able to have a hands-on experience during training.

**knowledge-of-predictor bias**   A form of bias occurring when an interviewer is aware that the candidate has scored particularly high or low on an assessment and allows this knowledge to influence the selection process.

**KSAs**   The knowledge, skills, and abilities required for successful job performance.

# L

**labor market**   The sources from which an organization recruits new employees; a single organization may find itself recruiting from several different labor markets depending on the availability of skills for different positions.

**layoff**   This occurs when an organization eliminates jobs and terminates employees for economic reasons, a change in strategic direction, or other business reasons. Also known as a reduction-in-force.

**leadership development**   A process that identifies employees who show promise as potential leaders; provides training, mentoring, and coaching for them; and ensures that they have experience in a broad range of areas within the organization.

**leapfrogging**   See *parallel bargaining.*

**learning curve**   A graphical representation of the rate of learning over time.

**learning evaluation method**   The second level of Donald Kirkpatrick's training evaluation model, the learning evaluation method uses a test to measure whether or not the participants learned the information that was presented.

**learning organizations**   Innovative environments in which knowledge is originated, obtained, and freely shared in response to environmental changes that affect the ability of the organization to compete.

**lectures**   A training method in which speakers address an audience to inform and answer questions. Lectures are often used in combination with other training methods, such as demonstrations.

**leniency bias**   A bias that occurs when an interviewer or reviewer tends to go easy on a candidate and give a higher rating than is warranted.

**liability**   A duty or responsibility owed by one party to another. A liability can result from an agreement or a contract or can be created through a tort.

**line functions**   Departments in an organization that are concerned with making decisions about operating needs, such as production and sales.

**line of sight**   Occurs when employees know that their performance, good or bad, impacts their base or variable pay.

**lobbying**   Activities designed to influence new laws and regulations.

**lockout**   A situation that occurs when management shuts down operations to keep the union from working.

# M

**maintenance of membership**   A clause in a union contract that allows employees to choose whether or not to join the union, but once they join, requires that they remain members until the expiration of the contract. The employee must notify the union to discontinue membership within 30 days of the contract expiration.

**Management By Objectives (MBO)**   A process that is built on the concepts of mutual involvement in setting performance goals, ongoing communications during the performance period (usually a year), and measurement and reward for accomplishments at the end of the period. MBO aligns individuals with organization goals and measures the successful attainment of objectives as well as the quality and/or quantity of performance.

**management development**   A program that seeks to upgrade the manager's skills so that they can better motivate employees, delegate work, manage time and productivity, set goals, plan, and communicate effectively.

**marketing**   The function of an organization that promotes and distributes products in the marketplace, provides support for the sales staff, conducts research to design products that customers will be interested in purchasing, and determines the appropriate pricing for the product.

**material safety data sheets (MSDS)**   Documents provided by chemical manufacturers that identify the ingredients in a chemical substance, how the substance reacts to changes in the atmosphere, and its explosive and flammable qualities. An MSDS tells employees whether the material is stable or unstable, what materials it must not be in contact with, and what additional hazards are present when the substance decomposes or degrades.

**mean average**   In quantitative analysis, the sum of the values in a set of numbers, divided by the number of values in the set.

**median**   In quantitative analysis, can be found by putting the numbers in a set in sequential order. The median is at the physical center, so half the numbers are below it and half are above it.

**mental models**   One of Peter Senge's five disciplines of learning organizations used to describe deep-seated beliefs that color perceptions and affect how individuals see the world around them and react to it.

**mentoring programs**   Mentoring programs match an experienced individual who acts as a teacher, guide, counselor, sponsor, or facilitator and provides personalized feedback and guidance for a more junior colleague.

**merit pay**   Compensation that rewards employee performance by increasing base pay.

**mass layoff**   A layoff in which either 500 employees are laid off or 33 percent of the workforce and at least 50 employees are laid off within a 90-day period.

**Mine Safety and Health Administration (MSHA)**   Established by the Mine Safety and Health Act of 1977 to monitor the safety of mining operations.

**mode**   In quantitative analysis, the number that occurs most frequently in a set of numbers.

**money purchase plan**   A defined contribution plan that uses a fixed percentage of employee earnings to defer compensation; works well for organizations with relatively stable earnings from year to year because the percentage is fixed and, once established, contributions must be made every year. The contribution limits are the same as for profit sharing plans.

**motivation/hygiene theory**   In the 1950s, Fredrick Herzberg theorized that two factors can be used to motivate people: challenging work (motivation) or the desire to avoid unpleasant experiences (hygiene). Also known as the two-factor theory.

**moving average**   Also called a rolling average, the moving average calculates an average for a specific period, for example, the average number of new hires each month for the past twelve months. As the number for the most recent month is added, the oldest number is dropped.

**multi-employer bargaining**   Bargaining in which the union negotiates with more than one employer in an industry or region at a time.

**multi-unit bargaining**   Also known as coordinated bargaining, multi-unit bargaining occurs when several unions represent different bargaining units in the company and the employer negotiates with the unions for more than one bargaining unit at the same time.

**multiple linear regression**   A quantitative analysis tool used to measure the relationship between several variables to forecast another.

**musculoskeletal disorder (MSD)**   The result of repeated stress to various parts of the body, including the back, arms, shoulders, and other areas, that is caused by the way tasks are performed. MSD injuries that can result from poor ergonomics in the workplace include tendonitis, bursitis, and carpal tunnel syndrome. Also referred to as cumulative trauma injury (CTI) and repetitive stress injury (RSI).

# N

**National Institute of Occupational Safety and Health (NIOSH)**   The OSH Act created NIOSH as part of the Department of Health and Human Services. NIOSH is charged with researching and evaluating workplace hazards and recommending ways to reduce the effects of those hazards on workers. NIOSH also supports education and training in the field of occupational safety and health by developing and providing educational materials and training aids.

**National Labor Relations Board (NLRB)**   Established by the National Labor Relations Act to enforce its provisions. This board is charged with conducting elections and preventing and remedying unfair labor practices. The NLRB does not instigate actions on its own, it only responds to charges of unfair labor practices or petitions for representation elections filed in one of its offices.

**needs analysis**   Also called needs assessment, needs analysis is a method for obtaining the information necessary to make decisions that best meet an organization's goals. These methods can be used to measure needs in any area of business; in HR they are often employed in the areas of training and development, staffing projections, and benefit planning for an organization, but they can be utilized to gather information for any program.

**needs assessment**   See *needs analysis*.

**negative emphasis bias**   This bias occurs when an interviewer or reviewer allows a small amount of negative information to outweigh positive information about the candidate or employee.

**negatively accelerating learning curve**   A learning curve in which learning increments are large in the beginning but become smaller as practice continues. This is the most frequent type of learning curve.

**nominal group technique**   A structured meeting format designed to elicit participation from all members of a group in order to arrive at the best possible solution to a problem. The process requires a facilitator and begins with a period of time for individuals to think about and write down all their ideas about the issue. Each participant then presents one idea, which is recorded by the facilitator for later discussion. When all of the ideas have been presented, the process of prioritizing and consensus building takes place until a resolution is agreed upon.

**nonbinding arbitration**   Arbitration in which either party may reject the arbitrator's decision and continue the dispute by filing a lawsuit.

**Non-Disclosure Agreement (NDA)**   A written agreement in which one party agrees to share proprietary information with another party and the other party agrees not to disseminate the information to anyone else.

**nonessential job functions**   A job function that is not necessary to a particular job but may be transferred to another job without adversely impacting the organization.

**nonexempt**   Employees who are covered by requirements of the Fair Labor Standards Act such as overtime pay for any hours worked in excess of 40 per week.

**nonforfeitable**   In deferred compensation, a nonforfeitable claim is one that exists due to a participant's service. Nonforfeitable claims are unconditional and legally enforceable.

**nonqualified retirement plan**   In deferred compensation, a plan in which the benefits exceed the limitations of qualified plans or do not meet other IRS requirements for favorable tax treatment.

**nonqualified (NQ) stock options**   A corporate benefit in which an employer offers organization stock to employees at market or even a reduced price. Employers can benefit from the possibility of an increase in stock value without risking a large amount of cash. Nonqualified stock options are the most common type of stock options and can be used for consultants and external members of the board of directors as well as employees.

**nonverbal bias**   A bias that occurs when an interviewer is influenced by body language. For example, a candidate who frowns when answering questions could be rated negatively even though the answers were correct.

# O

**objective**   In the strategic planning process, a specific description of the practical steps that will be taken to achieve business goals.

**Occupational Safety and Health Administration (OSHA)**  Established by the Occupational Safety and Health Act of 1970, this group is charged with the responsibility of creating and enforcing safety standards.

**occupational safety and health standards**  The OSH Act required OSHA to develop standards to prevent illness and injury to workers. Some of the standards that have been developed include the general duty standard, noise exposure, and personal protective equipment.

**Occupational Health, Safety, and Security**  The functional area of the HR body of knowledge covering the regulations and practices for ensuring a safe, secure, and healthful work environment for employees.

**Office of Federal Contract Compliance Programs (OFCCP)**  The agency of the federal Department of Labor charged with enforcing equal employment opportunity laws for federal contractors and subcontractors.

**Old Age, Survivors, and Disability Insurance (OASDI)**  Part of the Social Security Act of 1935 (SSA), this insurance is to be paid to qualified workers upon retirement or disability or to their surviving dependents in the event of a worker's death.

**ombudsman**  Also called an ombuds, an ombudsman is an impartial person not involved in a dispute who can speak with the parties and suggest alternative solutions.

**on-call pay**  Extra pay provided to employees who are required to be available via pager, telephone, e-mail, and so on to respond to work-related issues.

**on-call workers**  Employees who are available to work on short notice and called to work only when they are needed.

**one-on-one training**  Training in which an inexperienced worker is paired with an experienced supervisor or coworker who utilizes a variety of techniques to provide the worker with the information and hands-on experience necessary to do the job.

**opening conference**  The first step in an OSHA inspection, in which the inspector explains why the site was selected, the purpose of the visit, and the scope of the inspection and discusses the standards that apply to the worksite.

**operations**  The business function that encompass all of the activities necessary to produce the goods or services of the business, such as product design, capacity, production layout, schedules, quality, inventory, technology, and cost control.

**organization climate**  The climate created by the culture, behaviors, leadership, and management styles and the level of bureaucracy within an organization.

**organization culture**  The atmosphere, values, and beliefs that are shared at all levels and reflected in the behavior of individuals throughout the organization.

**organization development (OD)**  A systematic method for examining an organization's technology, processes, structure, and human resources.

**organization development (OD) interventions**  An action strategy used to improve the way an organization achieves its goals.

**organization incentives**   See *group incentives*.

**organizational level training**   Training that focuses on preparing for future needs. It may encompass the entire organization or a single division or department.

**organizational picketing**   Picketing that occurs when the union wants to attract employees to become members and authorize the union to represent them to the employer.

**OSHA Alliance Program**   A program that provides an avenue for small business owner associations to collaborate with the government in promoting workplace health and safety issues. The program is open to trade and professional organizations, businesses, labor organizations, educational institutions, and government agencies, among others.

**outplacement**   Services to transition employees who are leaving the company, most often as the result of a downsizing or layoff. These services assist employees with updating resumes, preparing for interviews, and searching for a new job.

**outsourcing**   A process that moves an entire function out of the organization to be handled by a company specializing in the function. This solution can be beneficial by allowing the organization to focus on its basic business operations.

**overtime**   Extra pay for extra work. Defined as one and one-half times an employee's regular wage rate for hours worked exceeding 40 hours a work week.

# P

**parallel bargaining**   Also known as pattern bargaining, whipsawing, or leapfrogging, parallel bargaining occurs when the union negotiates with one of the employers in an industry at a time. Once a contract has been reached with the first employer, the union uses the gains made during the negotiation as a base for negotiating with the next employer.

**parent-country nationals (PCNs)**   Employees who originate from the organization's home country; also known as expatriates.

**Pareto chart**   A graphical representation of the 80/20 rule: 80 percent of the problems are caused by 20 percent of the reasons. The Pareto chart points out which areas of concern will provide the greatest return when corrected.

**partially self-funded plan**   A health and welfare benefit plan in which the employer utilizes stop-loss insurance and agrees upon a preset maximum coverage amount that will be paid from the claim fund for each participant before the insurance company begins to pay the claim.

**participant**   In reference to benefits, a participant is someone who is enrolled in a specific benefit program. A participant can also be a member of a union or work team.

**part-time employees**   Employees who work less than a regular work week. They can be a cost-effective solution for organizations needing particular skills on an ongoing but not full-time basis.

**party in interest**    A pension plan participant, such as fiduciary, a person or entity providing services to the plan, an employer or employee organization, a person who owns 50 percent or more of the business, relatives of any of the above, or corporations that are involved with the plan in any of these functions.

**passive training methods**    Training in which the learner listens to and absorbs information. These methods are instructor-focused and require little or no active participation from the learner. Passive training methods include conferences, lectures, and distance learning.

**patent**    Exclusive rights granted to inventors that provide the benefits of an invention for a defined period of time.

**pattern bargaining**    See *parallel bargaining*.

**pay differential**    Additional compensation for work that is considered beyond the normal work for an organization.

**pay equity**    See *comparable worth*.

**pay for performance**    Compensation based on individual and organizational results; see also *merit pay*.

**pay grade**    In job pricing, the name or title given to the associated pay range.

**pay range**    In job pricing, the span between the minimum and maximum pay rate (hourly or annual) for all jobs in a particular pay or salary range.

**payrolling**    Allows the organization to refer individuals they want to hire to an agency. The agency hires them to work for the organization and provides payroll and tax services for either a fixed fee or percentage of the salary, which is generally less than a traditional temp agency fee.

**pay structure**    The way in which pay ranges and grades are constructed in an organization.

**pedagogy**    The study of how children learn. Specifically, education in which a teacher decides what will be taught and how it will be delivered.

**peer review panel**    A form of alternative dispute resolution in which management and nonmanagement employees trained in company policies, procedures, and work rules, hears disputes and makes decisions which, depending upon the individual program, can be final and binding on both parties to the dispute.

**performance appraisal**    Also called performance evaluation or review, the process of reviewing how well employees perform their duties during a specified period, usually one year.

**performance-based pay**    Merit increases or promotions, based on how an individual employee performs against the company's process for measuring performance.

**performance-based philosophy**    An approach to compensation that rewards employees for their accomplishments.

**performance-based training (PBT)**    Often utilized to correct performance problems in highly technical or hazardous professions. The trainee is provided with opportunities to practice and demonstrate the necessary skill or knowledge until the required level of proficiency is mastered.

**performance evaluation**    See *performance appraisal.*

**performance management**    An ongoing process of providing feedback to employees about their performance, developing them into increasingly productive contributors to the organization.

**permanent arbitrator**    A person who is viewed by the parties to an agreement as fair and impartial and able to resolve any disputes arising between them.

**perquisites**    Additional benefits provided for senior management and executives. Perquisites may include generous pensions plans, access to the company jet, club memberships, or limousine service.

**personal mastery**    One of Peter Senge's five disciplines of learning organizations, used to describe a high level of expertise in an individual's chosen field and a commitment to lifelong learning.

**PEST analysis**    Also referred to as a STEP analysis (depending on how the words are arranged), a PEST analysis scans the external environment to identify opportunities and threats as part of the SWOT analysis. PEST is an acronym for political, economic, social, and technological factors.

**phantom stock**    A stock option plan that provides the benefits of employee ownership without granting stock. Executives and outside members of the board of directors are the most common recipients of phantom stock.

**physical health hazards**    A type of environmental hazard that can cause physical injury such as excessive noise, extreme temperature, chemical explosion, or poor ergonomic design.

**picketing**    Occurs when a group of employees demonstrate at the entrance to a business to inform customers and the public about disputes, or to prevent deliveries to a business that the union is trying to influence in some way.

**plan administrator**    In deferred compensation, the person designated by the plan sponsor to manage the plan.

**plan sponsor**    In deferred compensation, the entity that establishes the plan. This may be a single employer, a labor organization or, in the case of a multi-employer plan, a group representing the parties that established the plan.

**planned retirements**    Usually occurs when an employee reaches normal retirement age and decides to stop working full time and pursue other interests.

**plant closing**    As defined by the WARN (Worker Adjustment and Retraining Notification) Act, a plant closing occurs when 50 or more full-time employees lose their jobs because a single facility shuts down, either permanently or temporarily.

**plant patent**    A patent that protect the invention or discovery of asexually reproduced varieties of plants for 20 years.

**point factor**    A job classification method that provides companies with a system of points that are assigned to the position being evaluated. Based on the total number of points a position receives, a pay grade/range is assigned to the position.

**policies**   Broad guidelines developed by the employer to guide organizational decisions.

**polycentric**   A global staffing strategy in which management positions in the host country are filled by home country nationals and corporate positions in the home country are filled with expatriates.

**positional bargaining**   Also known as distributive bargaining or hard bargaining, a negotiating position in which for one side to gain something, the other side must lose something.

**positively accelerating learning curve**   A learning curve that begins slowly with smaller learning increments but increases in pace with larger increments as learning continues. This curve occurs in situations when the material to be learned is difficult or complex.

**pre-employment testing**   Any testing that is done prior to employment to ascertain a candidate's ability to successfully perform a job.

**predictive validity**   A type of criterion validity that predicts whether a test measurement accurately predicts behavior. In predictive validity, a test is given and the behavior is measured at a later time.

**pre-existing conditions**   Health issues or ailments that affect a patient within six months of enrollment in a health plan. Insurers may exclude those conditions from coverage for 12 months, or in the case of a late enrollment, for 18 months.

**primary research**   Research conducted using original studies and experiments. See also *secondary research*.

**principled bargaining**   A negotiating strategy characterized by parties who are more interested in solving a problem than they are in winning a position. The parties remain open to looking at problems in new ways and brainstorming for ideas and often come up with an agreement that solves the original problem in a way that was not originally contemplated by either side.

**privacy concern cases**   New protections designed by OSHA to protect employee privacy by substituting a case number for the employee name on the OSHA 300 log.

**procedures**   The details of how policies are to be applied.

**process control charts**   A quality management tool that provides a graphical representation of elements that are out of the acceptable range by setting parameters above and below the range.

**production**   The business function responsible for creation of the product or service offered to customers. Traditionally, this means manufactured goods, but with the growth of service and information businesses, it has come to include some services as well.

**professional employer organization (PEO)**   A PEO operates as the organization's HR department. The PEO becomes the employer of record and then leases the employees back to the organization. PEOs provide full-service HR, payroll, and benefit services and can be a cost-effective solution to enable smaller companies to offer benefits comparable to those offered by much larger organizations.

**profit and loss statement (P&L)**   See *income statement*.

**programmed instruction**   Also called self-paced training, programmed instruction is the forerunner of computer-based training. In programmed instruction, the learner progresses from lesson to lesson in a predesigned course of instruction as mastery of the objectives is attained, allowing learners to progress at their own rate.

**project management**   The process of initiating, planning, executing, controlling, and closing an assignment that is temporary in nature.

**Professional in Human Resources (PHR)**   This level of certification measures a candidate's ability to apply HR knowledge at an operational or technical level. Candidates should be able to develop solutions by drawing on a variety of sources and knowledge that apply to a particular situation.

**Professional Examination Service (PES)**   A service that administers the PHR and SPHR examinations on behalf of HRCI.

**profit sharing**   A qualified, incentive-based program, available in many industries and at all corporate levels, that shares company profits.

**profit-sharing plans**   See *discretionary contributions*.

**protected classes**   Title VII of the Civil Rights Act of 1964 identified five protected classes: race, color, religion, national origin, and sex.

**protected health information (PHI)**   The Department of Health and Human Services (HHS) identifies protected health information (PHI) as patient information that must be kept private, including physical or mental conditions, health care given, and payments that have been made.

**prudent person standard of care**   In relation to fiduciary responsibility over a pension fund, a common law concept that requires all actions on behalf of the fund to be taken with care and due diligence.

**public domain**   In the context of copyrighted material, a work in the public domain is one for which the copyright period has expired or one that was produced as part of the job duties of a federal official.

**publicity picketing**   See *informational picketing*.

# Q

**Qualified Domestic Relations Orders (QDRO)**   Legal orders issued by state courts or other state agencies to require pension payments to alternate payees. An alternate payee must be a spouse or former spouse or child or other dependent of a plan participant.

**qualified plan**   A pension plan that meets ERISA (see Appendix A) requirements and that provides tax advantages for both employees and employers. Qualified plans cannot provide benefits for officers, shareholders, supervisors, or other highly compensated employees that exceed benefits for other employees.

**qualified stock options**    Also known as incentive stock options, qualified stock options are taxed at the capital gains rate when they are exercised, instead of at the ordinary income tax rate. They are riskier for the holder than nonqualified stock options because they must be held for a longer period of time to receive the tax advantage.

**qualitative analysis**    Analysis based on subjective judgments. These judgments may be very informal; for example, an experienced sales manager may be able to predict by the end of the first month of a quarter quite accurately whether or not the sales goal will be met.

**qualitative assessment tools**    Subjective evaluations of general observations and information, including various types of judgmental forecasts. These tools can be as simple as an estimate made by a knowledgeable executive or as involved as formalized brainstorming using a Delphi or nominal group technique.

**quantitative analysis**    Analysis based on mathematical models that measure historical data. Some of the models used are correlation measures, regression analysis, and measures of central tendency.

**quantitative assessment tools**    Objective measures of historical data that are analyzed using a variety of statistical measures. These tools are used to measure trends such as turnover or absenteeism.

**question inconsistency bias**    This occurs when an interviewer asks different questions of each candidate. While this is acceptable to a certain extent in order to delve more deeply into each candidate's qualifications, there is no baseline for comparison if there are no questions asked of all candidates.

**quid pro quo**    A legal term which means, in Latin, "this for that." Quid pro quo harassment, therefore, occurs when a supervisor or manager asks for sexual favors in return for a favorable employment action.

# R

**random drug testing**    Drug tests conducted on an arbitrary, unscheduled basis.

**ranking method**    A technique in which a manager compares the value of jobs in the organization and places them in order from most to least important to the organization.

**reaction evaluation method**    The first level of Donald Kirkpatrick's training evaluation model; it measures the initial reaction of the participants and is the least meaningful method of evaluation.

**realistic job preview (RJP)**    An accurate picture of a typical day on the job designed to give candidates an opportunity to self-select out if the job is not what they expected it would be.

**reasonable accommodation**    A requirement of the Americans with Disabilities Act that employers must provide workplace facilities that are accessible to persons with disabilities and to adjust the requirements of positions to accommodate qualified persons with disabilities. See also *undue hardship*.

**reasonable suspicion drug testing**    Reasonable suspicion drug testing can be used any time there has been an accident in the workplace or when a supervisor suspects, based on behavior, that an employee is under the influence of drugs.

**recency bias**    Occurs when an interviewer or reviewer recalls the most recently interviewed candidate more clearly than earlier candidates.

**recognitional picketing**    Occurs when a union wants an employer to recognize it as the employees' representative for collective bargaining purposes. The NLRA places a limit of 30 days on recognitional picketing, after which a petition for an election must be filed.

**red circle**    Refers to salaries that are above the maximum of the salary range.

**reduced FMLA leave schedule**    A reduced FMLA leave is one in which the employee's regular work schedule is reduced for a period of time. This can mean a reduction in the hours worked each day or in the number of days worked during the week.

**reduction in force (RIF)**    See *layoff*.

**regiocentric**    A global staffing approach that fills positions within a trade region, such as the European Union, with nationals from countries within that region.

**repetitive stress injuries (RSI)**    See *musculoskeletal disorder (MSD)*.

**replacement chart**    A chart used at all levels within an organization to categorize employees as ready for promotion, to be developed for future promotion, satisfactory in current position, or to be replaced.

**reporting premium**    When employees arrive at work for their regularly scheduled shift but there is no work to be done, they may be paid for a minimum number of hours based on employment agreements or state laws. Reporting pay is not required by the FLSA.

**request for proposal (RFP)**    A process in which vendors are asked to propose a plan and define costs for services needed by the organization. A well-constructed RFP serves as the basis on which the product or service is obtained, a means for controlling expenses, a guide to ensure that the delivery meets the organization's requirements, and a method of evaluation at the end of the project.

**resignations**    These occur when an employee voluntarily decides to leave the organization and pursue other interests.

**restricted stock**    Stock that is subject to special SEC regulations before it may be sold. Often awarded to insiders as the result of an acquisition or merger to prevent an adverse impact on the market price of the stock by requiring that it be held for a period of time.

**results evaluation method**    The fourth level of Donald Kirkpatrick's training evaluation model; provides the feedback most meaningful to the business: did the training have an impact on the business results?

**risk assessment**    The process by which an employer determines how likely it is that an emergency will occur, the cost of an emergency to the business should it occur, and the impact it would have on the ability of the business to continue operations. With this knowledge, it is possible to identify what controls must be in place to protect the company and which emergencies are most likely to occur so that preventive measures can be taken to protect the company.

**risk management**   The process of identifying risks and taking steps to ensure that those risks are minimized.

# S

**S-shaped learning curve**   This learning curve has characteristics of both positively and negatively accelerating learning curves. Learning initially progresses slowly and then accelerates but begins to slow down again after a period of time.

**safety**   A process of identifying possible hazards in the workplace and reducing the likelihood that an accident will happen by correcting the hazard. Management and employees are partners in this process.

**Safety and Health Achievement Recognition Program (SHARP)**   A program that recognizes small, high-hazard employers who have requested a comprehensive OSHA consultation, corrected any violations, and developed an ongoing safety management program.

**salary surveys**   A study of compensation and benefits that is collected by government agencies or private firms to assess current market trends. Salary surveys are commonly provided by a professional services vendor who is responsible for confidentially collecting and administering the salary survey data from companies and compiling this data in a format that is usable by the organization. Salary surveys are critical to ensuring the company's total compensation package continues to be aligned the organization's compensation philosophy.

**sales**   The business function responsible for transferring the product or service from the business to the customer.

**Scanlon Plan**   A type of gainsharing plan created in the 1930s by Joseph Scanlon to increase productivity and decrease costs through employee involvement. A Scanlon Plan is administered by a committee made up of employees and management and requires that the company's financial information and productivity metrics be disclosed to the employee population. See also *gainsharing*.

**scheduled drug testing**   Used for monitoring the rehabilitation progress of employees. Scheduled drug testing has limited value because employees who may be currently using drugs are generally able to stop long enough before the test to clear their systems of the drugs.

**scientific method**   A method of primary research, the scientific method has five steps that can be used in solving HR problems: identify the problem, create a hypothesis, decide a method for testing, collect data, and draw conclusions.

**seasonal staffing requirements**   Annual staffing requirements that differ from the general staffing trend in response to external factors or customer demands.

**seasonal workers**   Workers who are hired only at times of the year when the workload increases, such as the Christmas shopping season or when it is time to harvest agricultural products.

**secondary research**   Research based on information that has been collected or reported by others, such as books or articles by primary researchers, industry standards, or analysis of trends within an organization.

**self-study**   A type of active training directed entirely by the learner, who determines what, when, and where learning will occur. It may be based on a defined program and involve a trainer or mentor, but it is controlled by the learner.

**security**   Workplace security protects the company from threats of one kind or another, including fires, earthquakes, hurricanes, tornadoes, and other natural disasters; manmade threats such as terrorist attacks, computer hackers, workplace violence and theft; or the unintentional release of trade secrets or confidential information.

**Section 125 plans**   Allows employees to set aside pretax funds for medical expenses they plan to incur during the calendar year. See also *flexible spending account*.

**self-funded plan**   An insurance plan in which the employer creates a claim fund and pays all claims through it. Self-funded plans must conduct annual discrimination tests to ensure that HCEs (highly compensated employees) are not utilizing the plan disproportionately to non-HCEs.

**Senior Professional in Human Resources (SPHR)**   This level of certification measures a candidate's strategic perspective and ability to pull information from a variety of sources to address issues with organization-wide impact. The SPHR exam measures the candidate's ability to apply HR knowledge and experience in developing policies that will meet the organization's long-term strategic objectives and have an impact on the entire organization.

**seniority-based compensation**   A system in which pay decisions are based on length of time in the position, typically found in organizations with an entitlement culture.

**shared vision**   One of the five elements of a learning organization. Peter Senge's shared vision goes beyond the corporate vision statement to inspire commitment of all individuals in the organization.

**shift**   A block of time that is scheduled for work or duty.

**shift premium**   Additional compensation provided for employees who work other than the day shift. It may be paid as a percentage of base pay or factored into the hourly rate.

**similar-to-me bias**   A bias that occurs when the candidate has interests or other characteristics that are the same as those of the interviewer and which cause the interviewer to overlook negative aspects about the candidate.

**simple linear regression**   A measurement of the relationship between one variable (such as staffing) and another (such as production output) that allows future prediction.

**simulation training**   An interactive training method that provides the learner with opportunities to "try out" new skills or practice procedures in a setting that simulates the work environment but does not endanger the inexperienced trainee, coworkers, or the public.

**sit-down strike**   An unlawful strike in which employees stop working and stay in the building.

**skills inventory**   A collection of information about the organization's workforce including special skills or knowledge, performance appraisals, fluency in foreign languages, educational qualifications, previous experience in or outside of the company, credentials or licenses that may be required, and any continuing education the employee has obtained through training classes, seminars, or educational institutions.

**skip-level interview**   A process in which employees are interviewed by their manager's manager to provide insight into employees' goals and job satisfaction, as well as an opportunity for career counseling.

**Society for Human Resource Management (SHRM)**   SHRM is the largest organization of Human Resources professionals.

**span of control**   The number of employees that one manager can directly supervise.

**staff functions**   Those functions not involved with making operating decisions but involved with advising line managers.

**staffing needs assessment**   A determination of the numbers and types of jobs needed to successfully achieve business goals; the cornerstone of the workforce planning process.

**state unemployment insurance (SUI)**   The SSA (Social Security Act) of 1935 mandated the states to provide unemployment insurance for displaced workers. Each state develops its own UI program, so eligibility requirements for SUI vary between states, as do the SUI tax rates. The state rates vary between employers as well because states increase or decrease the amount of tax charged to individual employers based on the number of employees who file claims for unemployment during the year.

**statement of cash flows**   A report detailing the facts about money that flows through the business during the accounting period. This statement shows how much cash was a result of sales, how much was spent to produce the products that were sold, how much was borrowed or came in as a result of new capital investments, and how much was invested in assets.

**stereotyping bias**   This occurs when an interviewer or reviewer assumes a candidate has specific traits because they are a member of a particular group.

**stock option**   The right to purchase an employer's stock at a certain price, at a future date, and at a given price for a specific period of time.

**stop-loss insurance**   Insurance purchased by self-funded employers to prevent a single catastrophic claim from devastating the claim fund. The employer agrees upon a preset maximum coverage amount that will be paid from the claim fund for each participant before the insurance company begins to pay the claim.

**Strategic Management**   The functional area of the HR body of knowledge area that is concerned with the "big picture" of an organization and requires an understanding of overall business operations, basic knowledge of other functional areas in the organization, and the ability to interact and work effectively with those functions.

**Strategic Partnership Program**   A means for businesses and employees to participate in solving health and safety problems with OSHA. Partnerships currently exist for metal recycling, grain handling, and janitorial contractors working to develop solutions specific to their businesses.

**strategic planning**   A dynamic, systematic way of setting the direction for an organization and developing strategies, tactics, and operational plans that ensure its success.

**strategy**   A plan that uses the strengths of a business to its competitive advantage in the marketplace.

**stratification chart**   A quality management tool that shows problems in priority order and identifies possible strategies for correcting problems.

**stress**   According to NIOSH, job stress occurs when job requirements do not match the capabilities, resources, or needs of a worker, resulting in harmful physical and emotional responses.

**strike**   A strike occurs when the union decides to stop working.

**strike price**   Also known as the grant price, the strike price is the price at which stock options may be purchased or sold by the holder of the options when they are exercised.

**subject matter experts (SME)**   Professionals who are most qualified to ensure the maintenance and documentation of a particular topic or discipline.

**succession plan**   A plan that identifies individuals within the organization who have the talent and ability to move into other positions in one to five years.

**summary plan description (SPD)**   Provides benefit plan participants with information about the provisions, policies, and rules established by the plan and advises them on actions they can take in utilizing the plan. ERISA (see Appendix A) requires that the SPD include the name and other identifying information about plan sponsors, administrators, and trustees, along with any information related to collective bargaining agreements for the plan participants.

**supervisory training**   Training on topics related to interactions with employees, such as progressive discipline, performance appraisals, workplace safety, interviewing, and training.

**suspension**   A type of punishment that forces the offending employee to be absent from the organization (with or without pay) for varying periods of time, depending on the seriousness of the offense and other considerations. A suspension should be accompanied by a written document spelling out all the steps previously taken to resolve the issue, the reason for the suspension and a statement that continued nonconformance may result in termination.

**SWOT analysis**   Research that examines the strengths, weaknesses, opportunities, and threats (SWOT) that face the organization. Strengths and weaknesses are internal factors that can be controlled by the organization; opportunities and threats are external factors that may impact an organization's plans.

**systems thinking**   One of Peter Senge's five disciplines of learning organizations, systems thinking describes the ability of individuals and organizations to recognize patterns and project how changes will impact on them.

# T

**tangible employment action (TEA)**   As defined by the Supreme Court, "A significant change in employment status, such as hiring, firing, failing to promote, reassignment with significantly different responsibilities, or a decision causing a significant change in benefits."

**task level training**   Training involving processes performed in a single job category.

**target benefit plan**   A hybrid pension plan with similarities to both a defined benefit plan and a money purchase plan.

**telecommuting**   A way for employees to work at home and connect to the office electronically. This has become a viable solution for employees who do not wish to commute or who have other reasons to work at home.

**temp**   A temp, or temporary employee, is employed by an agency that screens and tests candidates prior to sending them to a work site for variable periods of time, from short, one-day assignments to longer assignments.

**temp-to-perm**   A type of assignment that allows organizations to observe and evaluate a worker's performance prior to making an offer of full-time employment.

**team learning**   One of Peter Senge's five disciplines of learning organizations, team learning refers to the ability of a team to share and build upon their ideas without holding anything back.

**teratogens**   Chemicals that do not affect a pregnant woman but can harm an unborn child.

**termination**   The firing of an employee.

**Theory X and Theory Y**   Douglas McGregor described the behavior of managers in their relationships with their employees by determining that there are two distinct management approaches, Theory X and Theory Y. Theory X managers have a world view of employees as lazy and uninterested in work and needing constant direction for the work to be completed. Theory X managers also believe that employees do not want to take responsibility and are interested in job security above all else. Theory Y managers believe that, given the opportunity, employees will seek out challenging work and additional responsibility if the work is satisfying.

**third-country nationals (TCNs)**   An employee from any country other than the home country or the host country.

**third party administrator (TPA)**   An entity that provides claim management services for benefit plans such as medical, dental, and vision insurance; pension plans; and Section 125/129 plans.

**third party contract**   In a third party contract, some part of the transaction is provided by an entity other than those who have signed the contract.

**time-and-a-half**   The overtime rate specified by the FLSA for nonexempt employees who work more than 40 hours per week.

**time series forecasts**   A quantitative method of analysis that can be used to measure historic staffing levels and provide a basis from which expected future needs can be calculated.

**TIPS**   An acronym used to remind employers of actions to avoid to prevent charges of unfair labor practices during unionizing efforts. That is, employers may not threaten, interrogate, promise, or spy on employees.

**tort**   Legal term that describes an action that injures someone. Torts are not related to laws or contracts but can result in legal action: the party who has been injured can sue the wrongdoer and collect damages for the injury that has been done.

**total compensation**   All forms of remuneration paid to employees, including cash compensation, equity, benefits, perquisites, and nonmonetary rewards. Total compensation is the entire package, the items that attract, motivate, and retain employees.

**total quality management (TQM)**   A process that focuses all resources within the organization on providing value for customers.

**totality of agreement**   See *zipper clause*.

**transfer of training**   This occurs when learning that took place away from the regular work environment is applied to the real job situation.

**trend analysis**   A quantitative analysis method that compares the changes in a single variable over time and, over a period of years, generally moves upward or downward. *Cycles*, also become apparent in a trend analysis.

**tripartite arbitration panel**   A panel consisting of three arbitrators who hear the issues and reach a joint decision regarding disputes.

**two-factor theory**   See *motivation/hygiene theory*.

# U

**undue hardship**   The ADA does not require employers to accommodate disabled individuals if the accommodation places an excessive financial burden on the employer. The cost of the accommodation is weighed against the size of the organization and other similar factors.

**unfair labor practice (ULP)**   An action by an employer or a union that restrains or coerces employees from exercising their rights to organize and bargain collectively or to refrain from doing so.

**union shop clause**   A clause that requires all employees to join the union within a grace period specified by the contract, but no fewer than 30 days, or, in the construction industry, 7 days.

**unlawful employment practices**   As defined by Title VII of the Civil Rights Act of 1964, practices that discriminate against a member of a protected class in recruiting, selection, hiring, compensation, benefits, training, apprenticeship, or any other terms and conditions of employment.

**utility patent**    A patent that protects the invention of a machine, a new and useful process, or the manufacture or composition of matter or of new and useful improvements to the same. Utility patents are limited to 20 years.

# V

**validity**    The assessment of whether or not a test is an accurate measure of the characteristics that it is supposed to measure.

**variable pay**    See *incentive pay*.

**verbal warning**    In documenting performance issues, before formal disciplinary action can begin, an employee must hear from a manager, verbally, that there is a performance issue. A manager must keep written documentation of the verbal warning.

**vestibule training**    A form of the simulation method, vestibule training allows inexperienced workers to become familiar with and gain experience using equipment that is either hazardous or requires a level of speed that can only be attained with practice.

**vesting**    The point at which employees own the contributions their employer has made to the pension plan on their behalf, whether or not they remain employed with the company. The vesting requirements established by ERISA (see Appendix A) refer only to funds that are contributed by the employer. Employees are always 100 percent vested in funds they have contributed, but they must earn the right to be vested in the employer's contribution.

**vicarious liability**    A legal concept that holds an employer accountable for the harmful actions of its employees, whether or not the employer is aware of those actions.

**visual learners**    Learners who learn best when they are able to see or read information.

**voluntary arbitration**    Occurs when both parties to a disagreement agree to submit the conflict to an arbitrator for resolution.

**Voluntary Protection Program (VPP)**    Employers with tough, established safety programs who meet OSHA criteria for the VPP program are removed from routine scheduled inspection lists.

# W

**wage compression**    Occurs when newly hired employees are hired at a pay rate that is greater than incumbent pay for similar skills, education, and experience. These situations occur during periods of high economic growth or when certain skill sets are in high demand.

**wage garnishment**    The result of a court or government order requiring a portion of an employee's earnings to be paid to another person or entity for the payment of a debt. Wage garnishments may be imposed by the IRS, a state tax collection agency, or by a court to enforce payment of child support or a debt.

**weighted average**   In quantitative analysis, a weighted average is used to compensate for data that may be out of date; the more current data is increased because it better reflects the current situation.

**weighted moving average**   An average calculated for a specific period that assigns more weight to current data. See also *moving average* and *weighted average*.

**whipsawing**   See *parallel bargaining*.

**wildcat strike**   A strike that occurs in violation of a contract clause prohibiting strikes during the term of the contract.

**Workforce Planning and Employment**   The functional area of the HR body of knowledge area that covers activities related to planning for and managing entry into and exit from the organization to meet changing business needs.

**workplace diversity**   The practice of employing individuals with diverse cultural, racial, and ethnic backgrounds and understanding the differences between people.

**workplace investigation**   A formal report or research into suspected illegal activity or serious violations of company policy taking place within an organization.

**workplace violence**   Occurs when an employee with poor behavior control becomes highly stressed. The stress may or may not be work related, but it is often set off by an incident in the workplace. Under OSHA's General Duty Clause, employers are required to be aware of employees exhibiting the signs of possible violent behavior and take steps to prevent its occurrence.

# Y

**yellow dog contracts**   These contracts were used by employers to prevent employees from joining unions by requiring them to sign an agreement that the employee was not a member of a union and would not become one in the future, and that joining a union would be sufficient grounds for dismissal in the future. They were prohibited by the Norris-La Guardia Act.

# Z

**zipper clause**   Also known as a totality of agreement clause, a zipper clause is an agreement between the parties to a collective bargaining agreement that the contract is the entire agreement between them and that anything not in it is not part of the agreement. The purpose of this clause is to prevent reopening of negotiations during the term of the contract.

# Index

Note to the Reader: Page numbers in **bold** indicate the principle discussion of a topic or the definition of a term. Page numbers in *italic* indicate illustrations.

## Numbers

# E

# G

# H

# J

# K

## P

Compensation and Benefits, 377
Employee and Labor Relations, 377–378
Human Resource Certification
    Institute, 374
Human Resource Development, 376
Internet search engines, 374
occupational Health, Safety, and
    Security, 378
overview of, 374
PHR & SPHR Certification Handbook
    ideal candidate profiles, 9
    overview of, 6
    professional standards, 46
    recertification, 9
    test specs, 8
PHR & SPHR Recertification Guide, 10
professional associations, 122, 374–378
Strategic Management, 375
test information, 374
Workforce Planning and
    Employment, 376
respect and trust, mutual, **277–278**
restricted stock, **218, 417**
results evaluation method, **186, 417**
retirement ages, **232–233**
retirement legislation. *See* ERISA; OASDI
retirement plans. *See* deferred compensation
retirements, planned, 143
Revenue Act of 1978, **359**
reverse mentoring, **170**
RFPs (requests for proposals), **26–27**
RIF (reduction in force), **145,**
    *See also* layoffs
risk assessment, **339–340, 417–418**
risk management, **54, 418**
risk, voluntary assumption of, **316**
RJPs (realistic job previews), **134**
Rogers, David, 38
The ROI of Human Capital (Fitz-Enz),
    375, 376
rolling averages, **52**
Roosevelt, Franklin Delano, 231, 287
Rosenfeld v Southern Pacific (1968), **363–364**
RSIs (repetitive stress injuries), **332**

# S

S-shaped learning curves, *182*, **182, 418**
sabbaticals benefit, **255**
Safety and Health Achievement Recognition
    Program (SHARP), **329, 418**
safety. *See* OHSS
St. Mary's Honor Center v Hicks (1993),
    **370–371**
salary surveys, **222, 223–224, 418**
sales bonuses, **219**
sales exemptions in FLSA, **205**
sales function, **68**
salting, **292**
sanitation standards, **319**
Sarbanes-Oxley Act of 2002, **88–89**
SARS (Severe Acute Respiratory Syndrome),
    **333–334**
Saunders, Bernard, 376
SBREFA (Small Business Regulatory Enforce-
    ment Fairness Act) of 1996, **316, 362**
SCA (Service Contract Act) of 1965, **202,
    356, 386**
Scalia, Justice Antonin, 272, 273
Scanlon Plan, **216, 418**
scatter charts, *51–52*, 168
scheduled drug testing, **336, 418**
School Board of Nassau v Arline
    (1987), **367**
Schreyer, Ray, 376
scientific method, **49, 418**
scope of duties clauses, **138**
"scoping" projects, **26**
screening applicants, *See also* WFP
    using applications, 123–124
    and communicating with them, 124
    in interviews, 124
    overview of, 122
    using tests, 125–129
    Uniform Guidelines for, 122–123, *123*
seamless management structures, **84**
search engines, 374
seasonal staffing requirements, **114, 418**
seasonal workers, **119, 418**

# T

# X

# Y

# Z

# TELL US WHAT YOU THINK!

Your feedback is critical to our efforts to provide you with the best books and software on the market. Tell us what you think about the products you've purchased. It's simple:

1. Go to the Sybex website.
2. Find your book by typing the ISBN or title into the Search field.
3. Click on the book title when it appears.
4. Click **Submit a Review**.
5. Fill out the questionnaire and comments.
6. Click **Submit**.

With your feedback, we can continue to publish the highest quality computer books and software products that today's busy IT professionals deserve.

## www.sybex.com

SYBEX Inc. • 1151 Marina Village Parkway, Alameda, CA 94501 • 510-523-8233

SYBEX®